DISCOVER VISUAL CAFÉ

DISCOVER VISUAL CAFÉ

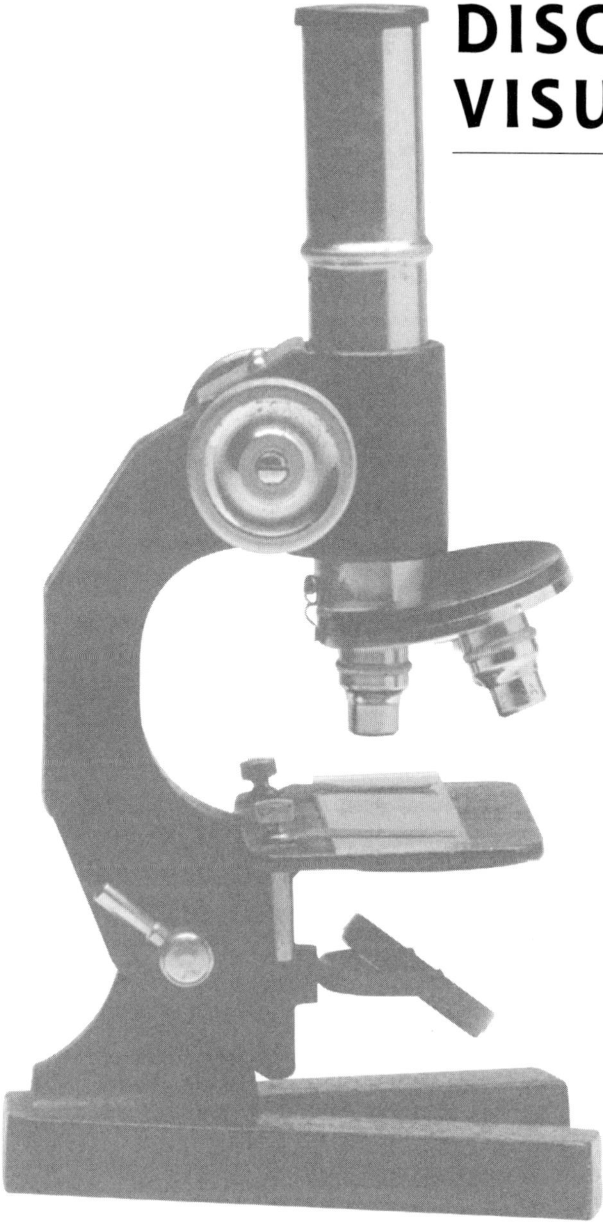

BY DAVID A. WALL
AND ARTHUR GRIFFITH

IDG BOOKS WORLDWIDE, INC.

AN INTERNATIONAL DATA GROUP COMPANY

FOSTER CITY, CA • CHICAGO, IL • INDIANAPOLIS, IN • SOUTHLAKE, TX

Discover Visual Café

Published by
IDG Books Worldwide, Inc.
An International Data Group Company
919 E. Hillsdale Blvd., Suite 400
Foster City, CA 94404

`http://www.idgbooks.com` (IDG Books Worldwide Web site)

Library of Congress Catalog Card No.: 96-79766

ISBN: 0-7645-3062-3

Printed in the United States of America

10 9 8 7 6 5 4 3 2 1

1IPC/RU/QT/ZX/FC

Distributed in the United States by IDG Books Worldwide, Inc.

Distributed by Macmillan Canada for Canada; by Contemporanea de Ediciones for Venezuela; by Distribuidora Cuspide for Argentina; by CITEC for Brazil; by Ediciones ZETA S.C.R. Ltda. for Peru; by Editorial Limusa SA for Mexico; by Transworld Publishers Limited in the United Kingdom and Europe; by Academic Bookshop for Egypt; by Levant Distributors S.A.R.L. for Lebanon; by Al Jassim for Saudi Arabia; by Simron Pty. Ltd. for South Africa; by Pustak Mahal for India; by The Computer Bookshop for India; by Toppan Company Ltd. for Japan; by Addison Wesley Publishing Company for Korea; by Longman Singapore Publishers Ltd. for Singapore, Malaysia, Thailand, and Indonesia; by Unalis Corporation for Taiwan; by WS Computer Publishing Company, Inc. for the Philippines; by WoodsLane Pty. Ltd. for Australia; by WoodsLane Enterprises Ltd. for New Zealand. Authorized Sales Agent: Anthony Rudkin Associates for the Middle East and North Africa.

For general information on IDG Books Worldwide's books in the U.S., please call our Consumer Customer Service department at 800-762-2974. For reseller information, including discounts and premium sales, please call our Reseller Customer Service department at 800-434-3422.

For information on where to purchase IDG Books Worldwide's books outside the U.S., please contact our International Sales department at 415-655-3172 or fax 415-655-3295.

For information on foreign language translations, please contact our Foreign & Subsidiary Rights department at 415-655-3021 or fax 415-655-3281.

For sales inquiries and special prices for bulk quantities, please contact our Sales department at 415-655-3200 or write to the address above.

For information on using IDG Books Worldwide's books in the classroom or for ordering examination copies, please contact our Educational Sales department at 800-434-2086 or fax 817-251-8174.

For press review copies, author interviews, or other publicity information, please contact our Public Relations department at 415-655-3000 or fax 415-655-3299.

For authorization to photocopy items for corporate, personal, or educational use, please contact Copyright Clearance Center, 222 Rosewood Drive, Danvers, MA 01923, or fax 508-750-4470.

ABOUT IDG BOOKS WORLDWIDE

Welcome to the world of IDG Books Worldwide.

IDG Books Worldwide, Inc., is a subsidiary of International Data Group, the world's largest publisher of computer-related information and the leading global provider of information services on information technology. IDG was founded more than 25 years ago and now employs more than 8,500 people worldwide. IDG publishes more than 275 computer publications in over 75 countries (see listing below). More than 60 million people read one or more IDG publications each month.

Launched in 1990, IDG Books Worldwide is today the #1 publisher of best-selling computer books in the United States. We are proud to have received eight awards from the Computer Press Association in recognition of editorial excellence and three from *Computer Currents*' First Annual Readers' Choice Awards. Our best-selling ...*For Dummies*® series has more than 30 million copies in print with translations in 30 languages. IDG Books Worldwide, through a joint venture with IDG's Hi-Tech Beijing, became the first U.S. publisher to publish a computer book in the People's Republic of China. In record time, IDG Books Worldwide has become the first choice for millions of readers around the world who want to learn how to better manage their businesses.

Our mission is simple: Every one of our books is designed to bring extra value and skill-building instructions to the reader. Our books are written by experts who understand and care about our readers. The knowledge base of our editorial staff comes from years of experience in publishing, education, and journalism — experience we use to produce books for the '90s. In short, we care about books, so we attract the best people. We devote special attention to details such as audience, interior design, use of icons, and illustrations. And because we use an efficient process of authoring, editing, and desktop publishing our books electronically, we can spend more time ensuring superior content and spend less time on the technicalities of making books.

You can count on our commitment to deliver high-quality books at competitive prices on topics you want to read about. At IDG Books Worldwide, we continue in the IDG tradition of delivering quality for more than 25 years. You'll find no better book on a subject than one from IDG Books Worldwide.

John Kilcullen
CEO
IDG Books Worldwide, Inc.

Eighth Annual Computer Press Awards 1992

Ninth Annual Computer Press Awards 1993

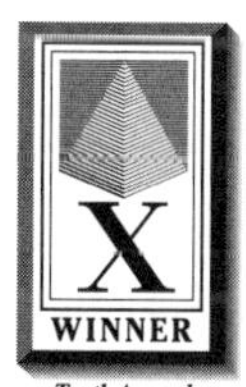

Tenth Annual Computer Press Awards 1994

Eleventh Annual Computer Press Awards 1995

IDG Books Worldwide, Inc., is a subsidiary of International Data Group, the world's largest publisher of computer-related information and the leading global provider of information services on information technology. International Data Group publishes over 275 computer publications in over 75 countries. Sixty million people read one or more International Data Group publications each month. International Data Group's publications include: **ARGENTINA:** Buyer's Guide, Computerworld Argentina, PC World Argentina; **AUSTRALIA:** Australian Macworld, Australian PC World, Australian Reseller News, Computerworld, IT Casebook, Network World, Publish, Webmaster; **AUSTRIA:** Computerwelt Osterreich, Networks Austria, PC Tip Austria; **BANGLADESH:** PC World Bangladesh; **BELARUS:** PC World Belarus; **BELGIUM:** Data News; **BRAZIL:** Annuário de Informática, Computerworld, Connections, Macworld, PC Player, PC World, Publish, Reseller News, Supergamepower; **BULGARIA:** Computerworld Bulgaria, Network World Bulgaria, PC & MacWorld Bulgaria; **CANADA:** CIO Canada, Client/Server World, ComputerWorld Canada, InfoWorld Canada, NetworkWorld Canada, WebWorld; **CHILE:** Computerworld Chile, PC World Chile; **COLOMBIA:** Computerworld Colombia, PC World Colombia; **COSTA RICA:** PC World Centro America; **THE CZECH AND SLOVAK REPUBLICS:** Computerworld Czechoslovakia, Macworld Czech Republic, PC World Czechoslovakia; **DENMARK:** Communications World Danmark, Computerworld Danmark, Macworld Danmark, PC World Danmark, Techworld Denmark; **DOMINICAN REPUBLIC:** PC World Republica Dominicana; **ECUADOR:** PC World Ecuador; **EGYPT:** Computerworld Middle East, PC World Middle East; **EL SALVADOR:** PC World Centro America; **FINLAND:** MikroPC, Tietoverkko, Tietoviikko; **FRANCE:** Distributique, Hebdo, Info PC, Le Monde Informatique, Macworld, Reseaux & Telecoms, WebMaster France; **GERMANY:** Computer Partner, Computerwoche, Computerwoche Extra, Computerwoche FOCUS, Global Online, Macwelt, PC Welt; **GREECE:** Amiga Computing, GamePro Greece, Multimedia World; **GUATEMALA:** PC World Centro America; **HONDURAS:** PC World Centro America; **HONG KONG:** Computerworld Hong Kong, PC World Hong Kong, Publish in Asia; **HUNGARY:** ABCD CD-ROM, Computerworld Szamitastechnika, Internetto online Magazine, PC World Hungary, PC-X Magazin Hungary; **ICELAND:** Tolvuheimur PC World Island; **INDIA:** Information Communications World, Information Systems Computerworld, PC World India, Publish in Asia; **INDONESIA:** InfoKomputer PC World, Komputek Computerworld, Publish in Asia; **IRELAND:** ComputerScope, PC Live!; **ISRAEL:** Macworld Israel, People & Computers/Computerworld; **ITALY:** Computerworld Italia, Macworld Italia, Networking Italia, PC World Italia; **JAPAN:** DTP World, Macworld Japan, Nikkei Personal Computing, OS/2 World Japan, SunWorld Japan, Windows NT World, Windows World Japan; **KENYA:** PC World East African; **KOREA:** Hi-Tech Information, Macworld Korea, PC World Korea; **MACEDONIA:** PC World Macedonia; **MALAYSIA:** Computerworld Malaysia, PC World Malaysia, Publish in Asia; **MALTA:** PC World Malta; **MEXICO:** Computerworld Mexico, PC World Mexico; **MYANMAR:** PC World Myanmar; **NETHERLANDS:** Computer! Totaal, LAN Internetworking Magazine, LAN World Buyers Guide, Macworld Netherlands, Net, WebWereld; **NEW ZEALAND:** Absolute Beginners Guide and Plain & Simple Series, Computer Buyer, Computer Industry Directory, Computerworld New Zealand, MTB, Network World, PC World New Zealand; **NICARAGUA:** PC World Centro America; **NORWAY:** Computerworld Norge, CW Rapport, Datamagasinet, Financial Rapport, Kursguide Norge, Macworld Norge, Multimediaworld Norge, PC World Ekspress Norge, PC World Nettverk, PC World Norge, PC World ProduktGuide Norge; **PAKISTAN:** Computerworld Pakistan; **PANAMA:** PC World Panama; **PEOPLE'S REPUBLIC OF CHINA:** China Computer Users, China Computerworld, China InfoWorld, China Telecom World Weekly, Computer & Communication, Electronic Design China, Electronics Today, Electronics Weekly, Game Software, PC World China, Popular Computer Week, Software Weekly, Software World, Telecom World; **PERU:** Computerworld Peru, PC World Profesional Peru, PC World SoHo Peru; **PHILIPPINES:** Click!, Computerworld Philippines, PC World Philippines, Publish in Asia; **POLAND:** Computerworld Poland, Computerworld Special Report Poland, Cyber, Macworld Poland, Networld Poland, PC World Komputer; **PORTUGAL:** Cerebro/PC World, Computerworld/Correio Informático, Dealer World Portugal, Mac*In/PC*In Portugal, Multimedia World; **PUERTO RICO:** PC World Puerto Rico; **ROMANIA:** Computerworld Romania, PC World Romania, Telecom Romania; **RUSSIA:** Computerworld Russia, Mir PK, Publish, Seti; **SINGAPORE:** Computerworld Singapore, PC World Singapore, Publish in Asia; **SLOVENIA:** Monitor; **SOUTH AFRICA:** Computing SA, Network World SA, Software World SA; **SPAIN:** Communicaciones World España, Computerworld España, Dealer World España, Macworld España, PC World España; **SRI LANKA:** Infolink PC World; **SWEDEN:** CAP&Design, Computer Sweden, Corporate Computing Sweden, Internetworld Sweden, it.branschen, Macworld Sweden, MaxiData Sweden, MikroDatorn, Nätverk & Kommunikation, PC World Sweden, PCaktiv, Windows World Sweden; **SWITZERLAND:** Computerworld Schweiz, Macworld Schweiz, PCtip; **TAIWAN:** Computerworld Taiwan, Macworld Taiwan, NEW ViSiON/Publish, PC World Taiwan, Windows World Taiwan; **THAILAND:** Publish in Asia, Thai Computerworld; **TURKEY:** Computerworld Turkiye, Macworld Turkiye, Network World Turkiye, PC World Turkiye; **UKRAINE:** Computerworld Kiev, Multimedia World Ukraine, PC World Ukraine; **UNITED KINGDOM:** Acorn User UK, Amiga Action UK, Amiga Computing UK, Apple Talk UK, Computing, Macworld, Parents and Computers UK, PC Advisor, PC Home, PSX Pro, The WEB; **UNITED STATES:** Cable in the Classroom, CIO Magazine, Computerworld, DOS World, Federal Computer Week, GamePro Magazine, InfoWorld, I-Way, Macworld, Network World, PC Games, PC World, Publish, Video Event, THE WEB Magazine, and WebMaster; online webzines: JavaWorld, NetscapeWorld, and SunWorld Online; **URUGUAY:** InfoWorld Uruguay; **VENEZUELA:** Computerworld Venezuela, PC World Venezuela; and **VIETNAM:** PC World Vietnam.

2/14/97

Welcome to the Discover Series

Do you want to discover the best and most efficient ways to use your computer and learn about technology? Books in the Discover series teach you the essentials of technology with a friendly, confident approach. You'll find a Discover book on almost any subject — from the Internet to intranets, from Web design and programming to the business programs that make your life easier.

We've provided valuable, real-world examples that help you relate to topics faster. Discover books begin by introducing you to the main features of programs, so you start by doing something *immediately*. The focus is to teach you how to perform tasks that are useful and meaningful in your day-to-day work. You might create a document or graphic, explore your computer, surf the Web, or write a program. Whatever the task, you learn the most commonly used features, and focus on the best tips and techniques for doing your work. You'll get results quickly, and discover the best ways to use software and technology in your everyday life.

You may find the following elements and features in this book:

Discovery Central: This tearout card is a handy quick reference to important tasks or ideas covered in the book.

Quick Tour: The Quick Tour gets you started working with the book right away.

Real-Life Vignettes: Throughout the book you'll see one-page scenarios illustrating a real-life application of a topic covered.

Goals: Each chapter opens with a list of goals you can achieve by reading the chapter.

Side Trips: These asides include additional information about alternative or advanced ways to approach the topic covered.

Bonuses: Timesaving tips and more advanced techniques are covered in each chapter.

Discovery Center: This guide illustrates key procedures covered throughout the book.

Visual Index: You'll find real-world documents in the Visual Index, with page numbers pointing you to where you should turn to achieve the effects shown.

DISCOVERY CENTRAL

DISCOVER VISUAL CAFÉ

Java Versus C

The following two programs do exactly the same thing—one in C and one in Java. Each reads its own source code file, character by character, and prints it to standard-out. They are written to be as much alike as possible to demonstrate both similarities and differences.

Program Written in C

```
#include <stdio.h>
#include <stdlib.h>

void main(int argc,char *argv[])
{
    FILE *fd;
    int character;

    fd = fopen("SeeMe.c","r");
    if(fd == NULL) {
        perror("Unable to open SeeMe.c");
        exit(1);
    }

    while((character = fgetc(fd)) != EOF)
        printf("%c",character);

    fclose(fd);
}
```

Same Program Written in Java

```
import java.io.*;

public class SeeMe {
    public static void main(String arg[]) {
        File file = new File("SeeMe.java");
        try {
            FileInputStream filein = new FileInputStream(file);
            while(true) {
                int character = filein.read();
                if(character == -1) {
                    filein.close();
                    return;
                }
                System.out.print((char)character);
            }
        } catch(IOException e) {
            System.err.println(e);
        }
    }
}
```

Visual Cafe Toolbar

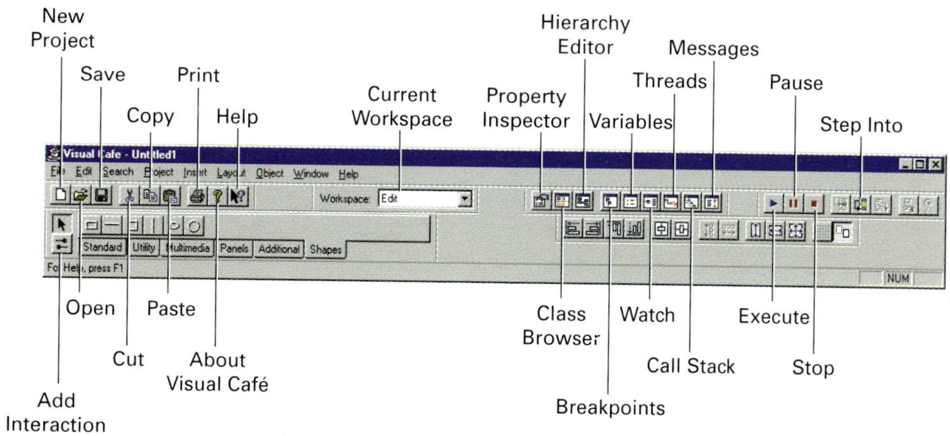

Java Interface Components

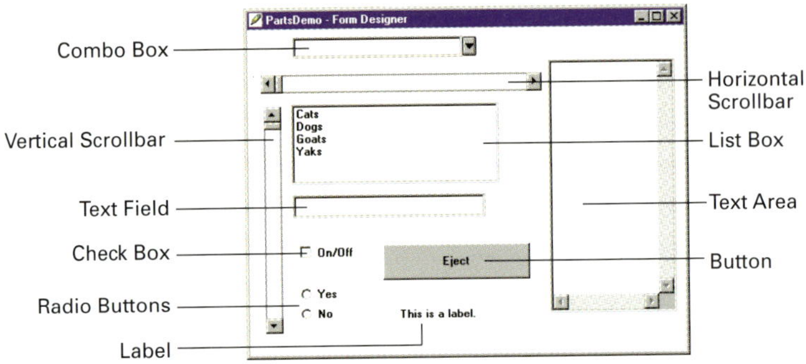

Using the Interaction Wizard

1. Start the Interaction Wizard by either
   a. clicking the Interaction Wizard button on the toolbar, then dragging the component that will experience an event to the component that will perform a behavior in response to the event.
   b. selecting Object → Add Interaction.
   c. right-clicking (or, in the case of Macintoshes, long-click) the component that is to experience a triggering event.
2. Specify the triggering event in the "Start an interaction for…" list box.
3. Specify a resultant behavior in the "Choose what you want to happen" list box.
4. Click the Finish button.

Quick Debugging Tips

To test-run your applets and applications, click the Run button.

To set a breakpoint, open the source code editor, position your cursor on the line before which you want the breakpoint to occur, and press F9.

To open the Breakpoints window, choose Window → Breakpoints or press Ctrl + Shift + B.

Visual Café has four major monitoring features:

- The *Watch window* displays the contents of any variable you specify. Open the Watch window by choosing Window → Watch or pressing Ctrl + Shift + W.
- The *Variables window* displays the contents of all the variables your program is using at the moment. Open the Variables window by choosing Window → Variables or pressing Ctrl + Shift + D.
- The *Call Stack window* shows references among classes in your program. To open the Call Stack window, choose Window → Call Stack or press Ctrl + Shift + L.
- The *Threads window* lets you follow multiple strands of execution in your program. Open the Threads window by choosing Window → Threads or pressing Ctrl + Shift + T.

IDG BOOKS WORLDWIDE

For more information about IDG Books call **1-800-762-2974.**

ISBN 0-7645-3062-3

Throughout the book, you'll also notice some special icons and formatting:

FEATURE FOCUS **A Feature Focus icon highlights new features in the software's latest release, and points out significant differences between it and the previous version.**

WEB PATH **Web Paths refer you to Web sites that provide additional information about the topic.**

TIP **Tips offer timesaving shortcuts, expert advice, quick techniques, or brief reminders.**

X-REF **The X-Ref icon refers you to other chapters or sections for more information.**

Pull Quotes emphasize important ideas that are covered in the chapter.

NOTE **Notes provide additional information or highlight special points of interest about a topic.**

CAUTION **The Caution icon alerts you to potential problems you should watch out for.**

The Discover series delivers interesting, insightful, and inspiring information about technology to help you learn faster and retain more. So the next time you want to find answers to your technology questions, reach for a Discover book. We hope the entertaining, easy-to-read style puts you at ease and makes learning fun.

Credits

ACQUISITIONS EDITOR
Mike Roney

DEVELOPMENT EDITOR
Ralph Moore

TECHNICAL EDITOR
John Cole

COPY EDITORS
Luann Rouff
Katharine Dvorak

PROJECT COORDINATOR
Susan Parini

QUALITY CONTROL SPECIALIST
Mick Arellano

GRAPHICS AND PRODUCTION SPECIALISTS
Mario F. Amador
Laura Carpenter
Renée Dunn
Jude Levinson
Stephen Noetzel
Ed Penslien
Mark Schumann

PROOFREADERS
Desne Border
Andrew Davies
Stacey Lynn
Candace Ward
Anne Weinberger

INDEXER
Ty Koontz

BOOK DESIGN
Seventeenth Street Studios
Phyllis Beaty
Kurt Krames

About the Authors

David Wall works as a writer-errant, writing books, stories, and articles of all kinds while moving from one city to the next. He is the author of *Netscape Plug-in Power (IDG Books Worldwide, 1996)*, which explains how to use more than 100 browser plug-ins to enhance productivity and improve the presentation of multimedia. At the moment he lives near Salt Lake City, Utah, where he enjoys skiing, bicycling, and walking in the mountains.

Arthur Griffith lives in Dallas, Texas, where he has worked as a software developer and consultant for 20 years. Arthur's software development includes compilers, interpreters, linkers, object librarians, and other system-level utilities. Over the years, he worked professionally with more than 30 computer languages. He enjoys acting and has landed small roles on network television.

David and Arthur have recently joined forces again to write *101 Freeze-Dried Java Applets* for IDG Books Worldwide. Look for it in the spring of 1997.

FOR MY FAMILY

—DW

FOR MARY

—AG

FOREWORD

In late 1995, when Sun announced their Java initiative, we immediately recognized the design benefits of the Java language. We also recognized the opportunity for application portability that the Java technology offered. But even we were surprised by the speed of the industry's adoption of Java. To state that a new programming language would eclipse other languages as the choice for most new project development, a mere 18 months after it's introduction, is startling and unprecedented.

We immediately began writing a Café for Java developers. It has an optimized bytecode compiler, a Java Just-In-Time compiler, a GUI debugger, and a form designer which generated Java code using standard AWT components. We released Café in March of 1996. Needless to say, the product was an overnight success.

Everyone was using Café to develop their Java applications. Symantec became the leader in Java tools virtually overnight. But we weren't done yet. We realized that Java would burst into the mainstream programming market and would soon be embraced by MIS and Web developers alike. They needed a RAD tool to get their applets built and deployed quickly. In parallel with the Café development, we had spawned number of other teams of developers to create a new breakthrough RAD tool. This product would take advantage of all of Java's capabilities and raise the bar in development tools technology.

Hence Visual Café was born. It's the focus of this book, and the tool with which you can expand both your knowledge and usage of Java. The two-way source and visual tool synchronization technology teaches Java to the newcomer and allows the power user to design in either tool without fear of overwriting code. The live-Java form designer lets you see the components and layouts that you select without having to compile and run. The Interaction Wizard allows you to create programs without coding. This wizard technology takes Visual Café beyond the prototyping stage and allows Java novices to deploy functional applets within minutes. This product indeed has many features for you to discover.

We hope you enjoy *Discover Visual Café* as much as we did. We welcome you to the threshold of a new beginning: The beginning of global information access. The beginning of end-user empowerment. The beginning of Ultra thin-client computing. The beginning of intelligent information publishing. All of the benefits of Java await you inside.

We wish you success.

Roger Bowman
Developer Relations Manager
Symantec Internet Tools

PREFACE

Thanks for reading *Discover Visual Café*! In this book you'll get to know Java, the greatest programming language to hit the computer community since C, and learn to use Visual Café, Symantec's outstanding Java development environment, to help you write Java applets and applications. By the time you finish *Discover Visual Café*, you'll be aware of the ins and outs of `java.awt`, `for...while` loops, and the rest of the Java language, and you will be able to use the Form Editor, the Interaction Wizard, and the rest of Visual Café to make Java components do your bidding. *Discover Visual Café* means to give you an in-depth look into the Java language. But at the same time, it tries to show you how Visual Café can make programming projects go faster and with less difficulty. Between Visual Café and this book, you're on the right track to learning Java.

How This Book Is Organized

This section introduces you to the organization of *Discover Visual Café* and should give you some guidance in deciding how to use this book to meet your goals. Consult the Table of Contents, too, when planning your attack.

Quick Tour

Discover Visual Café opens with a section called Quick Tour, which glosses over the details of Visual Café and Java to show you how to develop a simple Java applet quickly with the aid of Visual Café's Interaction Wizard. Without writing a single line of code by hand, you'll develop an applet that starts and stops a display of fireworks embedded in a Web page.

Quick Tour is meant to get you going with Visual Café, not to provide you with deep coverage. By giving you confidence in your Visual Café skills and showing you a little bit of Visual Café's powerful programming repertoire, Quick Tour encourages you to dig deeper into this book and learn more about Java and Visual Café.

Real Life Visual Café

Twice in this book, once at the beginning of each of the two major parts, you'll find sections called Real Life Visual Café. These short sections provide insights into the people and organizations behind Java and Visual Café. Based on a trip to Symantec's headquarters in Cupertino, in California's Silicon Valley, these sections help illustrate that by taking the time to learn Java and Visual Café, you're becoming part of an exciting, growing community.

Part One: Java and Visual Café

The first part of *Discover Visual Café* takes you on an adventure into the depths of the Java language. Explaining everything from what a thread is to how to declare variables of the string datatype and write complicated applets and applications, Part One gets you tuned in to the large and small issues the Java programmer must face.

Part One isn't ignorant of Visual Café, of course. All of the demonstrations take place in Visual Café, so you can begin to learn Visual Café procedures even as you're just beginning to learn Java structure and syntax.

Part Two: Programming With Visual Café

The second part of *Discover Visual Café* deals more with the details of Visual Café than with Java. The idea is that you can take the knowledge you acquired in Part One and continue exploring ways to make Visual Café ease the development process for you. In Part Two, you'll explore Visual Café's programming tools one by one, and learn how to use them together to write, debug, and release excellent programs in a hurry.

Discovery Center

Toward the end of *Discover Visual Café*, you'll find the Discovery Center, a graphical guide to important nuggets of knowledge contained in the text. You may find Discovery Center to be useful in reviewing one chapter before going on to the next, or as a quick reference to the Visual Café interface and Java programming style.

The CD-ROM

Discover Visual Café comes with a companion CD-ROM that is contained in a plastic pouch inside the back cover of the book. Read the CD-ROM License Agreement, open the pouch, load the CD-ROM into your computer's CD-ROM drive, and make sure that it got to you intact. Then, start exploring its contents.

Source Code

The CD-ROM contains all of the sample Java code covered in the first part of this book, plus supplementary source code for you to play with. Each sample is provided as a source code file, a compiled class, and a Visual Café project file that incorporates the other files. Some demonstrations also come with graphics files and other additional materials the programs require.

Acknowledgments

This book, at times, may sound as if it's trying to promote Visual Café and Java rather than merely describe and explain them. That's not because we didn't employ high standards of research on this project; we've pointed out the shortcomings of our subjects. Rather, the occasionally rah-rah tone of *Discover Visual Café* stems from the facts that Java represents the next generation in computer programming languages and that Symantec has a great product in Visual Café. We have very high expectations of both Visual Café and Java.

We owe a debt of gratitude to everyone who helped put this project together. Mike Roney at IDG Books Worldwide suggested this book and put the two of us together as a team. John Cole did a great job of keeping the content technically accurate, Luann Rouff edited the copy, and Tracy Cramer did her usual knockout work on the CD-ROM. The IDG Production group made everything look great. Ralph Moore did an outstanding job of coordinating everyone's efforts.

Without the assistance of Roger Bowman and others at Symantec, this book would have been much weaker.

David Wall thanks his family, as well as Adam Bergman, Adam Bernstein, Juliet Bishop, Ellen Marcus, Bryan Pfaffenberger, and Bruce Woodard for their support and friendship during the writing of this book.

Arthur Griffith thanks his wife, Mary, who, when told, "I am going to write a book," asked the question, "Does this mean you're going to quit your job?"

David Wall
Salt Lake City, Utah

Arthur Griffith
Dallas, Texas

CONTENTS AT A GLANCE

PART TWO—PROGRAMMING WITH VISUAL CAFÉ

CONTENTS

VISUAL CAFÉ QUICK TOUR

PRACTICE USING THESE SKILLS

Welcome to Visual Café!

By taking the time to explore Java programming and learn Visual Café, you've demonstrated a powerful enthusiasm for what's happening at the cutting edge of programming and network technology. You've positioned yourself to be supremely competitive in the networked workplace of the future. Java promises to completely change the way we think about computers and computer programming, while Visual Café boasts Java programming tools unsurpassed by any others available. The two technologies represent a powerful combination in the hands of a skilled user.

This book, *Discover Visual Café*, will turn you into a knowledgeable Java programmer and a top-flight Visual Café operator. The first section of this book teaches you Java, while the second half leads you through the intricacies of Visual Café.

But let's not wait to create a Java applet with Visual Café! The Visual Café Quick Tour leads you through the process of creating a simple applet using Visual Café programming tools.

Getting Ready to Go

We'll go on the assumption that you've already installed Visual Café on your computer and are ready to begin programming.

TIP **If you have installation troubles, find a bug, or run into any exotic difficulties as you explore and use Visual Café, send an e-mail message to the Visual Café support team at `vcafe@symantec.com`. They're busy, but they're the best, and they'll answer your questions promptly and accurately.**

Our guide for this trip through Visual Café is Roger Bowman, a developer relations spokesman for Symantec. This chapter derives from a tour of a preliminary version of Visual Café he gave in October of 1996.

Creating an Applet

After starting Visual Café, Bowman chooses **File** → **New Project** and chooses the "Basic Applet" template from the New Project dialog box that appears. He chooses **Window** → **Form Editor - Applet1** and gets a clean slate, like the one shown in Figure 1. The Form Editor and Project Manager are active.

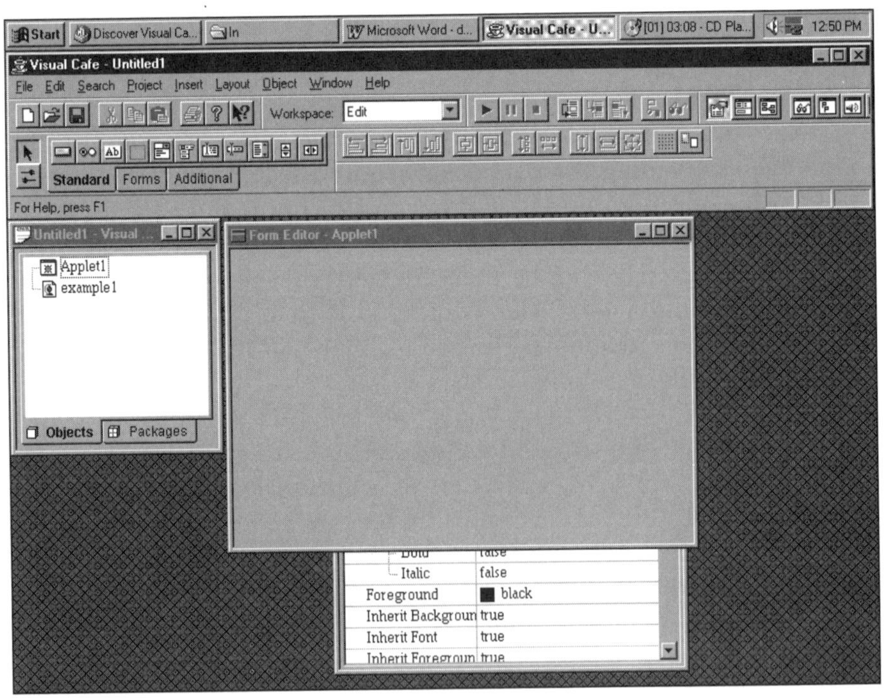

Figure 1 Visual Café stands ready to create an applet — quickly.

The Form Editor

On the toolbar, he clicks the Button button (not a redundancy — it's the toolbar button that you use to create a push-button in your applets and applications) and drags out a rectangle on the Form Editor with his mouse pointer to define the space the button will occupy. A push-button appears in the space he dragged out. He repeats the process to create a second button.

Then Bowman drags his mouse pointer to surround the two buttons with a temporary gray rectangle, selecting them. He chooses Layout → Align → Left to align the left edges of the buttons, making them look neater. Then he chooses Layout → Make Same Size → Both to give both buttons the same dimensions, further improving the appearance of the applet interface he's creating in the Form Editor.

His Form Editor now looks like the one shown in Figure 2.

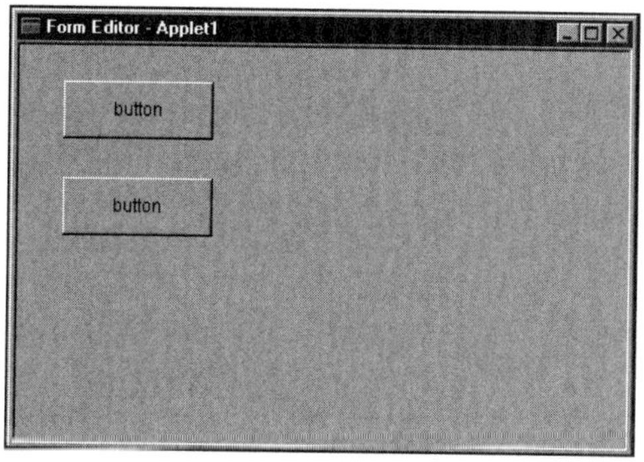

Figure 2 These buttons that appear in the Form Editor will soon get new labels.

The Property List

"The buttons need to say something other than 'button,'" he says. He highlights the top button by clicking it, then goes to the Property List, shown in Figure 3. He scrolls down the list of the button's properties — each one controlling some aspect of the button's appearance or behavior — to the one called "Label." Bowman changes the contents of the right column from "button" to "Freeze" — for a reason you'll understand in a moment. Immediately, the upper button in the Form Editor gets the "Freeze" label.

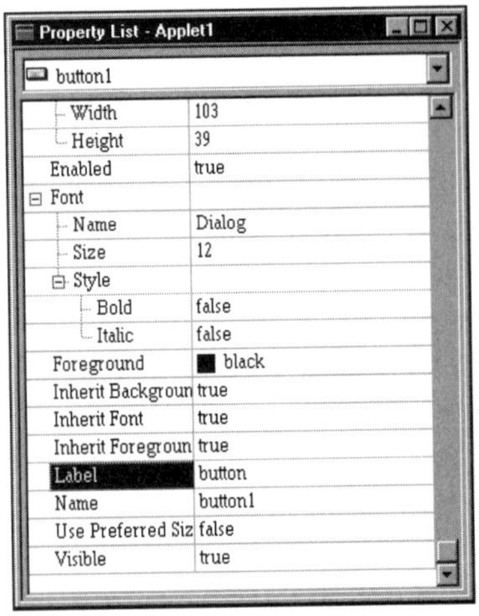

Figure 3 The Property List changes the attributes of items in the Form Editor.

He repeats the process for the lower button, labeling it "Thaw."

After editing the buttons — and note that he hasn't written a single line of code yet — Bowman clicks the Additional tab on the Palette toolbar, then clicks the Firework button on the toolbar. He returns his mouse pointer to the Form Editor and drags out a rectangle for the Firework class — a Symantec applet that comes with Visual Café whose function you will see in a second — on the form, to the right of the Freeze and Thaw buttons.

As soon as he releases the mouse button, the Firework class "goes live." It does what it will do in the final applet; namely, it displays images of fireworks arcing and exploding in a night sky. Figure 4 shows Bowman's applet at this stage.

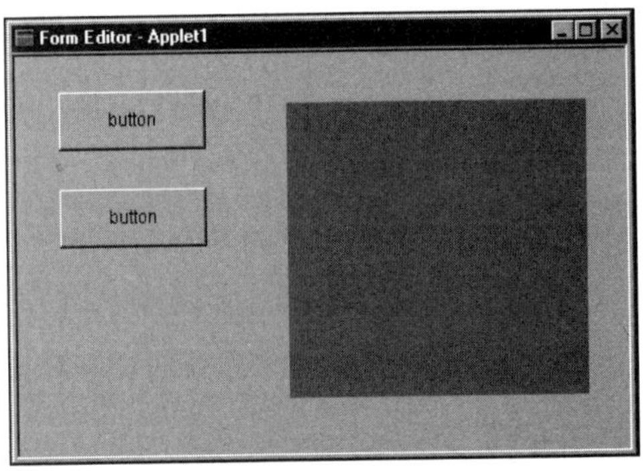

Figure 4 Bowman's applet, with all its components in place, is ready to be brought to life by the Interaction Wizard.

The Interaction Wizard

He's laid out a cool-looking class and two buttons, but the buttons don't do anything yet. That's where the Interaction Wizard comes into play. The Interaction Wizard represents Visual Café's most powerful tool for the novice Java programmer.

Bowman clicks the **Interaction Wizard** button on the toolbar. His mouse pointer becomes an icon that looks like a length of cord with a plug on each end.

With the Interaction Wizard pointer, Bowman clicks the Freeze button and holds down his mouse button. A thick black line appears from the button to the pointer and follows the pointer as he moves it. Carefully, he drags the pointer end of the line to the interior of the Firework box and releases his mouse. The Interaction Wizard, shown in Figure 5, appears.

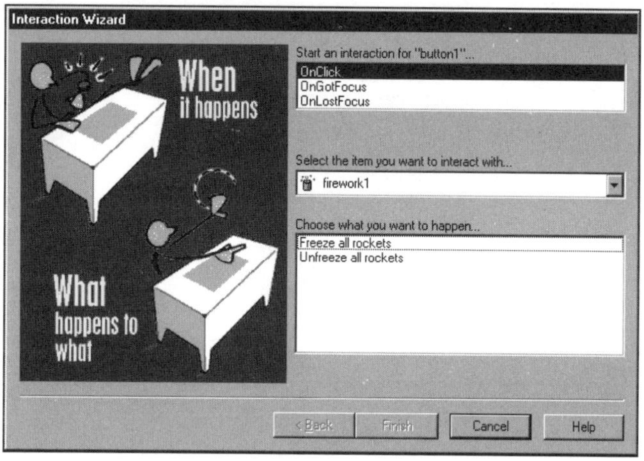

Figure 5 The Interaction Wizard is Visual Café's ace — it adds interactivity to your programs with a minimum of hassle.

The Interaction Wizard lists everything that can happen to the button (all the events that can occur there) and all the things the Firework class can do in response to those events. The Interaction Wizard tells him that three events can involve the button: OnClick (meaning that the user clicks the button with the mouse), OnGotFocus (meaning that the button gets the focus, as when the user tabs through the controls in a window), and OnLostFocus (which occurs when the button loses the focus, again with the tab key). He selects OnClick because he wants something to happen when the user clicks the button.

The bottom part of the Interaction Wizard lists all the things the Firework class can do in response to the button being clicked. Firework has only two actions: "Freeze all rockets" and "Unfreeze all rockets." To correspond with the Freeze button's label, he selects "Freeze all rockets" as the action to be taken if the user clicks the Freeze button.

He repeats the process for the Thaw button, carefully linking the Thaw button to the Firework box and specifying the "Unfreeze all rockets" action in the case of the "OnClick" event.

The Applet Viewer

Bowman's applet now looks exactly as it did in Figure 4, but underneath the surface, things have changed — thanks to the Interaction Wizard. It's time to compile the applet and see how it works. Bowman clicks the **Run** button to test his work.

The program compiles and begins to run in the Applet Viewer, as shown in Figure 6. Here Bowman can interact with his applet the way a user would. When he clicks the Freeze button, all the rockets stop. When he clicks the Thaw button, the bombs resume bursting in air. It's a success — and without touching a single line of code.

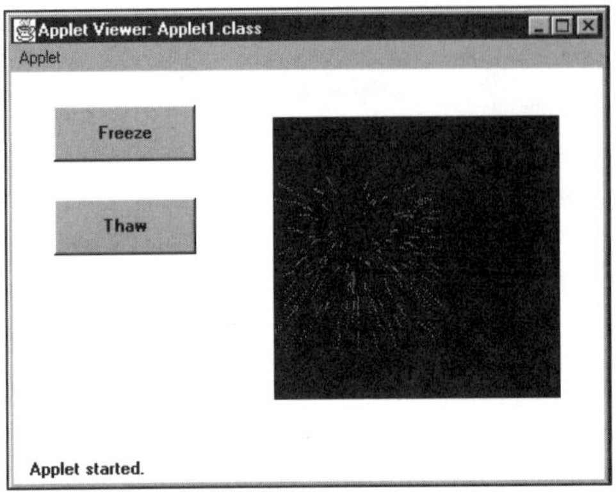

Figure 6 The Applet Viewer displays your applets without the hassle of running a full Web browser.

You understand that not all programming projects are as basic as this one, and you'll certainly have to edit Java source code before you get too far into exploring Java and Visual Café. But the Form Editor and Interaction Wizard provide you with a taste of how Symantec designed Visual Café to automate programming as much as possible — a feature that will save you time and effort down the line.

PART ONE

JAVA AND VISUAL CAFÉ

THIS PART CONTAINS THE FOLLOWING CHAPTERS

This first part of *Discover Visual Café* introduces you to the Java language. You'll find out the details of Java applets and applications. You'll discover the data types Java employs, and spend extra time learning about strings. You'll see how Java uses expressions, operators, and methods, then move on to the more complex issues of exceptions, threads, even handling and drawing. Finally, you'll learn about animation, input and output, javadoc, and the utility API.

REAL LIFE VISUAL CAFÉ: CAFEBABE

CUPERTINO, Calif. — Perhaps the success of Café and Visual Café was fated by the stars.

Unbeknownst to most Visual Café users — and indeed, most Java programmers in general — the Java specification for .class files includes an unintentional reference to Symantec's line of Java development environments.

At the beginning of every Java .class file — every file containing Java bytecodes ready for interpretation by an applet viewer or browser — there's what is called a *bytecode signature,* a string of hexadecimal numbers that identifies the file as Java code.

Most computer files have bytecode signatures that identify them to applications and operating systems. That's how, for example, Microsoft Word knows that it's dealing with a WordPerfect file it has to translate, or how QuarkXPress knows it has encountered a file in an incompatible format and must send the user an error message.

But compiled Java files — .class files — have a bytecode signature with special significance to the users of Symantec's Java development tools — even though the bytecode signature was created by Sun Microsystems engineers long before Symantec's first Java tools came out.

The first eight hexadecimal numbers of the Java bytecode signature, when translated into ASCII characters, spell "CAFEBABE." Every Java class in existence, without exception, opens with those eight characters.

The original significance of that signature has already been lost to the rapidly shifting sands of the computer industry. One can only imagine the Java team visiting a coffeehouse late at night, with the caffeine-fogged memory of a pleasant *barista* later finding its way out of a programmer's head and into the Java language specification. Or perhaps the bytecode signature was established soon after a baby joined one of the team members' families. It's not possible to know with certainty.

But we can take it as a happy omen that Visual Café is the right development environment for you as you explore Java programming.

CHAPTER ONE

THE STORY OF JAVA AND VISUAL CAFÉ

IN THIS CHAPTER YOU LEARN THESE KEY SKILLS

Nothing can generate hype like the computer community — especially now that so many are connected by the Internet. Often the hype gets focused on something that's not worth it — recall the initial excitement about Internet telephony. Other times a company will promote a so-so product to such an extent that the marketing outshines the product.

Java is the exception. It's been hyped worldwide, but the excitement is well-founded. It has the potential to revolutionize programming — no mean feat at all. Visual Café, which brings Java programming into the hands of less experienced programmers, is almost as exciting. This chapter explains the origins and characteristics of both Java and Visual Café.

The Language That's a Tourist Attraction

A few blocks from Symantec's headquarters on Stevens Creek Boulevard in Cupertino, California, Sun Microsystems' JavaSoft subsidiary has set up shop. In front of the JavaSoft building is a sign featuring the Java steaming coffee-cup logo. It's become a tourist attraction, with people coming from far away to have their pictures taken next to the JavaSoft sign.

That's how big a deal the Java programming language has become. It made its debut at the end of 1995 and already has begun to unseat C and C++, the long-reigning kings of software development. Let's see why.

What's So Great About Java?

Java code can execute on any kind of processor. A program you write in Java can run just as well on a Solaris workstation as on a Macintosh or a Windows 95 machine. Any system with a Java interpreter, and that includes most systems nowadays, can run any given Java program. There's no such thing as a "Macintosh executable" as distinguished from a "Windows executable" and from a "DOS executable" in Java, as there is with C++ programs. Every Java program works with every Java-aware platform. That's a big attraction to software developers, because it means that they no longer have to support parallel development efforts to create a particular program for different platforms.

In addition to its multiplatform capabilities, Java's technical features blow C and C++ away. Java incorporates most of the handiest features of C++, which guarantees that a significant number of programmers — 2.5 million or more — have some idea of what's going on in Java code. Java, like C++, is object-oriented, which means it's modular and easily expandable.

But Java does away with some of C++'s most confusing and error-prone features. It's much harder to create a memory leak — a set of instructions that uses up more and more memory, for no good reason, over time — with Java than with C++. That's because Java, at least on the surface, has no pointers, variables whose contents "point" to other locations in memory. Without pointers, programmers don't have to concern themselves much with memory management — Java takes care of it for them in the background. Furthermore, the absence of pointers makes it harder for a malicious programmer to hijack legitimate programs for the purpose of stealing information or wreaking havoc. Java is a very secure language.

Java really comes into its own on a network. Because programs written in it can run on many different kinds of computers, Java programs can be kept on a server, then parceled out to any computer that asks for them. A special kind of Java application, called an applet, is designed to be embedded in a Web page. Applets can do everything from make calculations based on user input to search the Web for user-specified information. Most Java uses so far have been as Web applets.

"Your Mother Was a Toaster..."

How did Java get to be such a great language? Initially it was designed as a language for smart appliances — a language for programming VCRs, stereo gear, toasters, and the like. Toasters simply *cannot* crash. If an appliance were to fail because of its software, it would have to go back to the manufacturer for repair — an expensive and inefficient proposition. The programs appliances run have to be, as programmers say, bulletproof. A team at Sun Microsystems, led by James Gosling (now a Sun vice president), created Java to fill this need for a hassle-free appliance language.

At first they called their language Oak, after a large oak tree that grew outside Gosling's office window. But that name ran into copyright trouble, and Sun's marketing people attached the name Java to the language, capitalizing on the trendiness of coffee and coffee culture.

Now Java's the main buzzword in Internet (and cyberposer) circles. It's even been written up in *USA Today* and other mainstream publications. Java — almost certainly with a fair amount of accuracy — is being cited as the next wave in everything from operating systems to stand-alone applications. Some colleges have even begun to teach Java as a first programming language.

Enter Symantec

In the winter of 1995 – 1996, Symantec's Internet and Developer Tools division was on fire with Java enthusiasm; the Symantec team saw Java's potential and, significantly, acted upon it sooner than other companies. Before the company got into the Java development tool business, though, a single man had to point out the strategic advantage Symantec had.

The Vision of One

Mansour Safai worked for Symantec as a general manager, leading the teams that developed Symantec's C++ coding and debugging environments for Windows and the Macintosh. Safai went to Sun Microsystems' Developers' Conference in September of 1995 and was present for the public unveiling of Java. He liked the language. But more than that, he saw how Symantec's C++ tools were the ideal starting point for creating a graphical development environment for Java.

Safai saw that, unlike Microsoft's C++ compiler, Symantec's compiler was truly modular and easily adaptable to the clean, efficient Java language. He realized that it would be relatively easy for Symantec to prepare its C++ tools for Java work — and get a big-time jump on the competition.

Safai went to Symantec president Gordon Eubanks and proposed that the company exploit its technical advantage and put out a Java development environment right away. Eubanks wasn't sure the idea would work, so he told Safai he needed more information.

Safai recruited Kenneth Kiraly, one of the lead architects of Symantec's C++ tools, and set to work at the division level, without any particular encouragement from upper management. Six weeks later, the two had converted the Sun

Java compiler into a Windows .DLL file, suitable for incorporation into the existing Symantec C++ development environment as an add-in expansion module.

Safai went back to Eubanks with this proof-of-concept product in mid-October 1995. The demonstration convinced the chief executive, and Symantec promptly licensed Java from Sun. It was one of the first companies to do so.

"We decided to bet our marketing on an integrated development environment for Java," Symantec spokesman Roger Bowman says.

Espresso and Beyond

Symantec placed its first chips on the table when Safai's add-in module, Espresso, went to market in December 1995. A similar Macintosh product, Caffeine, started selling in February 1996. Both products moved well — largely because they were the first graphical Java development tools (the only alternative was the command-line-driven Java Development Kit from Sun) and Symantec gave them to registered owners of its C++ products. "We wanted to be the first," Bowman says.

But it was Café, released for Windows in March 1996, that established Symantec as leader of the Java development tools market. Café was (and remains) a stand-alone development tool for Java. What really caused Café to take off, Bowman says, was its graphical debugger, the first such product for the Java language. Symantec later released a version of Café for the Macintosh and soon afterward put out Windows and Macintosh versions in Japan, tailored for the three Japanese character sets.

Café got a big boost when James Gosling, the father of Java, started using Café to demonstrate the capabilities of Java in public presentations and published articles. He praised the product and sales soared.

Of course, the competition wasn't sitting idly by as Symantec turned out Java products. Borland announced its plans to release JBuilder (formerly called Latté), a Java development environment that would itself be written in Java, before Safai even demonstrated his add-in to Eubanks. Borland later abandoned the idea of coding JBuilder in Java and started over in Delphi. As of this writing, JBuilder has yet to see the light of day, though Borland has a Java add-in for its C++ development environment.

Microsoft wasn't sitting still either. It released J++, a Java development environment with special support for Microsoft's ActiveX Controls standard, in the summer of 1996.

Most reviewers say J++ isn't as good as Café. It's troubled by the fact that it will let you insert an ActiveX Control (a button, for example) into an application without telling you that you're inserting an ActiveX Control. Then, when you try to run your applet on a browser that doesn't understand ActiveX (and that's most every browser except Microsoft Internet Explorer, including the popular Netscape Navigator), certain controls won't show up.

"But they do have great marketing," Bowman says, only partly joking.

A Mandate for Visual Café

Café, J++, and JBuilder treat Java as what's called a *third-generation language,* or *3GL.* In a 3GL environment, programmers have a great deal of control over the internal structure of programs, but they get very little hand-holding from the programming tools. Café is best suited to C++ programmers, who are used to turning out complicated programs without much assistance from their software tools. The world population of such programmers is about 500,000.

Many more people — about five times as many — can create programs with fourth-generation languages, or 4GLs. Delphi and Visual Basic are the most popular 4GLs at the moment.

Though they're not as powerful as 3GL environments and they insulate the programmer from certain low-level tasks, 4GL environments make it possible for less skilled programmers to quickly generate simple to moderately complex programs. These 4GLs usually feature a *form designer,* with which users can design windows visually by dragging elements like buttons and list boxes onto a grid. Often, 4GLs feature some kind of intelligence, or at least an assistant, that helps a semi-skilled user write programs that do what he or she wants.

Because there was originally no such product for Java, and the market demanded one, Symantec took its Java-integrated development environment lead and again parlayed it into commercial success, developing Visual Café for both Windows and Macintosh systems.

Summary

Java, you've seen, is the talk of the programming and Internet communities because it combines excellent attributes for a programming language — modularity, security, error resistance, relative simplicity, and cross-platform compatibility — with extreme network friendliness. Since Sun Microsystems unleashed Java in late 1995, it's been the biggest deal since the Web browser.

Web publishers have rushed to create applet-enhanced Web pages. These often gimmicky pages, usually featuring animation and forms, are just the beginning. Many experts predict that soon the network will *be* the personal computer, with the applications you use every day tapping resources far and wide across the Internet with the aid of Java.

Symantec took its C++ development environment — which was winning accolades but losing in the marketplace to the marketing sledgehammer that backs Microsoft products — and adapted it to write Java code. First as an add-in for its C++ environment, then later as a stand-alone product called Café, Symantec's Java products began to catch on among programmers. Initially the support came because Symantec's products got to market first. Later, Symantec kept its lead over Borland and Microsoft because it had a superior product.

Then Symantec decided to release a RAD — a Rapid Application Development environment — for Java. Visual Café is the result. Released at the end of 1996, Visual Café boasts an ease of use far greater than that of any other Java development environment. To a certain extent you can create Java programs in Visual Café without seeing a bit of source code.

Now you're ready to look behind the curtain. The next chapter begins a detailed look at Java. Later, in Chapter 12, "Understanding the Visual Café Interface," you'll begin to learn the details of Visual Café and how to use it.

CHAPTER TWO

THE JAVA NICKEL TOUR

IN THIS CHAPTER YOU LEARN THESE KEY SKILLS

Describing a computer language is simultaneously very easy and very difficult. It is easy in the sense that a computer language definition is very exact — there are no shadings of meaning in the parts that are defined. The difficulty in describing a computer language is that there is no clear place to start — every part relates to some extent to every other part. Finding a starting point is like finding the lead horse in a merry-go-round. When you read about a new computer language, you go along just fine until all of a sudden, wham! — there is a reference to something that you have never heard of. That's what this chapter is trying to prevent. It is a general introduction to the Java language. A general understanding of the material in this chapter will provide a framework for the details presented in the chapters that follow.

Java is eclectic. Like all computer languages since COBOL and FORTRAN, Java has the advantage of being able to draw features and characteristics from previous languages. Java has chosen from the best. Much of Java comes directly from C without change. Parts of it are variations on a theme from C. Other parts are concepts that come from other languages (exceptions seem to have a tinge of Ada and object manipulation seems to have a pinch of Smalltalk). These elements are all combined in such a way that we have what appears to be an entirely new language. Once you get the gist of its construction, you will see that it is really a very simple language.

The principal predecessor to Java is C — if you can keep C syntax and semantics in mind as you study Java you will be on the right track. While it is true that there are also certain similarities between Java and C++, the two languages are not similar enough for us to be able to use C++ as a basis for any of the descriptions; as a matter of fact, it can be confusing trying to keep them sorted out because some things that look alike actually work differently.

TIP **If your knowledge if C is limited, don't be concerned — everything is explained. There are references to C throughout the text, but these are there so that those who already know C can relate to a concept quickly and apply their existing knowledge.**

Things in C That Are Not in Java

And now, ladies and gentlemen, sit back and relax and allow us to be your tour guide through some strange and fascinating terrain. As we ruthlessly ride off into the new world of Java, we take a quick glance into the rearview mirror and, with a moment of sadness and reverie, bid a fond farewell to many elements of C that we have come to understand and cherish. Let us pause now to pay our respects to each of these and make our plans for how we will be coping without them in the future.

TIP **Actually, C is not being left behind at all. Java and C serve two entirely different purposes. C is an excellent systems-level language; Java is an outstanding applications programming language. C doesn't have the safety and object-orientedness of Java, and nothing — not even Java — can get as down and dirty inside the machine as C.**

Functions

Java has no functions. Well, it does, but they are a little different. Well, they're not really *that* different, but they are in a different place. In Java, a function-like thing is called a *method* and can only be defined as part of a class. There is no way to define a method outside of a class. However, it is possible to define a method within a class as being `static`, and it can be accessed globally just as if it were a function. So I suppose we really haven't *lost* functions; we just changed the way in which they are declared. Also, methods have some special powers when it comes to classes, as will be explained when we start dealing with classes. The entire Java API exists as a set of methods defined inside classes. For example, there is a `Math` class that has the methods `sin()` and `cos()` that work just like the C functions in `stdlib`.

2

Prototypes

It may be that we still have functions (now called methods, of course), but we certainly don't still have prototypes. Every method is declared in exactly one place. Because every method must reside in a class, it must be defined inside that class. Whenever a call is made to a method in another class, the compiler is smart enough to go and look in the other class to find the method definition. (Sometimes we have to help it a bit so that it can find the class — more on this in Chapter 6, "The Structure of a Java Program.")

This eliminates the whole undefined-forward-reference thing. In Java, there is no need to worry about the order in which things are defined. The compiler is smart: whenever it comes across something that is not defined, it will look through all the classes it knows about to find whatever it needs.

TIP **The Java compiler does whatever it can to find a definition for the names it finds in a class. It may, in the middle of compiling a class, find that it needs to compile another class to get a name resolved. It will stop right in the middle of one compile, go do another one, and then come right back. This way, two classes can refer to each other and the compiler will sort it all out.**

Header Files

There are no header files in Java. There is no `include` directive. We don't have function prototypes, so we don't need their type definitions. The compiler will look inside any class files to find all the definitions that it needs, so there is simply no need for header files for prototyping. Because Java will look ahead for you, there is no need for prototyping things that appear later in the same file — or even in another file.

Preprocessor

There is no preprocessor in Java. Because there are no header files, a preprocessor is not needed to include other source files. Java has the capability to define named constants as part of classes, so header files are not needed for that either.

Things that are done in C with macros can be done just as easily in Java with methods — an optimizing compiler will put code inline automatically.

Without a preprocessor, there is no conditional compilation. In C, conditional compilation is used for portability — enabling the code to compile on different machines or with different compilers. Because Java code is completely portable across platforms (the executable form is exactly the same regardless of the computer that it is compiled on), there is no need for conditional compilation.

TIP **If you are in the habit of using an `#if` and `#endif` pair to temporarily disable blocks of code, you will miss the preprocessor — I know I do. To retain the ability to comment out entire Java methods, it is necessary to use only the // form of comments inside a method, which leaves the /* and */ pair free to comment out its entire body. Just like C, the comments do not nest, but unlike C, the special // comment simply makes the rest of that one line a comment.**

We have all been doing a couple of things during software development that require conditional compilation. It is fairly common practice to compile the source with macros that call debug or trace functions. Then, by simply having the macro expand to nothing, the statements were removed by the compiler. This can still be done. Write the code to use the methods in some special trace or debug class and then, for the production version, change the class to one with empty methods. The compiler should optimize the calls right out of existence.

Typedefs

There is no typedef — nor anything like it — in Java. Everything must be explicitly defined using keywords of the Java language. There will be circumstances where it means that more typing needs to be done, but it also makes it very easy to read the definition of whatever is being defined. Anyway, since everything is defined in exactly one place, there is no need to typedef.

The int Default

In the C language, declarations always default to `int` unless otherwise specified. Also, the keywords `short` and `long` are reduced to the status of adjectives. In Java, there is no default type — everything must be declared as a specific type. Also, the keywords `short` and `long` are full-fledged data types, not just adjectives thrown in to modify an `int`.

Variable Argument Lists

All method arguments must be completely defined at compile time. There may be other times when you wish this was true, but experience has shown that it is almost always used for one of two purposes. Mostly it is used to format data into a string (as in C with `printf`), but with the string conversions and concatenations built into Java, there is no need for a variable argument list to achieve this. The other common use is in error handling, which Java takes care of with its built-in exceptions.

Bit Data Types

The bit data types of C are completely missing in Java. There is no way to assign a name, for example, to a two-bit integer. However, because the shift and masking operators still exist, it is quite straightforward to insert and extract bit patterns inside the integral data types — simply build a class as a wrapper around an integer and write bit-extraction and bit-insertion methods to your heart's content. The Java API supplies a class called `BitSet` that quite efficiently handles operations on variable-length arrays of bits.

Pointers

Java has no pointers. It does, however, have references. In reality, a reference is the same as a pointer, but with some *very* strict limitations. References are central to the operation of Java and they will be explained in great detail in the next few chapters. But when you are programming in Java, never think in terms of the address of anything; just use whatever name you assign to it and let Java find it for you. It makes things much friendlier to use.

Not having pointers is a bit disconcerting to those of us who have been armpit deep in C for all this time. My first pouty reaction was, "How can you do anything really serious in a language that forbids addressing?" As it turns out, Java does some RNS (Real Neat Stuff) with references combined with the appearance/disappearance of objects. If you are not familiar with the way Java handles references, keep reading — you have a real treat in store. (Hint: No more memory management code — ever!)

Structs

In one sense, there are no structs in Java, but because Java is composed entirely of classes, and because classes can be considered enhanced structs, in another sense Java is nothing but structs. Everything in Java resides inside one class or another. It is the primary unit of code organization. A class contains data, just as a C struct does, but it also contains all the functions (excuse me, methods) that operate on these data.

Unions

There are no unions in Java. You can use the superclass and subclass arrangement to do whatever it is you need to have done.

Enum

There is nothing in Java that is anything like the C `enum`.

Unsigned Integers

There is no way to declare an integer value as unsigned. All of them are signed (except for `char`, but it is normally used only for characters and strings). This should not be a problem; any value that can be expressed as an unsigned 32-bit number will fit easily into the Java 64-bit signed `long`.

Longjmp

Long ago it was found that programmers could get themselves into trouble deep down inside a multileveled function call and need to find some way of escape. The `longjmp` was thus invented and even though it's very manual in nature, it serves the purpose. An exception-handling scheme built into Java's language not only solves the problem of escaping from errors at the bottom level of a program, but also takes care of all sorts of other error-handling requirements.

SIDE TRIP

Two by Two

It seems that everything in Java comes in twos. It wasn't intentional, it just sort of worked out this way. Two basic components make up a class: the data and the methods. There are two kinds of primitive data types: the numeric types and the references. There are two kinds of primitive numeric data types: integer and real. There are two places that variables can be declared: at the class level or inside a method. There are two storage locations for data: static data is kept in the class while nonstatic data is duplicated in each object.

Two kinds of programs can be written in Java: an applet and an application. An applet is a graphical "programlet" that you can embed in the HTML of your Web site. An application is a full-blown, stand-alone program that you can run with the Java interpreter. There are two language facilities that can be used to design a class based on previously written code: *extension* (which is inheritance) and *interface* (which is a standard set of methods). There are two types of classes: regular classes, which can be instantiated into objects; and abstract classes, which cannot. Two categories of classes make up the Java standard library: those that are such an integral part of the language that Java will not work without them, and the library classes, which are not known to the Java compiler. There are also two classes that are so special they can be automatically generated by the Java compiler: the string and the array.

Objects Appear and Disappear

A Java program begins execution by having an object created and having a method within that object called by whatever started the program. If the program is an application, this startup method is called `main()`. If the program is an applet, the startup method is called `init()`. For a little program, this method could run to its conclusion and stop. The more common case is to have the executing method create another object (or objects) and pass execution to them. These objects in turn create other objects, which create still others, and so on down the line.

An object is created by using the keyword `new`. The following statement will create a `String` object:

```
new String("The string characters.");
```

This will create the `String`, but once we have it nothing else can be done with it because we didn't keep track of our creation. In order to be able to use it, we must have a reference to it:

```
String stref;
stref = new String("The string characters.");
```

The String object comes into existence and the reference variable named `stref` contains a reference to it. Now we have a way of doing things to it, such as printing its value:

```
System.out.println(stref);
```

OK. Now you know how to create an object. The next step is to find out how to delete one. The process is very simple — do nothing at all. That's right, nothing. The Java system tracks all objects and automatically destroys any that no longer have references to them. Java, by definition, cannot have memory leaks. You can freely exit the function where the reference is defined, you can set the reference to `null`, or you can even overwrite the value in the reference with information about a new object. Java will track it for you and take care of all cleanups. No stray memory can ever escape the watchful eye of the Java interpreter!

An object constructed from a class is said to be an *instance* of that class. The act of constructing an object is known as *instantiation*.

Classes and Methods

A Java program is composed entirely of classes. Java can be thought of as a toolkit that enables a programmer to interrelate classes. Object-oriented programming — at its most fundamental level — is nothing more than a particular way of organizing the code in a program. Object-oriented programming can be (and has been!) done in any language. Java has built-in facilities that simplify this particular type of code organization — the foundation of object-oriented programming in Java is the `class`.

TIP **A class is the floorplan for a set of data items and methods. That's really all that it is — the blueprint of an object. Everything else about a class has to do with the details of how it carries out its one purpose — to act as the planning committee during the construction of objects.**

In every class is one special method called a *constructor*. The constructor is easy to spot because it always has the same name as the class. A constructor may or may not take arguments, but it never returns a value. If, when you write a class, you do not write a constructor, the Java compiler will generate one for you — one that has no arguments and allows all the data items in the class to assume their default values. This is known as the *default constructor*. (Actually, any constructor without arguments is a default constructor — it's just that a default constructor is the only kind that Java will automatically generate.)

The constructor, which is called whenever an object is instantiated from a class, assumes the responsibility of initializing the new object. There can be several constructors in the same class as long as each requires a different set of arguments. Different constructors within a class can be used to initialize the objects in different ways. The following class has three constructors:

```
public class Fred {
  int fvalue;
  public Fred() {
   fvalue = 0;
  }
  public Fred(int a) {
   fvalue = a;
  }
  public Fred(int a,int b) {
   fvalue = a + b;
  }
}
```

The class `Fred` can be initialized in three entirely different ways. The first constructor — the one without an argument — is the default constructor and always sets the internal value to zero. The second constructor requires a single `int` argument, and the last one takes a pair of `int`s. All of them do the job of initializing `fvalue`. How does Java tell them apart? The same way you do — by looking at the argument list.

Having two methods with the same name (whether they are constructors or just plain old methods) is a fairly common practice. Java can always tell them apart by looking at the ordered list that designates the number and type of the arguments. This is called *overloading* — the same name has more than one meaning. It has some very nice uses, as we will discover in the coming chapters.

All sorts of scoping and privacy rules govern class definitions (and all of these will be discovered as we go along), but there is one concept that you will need right up-front: You need to have an idea of what is meant by a `static` method or `static` data member. Each time a new object is constructed from a class, each object is given its own copy of all the data items. This makes sense because, after all, the class is just a blueprint, right? Well, `static` is an exception. Declaring something as `static` means that there is only one copy of it — ever. And that one copy is used by all the objects of that class. The upshot of this is that if one object sticks a value into the static data member, all the objects of that class have the same value. Look at the difference between static and non-static data:

```
public class Fred {
  int avalue;
  static int bvalue;
}
```

In this example, there will be a separate copy of `avalue` in every object that is created, and each of these `avalue`s could hold a different value — each will be local to its object. On the other hand, there will only be one copy of `bvalue` no matter how many objects are created. If any of the objects stuffs a number into `bvalue`, all the other objects will get the changed value when they read it.

Not only is there static data, there are also static methods. Simply put, a static method knows nothing about the objects derived from the class, so it can only operate on the static data.

Inheritance and Interfaces

Defining one class as an extension of the definition of another class is known as *inheritance*. The class being inherited from is called the *superclass* and the class doing the inheriting is called the *subclass*. Another word for superclass is *base* class. Another word for subclass is *derived* class. Effectively, the subclass extends the capabilities of the superclass by adding methods and/or data to the ones that already exist. The Java keyword for inheritance is `extends`. A Dalmatian is a kind of dog, so you would define the subclass `Dalmatian` as an extension of the superclass `Dog`:

```
class Dalmatian extends Dog {
...
}
```

There could be other classes extending the same superclass:

```
class Pomeranian extends Dog {
...
}
```

The classes `Dalmatian` and `Pomeranian` are both extended from `Dog`, so they both are likely to have some methods and data in common. Writing your program in a way that takes advantage of this commonality is call *polymorphism*. (A loose definition of the word polymorphism might be, "A bunch of things, some of which are sort of alike.") You will see some examples of the advantages of polymorphism in the following sections.

Whenever you write a class without specifying another class to be extended, Java will automatically extend your class from the superclass `Object`. At some point back in its family tree, every class in Java can trace its ancestry back to the great base class — `Object`. There are no exceptions. This means that, due to polymorphism, certain characteristics are common to all classes.

TIP **The `Object` class has a method called `toString()` that generates a `String` object from the information inside the object. Because every class is derived from `Object`, every class can be printed as a string in a statement:**

```
System.out.println(object);
```

The information from some objects is more useful than the information from others, but every object in Java will print just fine.

Packages

As we said earlier, a Java program is made up of classes. These classes are organized into groups known as `packages`. If you want the class you are writing to be part of a specific package, you only need to tell the compiler the package name at the top of the file:

```
package animals;
```

This will put the classes defined in the file into the `animals` package. Using the dot reference naming convention, you can put packages inside of packages:

```
package animals.cute;
```

If you don't specify a package for your class, your class will go into the default class `java`. It is the same as if you had written the following at the top of your file:

```
package java;
```

The Java API is a collection of subpackages inside the `java` package. Table 2-1 lists the standard packages and what they contain.

TABLE 2-1 Java API Packages

Name	Purpose
java.lang	Compiler-essential classes
java.io	Input and output
java.util	Miscellaneous utilities
java.net	Networking support
java.awt	Abstract Window Toolkit
java.awt.image	Image managing classes
java.awt.peer	Platform-specific graphics
java.applet	The basis of applet creation

To access a class from one of the standard API packages, you can put its name on an import statement:

```
import java.awt.*;
```

This allows your class to be on a first-name basis with any member of the `java.awt` package.

Comments and Documentation

There is one kind of comment in C and two in C++. There are three in Java — sort of. The first one is the `/*` and `*/` pair. These work the same way in Java as they do in C. This kind of comment can span several lines of code, and everything between them is a comment. Like C, they do not nest. Whenever the compiler encounters a `/*`, a comment starts and the compiler scans to the first `*/` it comes to and ends the comment.

The second kind of comment was introduced in C++. Anywhere in the code that the compiler encounters a `//`, it considers everything from that point to the end of the line to be a comment.

The third kind is new in Java, and it is really the same as the first except that it begins with `/**` and ends with `*/`. That special three-character beginning is a coded message to a utility called *javadoc* that can be used to automatically generate HTML-formatted documentation. To construct the documentation, it uses the text of the comment, the name of the method or class, and special commands that can be embedded in the text of the comment. You will see examples of this in later chapters.

The Application, the Applet, and Security

Java has two faces. An *application* can be written to be run from the command line, and an *applet* can be written that must be loaded and run in the execution of an HTML script — a Web page. Other differences are mostly related to security. An application can do anything that any program written in any language is capable of doing. Conversely, because an applet is constructed to be loaded from a remote location and then executed locally, some limits have to be put on what it is able to do. This is to protect the local computer from applets that have bad attitudes, carry weapons, or come from broken homes. Strictly speaking, there are no limitations imposed by the Java language — the limitations are imposed by your Web browser while it loads and interprets the Java bytecode.

TIP **You can look at the source code of a class and tell immediately whether it is an applet, an application, or just a plain ol' utility class. If you see a method named main(), you are looking at an application. If you see a method named init(), you are looking at an applet. (If you see both, it is both. More about that later.) If you don't see either main() or init(). it can only be a utility class that is part of a larger program.**

Java applets are said to run in a "sandbox" in the browser — that is, the applet is allowed to do only the things that the browser will allow it to do. Nothing else. Exactly what the limitations are will vary from one browser to the next — but there are always limitations and they are strictly enforced. An applet cannot read and write local disk files. There can be no Internet connections made other than to the server from which the applet was loaded. An applet cannot read local system properties, execute programs, or load libraries.

The subject of applet security is somewhat complicated and is constantly being revised. Everyone wants applets to be able to do as much as possible while being as safe as possible. Compromises must be made as to exactly where to draw the line in the bitmap. To keep up with the current state of applet security, take a look at `http://java.sun.com/sfaq`, where the FAQ is kept.

BONUS

HTML and the Java Applet

Java applets are executed by being included in an HTML Web page. Following is a simple example of how this is done:

```
<html>
<head>
<title>The ShowCircle Applet</title>
</head>
<body>
<applet code="ShowCircle.class" width=200 height=150>
</applet>
</body>
</html>
```

This is a complete — but very simple — Web page. As all Web pages do, it begins with `<html>` and ends with `</html>`. There is a region for a heading (between `<head>` and `</head>`) and a region for the body of the Web page (between `<body>` and `</body>`). Inside the heading is a single line of title text (defined between `<title>` and `</title>`). The body of the page is where the applet is buried.

The HTML tags `<applet>` and `</applet>` are used to specify the name of the applet and its display size. In our example, the name of the applet file is `ShowCircle.class`, and it is to be given a rectangle on the screen that is 200 pixels wide and 150 pixels high. That's it — a browser will pick this up and take it from here.

TIP **An applet never gets to choose its own size — that is always done in the HTML. Of course, care should always be taken to make sure that the sizes are compatible. The applet has methods available to it to find out what size it must fill.**

Summary

This completes our preliminary look into the world of Java. We have pointed out the major characteristics of C that were left out, and have given you an idea of how Java works and how it is organized to do what it does. We have skimmed along the top of things so you will have a framework in mind as you discover other parts of the Java programming language.

In the next chapter we bungee dive to the very bottom of Java and start discussing how some of the stuff in the basement works. We are going to take a look into the wonderful world of integers, characters, and real numbers, and discover the kinds of data that exist at Java's lowest level. There are only a few of these fundamental types, but they are all that is needed to construct a Java program. In the Java universe, bits are the atoms and we are going to explore the molecules.

CHAPTER THREE

DATA TYPES

IN THIS CHAPTER YOU LEARN THESE KEY SKILLS

This chapter covers Java's built-in data types. The data types fall into two categories: the primitive types — boolean, byte, char, short, int, long, float, double, and reference — and objects. Each of the primitive types is designed to hold a single data item. With the possible exception of the reference, you already know what these are. A reference is a sort of "handle" to an aggregate (an object or an array). The primitive types are constructed at compile time. The other category of data types, the objects, are constructed at run time. As the program runs, it creates and destroys objects using collections of primitives and other objects.

Example code is supplied for this chapter on this book's accompanying CD-ROM, located in the directory named Chap03. The examples consist of very simple Java application programs — along with Visual Café project files — that demonstrate some of the characteristics of the primitive data types.

Primitive Data Types

The primitive data types of Java (see Table 3-1) have specific sizes, value ranges, and internal representations that do not vary in any way from one platform to another — they are always the same. This is one of the main reasons for Java's portability — the ability of Java code to work on many different machines.

TABLE 3-1 The Primitive Data Types

Type	Size	Description
`boolean`	1 bit	Can be either `true` or `false`. It can take on no other value.
`byte`	8 bits	A signed 8-bit integer.
`short`	16 bits	A signed 16-bit integer.
`char`	16 bits	An unsigned 16-bit integer. It can represent any of the Unicode characters.
`int`	32 bits	A signed 32-bit integer.
`long`	64 bits	A signed 64-bit integer.
`float`	32 bits	An IEEE 754 single-precision floating point value.
`double`	64 bits	An IEEE 754 double-precision floating point value.
`reference`		A reference to an object. Similar to a C pointer.

The boolean Type

The `boolean` type is rather unique among the primitives. Not only is it the smallest — consuming a total of one bit — it cannot be converted directly to or from any of the other primitive types. There are predefined named constants for the two possible `boolean` values: `true` and `false`. The only ways to set a `boolean` variable are by direct assignment (assigning it a constant value of `true` or `false`), by executing a logical operation (such as an arithmetic comparison), or by assigning it a value from another `boolean` type.

The following statement will declare a `boolean` variable called `trigger` and set it to an initial value:

```
boolean trigger = true;
```

In Java, all logical expressions — comparison tests and the like — result in a `boolean` type. Only `boolean` types or expressions can be used in the conditional parts of `switch`, `if`, `do`, and `while` statements. There is no way to cast any other type to a `boolean` type. If you feel like you really need to, that is, if you really need to use a `boolean` value in an arithmetic expression, there are ways to convert, for example, an `int` to a `boolean` type:

```
int ivalue;
boolean trigger;
// Convert from int to boolean
trigger = ivalue != 0;
// Convert from boolean to int
ivalue = trigger ? true : false;
```

3

The byte Type

Variables of the `byte` type hold signed 8-bit integers. These values range from -128 to 127. You can use a literal constant to set initial values.

```
byte a = 12;
byte b = +12;
byte c = -12;
byte d = 0x0C;
byte e = -0x0C;
byte f = 014;
byte g = -014;
```

Each of these valid `byte` declarations has an initial value setting of either positive or negative 12. As in C, a number with a leading "0x" or "0X" is a hexadecimal number, and a leading zero is an octal number. Notice that, along with the traditional unary minus, we also have a unary plus.

The char Type

The `char` type defines variables that hold characters. Not only will `char` values hold the ASCII characters that we all know and love, but Unicode characters as well. Because of Unicode — which includes all of ASCII and several other character sets — you don't need to worry about translating among multiple character sets. The `char` data type is a 16-bit unsigned value, which means it can take on any of the Unicode values from 0 to 65,535. That's a maximum of 64K.

TIP **It is true that a char type is an integer on which arithmetic can be performed, and there will be times when you need to do that. However, because the Java internals will always interpret the contents of a char data type as a character, it is best to use one of the other types for integer values. In particular, whenever Java converts values to**

something displayable (as it does when converting to a String), the char type is always assumed to hold a displayable Unicode character.

Following is the declaration of a few `char` data types with initial values. All of the initial declarations have the same numeric value — the 16-bit Unicode value for the ASCII letter J.

```
char a = 74;
char b = 'J';
char c = 0x4A;
char d = 0112;
char e = '\112';
char f = '\u004A';
```

As you can see, all of these are the same as in C except for the last one, which is the Java form of a 16-bit Unicode character constant.

Like C, some predefined characters are constructed by using the backslash escape sequences, as shown in Table 3-2. Unlike C, these are all 16-bit values.

TABLE 3-2 Predefined Character Constants

Character Constant	Unicode Value	Meaning
`'\b'`	`'\u0008'`	Backspace
`'\t'`	`'\u0009'`	Horizontal tab
`'\n'`	`'\u000A'`	Line feed
`'\f'`	`'\u000C'`	Form feed
`'\r'`	`'\u000D'`	Carriage return
`'\"'`	`'\u0022'`	Double quote
`'\''`	`'\u0027'`	Single quote
`'\\'`	`'\u005C'`	Backslash

The short Type

The `short` type is a signed, 16-bit integer. It can take on values from -32,767 to 32,768. That's a maximum of 32K. It's true that it is the same size as a `char` type, but because it is a *signed* value it has a different range of values. Be careful when mixing the two, as some values will fit in one but not in the other.

The int Type

The `int` type defines a signed, 32-bit integer. It can take on values from -2,147,483,648 to 2,147,483,647. That's a maximum of 2 gigabytes.

The long Type

The `long` type defines a signed, 64-bit integer. It can take on values from -9,223,372,036,854,775,808 to 9,223,372,036,854,775,807. That's a maximum of 4 giga-gigabytes. Those are really, really big numbers. If you want to read 9,223,372,036,854,775,807 out loud you simply say, "Nine quintillion, two hundred twenty-three quadrillion, three hundred seventy-two trillion, thirty-six billion, eight hundred fifty-four million, seven hundred seventy-five thousand, eight hundred seven." That's more than the number of pennies in the U.S. national debt.

TIP **Java keeps track of time by counting the number of milliseconds since January 1, 1970. Using this method — and using a long to store the value — Java will be able to keep track of every millisecond until the year 2,922,708,260. That's more than two gigayears.**

The float and double Types

Java adopted an already existing standard floating point format for its `float` and `double` types — the IEEE 754-1985 standard. A `float` variable can represent values between 3.40282e+038 and 1.4013e-045. A `double` can represent values between 1.79769e+308 and 2.22507e-308. Any of the values anywhere in the range can be either positive or negative.

The reference Type

This is where the object-oriented stuff comes in. In the normal execution of a Java program, objects appear and disappear. Whenever an object appears (usually by using the keyword `new` to create it), the program needs a place to hold the address of the new object. This place is called a *reference*.

A reference operates much like a C pointer, except there is no such thing as "reference arithmetic." The only way to manipulate the contents of a reference is to specify the object that it addresses. While there is some similarity to a C pointer, a reference can't be treated like a C pointer. You can't add a value to a reference. Nor can you index from it as if it were an array. You can't even assign it a value that is incompatible with its type. You can think of a reference as sort of a pointer with seat belts and an air bag.

A reference has a type. That is, it can only refer to one kind of thing. (I would say "point to" instead of "refer to," but some folks are adamant in their opinion that Java does not have pointers. We have to watch our terminology or we could be subject to harassment by the language cops.) A reference refers to an object. The object can be the instance of a class or it can be an array, but the reference will always hold the address of an object of the correct type. More on all this later. Much more. As a matter of fact, most of this book is about manipulating references to objects with Visual Café and the Java language.

Creating Named Constants

Remember, there is no Java preprocessor that can be used to define constants. Instead, a method has been built into the compiler for naming constant values. In Java, a constant is simply any of the primitive types that is declared as `final`. Also whenever you declare a value as `static`, you are specifying that only one copy of the value will exist no matter how many objects are constructed from the class. Defining it as being `final` means that it has a constant value — set at compile time — that can never be changed. The syntax of the language requires that whenever a variable is declared as `final`, it also must have an initial value declared.

Here is a simple class with some constant values defined:

```
public class ConstantExample {
  final int jimbo = 5;
  static final double mm = 2.3;
  public static final long pd = 894;
}
```

Because all the variables in `ConstantExample` are defined as being `final`, they are all constants. The constant `mm` is also defined as being static, so only one copy of it will be used by all the objects created from `ConstantExample`. The constant value `pd` is also declared as `public`, which means that the methods in other classes are allowed to access it directly.

Declaring a variable as being `public static final` makes it a little bit special. There will always be just one copy of it — regardless of the number of objects derived from the class. A `static` variable is not located in any of the objects, but instead in the class itself. Because of this, it can be accessed directly through its class name without the involvement of an object. The following example shows that the constant `pd` is accessible from any other method in any other class:

```
public class ConstantRef {
  public static void main(String argv[]) {
   System.out.println("The value of pd is "
         + ConstantExample.pd);
  }
}
```

TIP Applications quite often need a set of program-wide constant values. In C, the usual solution is to construct a header file that holds them all so that potential changes can be made in one place. You can do the same thing in Java by creating a class that holds nothing but the global constant values.

BONUS

Constructing Arrays

An array is an object. Because it is an object, an array cannot be declared directly. To construct an array, you must first declare a reference, and then the keyword new can be used to construct the actual array. Once the array is constructed, the only way to access it is through its reference. Listing 3-1 illustrates how an array is created and referenced.

Listing 3-1 arrayShow.java

```
public class arrayShow {
  static int arr[];
  static public void main(String argv[]) {
   show_arr(1);
   arr = new int[5];
   show_arr(2);
   arr[3] = 12;
   show_arr(3);
  }

  static void show_arr(int call_number) {
   System.out.print("Call #" + call_number);
   if(arr == null) {
         System.out.println(
               " The array arr references is null");
         return;
   }
   for(int i=0; i<arr.length; i++)
         System.out.print(
               " arr[" + i + "]=" + arr[i]);
   System.out.print("\n");
  }
}
```

Executing arrayShow program produces the following output:

```
Call #1 The array arr references is null
Call #2 arr[0]=0 arr[1]=0 arr[2]=0 arr[3]=0 arr[4]=0
Call #3 arr[0]=0 arr[1]=0 arr[2]=0 arr[3]=12 arr[4]=0
```

The declaration of arr as an array is actually the declaration of a reference, not an array. Note that this reference definition has no size. Its brackets are empty. It is simply the definition of a reference to a one-dimensional array of ints, and can be used as the reference to an array of any size. That it is a reference with no object to refer to is demonstrated by the first call to show_arr, indicating that arr is null.

An actual array is constructed by specifying its size, its type, and using the keyword new. The results of the array construction are placed into the reference arr that we have already defined. We now have an actual array — and we have captured its address in our reference so we are able to use it. A second call made to show_arr demonstrates that we have an array of all zero values.

TIP **All the members of a newly created array are initialized to zero by new. One of the promises that new makes is to initialize the fundamental types to zero. This is unlike C, which initializes allocated memory to interesting values that are probably not what you want.**

You probably noticed that the loop that prints the members of the array uses the expression arr.length to determine the size of the array. This length value is a special attribute of all array objects. Handy, eh?

Both the reference and the array could have been declared on one line as follows:

```
int arr[] = new int[5];
```

This is probably the more common form. This way we can simply think of the reference as being the array. Once it is allocated, it is simply a matter of sticking the square brackets on the reference to index to any member of the array.

There is run-time checking on array bounds. Any attempt to try to access an element beyond the end of the array in either direction (that is, an index that is too large or is a negative number) will result in an exception. The exception thrown will either be the ArrayIndexOutOfBoundsException or the NegativeArraySizeException. (Don't you just hate these short names that give you no idea about what is being named?) There is also an ArrayStoreException that will be thrown if the program attempts to store the wrong kind of object into an array of objects.

Multidimensional arrays work the same way. A two-dimensional array is constructed as follows:

```
float falm[][];
falm = new float[10][8];
```

Summary

This chapter briefly covered the fundamental data types and the two special cases of array objects. Other than input and output, there is only one other fundamental element of the language: `Strings`, which will be covered in the next chapter. These are the building blocks from which all other classes are constructed. A `String` in Java is much more than a simple array of `char` data types. Much more.

You were very patient and read the entire chapter, so here is a cookie for you: Two people were seen entering a building and, a few minutes later, three people came out. A physicist remarked, "The initial measurement was in error." A biologist concluded, "They have reproduced." A mathematician stated, "Now, if exactly one person enters the building, it will be empty again."

CHAPTER FOUR

STRINGS

IN THIS CHAPTER YOU LEARN THESE KEY SKILLS

String manipulation, the subject of this chapter, is far and away the most common activity in all of computerdom. String and character manipulation is such a common occurrence in programs, developers built it right into Java. Supplied with Java is not only the String class, but also a lot of operators that will allow you to do almost everything you want to do with strings, and the StringBuffer class, which will let you do everything else. And to top it all off, all string operations are in Unicode, which makes internationalization a snap.

The String Class

If the `String` class is not the most frequently used thing in Java, it is certainly a contender for the title. As befits its very high standing, `String` objects are a very special case in Java. The `String` class is composed of data and methods just like any other object. What makes it special is that the `String` class is built right into the Java language. This is true to the extent that the operators "+" and "+=" work as type converters and concatenators for the `String` class. Also, any time a group of characters is placed between a pair of double quotes, the Java compiler creates a `String` object. But there's more. Built right into Java is the ability to have any object or primitive type converted directly to a String.

TIP **An array of `chars` is *not* a string, and a `String` is *not* an array of `chars`. If your background is in C, you have a bit of unlearning to do. You will need to forget about null terminated arrays of `char` — they have no meaning in Java.**

A `String` — being an object — can be created and destroyed in the same way as any other object, but the contents of a string object *cannot be modified.* The only way to change the characters in a string is to destroy the old string and build a new one. (Another class, called `StringBuffer`, *can* be modified; it is described in the section "The StringBuffer Class" later in this chapter.) This inability to modify a `String` may seem a bit odd at first, but it really isn't nearly as limiting you might initially think.

StringShow

Probably the best way to describe string operations is with an example. The class `StringShow` contains examples of string operations. This class consists of a `main` that manipulates some character strings and prints them out. This example can be found on the CD-ROM as the file `StringShow.java` in the directory Chap04.

```
public class StringShow {

  public static void main(String[] args)
  {
   String stref;
   String part1;
   String part2;

   // Assigning to a string reference
   stref = "Now is the time";
   System.out.println(stref);
   stref = "Then was the time";
   System.out.println(stref);
```

For our first trick, we bring about the automatic creation of a `String`. The compiler creates a `String` object anywhere in Java a quoted string of characters is encountered. This is done a couple of times in our example and the location of the new `String` objects are stuffed into the reference `stref`. It is done a second time just to demonstrate that the reference will point first to one `String` and then to the other. The first `String` still exists, but it no longer has a reference that knows where it is. Because it is without a reference, the first `String` object will be automatically reclaimed by the system. At first it may seem brutal to destroy poor little orphaned objects this way, but it is really for their own good, you know:

```
// Concatenating two strings from references
part1 = "Party of the first";
part2 = " and second parts";
stref = part1 + part2;
System.out.println(stref);
```

For our next trick, we construct two `String` objects and, using the + operator, glue them together to make one `String` object. Actually, it only appears that we are sticking them together. There is a bit of Java sleight of hand going on here. As we mentioned earlier, a `String` is a read-only object. This means that we cannot jam one `String` into another one. What the + operator does is create a new `String` object with a length equal to the sum of the lengths of the two it is combining. The address of the resulting `String` is returned and assigned to `stref`. Whenever it is performing string operations, the + is known as the *concatenation operator:*

```
// Concatenating quoted strings directly
stref = "The first part" +
            " and the second part";
System.out.println(stref);
stref = "Party" + " " + "many" + " " + "parts";
System.out.println(stref);
```

Just like arithmetic addition, it is valid to use the plus sign to combine a whole series of `Strings`. Also, because the compiler converts all quoted character strings into `String` objects anyway, it makes no difference whether the things being concatenated are from literals or `String` references. The line in the preceding example with the four concatenation operators will simply combine the first two members into a new `String` object, and then combine the results with the next `String` object, and so on, until there is one `String` object that holds the entire thing. (In reality, some optimization is done here that will prevent all this running around in circles, but the result will be the same.

```
// Using the other concatenation operator
stref = "The beginning, ";
stref += " the middle, ";
stref += " and the end";
System.out.println(stref);
```

Here we introduce a new player. This is the other form of concatenation, and it does the same job as the + operator. This is just Java showing its heritage and using C syntax. Nothing really new, but look at this:

```
// Implicit string conversion
System.out.println(987);
```

This prints out a String. No mystery, really. The method println is overloaded and recognizes all the primitive types and knows how to convert each one to a String. In the following example, an int is converted to a String, but it could be any of the basic types that gets converted. There are overloaded methods of println for every fundamental type:

```
// The + operator converts numbers
stref = "number: " + 123.456;
System.out.println(stref);
```

Here we have another way of converting a number to a String. The conversion rule goes something like this: Whenever there is a + operator, and an item on either side of it is a String, the non-String item is converted to a String, and the two are then concatenated into a resulting String:

```
// So does the += operator
stref = "number: ";
stref += 456.789;
System.out.println(stref);
```

This is similar to the previous example, except that it uses the += concatenation operator. In this case, the rule is that whenever there is a += operator and the item on the left is a String reference, the expression on the right — no matter what it is — is converted to a String:

```
// Any object can be automatically
// converted to a String
StringShow ss = new StringShow();
System.out.println(ss);
```

What we do in this example is create a new StringShow object and pass it to the println method to see what happens. You may get a slightly different set of numbers, but what came out of our test was the following:

```
StringShow@13939b0
```

TIP **Anything in Java can be converted directly to a String. This includes the fundamental data types, the classes supplied in the Java API, and any classes that you write. Anything. Whenever you write a class, you can supply a String conversion method, or one will be supplied for you. To write your own, simply overload the default toString method with one of your own that creates a string and returns it.**

Because we did not specifically put in a method to convert a StringShow to a String, it took the default action. It concocted a unique String by using the class name, an at sign (@), and a hexadecimal number. What is this mysterious number? Wait! It looks like a memory address! Could it be the contents of the reference? Could this mean that the contents of the reference is an address?

But no, that would mean that a reference is really a pointer after all and, as we know, Java doesn't have pointers. Ignore that man behind the curtain! Because anything can be converted to a `String`, let's try an array:

```
// An integer array converted to a string
int arr[] = new int[5];
System.out.println(arr);
```

Here we construct ourselves an integer array and just shove it right into the `println` method as if it were a printable object. It turns out that it is. Here's what we got:

```
[I@1393a20
```

What we have here is a left bracket (indicating that it is an array), then there is the letter 'I' indicating an `int`, then there is an at sign and another one of those mysterious hexadecimal identification numbers. Because an array is an object, and objects can only be accessed through a reference, and because the value in the reference looks like an address, it is becoming more and more obvious that we are dealing with some form of a pointer.

TIP **It appears that we are dealing with addresses when we are working with references, and that could well be the case. However, this addressing stuff is all internal to the local Java interpreter, which can, as long it follows the rules of program execution, do anything it wants to do. Don't count on this address value having any meaning or consistency from one interpreter to the next.**

```
        // Don't confuse cat with add
        System.out.println("front" + 100 + 201);
        System.out.println("front" + (100 + 202));
        System.out.println(100 + "middle" + 203);
        System.out.println(100 + 204 + "back");
        System.out.println(100 + (205 + "back"));
        System.out.println(100 + 206);
    }
}
```

We close out the example with a demonstration of something that can cause confusion if you are not careful. The + operator is capable of both adding numbers and concatenating `Strings`. The + operator looks around to see who its neighbors are and takes action accordingly. If either neighbor is a `String`, it will concatenate. If both neighbors are numbers, it will add. Following is the complete output from the example:

```
Now is the time
Then was the time
Party of the first and second parts
```

```
The first part and the second part
Party many parts
The beginning,  the middle,  and the end
987
number: 123.456
number: 456.789
StringShow@13939b0
[I@1393a20
front100201
front302
100middle203
304back
100205back
306
```

You might want to compare the last few lines of the output with the code that generated them. In some cases, the numbers were converted directly to `String`s; in others, addition was performed first. This is where the precedence and associativity stuff comes in, which we will discuss in Chapter 5. If you are not careful, surprises can happen. Of course, you can always use parentheses to make your code do exactly what you want it to.

MyStringShow

As we saw in the previous example, everything in Java can be automatically converted to a `String`. However, the default format of the `String` generated from one of your classes may not necessarily be what you would like for it to be. Here is a way of having a class generate its own identifying `String`:

```
public class MyStringShow {
  public static void main(String[] args)
  {
   MyStringShow mys;

   mys = new MyStringShow();
   System.out.println("As a string: " + mys);
  }

  public String toString()
  {
   String stref;

   stref = "Hi! I am MyStringShow.";
   return(stref);
  }
}
```

This class has a toString() method that is used to make the conversion. Here's how all this works: Every class is derived from the great base class in the Java sky named Object. The Object class has a toString() method in it — which is why every object in all of Java can be converted to a String. The MyStringShow class overrides the inherited method toString() with one of its own, so when a string conversion is requested and the Java interpreter invokes the toString() method, it gets the local one instead of the one in the Object class. If this all sounds like smoke and mirrors, just stay with us. All of it will be made clear by the time you reach the end of Chapter 6, "The Structure of a Java Program."

SIDE TRIP

Remember the Main!

You probably noticed that the class MyStringShow has a main function, and that it used new to create a version of itself. This can be confusing at first, but it's really quite simple. Whenever the Java interpreter begins execution of an application object file, it starts with the function named main. There can be hundreds of classes in a program, and every one of them can have its own main. Only one main will be executed — the one that the Java interpreter is told to execute. Because main is declared as static, it exists in the class and is in no way involved with an instance of the class, so when main creates an instance of its enclosing class, it does not create another instance of the main function.

The String Class Definition

Let's take a look at the parts of the String class. First, it has a respectable list of constructors. As you can see, Strings can be constructed from nothing, from arrays of bytes that hold ASCII characters, from other Strings and StringBuffers, and from arrays of chars holding Unicode characters:

```
public String();
public String(byte ascii[], int hibyte);
public String(byte ascii[], int hibyte,
   int offset, int count);
public String(char value[]);
public String(char value[], int offset, int count);
public String(String value);
public String(StringBuffer buffer);
```

Various methods can be used to extract information about the `String`. Remember, because it is read-only, there are no methods to write to it. Oh, sure, you will see methods — such as `replace` — that can be used to replace the contents of a `String`, but notice that the return value is always a new `String` object. It does not modify the one that already exists:

```
public char charAt(int  index);
public int compareTo(String  anotherString);
public String concat(String  str);
public static String copyValueOf(char data[]);
public static String copyValueOf(char data[],
   int offset, int count);
public boolean endsWith(String suffix);
public boolean equals(Object anObject);
public boolean equalsIgnoreCase(String  anotherString);
public void getBytes(int srcBegin, int srcEnd,
   byte dst[], int dstBegin);
public void getChars(int srcBegin, int srcEnd,
   char dst[], int dstBegin);
public int hashCode();
public int indexOf(int ch);
public int indexOf(int ch, int fromIndex);
public int indexOf(String str);
public int indexOf(String str, int fromIndex);
public String intern();
public int lastIndexOf(int ch);
public int lastIndexOf(int ch, int fromIndex);
public int lastIndexOf(String str);
public int lastIndexOf(String str, int  fromIndex);
public int length();
public boolean regionMatches(boolean ignoreCase,
   int toffset, String other, int ooffset, int len);
public boolean regionMatches(int toffset, String other,
   int ooffset, int len);
public String replace(char oldChar, char newChar);
public boolean startsWith(String prefix);
public boolean startsWith(String prefix, int toffset);
public String substring(int beginIndex);
public String substring(int beginIndex, int endIndex);
public char[] toCharArray();
public String toLowerCase();
public String toString();
public String toUpperCase();
public String trim();
public static String valueOf(boolean b);
```

```
public static String valueOf(char c);
public static String valueOf(char data[]);
public static String valueOf(char data[],
    int offset, int count);
public static String valueOf(double d);
public static String valueOf(float f);
public static String valueOf(int i);
public static String valueOf(long  l);
public static String valueOf(Object obj);
```

The StringBuffer Class

While the existing read-only String class fits most cases, it doesn't do for all of them. When you find yourself in a situation where you need to diddle with a string one character at a time, it will probably be cheaper and easier to use the StringBuffer class. It has none of the built-in advantages of concatenation and such that the String class has, but it has something the String does not — it is modifiable. It does allow the programmer to reach down inside and do things with the individual characters. Also, it can be made to do all the things that a String can do, but not automatically.

4

TIP **The truth is that the StringBuffer class is used by the system to do a lot of the String concatenation operations that we talked about earlier. Although a String data type is always the result of any system-level string operation, it turns out that StringBuffer objects are used for the intermediate work.**

The StringBuffer class keeps track of both the number of characters it contains and the number of characters for which it has space allocated. A string operation that requires more space than is already allocated will cause the allocation to automatically expand to accommodate the new size. There are three constructors. The default is to have an empty string with enough space allocated to hold 16 characters. A second constructor allows for the specification of the size of the allocation. Finally, there is a third constructor that will accept the characters from a String object as its initial value, and allocate whatever space it needs to hold them:

```
public StringBuffer();
public StringBuffer(int length);
public StringBuffer(String str);
```

You will notice that a number of methods deal with string append and insert operations. In every case, an append method will convert its argument to a string and attach the results to the right end of the existing string. Any insert method will convert its argument to a string, then break the existing string at the offset point, insert the new string, and then attach the detached portion of the original string on the end. Remember that there is no problem with overflow — the internal length is extended automatically:

```
public StringBuffer append(boolean  b);
public StringBuffer append(char  c);
public StringBuffer append(char  str[]);
public StringBuffer append(char str[],
        int offset, int len);
public StringBuffer append(double  d);
public StringBuffer append(float  f);
public StringBuffer append(int  i);
public StringBuffer append(long  l);
public StringBuffer append(Object  obj);
public StringBuffer append(String  str);
public int capacity();
public char charAt(int index);
public void ensureCapacity(int  minimumCapacity);
public void getChars(int  srcBegin, int  srcEnd,
        char  dst[], int  dstBegin);
public StringBuffer insert(int  offset, boolean  b);
public StringBuffer insert(int  offset, char  c);
public StringBuffer insert(int  offset, char  str[]);
public StringBuffer insert(int  offset, double  d);
public StringBuffer insert(int  offset, float  f);
public StringBuffer insert(int  offset, int  i);
public StringBuffer insert(int  offset, long  l);
public StringBuffer insert(int  offset, Object  obj);
public StringBuffer insert(int  offset, String  str);
public int length();
public StringBuffer reverse();
public void setCharAt(int index, char  ch);
public void setLength(int newLength);
public String toString();
```

`StringBuffer` is like the C notion of a string in that it is possible to poke around inside an array and access the individual characters. However, there is still no indication of null termination — the end of the string is specified by the `length()` method.

BONUS

Unicode and UTF-8

The reality is that unless you're really going to dig down inside things, you don't need to know all this Unicode and UTF-8 stuff. All of this is handled internally by the Java system, so unless you have some sort of curiosity problem, you may want to just skip this section.

In Unicode, all characters have a 16-bit internal representation that is intended to encompass — without overlap or conflict — all of the characters in the alphabets of many languages around the world. This is very good for internationalization of the software, but there is one side effect when it comes to the regular day-to-day ASCII string operations: All the sizes of all the characters are doubled.

UTF-8 to the rescue. The standard ASCII characters are only seven bits long and are normally kept in a single byte with the first bit set to zero. The ASCII characters were mapped onto Unicode without changing their numeric representation, so the first nine bits of the 16-bit Unicode form of an ASCII character are always zero. All we have to do is omit the leading zeroes to get us back to the same size we had before. To do this, however, there must be some way of determining, character by character, whether or not the leading zeroes have been dropped. That is, there needs to be a lucid way of mapping Unicode characters back and forth between the long and short forms.

Here's how that's done. As shown in Table 4-1, the leading bits of each byte are checked to determine what kind of character we have.

TABLE 4-1 Bit Positioning in Translations Between UTF-8 and Unicode

UTF-8 Value	Unicode Value
0abcdef	000000000abcdef
110abcde 10fghijk	00000abcdefghijk
1110abcd 10efghij 10klmnop	abcdefghijklmnop

In the table, the bit positions are labeled using letters. For example, the letter "e" represents the position of a bit in the UTF-8 value and the position of the same bit in a Unicode value. You can see from the table that it is a simple matter of checking the leading bits of any Unicode value to make the conversion to

UTF-8. Conversely, by checking the leading bits of a UTF-8 byte stream, the conversion can be made to Unicode. Note that the second and third byte values of the UTF-8 coding always begin with 10. It is done this way so that a program indexing into the middle of a UTF-8 array will be able to correctly skip forward or backward to the beginning of the next character.

Summary

This chapter has given you a look into character string manipulations in Java — the workhorse of most applets and applications. This chapter concludes our discussion of Java data types. We now move on to the structure of Java programs.

A Java program is made up of classes. Classes are made up of methods and the fundamental data elements that were discussed in this and the previous chapter. Now that we have discussed the data, we can start to look at ways of handling it.

CHAPTER FIVE

EXPRESSIONS, OPERATORS, AND METHODS

IN THIS CHAPTER YOU LEARN THESE KEY SKILLS

5

This chapter concerns itself with methods and what goes in them. We will look at the different types of executable statements and how they all can be hooked together to form a complete method. We are still working in the basement, but this chapter will bring us up to the entrance of the main floor of the Java building. By the end of this chapter, you will understand enough Java basics to be able to analyze the structure of a Java program and get down to the business of creating programs.

Reserved Words

Table 5-1 lists the words that have special meaning in Java. These are the words specifically defined as being a part of the core language and have a special meaning to the compiler. Many of these terms have already been discussed to some extent — especially the fundamental data types.

TABLE 5-1 Reserved Words in Java

Word	Description
abstract	An abstract class cannot be instantiated — it can only be used on the extend command to construct child classes.
boolean	A primitive data type that can only take on the value of true or false.
break	A control flow command used to exit from inside a for, while, do, or switch block.
byte	A primitive data type. It is a signed, 8-bit integer.
case	A control flow command used as the receiving location of the branch generated by a switch command.
catch	An exception handling command used following a try as the receiving location of the branch generated by a throw command.
char	A primitive data type. It is an unsigned, 16-bit integer intended to contain a single Unicode character.
class	The keyword used to declare a class.
const	Unused. Java reserves this word for possible future use.
continue	A control flow command used to begin the next iteration of a for, while, or do block.
default	A control flow command used as a receiving location of the branch generated by a switch command.
do	A control flow command used to construct a loop that always executes at least once.
double	A primitive data type. It is a 64-bit real number.
else	A control flow command that defines a block to be executed as an alternative to an if block.
extends	Used as part of a class declaration to specify the name of the superclass of the class being declared.

Word	Description
false	A constant boolean value.
final	Used in declarations. If applied to a variable, it makes it a constant. If applied to a class, the class cannot be used as a superclass to derive other classes. If used to define a method, the method cannot be overridden.
finally	An exception handling command that defines a block of code to be executed following a try/catch sequence.
float	A primitive data type. It is a 32-bit real number.
for	A control flow command that defines a loop with counters and tests for exiting the loop.
goto	Unused. Java reserves this word for possible future use.
if	A control flow statement that evaluates a boolean expression to determine whether to execute a block of code.
implements	Used in a class declaration to name an interface that is being locally implemented.
import	Used at the top of source modules to qualify the path of external searches for names.
instanceof	A boolean operator that tests for an object being of a certain class.
int	A primitive data type. It is a signed, 32-bit integer.
interface	The definition of a set of methods that can be implemented by any class wishing to have a standard interface.
long	A primitive data type. It is a signed, 64-bit integer.
native	When used as part of a method declaration, it means that the method itself is defined elsewhere and is machine-native executable code.
new	Used to allocate memory and execute constructor methods during object construction.
null	The value contained in a reference when it does not address an object.
package	When used at the beginning of a class definition file, it places the definition of any class or interface into the named package.
private	Used as part of a declaration to limit the scope to the single class.
protected	Used as part of a declaration to limit the scope to the single class and its derived classes.

(continued)

5

TABLE 5-1 Reserved Words in Java (*continued*)

Word	Description
public	Used as part of a declaration to remove scope limitations and make the name global.
return	A flow control statement used to exit from a method.
short	A primitive data type. It is a signed, 16-bit integer.
static	Used in a declaration to cause the declared item to exist in the class instead of in each generated object.
super	Used to address data and methods in the parent class.
switch	A flow control statement used in conjunction with case and break statements to select a single block of code for execution.
synchronized	Used as a modifier to mark a block of code as being uninterruptable during multithreaded execution.
this	Used to address data and methods in the current object. It is always the name of the current object.
throw	Used in exception handling. This statement will throw an exception that must be caught by a catch command.
throws	Used in a class declaration to specify that this class throws, but does not catch, a specific exception.
transient	Unused. Java reserves this word for possible future use.
true	A constant boolean value.
try	Used in exception handling to execute code that contains one or more throw statements.
void	Defines methods that do not return values.
volatile	When used to declare a variable, it is a warning to the compiler that the value may change unexpectedly from some external source.
while	A flow control statement used to define an iteration that is to continue as long as a boolean expression is `true`.

Operator Precedence

The operator precedence of Java is very similar to that of C, but there are a few differences. For one thing, there are a couple of new operators. Table 5-2 lists the operators in precedence order and shows their associativity. Simply put, things with higher precedence will be done first — associativity is the tie breaker.

TABLE 5-2 Java Operator Precedence and Associativity

<table>
<tr><th>Operator</th><th>Prec</th><th>Assoc</th><th>Description</th></tr>
<tr><td>() [] .</td><td>1</td><td>LtoR</td><td>The primary expression operators</td></tr>
<tr><td>++ —</td><td>2</td><td>RtoL</td><td>Unary post- and pre-increment</td></tr>
<tr><td>+ -</td><td>2</td><td>RtoL</td><td>Unary plus and minus</td></tr>
<tr><td>~</td><td>2</td><td>RtoL</td><td>One's complement</td></tr>
<tr><td>!</td><td>2</td><td>RtoL</td><td>Boolean complement</td></tr>
<tr><td>()</td><td>2</td><td>RtoL</td><td>Casting of types</td></tr>
<tr><td>* / %</td><td>3</td><td>LtoR</td><td>Multiplication, division, and modulo</td></tr>
<tr><td>+</td><td>4</td><td>LtoR</td><td>Addition and String concatenation</td></tr>
<tr><td>-</td><td>4</td><td>LtoR</td><td>Subtraction</td></tr>
<tr><td><< >> >>></td><td>5</td><td>LtoR</td><td>Shift left, shift right, shift right without sign extension</td></tr>
<tr><td>< > <= >=</td><td>6</td><td>LtoR</td><td>Less than, greater than, less than or equal to, greater than or equal to</td></tr>
<tr><td>instanceof</td><td>6</td><td>LtoR</td><td>Type comparison</td></tr>
<tr><td>== !=</td><td>7</td><td>LtoR</td><td>Equal, not equal</td></tr>
<tr><td>&</td><td>8</td><td>LtoR</td><td>Boolean AND and bitwise AND</td></tr>
<tr><td>^</td><td>9</td><td>LtoR</td><td>Boolean XOR and bitwise XOR</td></tr>
<tr><td>|</td><td>10</td><td>LtoR</td><td>Boolean OR and bitwise OR</td></tr>
<tr><td>&&</td><td>11</td><td>LtoR</td><td>Conditional AND</td></tr>
<tr><td>||</td><td>12</td><td>LtoR</td><td>Conditional OR</td></tr>
<tr><td>?:</td><td>13</td><td>RtoL</td><td>Conditional ternary operator</td></tr>
<tr><td>= *= /= %= += -= <<= >>= >>>= &= ^= ~=</td><td>14</td><td>RtoL</td><td>Assignment operators</td></tr>
</table>

The set of operator precedence and associativity rules is what Java uses to determine what it needs to do first to evaluate an expression. Take the following simple expression:

```
a = b + c * d;
```

The highest priority operator is the multiply, so it will be done first. Next is the addition, so that happens next. The assignment operator has the lowest priority of all, so it is done last. However, there are times when two operators have the same precedence:

```
a = b + c - d;
```

The question here is whether the addition or subtraction should happen first. The decision is made according to the defined associativity, which in this case is left to right. That means that the leftmost operation, the addition, is performed first.

Conversions of Primitive Data Types

Java features a rich collection of assignment operators. Assignment operators are used to stuff values into the fundamental types. The only one of these that can be used to stuff a reference is the simple '='. All the others perform arithmetic operations and, because we do not have pointer arithmetic in Java, they cannot be used on references. The single exception to this is our old friend the `String` class, which can be stuffed with the '+=' operator, but as we said earlier, he is Mom's favorite and gets special privileges.

Assignment sometimes requires data conversion. Conversion of data from one type to another that is an upgrade (that is, the new type can accept the data from the old type without loss of the magnitude of the data), is known in Java as *widening*. Similarly, moving data into a type in which the magnitude could be lost is called *narrowing*. Table 5-3 lists the conversions that are guaranteed to be magnitude safe. The same table reversed would illustrate the conversions that are magnitude unsafe. Converting anything to a `char` is always narrowing because a `char` is unsigned and cannot hold any of the negative values the others are capable of holding.

Among both integer and real primitive types, the assignment operators are used to convert data from one type to another. Widening is OK, and Java will accept it without complaint. If you want to do narrowing, you are going to have to tell Java to ignore the safety factors and plunge right in. The way to do this is by *casting* the results of an expression into the narrower type. This is demonstrated in Listing 5-1.

TABLE 5-3 Data Converted in This Direction Is Called Widening

From	To
byte	short, int, long, float, or double
short	int, long, float, or double
char	int, long, float, or double
int	long, float, or double
long	float or double
float	double

Listing 5-1 Conversion.java

```
public class Conversion {
  public static void main(String[] args)
  {
   double d;
   float f;
   long l;
   int i;
   short s;
   byte b;

   // Assigning integers by widening
   b = 10;
   s = b;
   i = s;
   l = i;
   System.out.println(
         "Assign 10 widening results in " + l);

   // Assigning integers narrowing
   l = 10;
   i = (int)l;
   s = (short)i;
   b = (byte)s;
   System.out.println(
         "Assign 10 narrowing results in " + b);

   // Assigning integers to reals (widening)
```

5

```
        l = 1234567890;
        f = l;
        d = l;
        System.out.println("The long value " + l);
        System.out.println(
                "  assigned to a float is " + f);
        System.out.println(
                "  and assigned to a double is " + d);

        // Assigning reals to integers (narrowing)
        l = (long)f;
        System.out.println("The float value " + f);
        System.out.println("  assigned to a long " + l);
        l = (long)d;
        System.out.println("The double value " + d);
        System.out.println("  assigned to a long " + l);
    }
}
```

Following is the result of the Conversion class. As you can see, widening is accepted by Java with no complaint, but it was necessary to use casting to force narrowing.

```
Assign 10 widening results in 10
Assign 10 narrowing results in 10
The long value 1234567890
  assigned to a float is 1.23457e+009
  and assigned to a double is 1.23457e+009
The float value 1.23457e+009
  assigned to a long 1234567936
The double value 1.23457e+009
  assigned to a long 1234567890
```

Note a special situation when converting integer data to floating point data. A floating point value can certainly include the entire range of any of the integer values, but loss of some of the digits of significance is possible. This is the one manner in which data could possibly be lost without the use of a specific cast.

Binary Arithmetic Operators

We now come to the activities of add, subtract, multiply, and divide. This pretty much works in Java the same as it does in C. No arithmetic is done on any data smaller than an int. Whenever arithmetic is to be performed on a byte or char, Java converts it to an int, does the arithmetic, and then converts it back. Java looks at the operands on each side of the operator and if they are not the same, the lesser one is widened to be the type of the greater one, and then the arithmetic is performed. This means that the resulting value of any expression will have the type of the widest data type found anywhere in the expression.

All this widening happens without you having to be aware of it. Narrowing requires a little more work. That's the nice thing about widening, narrowing, and the casting rules. As long as only widening is taking place, you can just keep programming away and pay no attention to all the automatic conversions that Java is doing for you. If, in the midst of your coding frenzy, you write something that could possibly cause loss of magnitude, the compiler will nag you about it until you either change it or cast it. Whenever you cast something, it is the same as telling the compiler, "Look, I know this could cause loss of data. I don't really care. Hush!"

Assignment Operators

One of the more interesting things about C has always been its collection of operators that can perform arithmetic during the same operation as an assignment. This actually came about because the designers of C wanted to have operators in the language that were capable of doing the same things as the hardware opcodes on their target machine. The operators caught on as being both very useful and very cute. It's somehow satisfying to write down a single operation that does two things at once. Good news. Java has adopted all those fancy assignment operators — and even added a new one. Listing 5-2 demonstrates each of the binary operators in Java:

Listing 5-2 Binop.java

```
public class Binop {
  public static void main(String[] args)
  {
   int a;
   int b;
   int c;
   int d;

   a = 5;
   b = 3;
   System.out.println("  a=" + a + " b=" + b);
   c = a + b;
   System.out.println("a+b=" + c);
   c = a - b;
   System.out.println("a-b=" + c);
```


5

```
        c = a * b;
        System.out.println("a*b=" + c);
        c = a / b;
        System.out.println("a/b=" + c);
        c = a % b;
        System.out.println("a%b=" + c);

        a = -1;
        b = 1;
        System.out.println("  a=" + a + " b=" + b);
        c = a >> 1;
        d = b >> 1;
        System.out.println("a>>1=" + c + " b>>1=" + d);
        c = a >>> 1;
        d = b >>> 1;
        System.out.println("a>>>1=" + c + " b>>>1=" + d);
        c = a << 1;
        d = b << 1;
        System.out.println("a<<1=" + c + " b<<1=" + d);
    }
}
```

I'm sure you spotted our new contestant right away. It's that triple shift thing, >>>. Actually, this new shift operator came about as a result of Java having dropped the ability to declare integer data types as unsigned. Sometimes it is necessary to perform an unsigned shift to the right. That's what our new player does — it will shift any of the integer primitives to the right without the sign extension that would normally happen. You can see the results here in the output of our example:

```
  a=5 b=3
a+b=8
a-b=2
a*b=15
a/b=1
a%b=2
  a=-1 b=1
a>>1=-1 b>>1=0
a>>>1=2147483647 b>>>1=0
a<<1=-2 b<<1=2
```

Unary Operators

The most interesting — and useful — of the unary operators are the pre- and post- increment and decrement operators. A pre-increment operator says, "I'll add one to it and then give it to you" while the post-increment operator says, "Right after I give you a copy, I will add one to it." All the Java unary operators are demonstrated in Listing 5-3.

Listing 5-3 Unop.java

```
public class Unop {
  public static void main(String[] args)
  {
   int a;

   a = 5;
   System.out.print("a=5; a++=" + a++);
   System.out.println(" leaving a=" + a);
   a = 5;
   System.out.print("a=5; ++a=" + ++a);
   System.out.println(" leaving a=" + a);
   a = 5;
   System.out.print("a=5; a-- =" + a--);
   System.out.println(" leaving a=" + a);
   a = 5;
   System.out.print("a=5; -- a=" + -- a);
   System.out.println(" leaving a=" + a);
   a = 5;
   System.out.print("a=5; ~a=" + ~a);
   System.out.println(" leaving a=" + a);
   a = 5;
   System.out.print("a=5; -a=" + (-a));
   System.out.println(" leaving a=" + a);
  }
}
```

Here is the output:

```
a=5; a++=5 leaving a=6
a=5; ++a=6 leaving a=6
a=5; a--=5 leaving a=4
a=5; --a=4 leaving a=4
a=5; ~a=-6 leaving a=5
a=5; -a=-5 leaving a=5
```

In each case, we start with the value 5 and take a look at the immediate results and the residual results. Notice that only the increment and decrement operators modify the original value.

Conditional Expressions and Boolean Operators

We now come to one of the areas in which Java veers off from C. In Java, all conditional expressions result in a `boolean` value. Unlike C, this `boolean` type is a bona fide, full-blown primitive language type. It cannot be converted to an integer, character, real number, or anything else without going through some form of transformation process. (Well, it can be converted directly to a String, but remember: the `String` class has a permanent hall pass and can do whatever it wants.) The addition of this new data type has caused a ripple effect through the logical operations that Java inherited from C. Let's take a look.

When we have an expression that uses a `boolean` operator, such as

```
avalue > bvalue
```

the result is *always* a `boolean` data type. This is the case for every logical operator in the entire language. One consequence of this is that a `boolean` data type is the *only* type that can ever appear in conditional expressions. It is an error to do something like the following:

```
int value = 44;
if(value) {       *** ERROR ***
  /* do something */
}
```

Because `value` is an `int`, it cannot be used directly as a boolean expression. A test for nonzero will need to be explicitly made to generate a `boolean` data type that can be tested by the `if`:

```
int value = 44;
if(value != 0) {
  /* do something */
}
```

This is the case for every boolean operation in Java, including the ones in `do`, `while`, and `for`. It also applies to the hook and colon expression:

```
int result;
int testval = 0;

result = (testval == 0) ? 99 : 100;
```

Even though everything else in the expression is an `int`, the expression preceding the hook must be a `boolean` data type. (I don't know exactly why, but one day my friend Roger just started calling the ? a hook. It stuck. I thought I would be cute and started calling the # a gridlet, but it never caught on like his hook did. Of course, the ! has a bunch of names — bang, ball-bat, or dammit.)

When blending integers with booleans, there is also a bit of anding and ampersanding ambiguity. (If you say that last sentence just right, you can do the Macarena.) With the new `boolean` data type, the operators that perform anding and oring have become a little more complicated. Table 5-4 lists the valid combinations and describes what happens in each case.

TABLE 5-4 Anding and Oring with Integer and Boolean Types

Operation	Results
integer & integer	Bit-by-bit anding giving an integer result.
integer | integer	Bit-by-bit oring giving an integer result.
boolean & boolean	Both boolean expressions are evaluated and if both are `true`, the result is `true`.
boolean | boolean	Both boolean expressions are evaluated and if either one is `true`, the result is `true`.
boolean && boolean	If both boolean expressions are `true`, the result is also `true`. If the left expression is `false`, the right one is never evaluated.
boolean || boolean	If either boolean expression is `true`, the result is `true`. If the left expression is `true`, the right expression is never evaluated.

5

Method Invocation

It just doesn't seem that long ago that "invoking a method" was known as "calling a function." Life was much simpler in the days before object-oriented programming. Some object-oriented circles use the phrase "send a message to the object," which means the same thing. The "send a message" phrase seems to be falling out of favor, however. This could be because it somehow sounds as if it were politically motivated.

All the methods in Java can be divided into two categories. Some are static, some are not. The category a method is in has an effect on how it can be invoked. (To explain this, we need to jump ahead just a bit. Bear with us. All of this stuff about the relationships of classes and objects will be cleared up in Chapter 6, "The Structure of a Java Program.") Take a look at the example in Listing 5-4.

Listing 5-4 Invoke.java

```
public class Invoke {
  int one_per_object;
  static int only_one;

  public static void main(String[] args)
  {
   Invoke invfive = new Invoke(5);
   Invoke invsix = new Invoke(6);

   only_one = 111;

   System.out.println("     invfive: ");
   invfive.showvalues();
   System.out.println("     invsix: ");
   invsix.showvalues();
  }

  Invoke(int value) {
   one_per_object = value;
  }

  void showvalues() {
   System.out.println(
          "The value of only_one: " +
          only_one);
   System.out.println(
          "The value of one_per_object: " +
          one_per_object);
  }

  public static int get_only_one() {
   return(only_one);
  }
  public static void set_only_one(int value) {
   only_one = value;
  }
}
```

Notice that there are two integers, one of which is declared as `static`. Each time an object is instantiated from this class, the new object gets its own copy of the nonstatic data, but there is always only one copy of the `static` data. Being `static`, there is a single copy of it created by the compiler and stored in the class, and that is the only one that ever exists. Therefore, there is no need to actually have an object come into existence in order to be able to access `static` data.

A static method is only a slightly different beast than static data. A static method can only access static data. The only way it can get its hands on non-static data is to create an instance of the object and have it do the dirty work.

TIP **Every nonstatic method has a reference to the current object passed to it as its first argument. You don't declare it when you write the code for your method, but it is always there. The name of the reference is this. A static method does not have a this reference passed to it. A static method only knows about objects that you specifically pass to it, or that you specifically create inside the method. Because it has no this reference, a static method can only find things in the class — and the only thing in the class is the static data.**

In Listing 5-4, the nonstatic data item one_per_class cannot be accessed directly from main because main is static. Each time an object is created, a new copy of the nonstatic data is created for it. The fact that there is more than one copy is demonstrated in the output of our example:

```
      invfive:
The value of only_one: 111
The value of one_per_object: 5
      invsix:
The value of only_one: 111
The value of one_per_object: 6
```

It may seem at first that it would be necessary to instantiate an object from a class before accessing its static data, so there would be some name to call it. Not so. It is perfectly valid to access a static data item through a static method using the name of the class. That is the purpose of set_only_one and get_only_one in our example. The following example illustrates how a call from some other object could be made to one of these functions:

```
Invoke.set_only_one(44);
int value = Invoke.get_only_one();
```

Notice that neither of these lines of code requires the existence of an object. It is the name of the class that is used. This is quite common in Java, and there are more examples in the chapters that follow.

Anatomy of a Method

Okay. You have the basic building blocks. We now take a look at how you can take what you've got, throw in a couple of other elements, and start constructing methods. The only missing elements are the argument lists, return values, iterators (for, while, and do), and conditionals (if and switch).

Argument Lists

The syntax of the argument list in Java is a subset of the one in C. It is actually such a small subset of the C calling conventions that there is almost no way to make a mistake — just name your arguments in the order you want them to appear. There is no structure passing and returning because we have no structures. There is no addressing indirection and de-referencing because we have no pointers. The primitives are all passed by value. The only other thing is a reference and, being quite primitive itself, it is also passed by value. The reference values are passed around just like `int`s and `float`s. Inside a method, a reference argument acts exactly the same as a locally declared reference — it is the same; it just came from somewhere else. Are you going to miss all those asterisks and ampersands in the argument list? I'm not.

Return Values

If a value is to be returned from a method call, there must be a return statement with an expression of the appropriate type inside the method. If you don't get it right, the Java compiler will tell you. The return value can be any of the primitive types, including references. Return values in Java are as simple as the argument list — it's hard to mess it up. Only `void` methods can have a return statement without an expression.

TIP **One really nice result of having automatic garbage collection is the ease of returning references from methods. It is perfectly safe for a method to create a new object and return its reference to the caller because nobody has to keep track of whose job it is to de-allocate the thing later — it just happens automatically whenever everybody's through with it. Also, there is no way to accidentally return the address of some stack variable that goes out of scope and gets all hosed up. With Java, we all live in a cleaner and safer environment. Just close your eyes and start coding! (Well, almost.)**

Braces — { and }

Squiggly braces indicate a new block of code. The entire body of a method has an enclosing pair of braces making it a single block. A block is always executed as a unit, starting at its top, as if it were one statement. Any data declared inside a block is local to the block.

TIP **A variable can be declared at any point in a block, as long as it is declared before it is referenced. The variable will only exist while execution is occurring inside the block, and will be automatically deleted on exiting from the block.**

To see how this works, take a look at Herbert in Listing 5-5. We declare three String references with the same names and then stuff them with String objects:

Listing 5-5 Herbert.java

```
public class Herbert {
   static String herbert = "herbert the first";
   public static void main(String[] args)
   {
    System.out.println("1: " + herbert);
    {
            String herbert = "herbert the second";
            System.out.println("2: " + herbert);
    }
    {
            String herbert = "herbert the third";
            System.out.println("3: " + herbert);
    }
    System.out.println("4: " + herbert);
   }
}
```

Output of the class looks like the following:

```
1: herbert the first
2: herbert the second
3: herbert the third
4: herbert the first
```

Notice that there is a completely different herbert inside each of the pairs of braces. The kingdoms of herbert the second and herbert the third are limited to only the blocks in which they are defined. Once the flow of execution has moved out of their domain, they no longer exist.

As you can see, the domain of herbert the first encompasses all that of herbert the second. The two have exactly the same name, but herbert the second is a local variable and is selected by Java to be king within his little domain. This is known as *data hiding* — or sometimes just *hiding*. It is quite common and usually causes no problem because a locally declared variable is the one most visible to the programmer, and it is the one the compiler will select.

TIP **Data hiding does not occur within a method. That is, a variable declared inside a method cannot be hidden by another variable declaration inside the method. Data hiding only works with data that is outside the method.**

Note something else brought out in this example. As you may recall, any place Java encounters a group of characters enclosed in double quotes, it creates a String object. This means that the statement

```
String herbert = "herbert the first";
```

is exactly the same as if it had been written

```
String herbert = new String("herbert the first");
```

Conditional Branches

The conditionals if and switch work in Java pretty much as they do in C, with a couple of minor variations. Remember that the expression evaluated by an if must be boolean. There is also an interesting data type constraint on the switch statement. The compiler verifies that any constant value used in a case statement is valid for the primitive type used in the switch statement. This is really just another of Java's friendly error checks because any case that doesn't meet this criterion could never be selected from the switch. Consider the following example:

```
byte b;

switch(b) {
case 812:      /*** ERROR ****/
  System.out.println("One overflow");
  break;
}
```

The value 812 will not fit into a byte, so the compiler generates an error, proving that Java is not asleep at the switch. Of course, using an int as the switch value would solve the problem. An int is the largest type allowed in a switch statement. (Can't you hear it now? Some guy who hates Java will be yelling, "What? I can only have four billion cases in a switch statement!?")

The for Statement

The most common of the loopers is the for statement we all know so well:

```
int i;
for(i=0; i<10; i++) {
  /* do something ten times */
}
```

Just as in C, there are three parts inside the for parentheses, separated with semicolons. The first part is the initial value setting, the second is the conditional to be checked at the top of the loop, and the third is the statement to be executed at the bottom of each loop.

Up to this point, everything is the same in Java as it is in C. That's about to change. Notice the location of the loop counter declaration in Listing 5-6.

Listing 5-6 ForLoop.java

```
public class ForLoop {
  public static void main(String[] args)
  {
   for(int i=0; i<2; i++) {
         System.out.println("First i: " + i);
   }
   // The variable i does not exist here
   for(int i=0; i<2; i++) {
         System.out.println("Second i: " + i);
   }
   // The variable i does not exist here
  }
}
```

This is a special case declaration. As you already know, it is possible to declare a variable at any point in the program, and that variable will remain in existence until the end of the block in which it was declared. And you also know that a block is defined by a pair of squiggly braces. Well, the `for` loop doesn't exactly break that rule, but it does stretch it a bit. Any variable declared inside the parentheses of the `for` statement has the same scope it would have if it were declared inside a block of code to be executed by the `for` statement. This bending of the rules could be considered less than cricket by the intergalactic computer language cops, but it sure is convenient. It's very nice to have local loop counters without having to declare unique names or reuse the same counter variable for several loops.

You can't nest them though. There is no such thing as overriding a variable inside its own method. This is an error:

```
for(int i=0; i<10; i++) {
  for(int i=0; i<15; i++) { // ***ERROR***
  }
}
```

Because the counter of the outer loop is available to the inner loop, there is a name conflict. This is that old hiding situation we discussed earlier.

There are some differences between C and Java in the way that a conditional expression is handled. There are three expressions inside the parentheses of the for control statement — and the one in the middle is a logical expression. In the `for` loop of Java, that middle expression must be one that has a `boolean` type as its result. You may also recall that C allowed commas to appear in a conditional expression such as the following:

```
for(i = 0; i<10, j >= 45; i++) ... // *** ERROR ****
```

Java does not allow this. Java does, however, allow commas in each of the other expressions. This *is* valid.

```
for(i = 0, j=0; i < 10; i++, j++) ...
```

The while Statement

The `while` statement is sort of a repeating `if`. It first evaluates a boolean expression and if the expression results in `true`, the block of code associated with it is executed. On completion of the execution of the block of code, the boolean is evaluated again, and the whole thing starts over. Following is a simple example that will execute three times:

```
int i = 3;
while(i > 0) {
  i--;
};
```

Once the value of `i` reaches zero, execution will stop. The following example will never execute:

```
int i = 3;
while(i > 10) {
  i--;
};
```

Because the boolean expression is `false` on the first try, it simply skips over the block of code. Except for the type requirements on the boolean expression, this is just like C.

The do Statement

The `do` is simply an inverted `while`. The boolean expression is evaluated at the bottom of the loop, which means the loop will always execute at least once. Our example executes three times:

```
int i = 3
do {
  i--;
} while(i > 0);
```

This example will execute once:

```
int i = 3;
do {
  i--
} while(i > 10);
```

The boolean expression will evaluate to `false` the first time through the loop, but this doesn't happen until after the loop has already executed once.

The break and continue Statements

These work the same way as they do in C, but with one major addition. They can optionally be supplied a label that can be used to specify the block depth of the break. This looks a bit arcane at first, but it's really quite simple to do. You simply put a label at the top of a loop at the `for`, `do`, or `while` statement and then use the label on the `break` or `continue` statement. Listing 5-7 shows a few ways that this can be done.

Listing 5-7 BreakContinue.java

```
public class BreakContinue {
  public static void main(String[] args)
  {
   simple: for(int i=0; i<10; i++) {
         System.out.println("simple: " + i);
         if(i == 3)
               break simple;
   }

   twofer: for(int i=0; i<10; i++) {
         for(int j=0; j<2; j++) {
               System.out.println(
                     "twofer i=" + i + " j=" + j);
               if(i == 2)
                     break twofer;
         }
   }

   outer: for(int x = 0; x<3; x++) {
         int y = 0;
         inner: do {
               if(y == 1)
                     continue inner;
               if(x == 2)
                     break outer;
               System.out.println(
                     "outer,inner x=" + x + " y=" + y);
         } while(y++ < 2);
   }

   int m = 12;
```

```
      ifblock: if(m > 6) {
            for(int i=0; i<10; i++) {
                  System.out.println(
                        "ifblock m= " + m + " i=" + i);
                  if(i == 1)
                        break ifblock;
            }
      }
    }
  }
```

This example shows ways that `break` and `continue` can be used to exit from inner and outer blocks. Following is the output from this example:

```
simple: 0
simple: 1
simple: 2
simple: 3
twofer i=0 j=0
twofer i=0 j=1
twofer i=1 j=0
twofer i=1 j=1
twofer i=2 j=0
outer,inner x=0 y=0
outer,inner x=0 y=2
outer,inner x=1 y=0
outer,inner x=1 y=2
ifblock m= 12 i=0
ifblock m= 12 i=1
```

The last block in the example — the one labeled `ifblock` — shows that even though the `break` and `continue` statements normally do not operate inside an `if` block, they can be used to cause an exit back to the top of an enclosing `if` block by using an inner iterative loop and putting the label on the `if` statement.

BONUS

Say Good-bye to Memory Leaks

Allocated memory returned from a Java method is much simpler to manage than memory returned from a C function. One of the most insidious errors in existence is the infamous memory leak. A memory leak occurs whenever RAM is allocated and never released. This sort of activity is difficult to track because it is so often necessary to allocate something in one place and de-allocate it in another. In C, the problem most often occurs when a function allocates something and returns a pointer to it. This action requires that the caller be responsible for de-allocation. If the caller forgets? Memory leak.

Java has plugged this hole. A Java method can dynamically allocate an object and return it without worrying about what happens to it. The following is a perfectly valid, and safe, Java method:

```
SomeObect builder() {
  return(new SomeObject());
}
```

This method constructs an object using `new` (which allocates the RAM to hold it) and returns the object to the caller. It doesn't matter what the caller does with the returned reference — there will be no memory leak because the system keeps track of these things and does automatic recovery.

Designs can be made simpler. It is no longer necessary to avoid memory allocation by passing structs to functions to have them filled in. There is no need to declare a static location to be used as a place to store a return value. It has become unnecessary to keep detailed documentation on which function allocates what. It is no longer necessary for all progress to stop while searches are made for memory leaks.

Summary

This chapter completes our coverage of those parts of Java derived from C. As you can see, virtually all of the low-level parts of Java are inherited directly from C. There are some variations here and there, but they are variations either necessary or convenient for the implementation of an object-oriented language.

Chapter 6 begins our exploration into the object-oriented parts of Java.

CHAPTER SIX

THE STRUCTURE OF A JAVA PROGRAM

IN THIS CHAPTER YOU LEARN THESE KEY SKILLS

In order to be able to write a Java program, you need to understand how one is structured — and Java's structure is unique. A Java program is written as a collection of classes. Remember that a class is built out of data items and methods that can be called to manipulate the data.

A class exists in three forms. It first comes into existence as source code. This is the stuff we edit when we say we are programming (well okay — hacking). This source code form resides in a file that ends with the extension .java. It is passed through a Java compiler to produce a .class file that holds the bytecode form of the class. Finally, there is the instantiated, or loaded, form that comes about at run time when the interpreter constructs an executable object from the bytecode form. In common parlance, either of the first two forms are referred to as a *class*. The third form is called an *object*.

During a single execution of a Java program, any number of objects can be instantiated from a single class.

Look at a class as a cookie cutter that is used to stamp out objects. The design of each cookie cutter is unique, but the objects coming out of any one cookie cutter are all the same. This object creation is the heart and soul of Java — a Java program runs by creating objects and then telling them what to do. It is up to you, the Java programmer, to design the cookie cutters and specify how they will be used. If you understand the dynamic interrelationship of objects, you will understand Java programming.

There are two kinds of Java programs: applets (designed to be executed by a Web browser as part of an HTML page) and applications (designed to be executed as stand-alone units by the Java interpreter). Each has its own peculiarities but, as you will see, they cross-pollinate quite easily. This chapter will show you how to write a program that is either an applet or an application — or even both.

Anatomy of a Class

A class contains two things — data and methods. The methods are used to manipulate the data, which is composed of a collection of primitive data types and object references. The data can be defined as being *private,* meaning it can only be accessed by the methods within the class (this is called *encapsulation* and is central to the concept of object-oriented programming). Data can also be declared as *public,* which means it can be reached from the methods of other classes (in the same way data is available in a C `struct`). As long as you don't infringe on the domain of the keywords of the language, you can pretty well name the data items anything you want.

Access to methods can also be controlled. The methods of a class can be declared `private` (only accessible from other methods inside the class) or `public` (available to other classes). The naming of methods requires a little more care. Some specific names have special meaning, and some methods have predefined names.

TIP **Along with `public` and `private`, there are a couple of other access specifications: `protected`, `private protected`, and a default setting that doesn't have a name. As we unfold more and more of the structure of a Java program, the meanings of these visibility modifiers will become clear. At the end of this chapter you will find a summary of all of them.**

Listing 6-1 illustrates a very simple class that defines a circle. It doesn't do anything with the circle, it just defines the circle.

All we need to know to define a circle is its diameter and the location of its center.

Listing 6-1 Circle.java

```
public class Circle {
  int diameter;
  int x_center;
  int y_center;
  Circle(int d, int x, int y) {
   diameter = d;
   x_center = x;
   y_center = y;
  }
  public int diameter() {
   return(diameter);
  }
  public int radius() {
   return(diameter / 2);
  }
  public int x_left() {
   return(x_center - radius());
  }
  public int y_top() {
   return(y_center - radius());
  }
}
```

Notice that the class itself is declared as `public`, and that it is given the name `Circle`. The class `Circle` contains three data items — the circle's diameter and the coordinates of its center. The data is declared as `private`, which means it can only be accessed by methods defined inside `Circle`.

TIP **The name of a public class is always the same as the name of the file in which it is kept. That is, given a public class named `HomeBrew`, its source form will be kept in a file named `HomeBrew.java`, and its bytecode form will be in `HomeBrew.class`. There can be other classes in the file with `HomeBrew`, but they cannot be public classes — they are only available to the `HomeBrew` class and to each other.**

The `Circle` class has a *constructor* method. This is a method that is called whenever an object is created from the class definition. Its purpose is to perform any necessary initialization. A constructor is easy to spot. It always has the same name as the class itself. In this case, our constructor initializes the circle's diameter and the location of its center from the arguments that are passed to it.

Four methods in the `Circle` class are used to access the encapsulated data. The `diameter()` and `radius()` methods can be used to discover the size of the circle. A couple of methods can be used to determine the location of the circle. These methods don't return the center of the circle, but instead can be used to return the upper left-hand corner of a square in which the circle resides. By sheer coincidence, this is exactly what the Java graphics routines need to draw a circle.

Object

The class definition itself doesn't do anything but lie there. It comes to life when it is used by the Java interpreter as the blueprint to construct an object. There is more than one way to do this, but the most common and visible way is to use the keyword `new`. So now, right before your very eyes, we are going to use our `Circle` class to construct one of the least interesting applets in the history of Java. Listing 6-2 draws a circle.

Listing 6-2 ShowCircle.java

```
import java.applet.*;
import java.awt.*;

public class ShowCircle extends Applet {
  public void init() {
   setBackground(Color.blue);
  }
  public boolean mouseDown(Event e,int x,int y) {
   Circle circle = new Circle(50,x,y);
   Graphics g = getGraphics();
   g.setColor(Color.white);
   g.drawOval(circle.x_left(),circle.y_top(),
         circle.diameter(),circle.diameter());
   return(true);
  }
}
```

The class `ShowCircle` in Listing 6-2 is a complete applet. It imports the `java.applet` package and extends the `Applet` class, which means it can be executed from within an HTML script being displayed by a browser. `ShowCircle` also imports the `java.awt` package, which it uses to draw graphics. There are two methods in this class. The `init()` method is a part of all applets that need to do some initialization when they are first started by the browser. In our example, we set the background to blue just to prove we could do it.

The other method in `ShowCircle` is named `mouseDown()`. Like `init()`, `mouseDown()` is also called by the browser. Every click of the mouse inside the rectangle displayed by the applet will cause `mouseDown()` to be called. Every time `mouseDown()` is called, it creates a new `Circle` object at the mouse location — by using the keyword `new` — and uses the values from it to draw a circle on the display. As the wandering mouse clicks and moves on, `new` builds one `Circle` object after another and draws it on the display. To convince a browser to execute the program, it must be embedded in an HTML script. For this purpose, we created a very simple one — shown in Listing 6-3 — to execute this example. You will notice that the size of the rectangle used by the applet is determined by the setting in HTML — the applet doesn't get to decide the size of its window.

Listing 6-3 ShowCircle.html

```
<html>
<head>
<title>The ShowCircle Applet</title>
</head>
<body>
<applet code="ShowCircle.class" width=300 height=150>
</applet>
</body>
</html>
```

Visual Café has a local browser built into it, so by including the HTML file as part of the project, and by running the project, the built-in browser loads and runs `ShowCircle.html`. This way you can see just what the applet will look like when it becomes a citizen of the world by appearing on your Web site. Figure 6-1 shows the results of a few random mouse clicks.

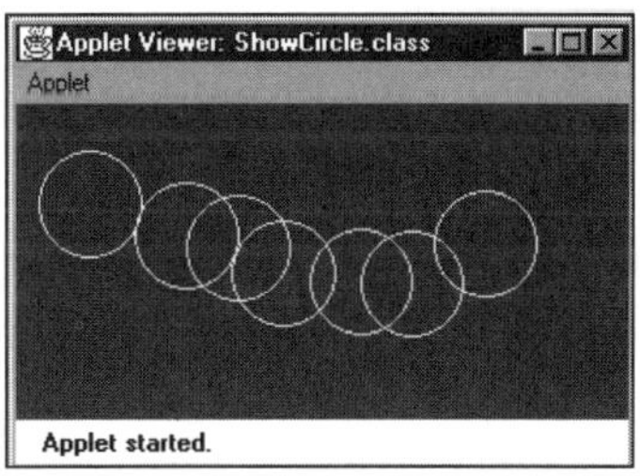

Figure 6-1 Typical output produced by ShowCircle.java

You may have noticed that no particular mouse button was specified — this is because they are all the same to Java. Java assumes a single-button mouse. Also, as you click away on the window, the program creates one `Circle` object after another and doesn't keep track of all the old `Circle` objects — once one is used for drawing, it is simply ignored. This is OK, because they are all accounted for and properly discarded by the Java interpreter during garbage collection. More about this later.

TIP **There is more to this mouse button thing than first meets the eye. If you don't do anything special in your program, Java assumes that all mouse buttons are created equal and does not discriminate. However, if you wish, you can actually tell them apart. All this is done in such a way that one-button mouse operators can participate. Pressing the right mouse button will set the bit** `Event.META_MASK` **in the variable** `Event.modifiers`**. The middle button will cause the bit** `Event.ALT_MASK` **to be set. This is exactly the same result that would occur if either the META or ALT key were held down during a mouse button press.**

Class Relationships with main() and init()

Every Java program — whether an applet or an application — is defined as a class. Every program must have a place to start, so if the program is an applet, it will begin execution with a method named `init()`. If it is an application, it will begin execution with a method named `main()`. A class can have both `init()` and `main()` methods, which means that it can be executed as either an applet or an application.

TIP **When you look at a class and see** `main()`**, it is an application. If you see** `init()`**, it is an applet. If you see them both, it is both. If you see neither, it is only a class and must be instantiated from either an application or an applet.**

Whenever an applet consists of multiple classes, it is abnormal if more than one of them has an `init()` method. On the other hand, it is quite normal for many of the classes to have a `main()`. Any class having a `main()` can be executed as a stand-alone program. This is a reasonable thing to do if you write, for example, a Java class that provides quick solutions to fourth order differential equations and the class is just one of several such classes in a larger application. It would be wise to insert a `main()` method in the class so it could be run alone for testing. Whenever the class is accessed from another class, the `main()` is ignored.

Anyway, once your class has been cranked up — through either `init()` or `main()` — it will begin creating objects from other classes as it needs them. These objects in turn create other objects. This goes on until your entire application is in full dynamic execution with all your objects working together. It's sort of like a football team with players running on and off the field between the plays. All we need now are the cheerleaders, "Shift to the left: shift to the right: come on boys: byte, byte, byte!"

Garbage Collection

Have you ever wanted to have a servant that would follow you around and clean up after you? Well, you've got one — the Java garbage collector. Create all the programmatic messes you want and whenever you discard anything, the garbage collector will automatically gather it up and dispose of it neatly.

Java is designed to do this cleanly. Whenever your program is running, this little Java guy is watching and making notes about the things you do. Every time you create an object, he makes a note of it. Every time you create a reference, he makes a note of that. At some point during the execution of your program, Java may determine that it is necessary to collect the garbage. To do this, Java compares the little guy's notebook with the list of references and finds all objects that you're not using. Java's reasoning? If you don't have a reference to it, you can't find it anyway, and so you will never miss it — recycle.

There are unseen forces at work here. Exactly what motivates Java to decide that the time has come to collect the garbage is a bit mysterious. The garbage collection intervals vary from one implementation of the Java interpreter to the next. We do know, however, that one of the prime motivators of garbage collection is running low on available RAM. There is also a system-level method that you can call that claims to have some effect on Java deciding to retrieve the old objects. The method is called `gc()` — which is short for garbage collect. In reality, however, calling this function is just a suggestion. It's like saying, "Mr. Java, sir, would you be kind enough to do some garbage collecting now?" There is no way for you to check to see what it has done because — by definition — it is working on things you know nothing about.

TIP **There is almost never a reason to be concerned about garbage collection. It happens smoothly in the background without any problems. The only thing that could be of concern is a discarded object that is still holding on to some system resource, such as a serial port. If this is a concern, the addition of a `close()` or `release()` method should do the trick. It is also possible to add a finalizer — discussed in the next section — to the class.**

Constructors and Finalizers

Every class has at least one constructor. As explained earlier, a constructor is a method with the same name as the class itself, and it is executed whenever an object is instantiated from its class.

In the `Circle` class of Listing 6-1, is a constructor that requires the size of the circle along with the *x* and *y* coordinates of its center. Every time a `Circle` object is constructed, all three of these values must be supplied. A class can have several different constructors that will enable an object to be constructed in several different ways. Listing 6-3 is a modified version of the `Circle` class with some added constructors to show how this works.

Listing 6-3 Circle2.java

```
public class Circle2 {
  private int diameter;
  private int x_center;
  private int y_center;
  public Circle2(int d,int x,int y) {
   diameter = d;
   x_center = x;
   y_center = y;
  }
  public Circle2(int x,int y) {
   diameter = 50;
   x_center = x;
   y_center = y;
  }
  public Circle2(Circle2 circle) {
   diameter = circle.diameter();
   x_center = circle.x_center();
   y_center = circle.y_center();
  }
  public int diameter() {
   return(diameter);
  }
  public int radius() {
   return(diameter / 2);
  }
  public int x_center() {
   return(x_center);
  }
  public int y_center() {
   return(y_center);
  }
  public int x_center() {
   return(x_center);
  }
  public int y_center() {
   return(y_center);
  }
  public int x_left() {
```

```
        return(x_center - radius());
    }
    public int y_top() {
        return(y_center - radius());
    }
}
```

Each of the constructors has the same name as the class. They differ only in their list of parameters. The `Circle2` class makes it possible to create a circle with a radius of 50 by specifying only its center:

```
Circle2 defcen = new Circle2(50,25,30);
```

It would then be possible to create a second circle identical to the first:

```
Circle2 sameas = new Circle2(defcen);
```

TIP **When there is more than one constructor in a class, Java determines which one to use by matching the argument types. This procedure, known as *overloading*, works with all methods, not just constructors.**

TIP **If you write a class and do not supply a constructor for it, Java supplies one for you. The supplied one is a very simple constructor with no arguments, and it initializes all the data members to their defaults of zeroes and nulls.**

A constructor has a counterpart method that is called at the end of the life of an object. Because Java is so neat and tidy about cleaning up after itself, it will be very rarely that you will ever use one, but if you want to write a *finalizer*, it's a simple matter. Say that you have a class that opens a file and keeps it open (or takes control of some other system resource that you want to make sure it eventually releases), simply include the following method in your class:

```
void finalize() {
    // Code to release system resource
}
```

Now, there is no guarantee about just when this method will be called. It will be called whenever the object is garbage collected, and there is just no telling when that will happen. The garbage may not be collected until the party is about over — when the program is ceasing execution — but it will execute eventually.

SIDE TRIP

Isa and Hasa

Do not confuse `extends` with `import` — they are very different animals. When one class `extends` another, the new class becomes a member of the family of the class being extended: this is called *isa,* because it "is a" member of the family. On the other hand, an `import` statement is used to access the definition of a class from some other file so it can create an object by using its definition: this is called *hasa,* since it "has a" member of the other family. A class can only have one heritage — that is, one `extends` statement — but it can do all the importing that the compiler will bear. There is more information on `import` later in this chapter.

Inheritance

Java has single inheritance. This means that a class can assume all the attributes and characteristics of — at the most — one other class. Once a class assumes all the attributes of another, it can add extensions to them to do something more, something different, or both. That is why the keyword for inheritance in Java is `extends`.

TIP **All classes in Java have the same root. They can all trace their ancestry to a class named `Object`. Whenever a class is written without a specific `extends` statement, by default it is actually an extension of `Object`. The class `Object` is the only one in all of Java that does not extend any other class.**

`Smiley.java` is shown in Listing 6-4 as an example of using `extends`. In this case, we have added eye and mouth locations to our `Circle` class to create the definition of a smiley face. To apply some terminology to this, `Smiley` is said to be a *subclass* of the *superclass* `Circle`.

Listing 6-4 Smiley.java

```
public class Smiley extends Circle {
  Smiley(int d, int x, int y) {
   super(d,x,y);
  }
  public int x_left_eye() {
   return(x_center - (radius() / 3));
  }
  public int x_right_eye() {
   return(x_center + (radius() / 3));
```

```
    }
    public int y_left_eye() {
     return(y_center - (radius() / 3));
    }
    public int y_right_eye() {
     return(y_center - (radius() / 3));
    }
    public int eye_width() {
     return(radius() / 8);
    }
    public int eye_height() {
     return(radius() / 5);
    }
    public int x_mouth_left() {
     return(x_center - mouth_radius());
    }
    public int y_mouth_top() {
     return(y_center - mouth_radius());
    }
    public int mouth_radius() {
     return((radius() * 2) / 3);
    }
}
```

Like its parent `Circle`, the class `Smiley` doesn't draw anything — it just defines the geometrics. The `Smiley` constructor has the same arguments as the `Circle` constructor because we had no need for any further information. If there had been a need for more data items, they could have been added, and there could have been initial value settings for them in the constructor. The first line of code in the constructor is a call to a method named `super()`. This is really a call to the constructor of `Circle`, because `Circle` is the superclass of `Smiley`.

6

TIP **Every constructor must include a call to a constructor of its superclass; that is, a call to `super()`. To make sure this happens, the Java compiler looks at the first line of code in every constructor it compiles and if it is not a call to `super()`, it inserts one. The compiler will always insert a call to the default constructor — the one without arguments. If you need to call a constructor that has arguments, you need to specify the call yourself as the first line of code in the constructor, as shown in Listing 6-4.**

We now have a new class named `Smiley`. It uses `Circle` as its superclass. All `Smiley` does is add some methods that can be used to locate the eyes and the distance from the center of the circle to the mouth (technically, I suppose, this could be called the *grin radius*). All the `Circle` information is still there — we have just added to it.

Listing 6-5 is the class ShowSmiley. It's very similar to ShowCircle, except that it makes use of the new information in creating the display.

Listing 6-5 ShowSmiley.java

```
import java.applet.*;
import java.awt.*;

public class ShowSmiley extends Applet {
  public void init() {
   setBackground(Color.blue);
  }
  public boolean mouseDown(Event e,int x,int y) {
   Smiley smiley = new Smiley(100,x,y);
   Graphics g = getGraphics();
   g.setColor(Color.yellow);
   g.fillOval(smiley.x_left(),smiley.y_top(),
         smiley.diameter(),smiley.diameter());
   g.setColor(Color.black);

   g.fillOval(smiley.x_left_eye(),smiley.y_left_eye(),
         smiley.eye_width(),smiley.eye_height());

   g.fillOval(smiley.x_right_eye(),smiley.y_right_eye(),
         smiley.eye_width(),smiley.eye_height());

   g.drawArc(smiley.x_mouth_left(),smiley.y_mouth_top(),
         smiley.mouth_radius()*2,smiley.mouth_radius()*2,
         190,170);
   g.dispose();
   return(true);
  }
}
```

Note that something has been added at the bottom of the mouseDown() method in ShowSmiley — it's sort of a safety feature. Whenever the mouseDown() method has finished with a Graphics object, it calls its dispose() method. The dispose() method causes the system to garbage collect the Graphics object. This means its finalizer will be called, which will free up any system resources being held by the Graphics object. It really doesn't affect the efficiency in our simple example, but in a larger applet that is doing lots of graphics, it could prevent the system from performing massive garbage collection all at once while the program is busy doing something else. There is also some evidence that the leftover allocation of too many simultaneous Graphics objects can cause troubles in Windows 95. Remember one important thing: Once dispose() has been called, you can no longer use the object — the value you now hold in your reference is invalid. Figure 6-2 is typical of what ShowSmiley looks like after a few mouse clicks.

Figure 6-2 Typical display of ShowSmiley.java

Overloading

In Java, the full name of a method includes its list of argument types. Two methods can have the same name as long as their *signature* is different. This is called *overloading*, and you saw an example of it earlier with the multiple constructors in `Circle2` in Listing 6-3. Overloading is normally used with constructors, but it will work for all methods.

One convenience of overloading is the ability to refer to one piece of data with the same name for both *setting* and *getting*. While it is common to prefix the data access functions with the words get or set (as in `setProperty()` and `getProperty()`), this is not strictly necessary. Take a look at `Cylinder.java` in Listing 6-6.

6

Listing 6-6 Cylinder.java

```
public class Cylinder {
  double height;
  double radius;
  static public void main(String argv[]) {
   Cylinder cyl = new Cylinder();
   cyl.height(30);
   cyl.radius(5);
   System.out.println("Height=" + cyl.height() +
         " Radius=" + cyl.radius() +
         " Volume=" + cyl.volume());
  }
```

```
    public double height() {
     return(height);
    }
    public void height(double height) {
     this.height = height;
    }
    public double radius() {
     return(radius);
    }
    public void radius(double radius) {
     this.radius = radius;
    }
    public double volume() {
     return( Math.PI * radius * radius * height);
    }
}
```

The methods `radius()` and `height()` are both overloaded. The ones that require arguments are used to set the values, and the ones without arguments are used to return the values. The `main()` method uses the *set* form of these methods to insert the values and then uses the *get* versions to return the values for printing. The output looks like this:

```
Height=30 Radius=5 Volume=2356.19
```

Actually, this class contains four different things all named `height`, and the compiler keeps them all straight. During compilation, the compiler first encounters the data declaration where the current value is kept. Second comes the method used to set the value. The compiler can easily distinguish between any future references to a method or a data item because of the parentheses — no problem so far. Third, there is the argument that we pass in to `height()` to set the value. The compiler uses its scoping rules to ignore the value outside the method, using the local one instead — still no problem. (You will notice that a reference to the outer scope required use of the magic word `this`.) Fourth, and finally, the compiler will come across another method named `height`. The compiler can easily distinguish the two by noting that one requires a `double` as an argument and the other has no argument. No problem — wherever the word `height` is used, the compiler will deduce exactly which one you are talking about.

TIP **Whenever a variable inside an inner scope has the same name as one in an outer scope, the one in the outer scope is said to be *shadowed* and it will not normally be seen. If a variable in a method shadows an object-level variable, it can be addressed by using `this`, as in `this.height` in Listing 6-6. Also, if a variable in the superclass is shadowed, it can be addressed by using `super`, as in `super.height`.**

There is something about overloading that you need to be careful about. The typematching between a method call and the method itself has a trap door through which a careless programmer may drop. In Listing 6-6, two calls set the values of `height` and `radius`, and in both cases integer values are used as the arguments. However, because there are no methods with those names that take integer values, the compiler chose the "closest fit." Recall that Java will perform automatic data conversions whenever there is no loss of magnitude. That's what happens here. It's a very handy thing to have the compiler do for you. Usually.

Let's say the height of these cylinders needed to be specified in two ways — either in decimal fractions of yards, or in inches. (I know that would be a screwy way to do things, but this *is* my example.) So we defined the height-setting methods as follows:

```
public void height(double height); // Fractions of yards
public void height(int height); // Inches
```

This will work fine. A call to `height(17.5)` will get the fraction-of-yards version, because Java will interpret 17.5 as being a `double` — it has the telltale decimal point. A call to `height(630)` will get you the inches version, because without a decimal point, Java interprets 630 to be an `int`. Just what you wanted. But you can see how easy it would be to write code that would call the wrong method. Also, any previously written code (such as the code in our `Cylinder.java` example) that was depending on the automatic conversion and assuming the fraction-of-yards version would get it wrong. Moral: Don't overload ambiguously.

Overriding

The ability of a subclass to override the methods of its superclass is one of the cornerstones of the object-orientedness of Java. Earlier — when we were dealing with inheritance — we discussed how it is possible to derive a subclass from a superclass and add things to it. With the magic power of overriding, it is also possible to change things that already exist in the superclass. Let's show how this works with a common application we are called on to write from time to time — the price of railroad crossties. We start off by defining `Crosstie` in Listing 6-7 — a class that defines our basic raw crosstie price. This very simple class contains only the standard price of a crosstie and a method for retrieving it.

6

Listing 6-7 Crosstie.java

```
public class Crosstie {
  protected double standard_price = 18.95;
  double price() {
   return(standard_price);
  }
}
```

But, as we all know, not all crossties are created equal. Next we define `CreosoteCrosstie`, shown in Listing 6-8, as the pricing subclass for a crosstie that has been properly creosote-treated and is ready to be shoved under a train.

Listing 6-8 CreosoteCrosstie.java

```
public class CreosoteCrosstie extends Crosstie {
  private double creosote_process_cost = 3.52;
  double price() {
   return(creosote_process_cost + standard_price);
  }
}
```

Both the superclass, `Crosstie`, and the subclass, `CreosoteCrosstie`, have methods named `price()`. The one that is called is determined by which of the classes is instantiated — which is exactly what we want to have happen. Let's create another kind of crosstie:

Listing 6-9 UsedCrosstie.java

```
public class UsedCrosstie extends Crosstie {
  private double discount_percent = 0.10;
  double price() {
   return(standard_price * (1.0 - discount_percent));
  }
}
```

The `UsedCrosstie` class in Listing 6-9 handles the pricing of the old crossties the railroad digs up (and which folks like to put in their gardens). This is just another subclass from our basic `Crosstie` class, and it also has its own `price()` method. This time the price is derived from the standard price in the superclass:

Listing 6-10 PriceList1.java

```
public class PriceList1 {
  public static void main(String argv[]) {
   Crosstie a = new Crosstie();
   Crosstie b = new UsedCrosstie();
   Crosstie c = new Crosstie();
   Crosstie d = new CreosoteCrosstie();
   Crosstie e = new CreosoteCrosstie();

   System.out.println(a.price());
   System.out.println(b.price());
   System.out.println(c.price());
   System.out.println(d.price());
   System.out.println(e.price());
  }
}
```

Listing 6-10 shows a class that is used to print out a list of the prices of various crossties. Notice that in `main()` there seems to be a conflict in definitions. Even though we are declaring some of each of our different kinds of crossties, we are stuffing them all into `Crosstie` references. We can do that because all of these objects are either `Crossties` or descendants of `Crossties`. The output from executing `PriceList1` is as follows:

```
18.95
17.055
18.95
22.47
22.47
```

Notice how Java is perfectly happy to refer to any kind of crosstie — used or creosote-treated — as simply being a crosstie. Because the pricing method has been overridden in the subclasses, the correct pricing method is called. The pricing method of the superclass has been overridden completely.

TIP **A reference is capable of referring to any object that has been subclassed from the reference's class. This mechanism, called *polymorphism,* can be used to handle objects in a general sort of way. It is not necessary to know exactly what type of object you are dealing with — you only need to know its family.**

In Listing 6-11, we do the same thing in a slightly different way. This time we put all references to the `Crosstie` objects in an array. The polymorphism resulting from overriding the `price()` method allows us to create an array of things that seem to all be alike, while each one knows — deep down inside where it counts — that they are all very different.

Listing 6-11 PriceList2.java

```
public class PriceList2 {
  public static void main(String argv[]) {
   Crosstie arr[];
   arr = new Crosstie[5];

   arr[0] = new Crosstie();
   arr[1] = new UsedCrosstie();
   arr[2] = new Crosstie();
   arr[3] = new CreosoteCrosstie();
   arr[4] = new CreosoteCrosstie();

   for(int i=0; i<5; i++)
         System.out.println(arr[i].price());
  }
}
```

Implementing Interfaces

In our crosstie example you saw what it means to have objects of similar parentage respond to the same command. What about those that don't have the same parentage? There will be cases when it would be very convenient to have objects of completely different heritage have some of the same methods so they can be handled in the same way. For example, you could have a collection of objects that all have the ability to display themselves, and you could install a method called `display()` in each one to do that. Even better, imagine the advantages of each of them having the same set of several methods that could be used to set their size, position, or whatever. Of course, you would have to keep track of all the methods in all these classes — if you make a method-calling change to one, you have to make the same change to all of them.

This is exactly what the Java interface is designed to do. You can think of an interface as a sort of class description that contains only abstract methods and has no variable data items. There is one other important difference between a class and an interface: While a class can only have one superclass, this same class can implement as many interfaces as it wants to.

TIP **In order for a class to fully implement an interface, it must supply a body for every method defined in the interface — leaving even one of the interface methods undefined causes the class to become abstract. That's fine, if that is what you intend to do, but an abstract class cannot be instantiated.**

Listing 6-12 is an example of an applet that uses three different objects that all implement the same interface. The output from it is shown in Figure 6-3.

Listing 6-12 ShowShapes.java

```
import java.applet.*;
import java.awt.*;

public class ShowShapes extends Applet {
  public void paint(Graphics g) {
   Rectangle r = bounds();
   int area = (r.width * r.height) / 12;
   Square square = new Square();
   Circle circle = new Circle();
   Triangle triangle = new Triangle();

   square.center(r.width/4,r.height/2);
   square.area(area);
   circle.center(2*r.width/4,r.height/2);
   circle.area(area);
```

```
    triangle.center(3*r.width/4,r.height/2);
    triangle.area(area);

    square.draw(g);
    circle.draw(g);
    triangle.draw(g);
  }
}

interface SetupAndDisplay {
  public void center(int x,int y);
  public void draw(Graphics g);
  public void area(int area);
}

class Square implements SetupAndDisplay {
  int x;
  int y;
  int width;
  public void center(int x,int y) {
   this.x = x;
   this.y = y;
  }
  public void draw(Graphics g) {
   int half = width / 2;
   g.drawLine(x-half,y-half,x+half,y-half);
   g.drawLine(x+half,y-half,x+half,y+half);
   g.drawLine(x+half,y+half,x-half,y+half);
   g.drawLine(x-half,y+half,x-half,y-half);
  }
  public void area(int area) {
   width = (int)Math.sqrt(area);
  }
}

class Circle implements SetupAndDisplay {
  int x;
  int y;
  int radius;
  public void center(int x,int y) {
   this.x = x;
   this.y = y;
  }
  public void draw(Graphics g) {
```

6

```
        g.drawOval(x-radius,y-radius,2*radius,2*radius);
    }
    public void area(int area) {
        radius = (int)Math.sqrt(area/Math.PI);
    }
}

class Triangle implements SetupAndDisplay {
    int x;
    int y;
    int width;
    public void center(int x,int y) {
        this.x = x;
        this.y = y;
    }
    public void draw(Graphics g) {
        int half = width / 2;
        g.drawLine(x-half,y+half,x,y-half);
        g.drawLine(x,y-half,x+half,y+half);
        g.drawLine(x+half,y+half,x-half,y+half);
    }
    public void area(int area) {
        width = (int)Math.sqrt(area * 2);
    }
}
```

The ShowShapes class is designed to display three shapes equally spaced and horizontally and vertically centered in the window. Each of the three shapes will enclose one-twelfth of the total area, and each one needs to respond to identical commands, so we declare ourselves an interface named SetupAndDisplay with the three methods area(), center(), and draw(). The area() method is used to tell the shape how much area it is to cover; the center() method is used to tell the shape where it is to draw itself; and the draw() method is used to command it to draw itself. With the interface defined, it is now a matter of constructing a class for each of the shapes. Because each of the shape classes implement the SetupAndDispay interface, the ShowShapes class knows exactly how to talk to them. They all speak the same language.

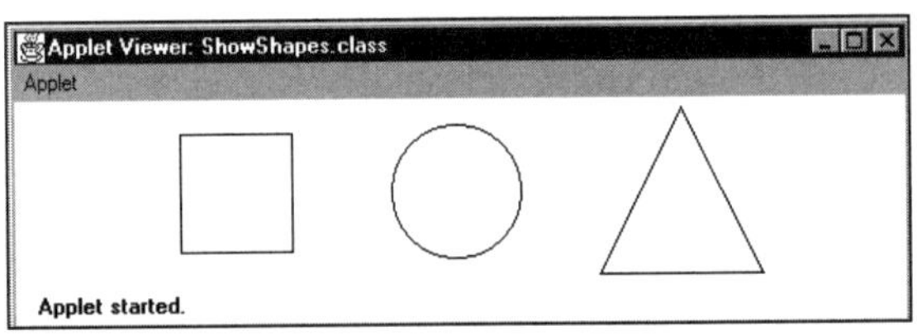

Figure 6-3 The display window of ShowShapes.java

TIP **Think of an interface as a contract agreed upon by specified objects. It is an agreed-upon definition of the way the objects will communicate with one another. The only way to modify this contract is to modify the interface — the contract. This will force every object using the interface to have its methods modified to exactly match the new contract. You can see how this could work in a large system with hundreds of classes. If it becomes necessary, say, to add a new method to an interface, the Java compiler will squeal to the programmer about every class that attempts to break the contract. This is an enormously handy safety mechanism in software development.**

The `ShowShapes` class only has a `paint()` method. Each time the `paint()` method is called, it calls `bounds()` to discover the size of the current rectangle available to the applet. The dimensions of the bounding rectangle are then used to create three shapes and tell each one of them where it should place its center and how much area it should enclose. Each of the three shapes is then told to draw itself. All of this is done using the interface that everyone has agreed to use.

TIP **As you can see from Listing 6-12, it is possible to have more than one class in a file. It is only possible to have one *public* class in any one file, and that public class must have the same name as the file. However, there can be any number of *nonpublic* classes and interfaces in a single file. These nonpublic classes are local to the file and cannot be accessed directly by any code outside the file.**

A class can choose to implement several interfaces and simultaneously extend a class. The syntax for this looks like the following:

```
public class Pentagon extends ShapeBase
   implements SetupAndGo, Rotate, Colorize {
...
```

6

The keywords `extends` and `implements` can each appear only once, but you can put all the interface names you want following `implements`.

While you cannot define variables in an interface, you can declare constant values. Use the same syntax you would use in a class:

```
public interface SeeSaw {
  static final int SEE_MAXIMUM = 100;
  static final int SEE_MINIMUM = 80;
...
```

Any constants defined this way are available to the methods of any class that implements the interface.

TIP **It is possible to define interfaces that contain nothing but constants. This way you can use a bunch of interfaces just as you would a bunch of header files in C — you can define named groups of constants.**

Packaging

Packaging is a method of organizing Java classes into groups. One advantage of putting classes in a package is the name space capability. Because all packages have their own name space, you have the freedom to name things whatever you would like. You can write classes that have the same names as those of another package. The classes that use the packages will make the name distinctions by specifying which packages are imported. If a couple of packages are imported that have some classes with the same names, the names will simply have to be qualified by using the package name on each reference. You have to use full names, just as you would when there are two women named Bertha — you have to call one Bertha Stone and the other one Bertha D. Blues.

To have Java compile a class into a package, just name the package at the beginning of the file:

```
package animals;
public class Flatworm {
...
}
```

Packages can be included inside other packages. This is done by using a dot reference and, just like the file system on your computer, can be used to create a hierarchy of packages. For example, we could subdivide our animals package:

```
package animals.ugly;
public class Warthog {
...
}
```

TIP **All classes are in a package. If the code you write does not contain a** `package` **statement, the classes are automatically included in the default package. The name of the default package is** `java`**.**

Once you put some classes into a package, you will need to tell the Java compiler that you want to use members of the package. This is done with the `import` statement. The `import` statement does not attach the package to your class (the way the `include` statement does in C). It is only information supplied to the Java compiler for it to use to resolve name references. Consider the following:

```
import animals.*;
import animals.ugly.*;
public class Ark {
  Flatworm fw;
  Warthog wh;
Ark() {
  fw = new Flatworm();
  wh = new Warthog();
...
  }
}
```

The Java compiler will run through this code once in its bare feet and discover that it has a couple of names left over. It has no idea what you meant by `Flatworm` or `Warthog`. It will then check to see what you specified to be imported, stick these names where the asterisks are, and then try to make sense of them that way. Voilá!

The way Java uses the import statement leaves you with a good bit of flexibility regarding how you are able to specify the packages. The previous example could have been written as follows:

```
import animals.Flatworm;
import animals.ugly.Warthog;

public class Ark {
  Flatworm fw;
  Warthog wh;
Ark() {
  fw = new Flatworm();
  wh = new Warthog();
...
  }
}
```

This is often handy when there is more than one `Warthog` or `Flatworm` in your universe and you want to specify which one you are talking about. Of course, if you want to use the `Warthogs` from two places at once, that can be done also, but you need to specify which one you are talking about and where:

```
import animals.ugly.Warthog;
import animals.mythological.Warthog;

public class Ark {
  ugly.Warthog uwh;
  mythological.Warthog mwh;
Ark() {
```

```
    uwh = new ugly.Warthog();
    wh = new mythological.Warthog();
...
    }
}
```

Java is pretty smart about matching up the names on the import statements with the names in your program. It will not allow any ambiguities. If you name things in such a way that it could be interpreted as valid references to more than one thing, the compiler will complain and refuse to compile your program.

BONUS

Access Roundup

Throughout all the previous chapters, such terms as `protected`, `private`, and `public` have been thrown around. If it seems confusing to you, that's a good sign — it is confusing. These words are used for *access control*. They are used to either limit or expand access to the names being defined in a Java program. Table 6-1 contains a list that you can use to try to get it all straight.

TABLE 6-1 Access Control Declarators

Declaration	**Means**
(DEFAULT)	If no access is specified for a class, it can be accessed only within its own package.
(DEFAULT) METHOD	If no access is specified for a method, it can be accessed where its class can be accessed, but not outside of its package.
(DEFAULT) VARIABLE	If no access is specified for a variable, it can be accessed where its class can be accessed, but not outside of its package.
PUBLIC CLASS	A public class is accessible everywhere.
PUBLIC METHOD	A public method has the same accessibility as its enclosing class.

Declaration	Means
PUBLIC VARIABLE	A public variable has the same accessibility as its enclosing class.
PROTECTED CLASS	There is no such thing.
PROTECTED METHOD	A protected method is accessible inside any of its subclasses and throughout its package.
PROTECTED VARIABLE	A protected variable is accessible inside any of its subclasses and throughout its package.
PRIVATE CLASS	There is no such thing.
PRIVATE METHOD	A private method is only visible within its own class.
PRIVATE VARIABLE	A private variable is only visible within its own class.
PRIVATE PROTECTED CLASS	There is no such thing.
PRIVATE PROTECTED METHOD	A private protected method is accessible only within its own class and its subclasses.
PRIVATE PROTECTED VARIABLE	A private protected variable is accessible only within its own class and subclasses. Also, while the object of a subclass can access the private protected variables it has inherited, it cannot, through polymorphism, access the same fields in an object of its superclass.

Summary

This chapter has covered the core concepts of the object-oriented language called Java. You now understand the basic parts and construction techniques that go into a Java program. You have enough information to take the fundamental parts and pieces — supplied as part of the Visual Café development environment — and build programs.

A Java class is the set of plans used to construct an object. A Java program comes out of the compiler and goes onto disk as a set of classes. When a Java program goes into execution (either inside a Web browser or under the control of a Java interpreter), it becomes a collection of objects interacting with one another. As the program runs, it creates objects. Whenever one of these objects is dropped by the program, the Java system automatically deletes it.

A Java class is a stand-alone unit that maintains its own internal data. Every class in Java has one parent — and the heritage of all classes can be traced back to the common ancestor called `Object`. The public and protected methods of the parent can be overridden in a child class, giving the child class the power to do things its parent is either unable to do or does differently. Every class has a constructor method that executes once whenever an object is instantiated — if you don't supply one, the Java compiler will.

A class operates on its internal data by using its methods. In fact, a class is often described as a list of data items and the methods to operate on that data.

The next chapter will start looking at some of the interplay that takes place during program execution. Because Java programs are very dynamic, there need to be structures and procedures that enable a Java program to do several things at once and not lose track of where it has been, where it is now, and where it needs to be.

CHAPTER SEVEN

EXCEPTIONS AND THREADS

IN THIS CHAPTER YOU LEARN THESE KEY SKILLS

Now that you understand the fundamental structure of a Java program, let's take a look at some of the fancy things that can be done with it. There are many nice features in the Java language — this chapter covers two of the most useful ones: the handling of exceptions and threads. (Hey, they took the best from every existing computer language on Earth. It has to be good!) The way Java handles exceptions and sets up for multithreaded execution are a couple of its best tricks. Both of these capabilities are add-ons in most languages that have them, but they are at the core of Java.

Java uses *exceptions* to handle error conditions, such as an index going past the end of an array or a ground ball going past the shortstop. You use exceptions to set things up so that errors are handled either right where they occur, or all the errors of a certain type are handled in one central location. Exceptions are such an integral part of the Java language that certain error conditions *must* be handled — the compiler will complain unless you do. We like this because it allows us to code away, without writing code to check for potential error conditions, knowing that the compiler will pull us up short if we leave something out.

Java *threads* allow a program to do several tasks at once — sort of like cloning itself for different chores. Imagine yourself walking into a grocery store and instantly cloning yourself. One copy of you could go to the meat section, another to the canned goods, and a third to the frozen foods. Each copy of you would do the shopping in that section, then you could all meet up with yourself at the checkout counter and recombine. Java programs can do that.

Exception Handling

Exception handling is the mechanism by which the Java programmer can deal with exceptional and error conditions. Used properly, it can take the hard work out of error handling. Basically, anywhere in the program that an error occurs, an exception is *thrown*. Whenever one is thrown, it must be *caught* — somewhere. A few default catchers are already set up for you to handle some of them, but you will have to put in some catchers of your own for certain exceptions. In fact, once you get into this and see how it works, you will probably want to create some exceptions of your own and start throwing them around.

TIP **There are times in C when it is necessary to use `longjmp`. Its purpose is to exit from down in the bowels of the program and arrive at some predetermined destination where some mess or other can be cleaned up. Sort of like the Starship Enterprise going into warp to get out of danger and go somewhere where cooler heads can solve the problem. Exceptions in Java can be used to do exactly the same thing, but in a much tidier and more efficient way. You might say that it is the next generation of programmatic warp engines.**

When you look at the code, you can't mistake exception handling for anything else because it has its own set of keywords built right into the language. These keywords all work together to construct the exception handling system. If instead of executing a program, Java was managing a subway excavation project, the keyword `try` would occur when one worker tells another, "I know there may be live steam in that pipe, Harvey — just close your eyes and cut it." The keyword `throw` occurs when Harvey says, "Oops. Live steam! Let's get the heck out of here." The keyword `catch` occurs when the foreperson on the job grabs Harvey on his way out of the tunnel and says, "Here is a clamp to put around the pipe to shut off the steam." The keyword `finally` occurs as the list of actions that will be taken by the foreperson — whether or not the original `try` succeeded. One more keyword, `throws`, is used like the sign at the entrance to a tunnel that says: DANGEROUS PEOPLE WORKING. BEWARE OF LIVE STEAM.

Handling an Exception Where It Occurs

Listing 7-1 is a very simple example of exception handling. All we do here is attempt to open a file that doesn't exist and catch the exceptions.

Listing 7-1 TryCatch1.java

```
import java.io.*;

public class TryCatch1 {
  public static void main(String[] args)
  {
   FileInputStream fin;

   try {
         System.out.println(
               "About to open the file.");
         fin = new FileInputStream("fred");
         System.out.println("The file opened ok.");
   } catch(FileNotFoundException e) {
         System.out.println("The file did not open.");
         System.out.println(e);
         return;
   } finally {
         System.out.println(
               "This will always print.");
   }
   System.out.println(
         "This will print only if the file opens.");
  }
}
```

The combination of `try`, `catch`, and `finally` looks very much like an `if-else` block, but don't be fooled by appearances — they are quite different. Execution begins, as you would expect, with the first statement in the try block. (In this example, we are simply attempting to open a file, but there could be several statements in the try block, and exceptions could be thrown by any of them — or all of them.) If there is no exception thrown in the try block, execution transfers directly to the finally block, and then drops through to the rest of the code of the method. In our example, when the file does not exist, a `FileNotFoundException` exception is thrown, which transfers control to the catch block. The code inside the catch block executes. Remember: Every object can be converted to a string by `println()`, and an `Exception` is no exception. The catch block prints the exception string and then executes a `return` statement — but it doesn't return immediately. There is a law that must be obeyed first. It goes something like this: Whenever a finally block is present, it *must* be executed. It doesn't matter what goes on inside the try and catch blocks — once you are in there, the only way out is through the finally block. So, in our example, the return statements have the effect of executing the finally blocks and then returning.

NOTE **The exception objects, like all other objects in Java, have a method named `toString()` that is invoked automatically by a call to `System.out.println()`. In Listing 7-1, the line of code `System.out.println(e)` is exactly the same as if it had been written `System.out.println(e.toString())`.**

TIP **There is only one try block. It is required and it comes first. There is only one finally block. It is optional and it comes last. There can be any number of catch blocks. If you want to be able to catch more than one type of exception, simply add a new catch block for each one.**

Two things can happen in our example — the file either opens or it doesn't. If the file doesn't exist, the following will be output from the program:

```
About to open the file.
The file did not open.
java.io.FileNotFoundException: fred
This will always print.
```

The exception was thrown by `FileInputStream`, then it was caught, and the finally block was executed on the return. By the way, it is not necessary to put a return statement in the catch block. If no return statement is present, the block will simply drop through the bottom after executing the `finally` block and continue with the method:

```
About to open the file.
The file opened OK.
This will always print.
This will print only if the file opens.
```

Even though no exception was thrown, the finally block executed anyway.

TIP **You can only have one exception in the air at a time. Once an exception is thrown, nothing else will happen until it is caught. The upshot of this is that whenever a statement in a try block throws an exception, none of the other statements in the try block that follow it will be executed — the try block is finished.**

Handling an Exception in Another Method

Listing 7-2 is an example of deferred exception handling. You can be several method calls deep and throw an exception that will be passed right back up through the call stack until some method or other catches it.

Listing 7-2 TryCatch2.java

```
import java.io.*;

public class TryCatch2 {
  private FileInputStream fin;
  public static void main(String[] args)
  {
   TryCatch2 fop = new TryCatch2();

   try {
         System.out.println("About to call startup.");
         fop.startup();
         System.out.println(
         "Back from startup - the file is open.");
   } catch(FileNotFoundException e) {
         System.out.println("The file did not open.");
         System.out.println(e);
         return;
   } finally {
         System.out.println(
               "This will always print.");
   }
   System.out.println(
         "This will print only if the file opens.");
  }

  public void startup() throws FileNotFoundException {
   openit("fred");
  }

  public void openit(String name)
         throws FileNotFoundException {
   fin = new FileInputStream(name);
  }
}
```

This is a lot like the previous example, except that there are a few method calls between the throw and the catch. Notice the way `openit()` handles the exception. It doesn't. Any method that is going to do something that could cause an exception can rid itself of any responsibility by simply announcing that the exception will be thrown in the `throws` statement. The method `openit()` demonstrates that the buck can be passed further up the line. This buck-passing has to stop somewhere — if it doesn't, the Java compiler will complain and refuse to compile the whole thing. In our example, it is stopped at the last possible method — in `main()`. Following is the output in the case of the file failing to open:

```
About to call startup.
The file did not open.
java.io.FileNotFoundException: fred
This will always print.
```

And this is the output when the file opens successfully:

```
About to call startup.
Back from startup - the file is open.
This will always print.
This will print only if the file opens.
```

You can see how something like this could be very handy. For example, if you have an application that is going to open and close files in several different places, you can centralize your error handling to just one place. This streamlines the methods because they don't have code in them to handle all the possible error conditions. It also enables the programmer to put all the error handling in one easy-to-maintain spot — one change fixes all.

TIP **The fact that the Java compiler will not allow thrown exceptions to be ignored is a great safeguard. Just go right ahead and write the code to open the file, write to it, and ignore the errors. If there isn't a method upstream somewhere that is going to catch all the possible exceptions, the program won't compile.**

The Catcher in the Java

A whole bunch of exceptions are defined for the Java API. We have already looked at the one for attempting to open a nonexistent file, but there are others. They are all extensions of the `Throwable` class — and there are two different kinds. Some are just plain ol' exceptions (like we have seen) from which any program can recover. Some, however, are classified as errors. These error types are the heavy hitters. They have to do with things such as overflowing the stack, running out of memory, or waking up with bubble gum in your hair — things you just can't recover from.

There *is* a default catcher. You don't have to go to all the trouble of catching all the exceptions that can be thrown — the default catcher is always on the job. Of course, you can catch them if you wish, because the default catcher simply prints out an appropriate message and causes the program to cease execution. That may not be what you want. However, it may not be a good idea to catch these error types, because they are internal to Java and there's just not a lot you can do about them. Just wave good-bye as they pass.

Rolling Your Own Exceptions

Once you begin to get familiar with the exception mechanism, you may want to start creating your own exceptions. You construct an exception as a regular Java object that has extended the `Exception` class. Listing 7-3 is an example of a homemade exception.

Listing 7-3 EvenOnly.java

```
import java.util.Date;

public class EvenOnly {
  public static void main(String argv[]) {
   try {
         EvenOnly eo = new EvenOnly();
   } catch(OddMinuteException e) {
         System.out.println(e);
   }
  }

  EvenOnly() throws OddMinuteException {
   Date date = new Date();
   if((date.getMinutes() & 0x01) != 0)
         throw new OddMinuteException(date);
   System.out.println("Success at " +
         date.toString());
  }
}

class OddMinuteException extends Exception {
  OddMinuteException(Date date) {
   super("Failure at " + date.toString());
  }
}
```

The class `EvenOnly` will throw an exception from its constructor if an attempt is made to create an object on an odd-numbered minute. To do this, the constructor creates a `Date` object and tests its minute value for being odd or even. If it is an odd number, an exception is instantiated right in the `throw` statement. Because this exception is not being caught locally, the constructor `EvenOnly()` returns immediately with the exception — just as in our previous examples. The `throw` statement is an order to start returning from method calls and keep doing it until one of them catches the exception.

TIP **Yes, you can throw an exception in a constructor. An exception can be thrown from any place in Java that instructions are executed. You can even throw an exception from inside a catch block — this can be the same exception that was just caught (sending the message on upstairs, so to speak), or it could be a completely different exception.**

The exception class `OddMinuteException` is defined by extending the `Exception` class. It has a single constructor that accepts a `Date` object. One of the `Exception` class constructors accepts a `String`, so it is invoked — using `super` — with an appropriately descriptive string.

That's all there is to defining an exception. Of course, because an exception is just another class, you could include all kinds of extended information and fancy interfacing. You could go so far as to give an exception its own dialog window that could be invoked by a method call, but that would be a bit baroque. About all you normally need is some text that describes what happened — but if you have an exception that can be thrown in a hundred places, and there is only one place where you catch them all, you might want to include some sort of location information in the exception class so you can trace it to its origin.

The `main()` of `EvenOnly` will always try to execute its constructor. If the clock comes up with an even-numbered minute, the output from `EvenOnly` looks like the following:

```
Success at Thu Oct 17 16:42:56  1996
```

Running the program during an odd-numbered minute causes the exception to be thrown, with the output as follows:

```
OddMinuteException: Failure at Thu Oct 17 16:43:07  1996
```

Threads

Java through space and time! Space exists so that everything doesn't happen in the same place. Time exists so it doesn't all happen at once. Threads exist in Java to help us overcome the separation imposed by time — a thread in Java is a way of doing two things at once. If you want to do Java animation, you will need to know about threads so you can continue to run your animation while the Web browser does other things.

The Balloon Race

Using a thread, you can instantiate an object and then send it off on its own to do its thing. Listing 7-4 shows a class that does just this. It is an application that builds a window and then starts three balloons floating — at different speeds — up through the window until they hit the top of the window.

Listing 7-4 BalloonRace1.java

```
import java.awt.*;

public class BalloonRace1 extends Frame {
  private int width = 160;
  private int height = 300;
  public static void main(String argv[]) {
   Frame frame = new BalloonRace1();
  }

  BalloonRace1() {
   super("BalloonRace1");
   resize(width,height);
   show();
   // Construct three balloons and start them moving.
   Graphics g = getGraphics();
   Balloon1 b1 =
         new Balloon1(g,450,Color.red,0,280,0);
   b1.start();
   Balloon1 b2 =
         new Balloon1(g,500,Color.black,50,280,0);
   b2.start();
   Balloon1 b3 =
         new Balloon1(g,400,Color.blue,100,280,0);
   b3.start();
  }
}

class Balloon1 extends Thread {
  int xtrack;
  int yend;
  int ycurrent;
  int nap;
  Color color;
  Graphics g;
  Balloon1(Graphics g,int nap,Color color,
         int xtrack,int ystart,int yend) {
   this.xtrack = xtrack;
   this.ycurrent = ystart;
   this.yend = yend;
   this.g = g;
   this.nap = nap;
   this.color = color;
  }
```

```
    public void run() {
     try {
           while(yend < ycurrent) {
                 // Erase the previous balloon
                 g.setColor(Color.white);
                 g.fillOval(xtrack,ycurrent,50,60);
                 // Draw the new balloon
                 g.setColor(color);
                 g.fillOval(xtrack,ycurrent -= 3,50,60);
                 sleep(nap);
           }
     } catch(InterruptedException e) {
           return;
     }
    }
}
```

The BalloonRace1 class is an application that extends Frame so it will have a window to use as a racetrack. The BalloonRace1 constructor sets the size of the window and then displays it. Then it creates three Balloon1 objects and releases them into the window. The Balloon1 class has inherited a method called start() from the Thread class, and it is used to start each of the threads into execution. The call to the start() method causes the Balloon1 class to be spun off into its own thread and then returns to the caller. After the call to start() returns, the threads all run on their own.

TIP **If you take a peek into the directory where this program is compiled, you will notice that there is, as you would expect, a file named BalloonRace1.class, which is the bytecode of the class. You might not have expected to find another file — Balloon1.class. Even though the class is private to the BalloonRace1.java file, it compiles into its own bytecode file. Care must be taken that two classes of the same name — even private classes — are not given the same name if they reside in the same directory. Every time you compile one, it would replace the output of the other.**

Once the start() method has spun the object off on its own — allowing it to leave home, so to speak — the thread needs to find something to do to fill its time. To find some busywork, it calls the run() method. As shown in Listing 7-4, the run() method of Balloon1 is a try block containing a loop that continuously erases and redraws a balloon — each time at new locations, moving it up through the window. The resulting exciting balloon race is captured in midflight in Figure 7-1. (Actually, it isn't really much of a race because the outcome is preset when the balloons are created.)

Figure 7-1 Output of the first balloon race

TIP **In our examples here, we use `start()` to kick off a thread. Then `run()` gets called to keep things rolling. We use `sleep()` inside the loop to suspend thread execution for a time. Several other methods in the thread class could be used to control its actions. For example, `stop()` can be called to immediately bring a thread to a halt. Calling `suspend()` will freeze a thread in its tracks until `resume()` is called. The `join()` method will wait until the thread has finished execution. And the `yield()` method will cause the thread to pause slightly and then continue again. The priority of execution of a thread can be changed with a call to `setPriority()`.**

As this runs, you may notice some problems. The most obvious one is that the balloons flicker from time to time, and, if you run it a few times, you may see the colors get themselves mixed up occasionally. (If you really want to see some confusion with the colors, load your machine with a bunch of stuff running so the threads are all interrupted a lot.) The flicker happens whenever a thread paints a balloon white and an interruption occurs before it can put the color back into it.

The color confusion is a little more complicated, but it has the same root cause — untimely interruptions. Because interruptions can come between any two statements, and because all the threads are using the same `Graphics` object, one of the threads can pick a color just as control switches to another thread for it to draw a balloon and — oops — wrong color.

Let's build another balloon race and fix these problems.

BONUS

A Better Balloon Race

Listing 7-5 is a modified version of BalloonRace1 with the highly original name BalloonRace2.

Listing 7-5 BalloonRace2.java

```
import java.awt.*;

public class BalloonRace2 extends Frame {
  private int width = 160;
  private int height = 300;
  public static void main(String argv[]) {
   Frame frame = new BalloonRace2();
  }

  BalloonRace2() {
   super("BalloonRace2");
   resize(width,height);
   show();
   // Create three balloons and start them moving.
   Graphics g = getGraphics();
   new Balloon2(g,450,Color.red,0,280,0).start();
   new Balloon2(g,500,Color.black,50,280,0).start();
   new Balloon2(g,400,Color.blue,100,280,0).start();
  }
}

class Balloon2 extends Thread {
  int xtrack;
  int yend;
  int ycurrent;
  int nap;
  Color color;
  Graphics g;
  Balloon2(Graphics g,int nap,Color color,
         int xtrack,int ystart,int yend) {
   this.xtrack = xtrack;
```

```
        this.ycurrent = ystart;
        this.yend = yend;
        this.g = g;
        this.nap = nap;
        this.color = color;
    }
    public void run() {
        try {
            while(yend < ycurrent) {
                synchronized(g) {
                    // Erase the previous balloon
                    g.setColor(Color.white);
                    g.drawLine(xtrack + 25,ycurrent +
                        115,xtrack + 25,
                        ycurrent + 120);
                    g.fillOval(xtrack + 22,
                        ycurrent + 60,6,3);
                    g.drawArc(xtrack,ycurrent--,
                        50,60,0,-180);
                    g.drawArc(xtrack,ycurrent--,
                        50,60,0,-180);
                    g.drawArc(xtrack,ycurrent--,
                        50,60,0,-180);
                    // Draw the new balloon
                    g.setColor(Color.black);
                    g.drawLine(xtrack + 25,
                        ycurrent + 60,
                        xtrack + 25,ycurrent + 120);
                    g.setColor(color);
                    g.fillOval(xtrack,ycurrent,50,60);
                    g.fillOval(xtrack + 22,
                        ycurrent + 60,6,3);
                }
                sleep(nap);
            }
        } catch(InterruptedException e) {
            return;
        }
    }
}
```

It runs much cleaner now. To stop the colors from swapping around from one balloon to another, it was necessary to add a `synchronized()` block. You can see how this is done in the `run()` method of Listing 7-5. Our problem with the first balloon race was that all of our threads were able to modify the

Graphics object without paying any attention to what the other threads were doing, so we put the Graphics object in the synchronized statement. Now Java, whenever it comes to the synchronized statement, will look around to see if any other thread of the Balloon2 class is using a block of code synchronized to this particular object. If there is, it will politely wait until the other one is finished. The result is that only one thread can be messing around with our Graphics object at any one time.

In our example, we have synchronized data (that is, the Graphics object). It is possible to have a method synchronized using syntax such as the following:

```
private synchronized void fred(int hoomer) {
  ....
}
```

Synchronized methods work pretty much the same as synchronized blocks of code — only one thread at a time can be executing the code in the method. If a static method is declared synchronized, it can only be executed by one thread at a time by any other object in the entire program.

Synchronization did not clear up the flicker because even though the code in the synchronized block could not be simultaneously executed by another thread of the BalloonRace2, the synchronized block could still be interrupted by another thread coming out of the sleep() method. Or, for that matter, by some entirely separate process on the same computer. We still had the flicker.

The solution to the flicker was not in the threading but in the drawing itself. There was no need to erase the entire balloon just to draw it again because it was mostly a matter of putting the pixels right back in where they had been taken out. The erasure code was changed to drawArc() to erase only the bottom portion of the balloon — the part that was to disappear. That worked out so well we got all excited about the little nozzle doohickey at the bottom and tied a string to the balloon (being careful to erase the bottom of the old string each time we drew a new one). Our new balloon race is shown in Figure 7-2.

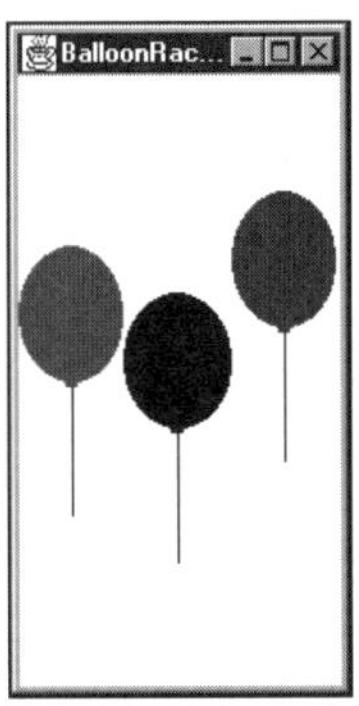

Figure 7-2 Output from BalloonRace2

One other change was made. The statements that create the three threads was simplified. This may look a bit peculiar at first, but it works. Because the `start()` method is being called on all three threads, and because `start()` returns immediately, it was appended directly to the end of the `new` command that creates the threads. This can be done because the return value from `new` is an object reference value, which uses a dot reference to call a method. With this done, there was no need to keep the references, so they were removed.

TIP **Under normal circumstances, an object without a reference will be automatically garbage-collected by Java. Because a thread is running — has its own life, you might say — it is OK to leave it without a reference. It will not be garbage-collected until it stops running.**

Summary

In this chapter, we discovered two things that are very much a part of the Java language — exceptions and threads. Even though these two are implemented as classes (`Exception` and `Thread`), they are both so close to the center of the Java language that they have their own special keywords (`try`, `throw`, `throws`, `catch`, `finally`, and `synchronized`). This is sort of like the `String` class we discussed earlier having its own overloaded operator, the plus sign.

The next chapter digs into more classes that are close to the heart of Java. It then moves on to other classes that are not as close to the center of the language definition, but are necessary for getting things done.

CHAPTER EIGHT

HANDLING EVENTS AND DRAWING

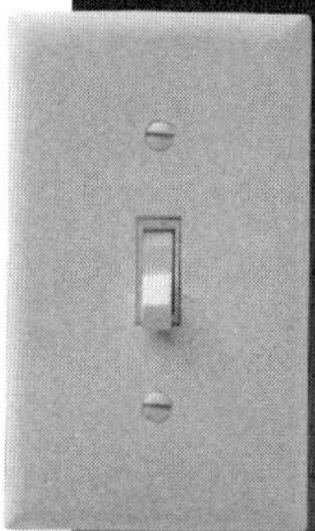

IN THIS CHAPTER YOU LEARN THESE KEY SKILLS

If you write your applet in such a way that it needs input from the user, you will need to know something about processing events. An *event* is something tossed at the applet any time a key on the keyboard is pressed or released, or any time a mouse button is pressed or released. An event occurs every time the mouse is moved — there is even a special one every time the mouse enters or leaves the applet window. From the viewpoint of your applet, the user is just an event machine gun.

In order to respond to user activities, your applet needs to:

* Receive an event
* Recognize what type of event it is
* Take the appropriate action in response to the event

This reminds me of a story. There was a guy who had been in the army for about a month when they realized he was just walking around picking up pieces of paper. That's all he did. He would look at each piece of paper and say, "That's not it," and drop it. He kept this up continuously — day in and day out. When the psychiatric bunch checked him out he just picked up the papers on their desks, one by one, and said, "That's not it." Well, he was eventually declared unfit for service and given a discharge order. He picked it up and said, "That's it!"

The Raw Mouse and Keyboard

Events happen. The user presses keyboard keys or grabs the mouse and squeezes its little buttons. But Java knows all and sees all when it comes to keyboards and mice. It knows because event objects are passed via calls to the `handleEvent()` method of the `Component` class. The `Component` class is the parent class of buttons, sliders, menus, and all things GUI. Listing 8-1 shows what you get when you overload the `handleEvent()` method of the superclass `Applet`.

Listing 8-1 RawEvents.java

```
import java.applet.*;
import java.awt.*;

public class RawEvents extends Applet {
  String line;
  public void paint(Graphics g) {
   g.setColor(Color.white);
   g.fillRect(0,0,size().width,size().height);
   g.setColor(Color.black);
   if(line != null)
         g.drawString(line,10,30);
  }

  public boolean handleEvent(Event e) {
```

```
        line = "id=" + e.id;
        line += " key=" + e.key;
        line += " modifiers=" + e.modifiers;
        line += " count=" + e.clickCount;
        line += " x=" + e.x;
        line += " y=" + e.y;
        line += " when=" + e.when;
        repaint();
        return(false);
    }
}
```

The sequence goes something like this: Deep in the heart of the Java interpreter, it is detected that a button is clicked (or the mouse is moved, or whatever). The interpreter creates an `Event` object and passes it to whichever displayed component happened to be the target of the keyboard or mouse — this is done by calling the component's `handleEvent()` method. Our example program in Listing 8-1 simply overrides the `handleEvent()` method, receiving all the `Event` objects and printing some of the values from it. With every `Event`, a new output line is created and a call is made to `repaint()` which, in turn, causes the `paint()` method to be called with a `Graphics` object. The `paint()` method paints the String on the applet window. The results are shown in Figure 8-1.

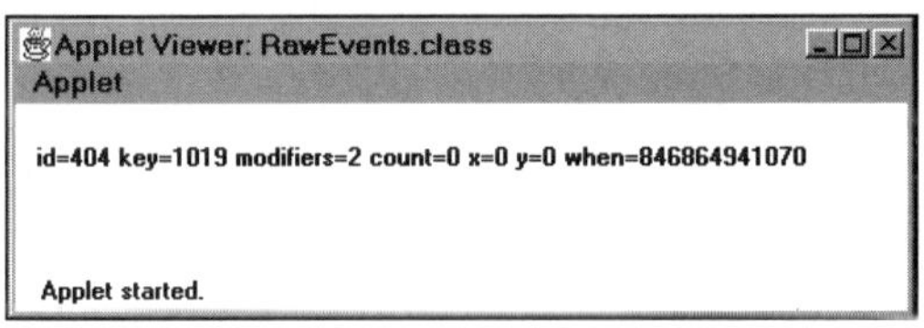

Figure 8-1 Output from RawEvents.java

The applet `RawEvents.java` simply prints out some of the more interesting values to be found in the event. The id number 404 indicates that this event is the release of some non-ASCII key. The key number of 1019 identifies the key as F12. The modifier value of 2 indicates that the control key was held down. There is no *x* or *y* position because we are not dealing with the mouse here. The last element is the enormous timestamp number (the number of milliseconds since January 1, 1970).

Overriding `handleEvent()` will cause every event to come to the applet. The return value is important. A return value of `false` — as we have in our example — sends a message back to the caller that the event was not handled. Our example doesn't handle any of the events (it just looks at them), so it always returns `false`. If you handle the event and don't want anything else to ever be done with it, you simply return `true`.

The Cooked Mouse and Keyboard

Recall that most things in Java come in twos. Event grabbing is no exception. We have a better mouse event trap. Look at EventList.java in Listing 8-2.

Listing 8-2 EventList.java

```
import java.applet.*;
import java.awt.*;

public class EventList extends Applet {
  static final int LINE_COUNT = 30;
  String line[];
  Rectangle rectangle;
  int y_start;
  int y_delta;

  public void init() {
   rectangle = bounds();
   line = new String[LINE_COUNT];
   Graphics g = getGraphics();
   FontMetrics fm = g.getFontMetrics(g.getFont());
   y_delta = fm.getHeight();
   y_start = rectangle.height - fm.getHeight();
  }

  public void paint(Graphics g) {
   g.setColor(Color.white);
   g.fillRect(0,0,size().width,size().height);
   g.setColor(Color.black);
   int y_walk = y_start;
         for(int i=0; (i<LINE_COUNT) && (y_walk>0); i++) {
         if(line[i] == null)
               break;
         g.drawString(line[i],10,y_walk);
         y_walk -= y_delta;
   }
  }

  public boolean mouseMove(Event e,int x,int y) {
   scroll();
   line[0] = "mouseMove(" + x + "," + y + ") ";
   line[0] += modifiers(e);
```

```
  repaint();
  return(true);
 }

 public boolean mouseDown(Event e,int x,int y) {
  scroll();
  line[0] = "mouseDown(" + x + "," + y + ") ";
  line[0] += modifiers(e);
  repaint();
  return(true);
 }

 public boolean mouseUp(Event e,int x,int y) {
  scroll();
  line[0] = "mouseUp(" + x + "," + y + ") ";
  line[0] += modifiers(e);
  repaint();
  return(true);
 }

 public boolean mouseDrag(Event e,int x,int y) {
  scroll();
  line[0] = "mouseDrag(" + x + "," + y + ") ";
  line[0] += modifiers(e);
  repaint();
  return(true);
 }

 public boolean mouseEnter(Event e,int x,int y) {
  scroll();
  line[0] = "mouseEnter(" + x + "," + y + ") ";
  line[0] += modifiers(e);
  repaint();
  return(true);
 }

 public boolean mouseExit(Event e,int x,int y) {
  scroll();
  line[0] = "mouseExit(" + x + "," + y + ") ";
  line[0] += modifiers(e);
  repaint();
  return(true);
 }
```

```
public boolean lostFocus(Event e,Object o) {
 scroll();
 line[0] = "lostFocus";
 repaint();
 return(true);
}

public boolean gotFocus(Event e,Object o) {
 scroll();
 line[0] = "gotFocus";
 repaint();
 return(true);
}

public boolean keyDown(Event e,int key) {
 scroll();
 line[0] = "keyDown" + key_id(e) + modifiers(e);
 repaint();
 return(true);
}

public boolean keyUp(Event e,int key) {
 scroll();
 line[0] = "keyUp" + key_id(e) + modifiers(e);
 repaint();
 return(true);
}

private final void scroll() {
 for(int i=LINE_COUNT-1; i>0; i--)
        line[i] = line[i-1];
}

private final String modifiers(Event e) {
 String retstring = "";
 if((e.modifiers & e.ALT_MASK) != 0)
        retstring += " Alt";
 if((e.modifiers & e.CTRL_MASK) != 0)
        retstring += " Control";
 if((e.modifiers & e.SHIFT_MASK) != 0)
        retstring += " Shift";
 if((e.modifiers & e.META_MASK) != 0)
        retstring += " Meta";
 return(retstring);
```

```
    }

    private final String key_id(Event e) {
     String retstring = "";
     retstring = " Key=";
     if((e.key < ' ') || (e.key >'~'))
           retstring += e.key;
     else
           retstring += "'" + (char)e.key + "'";
     retstring += " Id=" + e.id;
     return(retstring);
    }
}
```

This is a more elaborate version of our first attempt to herd the events. First, it uses an entirely different method for grabbing events; instead of overriding `handleEvent()`, this applet overrides each method responsible for handling the individual events. This seems to be the most sensible way to do it — leave all the sorting-out and bookkeeping to the component. The default `handleEvent()` method simply checks the event type and then calls one of these methods to handle that specific type. The work of figuring out just which event is coming has been done for us.

`EventList.java` overrides each of the methods in the `Component` class and displays the output by calling `scroll()` to empty the bottom line, creating a new line of text with information about the event, issuing a command to have the screen repainted, and returning `true` to indicate that the event has been handled.

TIP **In this simple applet, it really doesn't matter whether we return `true` or `false` from the event handlers — nothing else will be done with the events anyway. What does an Applet window care if you clicked a mouse button? If we were processing events from a button, for example, the return value would have meaning — the button knows what to do with a mouse click.**

Figure 8-2 shows some typical output from `EventList.java`.

Whenever you do anything with the mouse, the `mouseMove()` method is by far the busiest because it's called every time the mouse changes position. The `mouseDrag()` method takes over the job of tracking movement whenever a button is held down on the mouse. A couple of event handlers are called whenever the mouse leaves or enters the window: `mouseEnter()` and `mouseExit()`. There are also a couple of mouse button event handlers: `mouseDown()` is called whenever a button is pressed and `mouseUp()` is called whenever it is released. The event modifiers field can be used to determine which mouse button was pushed and whether any special keys (shift, control, alt, or meta) were being held down. This may seem a little clumsy, but if you think in terms of a one-button mouse (the lowest common denominator), it makes sense. All Java mouse button events can be generated by a multibutton mouse, or by a one-button mouse and a keyboard.

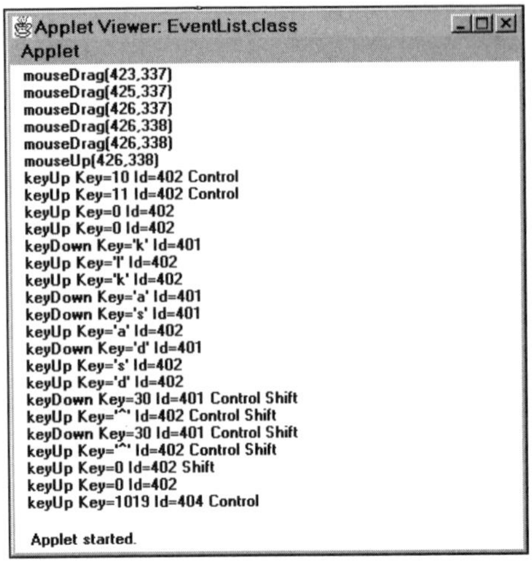

Figure 8-2 Output from EventList.java

The keyboard doesn't move and drag the way the mouse does, but it does go in and out of focus. Whenever you press a key on the keyboard, only one window on the operating system's display will receive it — the one with the focus. From inside your applet, you can detect those golden moments when you acquire or lose focus with the methods `gotFocus()` and `lostFocus()`.

CAUTION

Note that there is a potential problem with `gotFocus()` and `lostFocus()`. Some windowing systems don't adequately report this event to Java — and this makes it difficult for the Java.awt to always get it right. Be very careful if you are going to write something that depends on having these methods work correctly.

The only activity we have with a keyboard are those breathtaking moments when a key is either pressed or released. The event handling method for each of these events is `keyDown()` and `keyUp()`. The easy part is discovering that a key has been pressed. It is a little more difficult to find out exactly which key — and whether it has been escaped or controlled. Remember, we are dealing with Unicode here. The method `key_id()` in our example shows a very simple analysis of the keystroke — if it is ASCII, we print the character it represents; otherwise, we just print the number.

Boiling Down the Keyboard

A bit of information comes with each keystroke event, as is shown by the class `Keyboard.java` in Listing 8-3.

Listing 8-3 Keyboard.java

```
import java.applet.*;
import java.awt.*;

public class Keyboard extends Applet {
  static final int LINE_COUNT = 30;
  String line[];
  Rectangle rectangle;
  int y_start;
  int y_delta;

  public void init() {
   rectangle = bounds();
   line = new String[LINE_COUNT];
   Graphics g = getGraphics();
   FontMetrics fm = g.getFontMetrics(g.getFont());
   y_delta = fm.getHeight();
   y_start = rectangle.height - fm.getHeight();
  }

  public void paint(Graphics g) {
   g.setColor(Color.white);
   g.fillRect(0,0,size().width,size().height);
   g.setColor(Color.black);
   int y_walk = y_start;
         for(int i=0; (i<LINE_COUNT) && (y_walk>0); i++) {
         if(line[i] == null)
               break;
         g.drawString(line[i],10,y_walk);
         y_walk -= y_delta;
   }
  }

  public boolean keyDown(Event e,int key) {
   showkey("keyDown",e);
   return(true);
  }
```

```
public boolean keyUp(Event e,int key) {
 showkey("keyUp",e);
 return(true);
}

private final void showkey(String action,Event e) {
 switch(e.id) {
 case Event.KEY_ACTION:
        action += " KEY_ACTION";
        break;
 case Event.KEY_ACTION_RELEASE:
        action += " KEY_ACTION_RELEASE";
        break;
 case Event.KEY_PRESS:
        action += " KEY_PRESS";
        break;
 case Event.KEY_RELEASE:
        action += " KEY_RELEASE";
        break;
 default:
        action += " ?" + e.id;
        break;
 }
 action += modifiers(e);
 action += keyid(e);

 scroll();
 line[0] = action;
 repaint();
}

private final void scroll() {
 for(int i=LINE_COUNT-1; i>0; i--)
        line[i] = line[i-1];
}

private final String modifiers(Event e) {
 String retstring = "";
 if((e.modifiers & e.ALT_MASK) != 0)
        retstring += " Alt";
 if((e.modifiers & e.CTRL_MASK) != 0)
        retstring += " Control";
```

```
        if((e.modifiers & e.SHIFT_MASK) != 0)
            retstring += " Shift";
        if((e.modifiers & e.META_MASK) != 0)
            retstring += " Meta";
        return(retstring);
    }

    private final String keyid(Event e) {
        String retstring;
        switch(e.key) {
        case Event.F1: retstring = " F1"; break;
        case Event.F2: retstring = " F2"; break;
        case Event.F3: retstring = " F3"; break;
        case Event.F4: retstring = " F4"; break;
        case Event.F5: retstring = " F5"; break;
        case Event.F6: retstring = " F6"; break;
        case Event.F7: retstring = " F7"; break;
        case Event.F8: retstring = " F8"; break;
        case Event.F9: retstring = " F9"; break;
        case Event.F10: retstring = " F10"; break;
        case Event.F11: retstring = " F11"; break;
        case Event.F12: retstring = " F12"; break;
        case Event.DOWN: retstring = " DOWN"; break;
        case Event.END: retstring = " END"; break;
        case Event.HOME: retstring = " HOME"; break;
        case Event.LEFT: retstring = " LEFT"; break;
        case Event.PGDN: retstring = " PGDN"; break;
        case Event.PGUP: retstring = " PGUP"; break;
        case Event.RIGHT: retstring = " RIGHT"; break;
        case Event.UP: retstring = " UP"; break;
        default:
            if((e.key < ' ') || (e.key >'~'))
                retstring = " " + String.valueOf(e.key);
            else
                retstring = " '" + (char)e.key + "'";
            break;
        }
        return(retstring);
    }
}
```

Keyboard.java is a modification of EventList.java with the mouse stuff taken out and a more detailed analysis of keyboard events added. While there are only two keystroke event handlers, keyDown() and keyUp(), they each handle two Event id values — one for the regular displayable keys and one for the function keys and such. The regular ASCII keys will generate a KEY_PRESS going down and a KEY_RELEASE coming back up. All the other keys will generate a KEY_ACTION going down and a KEY_ACTION_RELEASE coming back up. Figure 8-3 shows some typical output from Keyboard.java.

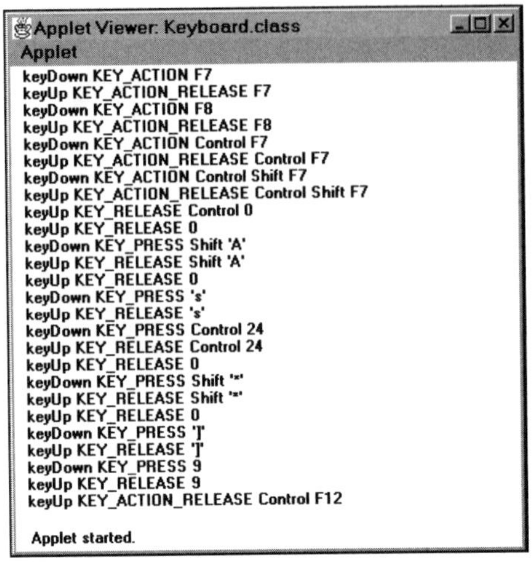

Figure 8-3 Output from Keyboard.java

> **TIP** **You will probably find that some keys are not included in the Java key definitions found in the Event class. Experimentation will show what values these missing keys generate. If you use this behavior in your code, you will be thwarting efforts toward portability that the Java designers worked so hard to achieve.**

Keyboard and Mouse Reactions

In previous examples we had our applets respond to events by creating some text and displaying it. Let's draw some pictures now. Listing 8-4 shows a simple graphics program that uses the mouse buttons to generate some concentric circles along with the most recent letter you typed.

Listing 8-4 BullsEyeLetter.java

```
import java.applet.*;
import java.awt.*;

public class BullsEyeLetter extends Applet {
  Rectangle rectangle;
  String letter;
```

```
    int x_center;
    int y_center;
    boolean have_coordinates;

    public void init() {
     rectangle = bounds();
     letter = "X";
     have_coordinates = false;
    }

    public void paint(Graphics g) {
     g.setColor(Color.white);
     g.fillRect(0,0,size().width,size().height);
     if(have_coordinates) {
            g.setColor(Color.blue);

            g.drawLine(0,y_center,rectangle.width,y_center);

            g.drawLine(x_center,0,x_center,rectangle.height);
            g.setColor(Color.red);
            for(int rad = 30; rad < rectangle.width; rad += 50)
                  g.drawOval(x_center-rad,y_center-
    rad,rad*2,rad*2);
            g.setColor(Color.black);
            g.drawString(letter,x_center,y_center);
     }
    }

    public boolean mouseDown(Event e,int x,int y) {
     have_coordinates = true;
     x_center = x;
     y_center = y;
     repaint();
     return(true);
    }

    public boolean keyDown(Event e,int key) {
     Character character = new Character((char)key);
     letter = character.toString();
     repaint();
     return(true);
    }
}
```

This is just about as simple an interactive graphics program as you can get. It responds to only two inputs — a mouse button and a keystroke. (I don't know about you, but this covers about 98 percent of what I will ever need.) The class `BullsEyeLetter` only stores the total size of the displayable rectangle, the last letter typed in, and the coordinates of the center of the last mouse shot. It also keeps a boolean value that it uses to determine whether or not you have ever clicked the mouse — if you never click the mouse, it will never draw anything. Each time `paint()` is called, the window is cleared and a bull's-eye target is drawn. The applet then carefully places the letter at the center of the bull's-eye. Figure 8-4 shows a typical display.

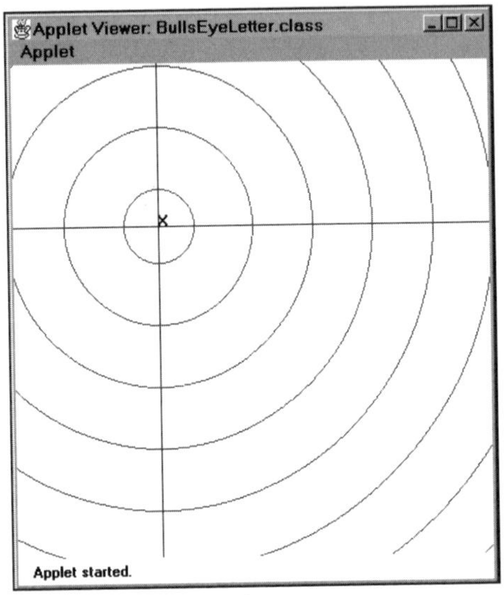

Figure 8-4 Output from BullsEyeLetter.java

TIP **You can see from Figure 8-4 that the letter isn't really centered in the bull's-eye. It appears to be above it and to the right. It is to the right, but it is not exactly above it. A letter is made up of ascenders and descenders. The ascenders of a letter start at the horizontal line and go up, and most letters only have ascenders. Descenders start at the same line and go down. A descender is that hanging-down part that shows up on letters like "g" and "y."**

Adding a Button

For our next trick, we are going to create a new version of `BullsEyeLetter` without touching it. We are going to create a new class that `extends` it to add an erase button. The resulting program is `ButtonBullsEye`, as shown in Listing 8-5.

Listing 8-5 ButtonBullsEye.java

```
import java.applet.*;
import java.awt.*;

public class ButtonBullsEye extends BullsEyeLetter {
  Button erase;

  public void init() {
   super.init();
   erase = new Button("Erase");
   add(erase);
  }

  public boolean action(Event e,Object what) {
   if(e.target == erase) {
         have_coordinates = false;
         repaint();
         return(true);
   }
   return(super.action(e,what));
  }
}
```

This applet has only two methods. It has an `init()` method — as all respectable applets do — to get things started. Because there is some stuff in the superclass (the superclass being `BullsEyeLetter`) that needs to get done, there is a call to `super.init()`. A button is then instantiated and added to the applet. The button is not positioned — the default location of the button is shown in Figure 8-5.

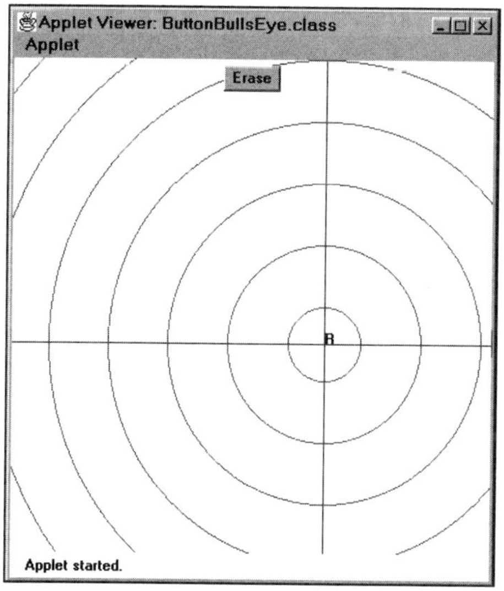

Figure 8-5 Output of ButtonBullsEye.java

The action() method is there to react to the button. Nothing mysterious here: the action() method is called by our old friend handleEvent(), just like the mouse and keyboard methods we looked at earlier. Whenever the button processes the event from the mouse, it issues a button event and calls action(). This means the button has been pressed by the mouse and the time has come to clear the display, which is done by simply setting the indicator to false and calling repaint().

Buttons and Layouts

What if you want to put the button in another location on the display? As it turns out, the Applet class extends the Panel class, and the Panel class has a layout manager. Specifically, the Panel class has a FlowLayout manager. It is a nice default because you can add a bunch of stuff to your applet and the FlowLayout manager will just arrange them in neat rows. Listing 8-6 is a simple applet designed to show how the FlowLayout manager will handle a number of buttons.

Listing 8-6 FlowButtons.java

```
import java.applet.*;
import java.awt.*;

public class FlowButtons extends Applet {
  public void init() {
   add(new Button("OK"));
   add(new Button("Cancel"));
   add(new Button("Hi Mom"));
   add(new Button("Press Your Luck"));
   add(new Button("Cockpit"));
   add(new Button("Snake Pit"));
   add(new Button("Arm Pit"));
   add(new Button("Lion Pit"));
   add(new Button("Peach Pit"));
  }
}
```

Figure 8-6 shows an arrangement resulting from running FlowButtons.java.

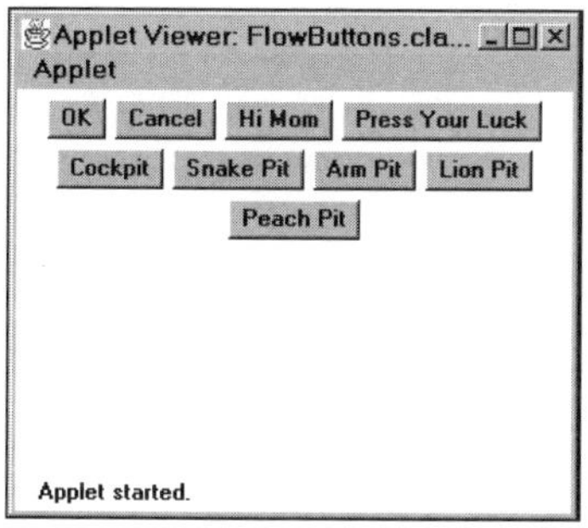

Figure 8-6 Output from FlowButtons.java

`FlowLayout` is very methodical. As many components (in this case, buttons) as possible are put on the top row; then the next row is filled up, and so on until either there is no more real estate or there are no more components. Try it yourself. Run this applet and notice that as you resize the window, the `FlowLayout` manager stays right with you and moves things around to fit whatever new size you come up with.

Layout Manager Options

There is more than one layout manager — and you get to decide which one to use. Listing 8-7 is a collection of five buttons laid out using the `BorderLayout` manager. It simply shoves the managed components to the four points of the compass and then places one in the center. As you can see, it has a "one size fits all" attitude and will stretch the component to fit the space.

Listing 8-7 BorderButton.java

```
import java.applet.*;
import java.awt.*;

public class BorderButtons extends Applet {
  public void init() {
   setLayout(new BorderLayout());
   add("West",new Button("OK"));
   add("East",new Button("Cancel"));
   add("Center",new Button("Hi Mom"));
   add("South",new Button("Press Your Luck"));
   add("North",new Button("Cockpit"));
  }
}
```

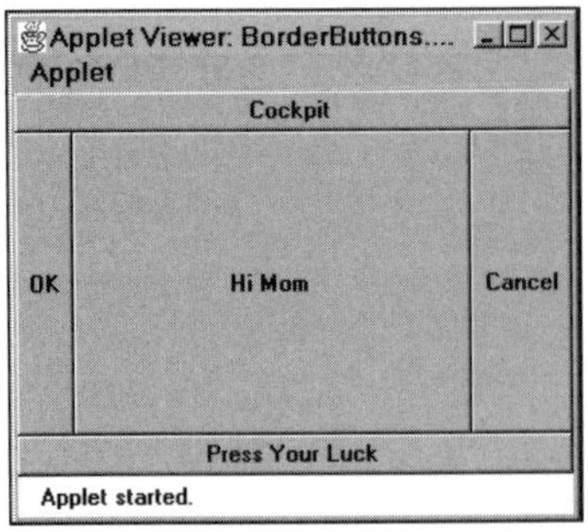

Figure 8-7 Output from BorderButton.java

There are other layout managers, some of which you will learn about in Chapter 13, "Building a User Interface." The `CardLayout` manager, for example, places things one on top of the other so the mouse can be used to flip from one component to the next. The `GridLayout` manager can be used to define a grid of certain size so that components can be attached — sort of like hanging pictures on a chicken-wire fence. There is also a `GridBagLayout` manager that can be used whenever the layout requirements become very complicated — it lets you hook one to another as if you were laying bricks of different sizes.

TIP **The layout manager is a convenience, not a necessity. If you take a look at the code generated by Visual Café — when you position your components with the form editor — there is no layout manager. It does this by calling `setLayout()` to nullify the default layout manager. The job of a layout manager is to call certain methods in each of the components to tell them where to go and how big to be and stuff like that. Visual Café just calls the positioning for these methods directly without the intervention of a layout manager.**

BONUS

Laying Out a Canvas with Buttons

In this chapter we've been looking at some pretty simple applets. For our next trick we will combine some layout managers with some buttons and drawing techniques to build an applet that has a bit more to it. Nothing stupendous — we are going to construct an applet that will make a circle at every point the mouse is clicked and then join the points together with lines. There will only be a fixed number of points; the oldest one will be erased if there are too many. A rubber band line will follow the line as the mouse moves to the next point.

In Java, if you want to draw something, grab a `Canvas` and start drawing. In the previous examples, we just started drawing on the window that Java gave us. This works for very simple applets, but it's a little sloppy. Instead, you can grab a `Canvas` object and, because it is a component just like a button or a label, you can size it and stick it on the face of your applet wherever you would like to put it.

TIP **The `Canvas` class is a subclass of the `Component` class, just like `Button`, `Label`, `Scrollbar`, and all the other GUI guys. Chapter 17 explains how all the `Components` are handled in Visual Café. Note, however, that there is nothing visual about a canvas until you put something on it.**

The applet `FollowMe` is shown in Listing 8-8. The `init()` method creates all the components and hooks them together. What we want is to have the buttons appear in a row across the bottom of the applet window with the `Canvas` covering the rest of it. This sounds like a job for a `BorderLayout` manager. The default `FlowLayout` manager is replaced with a new `BorderLayout` manager with a call to `setLayout()`. We then create a `Panel` container (which has, as its default, a `FlowLayout` manager) to hold the buttons; the buttons are then created and added to the panel. We put the panel, which now contains all the buttons, on the bottom of the applet window by telling `BorderLayout` to add it to the "South" of the window. All that is left to do is fill the rest of the display with a `Canvas`. This is done by creating a `Canvas` object and putting it in the "Center." This causes the `BorderLayout` manager to stretch the `Canvas` to cover all the unused area. The applet is now fully constructed.

Listing 8-8 FollowMe.java

```
import java.applet.*;
import java.awt.*;
```

8

```
public class FollowMe extends Applet {
  // The maximum number of points to draw.
  private final int POINTS = 10;
  // The area for drawing.
  Canvas canvas;
  // The buttons.
  Button red_button;
  Button blue_button;
  Button black_button;
  Button clear_button;
  Button quit_button;
  // The array of the points and colors.
  Point p[];
  Color c[];
  // The newest point that was added to the p array.
  Point newest_point;
  // The currently selected color.
  Color current_color;
  // The current location of the mouse.
  Point last_mouse;

  public void init() {
   // Initialize the arrays for points and colors.
   p = new Point[POINTS];
   c = new Color[POINTS];
   current_color = Color.black;
   // Use border layout to position components.
   setLayout(new BorderLayout());
   // Create a panel to hold all the buttons and
   // place it at the bottom of the window.
   Panel buttons = new Panel();
   red_button = new Button("Red");
   blue_button = new Button("Blue");
   black_button = new Button("Black");
   clear_button = new Button("Clear");
   quit_button = new Button("Quit");
   buttons.add(red_button);
   buttons.add(blue_button);
   buttons.add(black_button);
   buttons.add(clear_button);
   buttons.add(quit_button);
   add("South",buttons);
   // Placing the canvas in the center will cause it
   // to fill out the rest of the window.
```

```
    canvas = new Canvas();
    add("Center",canvas);
}

// Clear the display and paint all the circles and lines.
public void paint(Graphics g) {
    g = canvas.getGraphics();
    g.clearRect(0,0,canvas.size().width,canvas.size().height);
    int r = 10;
    for(int i=0; i<p.length; i++) {
        if(p[i] == null)
            break;
        g.setColor(c[i]);
        g.drawOval(p[i].x - r,p[i].y -r,r*2,r*2);
        if(i > 0)
            g.drawLine(p[i-1].x,p[i-1].y,p[i].x,p[i].y);
    }
    g.dispose();
}

// Respond to the buttons.
public boolean action(Event e,Object what) {
    if(e.target == quit_button) {
        System.exit(0);
    } else if(e.target == clear_button) {
        for(int i=0; i<p.length; i++)
            p[i] = null;
        newest_point = null;
        last mouse = null;
        repaint();
    } else if(e.target == red_button) {
        current_color = Color.red;
    } else if(e.target == blue_button) {
        current_color = Color.blue;
    } else if(e.target == black_button) {
        current_color = Color.black;
    }
    return(super.action(e,what));
}

// Add a new point every time the mouse clicks.
public boolean mouseDown(Event e,int x,int y) {
    if(e.target != canvas)
        return(false);
```

8

```
	newest_point = new Point(x,y);
	if(p[p.length-1] == null) {
		insert: for(int i=0; i<p.length; i++) {
			if(p[i] == null) {
				p[i] = newest_point;
				c[i] = current_color;
				break insert;
			}
		}
	} else {
		for(int i=1; i<p.length; i++) {
			p[i-1] = p[i];
			c[i-1] = c[i];
		}
		p[p.length-1] = newest_point;
		c[c.length-1] = current_color;
	}
	repaint();
	return(true);
}

// Rubberbanding from the last point to the mouse.
public boolean mouseMove(Event e,int x,int y) {
	if(e.target != canvas)
		return(false);
	if(newest_point == null)
		return(true);
	Graphics g = canvas.getGraphics();
	g.setXORMode(Color.white);
	if(last_mouse != null) {
		g.drawLine(newest_point.x,newest_point.y,
			last_mouse.x,last_mouse.y);
	}
	last_mouse = new Point(x,y);
	g.drawLine(newest_point.x,newest_point.y,
		last_mouse.x,last_mouse.y);
	g.dispose();
	return(true);
}
}
```

The `paint()` method ignores the `Graphics` object that is passed to it, as it is the one for the entire applet window. It uses the `Graphics` object from the canvas. The drawing is just a matter of looping through all the points and joining them together and drawing a circle around each one — in the right color, of course. An example of the output is shown in Figure 8-8.

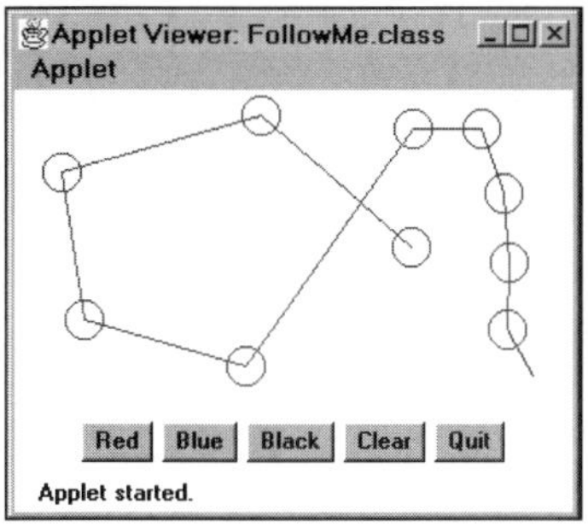

Figure 8-8 Output of FollowMe.java

The `action()` method is there to respond to the buttons. The color-setting buttons modify the value that will be added to the drawing array. The clear button sets all the mouse and point information back to their original values.

TIP **You will notice that the class `Point` is used for the objects that hold locations on the canvas. Java also has a utility class called `Dimension` that can be used to hold height and width. Another class — `Rectangle` — can be used to hold the definition of a rectangle's location as well as its size. These are very simple classes that come in handy when keeping track of where and how big things are.**

Whenever the mouse is clicked on the canvas, `mouseDown()` adds a new point to the array. If the array isn't full, the new point is added at the next available place; otherwise, the oldest point is deleted by shifting all the others down one position and the new point is added as the last one. The array of colors is maintained along with the array of points so the points and colors can be matched up for drawing. Once the arrays are updated, `repaint()` schedules a call to `paint()` so the new points will be drawn.

And now for the rubber stuff. As we saw earlier, the `mouseMove()` method is called every time the mouse changes position. The value of `newest_point` is always the coordinates of the last point drawn. The value of `last_mouse` is the last reported position of the mouse. Each time `mouseMove()` is called, any existing line from `newest_point` to `last_mouse` is erased. Then the `last_mouse` location is updated and a new line is drawn. The drawing is done in *exclusive-or* mode: each bit of the color being painted is exclusive-ored with the pixel value to be painted, and the result is placed in the pixel. This has the magical quality that if you do it twice, the pixel returns to its original value. In other words, to erase the previously painted line, just paint it again.

Summary

Java waits for user requests via two methods — the keyboard and the mouse. Messages from these two devices come to your program in the form of events. Just like everything else in Java, there is more than one way to field the events and deal with them — but this always involves overloading methods of the `Component` class. To prove its attentiveness to the user, an applet responds by displaying characters or other graphics. A basic `Graphics` class is used to write and draw to all the different types of displayable components. These displayable components are positioned and sized on the display under the control of layout managers.

In the next chapter we'll go into motion, exploring the anatomy of an animation applet.

CHAPTER NINE

THE JAVA APPLET AND ANIMATION

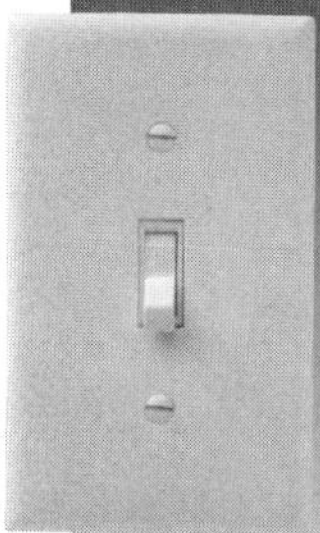

IN THIS CHAPTER YOU LEARN THESE KEY SKILLS

It's show time! This is the first thing we all noticed about Java — it moved. Suddenly there was movement on the Internet; Web pages sprang to life and things started moving around in our browsers.

If Java were a building, it would be a large one with several floors and hundreds of rooms — but animation would be the big showcase window facing the outside world.

Animation is simply the process of showing a bunch of pictures fast enough that the human eye smears them together and perceives movement. Java animation is very simple in comparison to the special effects we see every day on television and in the movies — but it happens right there on our computer screen. In this chapter we'll explore how to make this happen in your Web pages.

We will be looking at three animation applets in this chapter. The first two are simple examples of the two basic kinds of graphic animation. Bouncer is the first and the simplest. It demonstrates the use of the basic form of an animation applet, and uses Java's built-in drawing tools to create movement. FlyingSausage is the second. It uses the same basic structure of an animated applet, but with predrawn graphic files to create animation. The third example is our bonus. It uses the animation structure to demonstrate how to create animated text that moves its font and size (in other words, its appearance) changes.

Bouncer

Java is flexible — there is more than one way to do animation. Listing 9-1 shows only one way of doing it. We like this form for three reasons: it works, it's simple, and we understand it. The Bouncer applet is a very simple animation applet designed so the structure would be easy to see. There is not much drawing (just one little circle) so there is a minimum of clutter. If it were any simpler, it wouldn't do anything at all.

Listing 9-1 Bouncer.java

```
import java.awt.*;
import java.applet.*;

public class Bouncer extends Applet implements Runnable {
  private static final int UP = 1;
  private static final int DOWN = 2;
  private static final int RIGHT = 1;
  private static final int LEFT = 2;
  private static final int DOT_DIAMETER = 8;
  private static final Color BACKGROUND_COLOR = Color.black;
  private static final Color DOT_COLOR = Color.orange;
  private static final int PAUSE = 5;

  private int vertical;
  private int horizontal;
  private Thread thread;
  private Rectangle rectangle;
  private Dot dot;
  private Font font;

  public void init() {
   vertical = UP;
   horizontal = RIGHT;
   rectangle = bounds();
   font = new Font("TimesRoman",Font.BOLD,48);
   dot = new Dot(size().width / 2,size().height / 2,
         DOT_DIAMETER / 2);
  }

  public void start() {
   if(thread == null) {
         thread = new Thread(this);
         thread.start();
```

```
    }
  }

  public void run() {
    try {
           while(true) {
                  repaint();
                  Thread.sleep(PAUSE);
           }
    } finally {
           return;
    }
  }

  public void stop() {
    if(thread != null) {
           thread.stop();
           thread = null;
    }
  }

  public void update(Graphics g) {
    if(thread.isAlive()) {
           Rectangle clip = dot.rectangle();
           next_frame();
           clip = clip.union(dot.rectangle());
           g.clipRect(clip.x,clip.y,clip.width,clip.height);
           paint(g);
    }
  }

  public void paint(Graphics g) {
    g.setColor(BACKGROUND_COLOR);
    g.fillRect(0,0,size().width,size().height);
    g.setColor(Color.lightGray);
    g.setFont(font);
    g.drawString("Bouncer",5,40);
    g.setColor(DOT_COLOR);
    g.fillOval(dot.left(),dot.top(),
           dot.diameter(),dot.diameter());
    g.dispose();
  }

  private void next_frame() {
```

```
    if(horizontal == RIGHT) {
          dot.move_right();
          if(dot.right() >= size().width)
                horizontal = LEFT;
    } else {
          dot.move_left();
          if(dot.left() <= 0)
                horizontal = RIGHT;
    }
    if(vertical == DOWN) {
          dot.move_down();
          if(dot.bottom() >= size().height)
                vertical = UP;
    } else {
          dot.move_up();
          if(dot.top() <= 0)
                vertical = DOWN;
    }
   }
 }

 class Dot {
   private static final int DOT_MOVEMENT = 3;
   int x;
   int y;
   int radius;

   Dot(int x,int y,int radius) {
    this.x = x;
    this.y = y;
    this.radius = radius;
   }

   final public void move_down() {
    y += DOT_MOVEMENT;
   }
   final public void move_up() {
    y -= DOT_MOVEMENT;
   }
   final public void move_right() {
    x += DOT_MOVEMENT;
   }
   final public void move_left() {
    x -= DOT_MOVEMENT;
```

```
    }
    final public int top() {
     return(y - radius);
    }
    final public int bottom() {
     return(y + radius);
    }
    final public int left() {
     return(x - radius);
    }
    final public int right() {
     return(x + radius);
    }
    final public int diameter() {
     return(radius * 2);
    }
    final public Rectangle rectangle() {
     return(new Rectangle(x-radius,y-radius,radius*2,radius*2));
    }
}
```

Included with Bouncer is the nonpublic class Dot used to maintain the current position of the moving dot. All Bouncer does is bounce a dot against the edges of the window. Figure 9-1 shows the output from Bouncer.java.

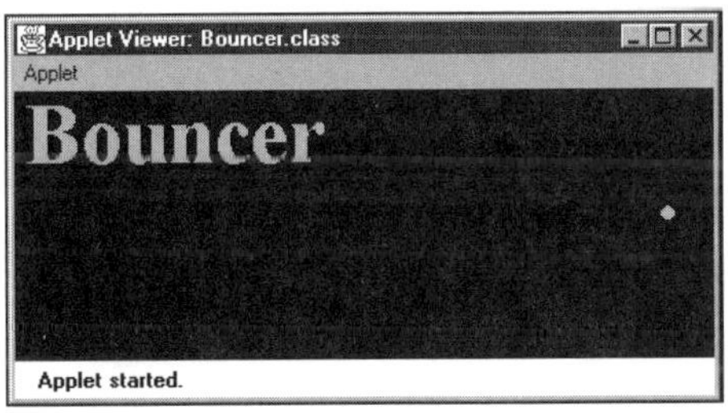

Figure 9-1 The applet Bouncer.java displays a moving dot.

Bouncer is an applet (because it extends the Applet class). It implements the Runnable interface; this is what enables the thing to run as a thread. Let's look at the Bouncer methods to see how each one is involved in the animation.

What Does init() Do?

The method init() is very much a one-time kind of guy. The browser calls this method exactly once — when the applet is first loaded. All it does is set up the initial values and return. It doesn't call a method to do any painting or animating; it just sets up the picnic tables for the other guests and then goes away. Oh, sure, it builds a Dot object, but it just leaves it on the table to be used later.

What Does start() Do?

Right after it calls `init()`, the browser calls `start()`. While `init()` is never called again, `start()` can be called over and over again — each time the browser comes back to the Web page with the applet there is another call to `start()`. The `start()` method will crank up a thread if one isn't already running. If the thread is already running, then there is nothing to be done.

CAUTION **Don't confuse the two `start()` methods. The method named `start()` being defined in `Bouncer` overrides the one in its superclass, `Applet`. The method named `start()` in `thread` is a completely different method — it is the one in the `Thread` class. (Don't you hate it when they do that?)**

Making a call to the `thread.start()` returns after it starts a whole new stream of Java execution. It is as if two copies of `Bouncer` are running in the same place. Now the thread finds itself with nothing but CPU time on its hands and, to fill this time, it calls the `run()` method of the object passed to it at creation. (Yes. It is possible to create a thread that runs another class. We told you there is more than one way to do animation.)

Actually, the new thread does more than just call the `run()` method; it swears a loyalty to it. It swears, "If the `run()` method returns, I will die!" And it does.

What Does run() Do?

The `run()` method goes into a loop and stays there. This is where all the timing and drawing and stuff is done. As you can see in Listing 9-1, a do-forever loop continuously calls `repaint()` at intervals timed with a call to `sleep()`.

TIP **It's OK for a thread to sleep for as long as you wish. Actually, this is the main reason for having a thread: It won't block the rest of the applet from running. A thread can take all the time it wants to do its work and it won't bother anything else.**

The `repaint()` method is a scheduler. What `repaint()` does is schedule a future call to the `update()` method. You can call `repaint()` as often as you like; it is possible for a bunch of calls to `repaint()` to culminate in a single call to `update()`.

The thread will quit whenever `run()` returns. The only way out of the `run()` method in `Bouncer` is for an exception to occur. In `Bouncer`, we simply exit no matter what kind of exception is encountered; but in a more complex applet, it may be necessary to handle some exceptions.

TIP **Whenever the thread ceases execution, a `ThreadDeath` exception is thrown. That is why the `run()` loop is nested in a try block. It is important that you do not catch this `ThreadDeath` exception — it must be passed on up so the thread will manage to pass away cleanly and**

not have parts of itself hanging around. There is no ghost more evil and devious than the active remains of a semi-dead thread; you don't want zombies in your browser.

What Does stop() Do?

The `stop` method can be called any time, but it is normally called by a browser when the page containing the applet is no longer being displayed — the fickle user has tired of the applet and moved on. It is the duty of the `stop()` method in the applet to call the `stop()` method of the thread. If it doesn't, the thread could live forever — or at least until the browser crashes.

Making a call to `thread.stop()` will cause the thread to begin termination procedures immediately. A `ThreadDeath` exception is thrown, which causes the `try` block in the `run()` method to exit.

CAUTION

Don't confuse the two `stop()` methods. The method named `stop()` in `Bouncer` overrides the one in its superclass, `Applet`. The method named `stop()` in `thread` is a completely different method — it is the one in the `Thread` class.

What Does update() Do?

The `update()` method is called each time the little orange dot is to move from one location to the next. It is the responsibility of `update()` to call `paint()`. This `update()` method is an override of the one in the `Container` class. The one in the `Container` class simply erases the entire window and then calls `paint()`.

We don't want to redraw the entire applet window every time the dot moves, so `update()` clips the drawing to just the parts we need. We know that the `paint()` method is going to erase and redraw the whole window using the `Graphics` object we pass it, so we limit the `Graphics` object to drawing only the portions we want — in this case, the place where the dot is now and the place we want it to be next. To do this, we build a clipping rectangle. Figure 9-2 shows how this is accomplished. A call is made to `dot.rectangle()` to get a rectangle that encloses the current position. The position of the dot is then moved to the next location with the call to `next_frame()`. The new `dot` rectangle is combined with the old `dot` rectangle to construct a rectangle that will include both of them. A call is made to the `clipRect()` method with this rectangle, which makes the `Graphics` object incapable of drawing outside the rectangle. The `paint()` method can do anything it wants to do, but nothing will have any effect outside of the clipping area.

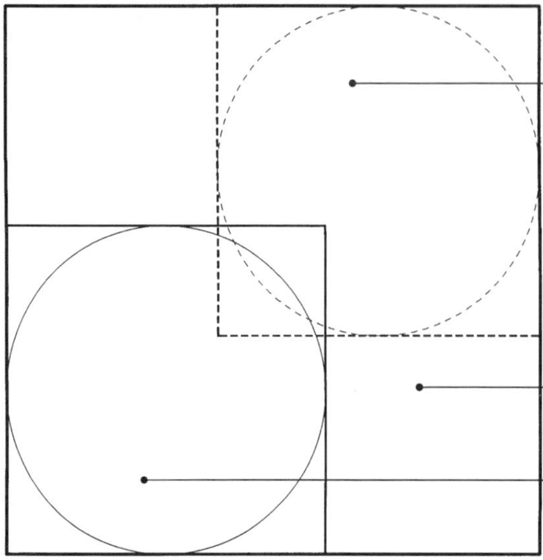

Figure 9-2 The clipping rectangle includes both old and new dot locations.

TIP **You probably noticed there is a call to `thread.isAlive()` at the beginning of `update()`. This is done to avoid the occurrence of a problem brought on by a race condition. It goes like this: You enter the Web page containing the applet and the applet loads and runs. The browser dutifully caches the Web page along with the applet. You leave this page to look at another and then come back to the one with the applet. The page and the applet both load from cache. The browser calls `init()` and then `run()`. The `run()` method calls `repaint()`, which causes a call to `update()`. If we come from cache, all this can happen quickly — so quickly in fact that the new thread hasn't had time to get itself ready to accept callers. The drawing goes awry and starts spewing pixels at random. This can cause a condition commonly known as "browser crash." It's a bug.**

What Does paint() Do?

The `paint()` method assumes the window is completely blank and tries to fill in the whole thing. This method is called by the browser any time it needs to display the whole applet. This happens once at the beginning when the applet first appears. It will also happen when the applet scrolls into view or when the browser is restored to a window from an icon. Good and faithful ol' `paint()` — always standing by to completely redraw the window.

Rotating Bitmaps

There is only so much that can be reasonably done with the pixel placement methods. There are times when more detailed pictures are needed. It is possible to generate animation by displaying a series of pictures from graphics files — like a motion picture. Figure 9-3 shows a sequence of pictures that can be used this way.

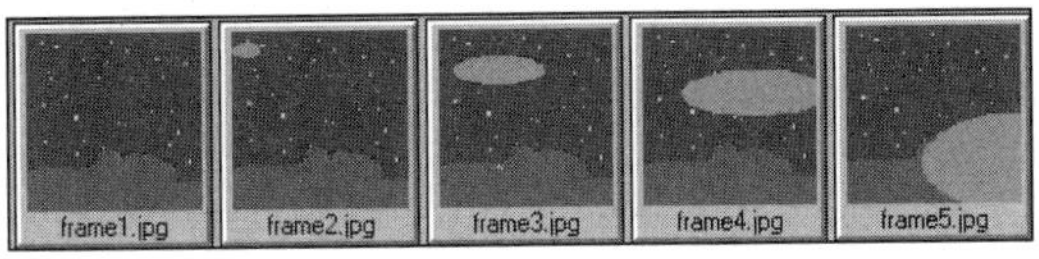

Figure 9-3 A sequence of still pictures can be displayed to give the appearance of motion.

Now that we have our pictures, our next trick is to display them. This is done with the `FlyingSausage` applet, shown in Listing 9-2.

Listing 9-2 FlyingSausage.java

```
import java.awt.*;
import java.net.*;
import java.applet.*;
import java.awt.image.*;

public class FlyingSausage extends Applet implements Runnable {
  private final int SHORT_PAUSE = 100;
  private final int LONG_PAUSE - 2000;
  private final int IMAGE_COUNT = 5;
  private Image[] image;
  private int index;
  private Thread thread;
  private boolean images_being_loaded;

  public void init() {
   URL url = getDocumentBase();
   images_being_loaded = true;
   index = 0;
   image = new Image[IMAGE_COUNT];
   image[0] = getImage(url,"frame1.jpg");
   image[1] = getImage(url,"frame2.jpg");
   image[2] = getImage(url,"frame3.jpg");
   image[3] = getImage(url,"frame4.jpg");
   image[4] = getImage(url,"frame5.jpg");
  }
```

```
public void start() {
 if(thread == null) {
        thread = new Thread(this);
        thread.start();
 }
}

public void run() {
 try {
        while(images_being_loaded) {
               index = 0;
               repaint();
               Thread.sleep(LONG_PAUSE);
               images_being_loaded = false;
               for(int i=0; i<IMAGE_COUNT; i++) {
                      if(image[i].getWidth(this) < 0)
                             images_being_loaded = true;
               }
        }
        while(true) {
               repaint();
               if(index == 0)
                      Thread.sleep(LONG_PAUSE);
               else
                      Thread.sleep(SHORT_PAUSE);
               if(++index >= IMAGE_COUNT)
                      index = 0;
        }
 } finally {
        return;
 }
}

public void stop() {
 if(thread != null) {
        thread.stop();
        thread = null;
 }
}
```

```
    public void update(Graphics g) {
     if(thread.isAlive()) {
            paint(g);
     }
    }

    public void paint(Graphics g) {
     g.drawImage(image[index],0,0,this);
     g.dispose();
    }
}
```

As you read through `FlyingSausage`, you will notice it has the same basic structure as `Bouncer`. Just like `Bouncer`, the `FlyingSausage` applet is threaded so it can go off and do its own thing with the animation.

The `init()` method loads the pictures and pops the popcorn. (Just kidding about the popcorn.) There are some rules about the location of loadable pictures. Remember, we have that security thing we have to deal with — an applet cannot read files from any location other than the one from which it was launched. We have to find out where the applet resides so we will know where the files are to be found. Everything could be local, or it could be we are loading stuff from across the Internet. A call to `getDocumentBase()` will give us the URL of the Web page, which will also be the URL of some files we can read. Now that we know where they are, `init()` can load each one as the member of an array of `Image` objects. We are ready to run our movie — almost.

The `run()` method checks the boolean value of `images_being_loaded` in a continuous loop. You see, the images probably didn't load immediately (hey, you know how the Internet is) when the call was made to `getImage()`. The loading is underway and, like all good little applets, `FlyingSausage` has to wait for them. The `run()` method waits impatiently. It continues to display the first frame over and over (by making sure the `index` remains at zero) while checking to see whether the other frames have been loaded. Attempting to display a frame before it is loaded is not an error — it just doesn't all show up.

TIP **There is a reason to hang on the first frame and wait until all frames are loaded. We could just go ahead with the animation — lots of applets do that. What happens is they get halfway through one of the frames and, because the whole frame is not loaded, they stop. Things look like they are all balled up. The animation will eventually cycle around to its beginning and, maybe, get a little further next time. Our preference is to have the first frame show up as a still picture until everything is loaded and we can go. Another option is to make a movie out of whatever frames have finished loading. It's all a matter of preference.**

TIP **It is very easy to tell whether or not an image is loaded. Until it is completely loaded, both the `getWidth()` and `getHeight()` methods return -1. Once either of these dimension values switches to a positive number, the image is loaded and ready to show itself.**

In the `run()` method, once all the images are loaded and ready to go, the program will drop into the second loop — the one that does the animation. All the second loop does is bump the index to the next frame and call `repaint()`; whenever `index` reaches the end of the array, it is reset to zero to start over. Two timers (values used by `Thread.sleep()`) define delays between frames. A short pause is used between frames as the sausage flies by. A longer pause is used to set the time between the end of one movie and the start of the next.

The `paint()` method uses `drawImage()` to display the current frame. The first argument passed to `drawImage()` is the image to be drawn, the second and third arguments are the x and y coordinates of where the image is to appear in the applet window, and the final argument is the applet itself.

TIP **Visual Café has a facility that can speed up your development of animation applets. It is the template selection — the one that appears each time you create a new applet. It is a simple matter of adding one or more of the applets from this chapter (modified to your liking, of course) to the list of available templates. This will give you the running start you need at the very moment you have that brilliant animated applet idea. Just load up the animation skeleton of your choice as a Visual Café template and start adding your pictures and painting methods. You'll learn how to create templates in Chapter 21, "Customizing Visual Café."**

BONUS

9

Text and Background Drawing

Java displays text very well. Several scaleable fonts are available and the `FontMetrics` class can be used to gather information about the dimensions of a particular font, enabling you to put things where you want them.

There is also an animation technique that can be used to generate flicker-free animation with vector drawings. The trick is to do all the clearing and drawing of pixels in RAM instead of in the displayable window. Once a frame of the animation sequence is finished in RAM, it is just a matter of displaying the whole thing all at once. This technique is really just a combination of our two previous examples. It enables you to draw each new frame at your leisure and then — wham! — put the whole thing on display at once. No flicker.

Our animated text applet is shown in Listing 9-3. It cycles through all the available fonts (which ones are available can vary from one implementation to another) and then displays each one in point sizes that vary from really tiny to pretty darn big.

Listing 9-3 LittleBigWord.java

```
import java.awt.*;
import java.net.*;
import java.applet.*;
import java.awt.image.*;

public class LittleBigWord extends Applet implements Runnable {
  private final int PAUSE = 25;
  private String word;
  private Thread thread;
  private Image workimage;
  private boolean shrinking = true;

  private int x;
  private int y;
  private Font font;
  private String[] fontname;
  private int font_index = 0;

  private int[] style;
  private int style_index = 0;
  private final static int STYLE_COUNT = 4;
```

```
private int fontsize = MINIMUM_FONTSIZE;
private static final int MAXIMUM_FONTSIZE = 60;
private static final int MINIMUM_FONTSIZE = 6;

public void init() {
 workimage =
        createImage(size().width,size().height);
 // Get the list of all available fonts
 Toolkit kit = Toolkit.getDefaultToolkit();
 fontname = kit.getFontList();
 // paint() could be called before run()
 word = fontname[0];
 // Construct an array of all possible styles
 style = new int[STYLE_COUNT];
 style[0] = font.PLAIN;
 style[1] = font.BOLD;
 style[2] = font.ITALIC;
 style[3] = font.BOLD + font.ITALIC;
}

public void start() {
 if(thread == null) {
        thread = new Thread(this);
        thread.start();
 }
}

public void run() {
 try {
        while(true) {
               if(shrinking) {
                      if(--fontsize <= MINIMUM_FONTSIZE) {
                             shrinking = false;
                             if(++style_index >=
                                           STYLE_COUNT) {
                                    style_index = 0;
                                    if(++font_index >=
                                           fontname.length)
                                           font_index = 0;
                             }
                      }
               } else {
                      if(++fontsize >= MAXIMUM_FONTSIZE)
                             shrinking = true;
```

```
                }
                font = new Font(fontname[font_index],
                       style[style_index],fontsize);
                word = fontname[font_index];
                repaint();
                Thread.sleep(PAUSE);
        }
   } finally {
        return;
   }
  }

  public void stop() {
   if(thread != null) {
        thread.stop();
        thread = null;
   }
  }

  public void update(Graphics g) {
   if(thread.isAlive()) {
        // Center the word
        FontMetrics metrics = g.getFontMetrics(font);
        x = (size().width - metrics.stringWidth(word)) / 2;
        y = size().height / 2;
        paint(g);
   }
  }

  public void paint(Graphics g) {
   // Do the drawing to the off-screen
   Graphics wg = workimage.getGraphics();
   wg.setColor(Color.lightGray);
   wg.fillRect(0,0,size().width,size().height);
   wg.setColor(Color.blue);
   wg.setFont(font);
   wg.drawString(word,x,y);
   // Put the off-screen image on the screen
   g.drawImage(workimage,0,0,this);
   wg.dispose();
   g.dispose();
  }
}
```

The `init()` method gets the default `Toolkit` object and uses it to get a complete list of the font names available to the applet. (The `Toolkit` is a low-level class you will only need for internal stuff, such as the list of font names.) An array of styles is constructed that contains the four possible settings that can be used to paint characters.

TIP **The `String` variable `word` is initialized to the name of the first font in the array. This is to prevent a fault coming out of the `paint()` method. You see, even though we are going to do animation and set things up so `paint()` is called through `update()`, the interpreter will blithely call `paint()` right after `init()` anyway. Our problem is that the call to `drawString()` in `paint()` needs a valid `String` object. In general terms, make sure your `paint()` method can be safely called right after `init()` and before anything else.**

The `run()` method checks the boolean value of `shrinking` and if it is `true`, it reduces the font size by one point. When the font size reaches our minimum setting, we set `shrinking` to `false` and move to the next style. If the style index recycles to zero, we move to the next font; this way we get all styles with all fonts. Whenever `shrinking` is `false`, the font size is incremented until the maximum size is reached. We then create a new font with the new settings, set the word to the name of the font, and schedule `update()`.

The `update()` method gets a `FontMetrics` object, based on this particular font, and uses it to set the values of x and y that will place the name of the font at the center of the window.

The `paint()` method does its drawing to the `Image` object `workimage`. The `workimage` is in RAM so the drawing has no effect on the display. Once the name of the font is drawn on a newly cleared RAM image, the method `drawImage()` is called to transfer the RAM image to the display. Because the RAM image is the same size as our window, we request that it be displayed in the upper left-hand corner of the window — replacing everything there. Figure 9-4 is a snapshot of the moving text.

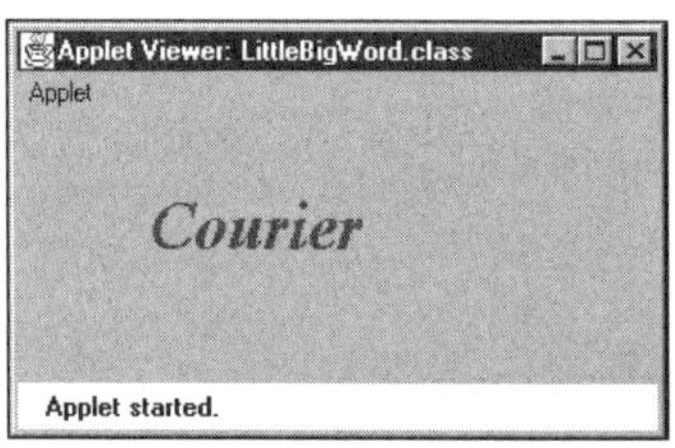

Figure 9-4 The output from LittleBigWord has text that continuously expands and contracts.

Summary

Animation in Java is easy because the Java interpreter does the work of threading the calls to the methods that do the drawing; the only real code to write is the actual drawing of the pictures. There are two basic kinds of animation: the kind that entails drawing and painting lines and pixels on the display and the kind in which a set of predrawn pictures are shown in succession, like television.

The draw-and-paint method is called *vector* graphics because it involves the layout of rows and columns of pixels. Using vector graphics in Java has the advantage of creating an applet that is quicker to load — no large graphics files need to be transmitted across the Internet. It has the disadvantage of not being able to include the details and subtle picture elements possible when loading images.

Graphics that use `.gif` and `.jpg` files are called *raster* graphics because they are so much like television — a series of complete pictures made up of row after row of pixels.

Java handles both of these very well. In fact, the two can be mixed together in a single Java applet because vector graphics can be applied to a loaded raster image.

Security precautions prevent Java applets from having the ability to read from or write to files, but Java applications have this power. The next chapter will show you how a Java application can stream input and output.

CHAPTER TEN

INPUT AND OUTPUT

IN THIS CHAPTER YOU LEARN THESE KEY SKILLS

In previous chapters we looked at input coming from the keyboard or the mouse and output going to the screen. This chapter is an introduction to input from and output to other locations. We will pay particular attention to file input and output, including examples of each.

After reading this chapter you will understand how the various Java classes of input and output can be connected together to construct a class that does exactly what you need to have done. Once you see how this is accomplished, you will be able to mix and match your own stream classes to build whatever you need.

Streams

Input and output in Java is defined in terms of *streams* of data. A *stream* is an orderly flow of data from a specific source to a specific destination. Different types of streams are defined by the form of the data being streamed and by the type of source or destination.

There is an advantage in using the stream concept as an abstraction. Once a stream is set up and operating, the operations on it are the same whether the other end of the connection is a file, another process, a location in RAM, or even a socket connection across a network.

A stream is a one-way apparatus. There are input stream classes that extend the abstract `InputStream` class, and there are output stream classes that extend the abstract `OutputStream` class. (The `RandomAccessFile` class that performs both input and output on a file isn't a stream.)

The File Class

The `File` class can be thought of as the name and descriptive information of a file. To construct one of these rascals, just give it a file name. Its constructors look like the following:

```
public File(File dir, String name);
public File(String path);
public File(String path, String name);
```

The file doesn't have to exist in order for a `File` object to be created, but once you have the `File` object, you can get a full pedigree of the file. Various methods can be used to find out whether the file exists, whether it is readable and/or writeable, how big it is, whether it is a directory, and more. You can even rename it or delete it. Following is a partial list of the methods:

```
public boolean canRead();
public boolean canWrite();
public boolean delete();
public boolean exists();
public String getAbsolutePath();
public String getName();
public String getPath();
public boolean isDirectory();
public boolean isFile();
public long lastModified();
public long length();
public boolean renameTo(File dest);
```

One of the main reasons for creating a `File` object is for it to be passed to one of the stream classes to set things up for some input and output.

Writing Raw Data to a File

Listing 10-1 uses simple byte stream input and output to a file. To open a file for writing, create a `FileOutputStream` object. To open a file for reading, create a `FileInputStream` object. There is more than one `read()` and `write()` method in these classes, but they all operate on a stream of raw byte data.

This example creates an output file and writes ten bytes to it. It then turns around and opens the file for reading and reads the bytes back in.

Listing 10-1 ByteInputOutput.java

```
import java.io.*;

public class ByteInputOutput {
  static public void main(String arg[]) {
   ByteInputOutput bio = new ByteInputOutput();
   bio.do_output();
   bio.do_input();
  }

  void do_output() {
   File file = new File("fred");
   try {
        FileOutputStream fileout =
                      new FileOutputStream(file);
        for(byte i = 0; i<10; i++)
                fileout.write(i);
        fileout.close();
   } catch(IOException e) {
          System.out.println(e);
          System.exit(1);
   }
  }

  void do_input() {
   File file = new File("fred");
   try {
        FileInputStream filein =
                      new FileInputStream(file);
        while(true) {
                int inbyte = filein.read();
```

```
                if(inbyte == -1) {
                      System.out.print("\n");
                      filein.close();
                      return;
                }
                System.out.print(" " + inbyte);
          }
    } catch(IOException e) {
          System.out.println(e);
          System.exit(1);
    }
   }
}
```

Output Strings to a File

The `PrintStream` class will write ASCII strings to an output stream. Whether you know it or not, you are already familiar with an object of this class — `System.out` is a `PrintStream` object that sends character data to the screen. Listing 10-2 uses a `FileOutputStream` object to demonstrate sending character data to a file.

Listing 10-2 StringOutput.java

```
import java.io.*;

public class StringOutput {
  static public void main(String arg[]) {
   StringOutput sio = new StringOutput();
   sio.do_output();
  }

  void do_output() {
   File file = new File("fred");
   try {
         FileOutputStream fileout =
                     new FileOutputStream(file);
         PrintStream pr = new PrintStream(fileout);
         pr.println("The toString of this: " + this);
         pr.close();
   } catch(IOException e) {
         System.out.println(e);
   }
  }
}
```

We create a stream that sends string output to a file by constructing it from parts as in a kit. Starting with the file name, we first create a `File` object named `file`. Then we use `file` to create a `FileOutputStream` object name `fileout`. We then use `fileout` to create a `PrintStream` object named `pr`. Now that we have `pr`, we can write all the strings we want to the file. This kit-like construction may seem a bit odd at first, but it allows you to mix and match different types of input and output streams to come up with whatever you may happen to need at the moment. You'll get the hang of it after you use it a couple of times.

10

Data Input and Output

If you want to read and write the Java fundamental data types, use the `DataOutputStream` and `DataInputStream` classes. These are similar to the `PrintStream` class in the previous section, but instead of character strings these classes write `floats`, `doubles`, `longs`, and the other fundamental types. Listing 10-3 is an example that writes some data out to a file and then reads it back in. You will notice the familiar kit-like construction of building a stream of the kind we want. The name of the file is used to construct a `File` object, which is used to construct a `FileOutputStream`, which is used to construct a `DataOutputStream`, which is used to write the data. The input stream is constructed the same way.

Listing 10-3 DataInputOutput.java

```
import java.io.*;

public class DataInputOutput {
  static public void main(String arg[]) {
   DataInputOutput dio = new DataInputOutput();
   dio.do_output();
   dio.do_input();
  }

  void do_output() {
   File file = new File("fred");
   try {
         FileOutputStream fileout =
                     new FileOutputStream(file);
         DataOutputStream dout =
                     new DataOutputStream(fileout);
         dout.writeBoolean(true);
         dout.writeInt(2345);
         dout.writeDouble(88.99);
         dout.close();
```

```
    } catch(IOException e) {
          System.out.println(e);
    }
  }

  void do_input() {
    File file = new File("fred");
    try {
          FileInputStream filein =
                      new FileInputStream(file);
          DataInputStream din =
                      new DataInputStream(filein);
          System.out.println("boolean value " +
                      din.readBoolean());
          System.out.println("int value " +
                      din.readInt());
          System.out.println("double value " +
                      din.readDouble());
          din.close();
    } catch(IOException e) {
          System.out.println(e);
    }
  }
}
```

Reading and Writing in RAM

It is possible to read and write data in RAM. Listing 10-4 shows how this is accomplished for raw byte input and output. Just create a `ByteArrayOutputStream` and start writing to it — it will automatically expand to include all the data you write to it. Any time you want a copy of what has already been written, just make a call to the `toByteArray()` method and a fresh copy of the internal byte array is allocated and returned to you.

Listing 10-4 RamInputOutput.java

```
import java.io.*;

public class RamInputOutput {
  byte[] barray;
  static public void main(String arg[]) {
   RamInputOutput rio = new RamInputOutput();
```

```
        rio.do_output();
        rio.do_input();
    }

    void do_output() {
        try {
            ByteArrayOutputStream ramout = new
                    ByteArrayOutputStream();
            for(byte i = 0; i<10; i++)
                ramout.write(i);
            barray = ramout.toByteArray();
            ramout.close();
        } catch(IOException e) {
            System.out.println(e);
            System.exit(1);
        }
    }

    void do_input() {
        try {
            ByteArrayInputStream ramin = new
                    ByteArrayInputStream(barray);
            while(true) {
                int inbyte = ramin.read();
                if(inbyte == -1) {
                    System.out.print("\n");
                    ramin.close();
                    return;
                }
                System.out.print(" " + inbyte);
            }
        } catch(IOException e) {
            System.out.println(e);
            System.exit(1);
        }
    }
}
```

TIP You can use these classes to do formatted reading and writing of simple byte arrays, formatting the data in all sorts of ways using the kit-like construction shown in the previous examples. Any place you can use a `FileOutputStream` you can also use a `ByteArrayOutputStream` — and any place you can use a `FileInputStream` you can use a `ByteArrayInputStream`.

BONUS

The RandomAccessFile Class

There is one class for input and output that doesn't fit with the others. So far every class we have dealt with has either been an input class or an output class. The `RandomAccessFile` class does both — it has both read and write methods. It can also be repositioned prior to any of these reads and writes. Another thing: it can't be used as part of a kit in building a stream like the others can. This is the Java file handling class that is probably most like the C functions of `fopen()`, `ftell()`, `fseek()`, and `fclose()`. The simple example in Listing 10-5 shows how it works.

Listing 10-5 RandomInputOutput.java

```
import java.io.*;

public class RandomInputOutput {
  static public void main(String arg[]) {
   File file = new File("fred");
   try {
         RandomAccessFile ra = new
                     RandomAccessFile(file,"rw");
         ra.writeChar('A');
         long position = ra.getFilePointer();
         ra.writeChar('B');
         ra.seek(position);
         System.out.println("Position=" + position
               + " Char=" + ra.readChar());
         position = 0;
         ra.seek(position);
         System.out.println("Position=" + position
               + " Char=" + ra.readChar());
         ra.close();
   } catch(IOException e) {
         System.out.println(e);
   }
  }
}
```

All you need is a `File` object and you're ready to go. The constructor takes two arguments: the `File` object and a mode string. The mode string is either "r" for read-only or "rw" for both read and write. The `RandomAccessFile` class implements the same interface as does `DataInputStream` and `DataOutputStream` so you are able to read and write the fundamental data types.

The interesting parts of `RandomAccessFile` are the positioning methods. A position in the file is defined as being an offset from the beginning of the file — position zero being the beginning of the file. The method `getFilePointer()` returns the current position, and the method `seek()` positions the file.

TIP **When you open a file that does not already exist, `RandomAccessFile` will create a new one. If the file does exist, it is not changed in any way. It is left completely intact; you can start reading and writing anywhere in the file. If you write beyond the end of the existing file, it will simply be extended to accommodate you.**

Summary

This chapter summarizes the more common forms of input and output in the Java API. Some raw data input and output classes can be used for the simple reading and writing of raw data. If more sophisticated reading and writing is needed, it is possible to superimpose a more sophisticated interface on top of the simpler ones by mixing and matching as if they were parts in a kit.

The same interfaces that are used to read and write files can be used to read and write to RAM. There are interfaces designed to communicate through pipes connected between threads, and special interfaces to do some special buffering — just hook up the ones you need and start streaming.

These input and output classes are only a few of the utilities supplied with the Java API. In the next chapter we take a swing through some of the others.

CHAPTER ELEVEN

JAVADOC AND THE UTILITY API

IN THIS CHAPTER YOU LEARN THESE KEY SKILLS

This chapter is about utilities. There are two kinds of utilities: those you can include as part of your program and those that operate "on the side" as stand-alone programs. For our "on the side" utility, we explore the exciting world of automatic document generation through the magical powers of javadoc.

Mostly, this chapter is about the utility classes that can be included in your applets and applications to generally make life easier. These classes are just sitting there in the Java class library waiting for you to put them to work.

"The purpose of any software project is documentation. Period." We first came across this statement years ago (we simply can't remember where), but we have never been able to prove it untrue. Documentation is necessary if for no other reason than to stipulate the interfaces. Undocumented software is software that will be thrown out, either because it can't be used or it can't be changed. One of the really nice things about Java is that it has come darn close to completely automating the documentation process.

Javadoc

Javadoc is a stand-alone program that is run from the command line. It reads through the source code looking in specific places for comments in specific formats. It converts these comments into HTML documentation. All comments to be converted to documentation have the following form:

```
/** Comment to become documentation. */
```

It's that little double asterisk trick at the beginning that tips off javadoc when it finds a documentable comment. For javadoc to know what you are talking about (after all, it can't really read), the comment must come right before a data declaration, a class definition, or a method. Consider this example:

```
/** The frog counter. Each time there is another frog,
this value will be incremented by one. */
public int FrogCount = 0;
```

Javadoc will assume the document-comment belongs with `FrogCount` because `FrogCount` immediately follows the comment.

Tags

Tags can be used to enhance the text of your documentation. There are tags to do all sorts of things, but they all have the same basic format — an *at* sign (@) followed by a keyword followed by the tag value.

The following example uses both kinds of tags to generate documentation for a class:

```
/**
This is a class to pop up a color selection wheel. It
presents a box of crayons on the screen to allow the user
to select his favorite color of wax.

An example of creating a Cray:
<pre>
    Cray cray = new Cray(parent);
    cray.show();
</pre>

@author P. T. Barnum
@see awt.Window
@see ColoringBox
@version 1.0 10/12/1997
*/
class Cray extends ColoringBox {
```

```
    ...
}
```

Each of the javadoc tags (the keywords preceded with an at sign) will generate a special entry in the documentation; the @see tags will create links to the named items. As you can see, it is also possible to insert certain of the HTML formatting commands. In this example we have used <pre> and </pre> to insert some preformatted text.

TIP **Take care when using HTML formatting tags. Javadoc itself generates HTML to surround and format the stuff from your comment, and you could wind up in conflict. Simple formatting works OK, but for other things you will need to experiment to see what happens.**

THE @author TAG

There can be one or more author tags in a documentation block. Following are some examples:

```
@author Bertha D. Blues
@author Phillip Space
```

This tag will cause the author's name to be displayed prominently in the documentation (so everybody will know who to blame).

THE @exception TAG

The @exception tag is for method documentation only. This tag will insert information describing which exceptions are thrown and why. There can be several of these tags because a method can potentially throw several exceptions. It looks like the following:

```
@exception IndexOutOfBoundsException Too many angels dancing on
  the head of a pin.
```

The format is simply the name of the exception being thrown and a description of why it is thrown.

THE @param TAG

The @param tag is for methods only. It can be used to describe the parameters. There can be several of these — one for each parameter:

```
@param Maximum The maximum number of angels allowed on the pin.
@param Width The total size of the pin head.
```

Javadoc expects there to be a parameter name followed by its description. For clarity, these tags should appear in the same order as the arguments of the method.

THE @return TAG

The @return tag can be used to specify the return value of a method. It has no particular form — just the tag followed by a descriptive comment:

```
@return An integer count of the actual number of angels on the pin.
```

THE @see TAG

The @see tag may be the most useful tag in the whole bunch. This tag can be used to generate links to other pages in the documentation. This is done whenever you want to make a reference to a class, interface, method, or even a field in another class. You can even insert a link to another Web page — and references can span the Internet. Following are some examples:

```
@see java.util.Properties
@see Amphibians.FrogCount
@see <a href="http://www.idgbooks.com">IDG Books</a>
```

THE @version TAG

There is no particular format for the @version tag — it can be a mixture of names and numbers.

```
@version 1.0 4/12/97
```

Javadoc Descends

Javadoc is run from the command line and it has a few options. The command line has the following form:

```
javadoc [options] packagename
javadoc [options] name.java [ name2.java ... ]
```

You can supply javadoc a package name or list one or more class file names. It accepts wild cards. If you have the source code for a bunch of classes in one directory, you can run javadoc on all of them:

```
javadoc *.java
```

Javadoc generates documentation that cross-references the classes. It also generates a Web page for each class. The output of javadoc is HTML containing links connecting all the pages together.

TIP **It is probably a good idea to construct some sort of command script to automate the running of javadoc. By doing this, you will be able to specify all the classes and packages and have javadoc create a single set of interlinked documents for you. You can run the script again and again to keep the documentation up to date.**

COMMAND-LINE OPTIONS

`-author`

Any `@author` tags found will be ignored unless the `author` option is specified.

`-classpath path`

The `classpath` option supplies javadoc with a list of semicolon-separated directory names to be searched for files. The `classpath` option overrides the environment variable `CLASSPATH`.

`-d directory`

This option will tell javadoc which directory should receive the generated documentation. If no directory is specified, javadoc puts its output into the current directory.

`-doctype typename`

Javadoc is capable of generating two types of documentation files: `html` or `mif` (the FrameMaker document format). The default is `html`.

`-noindex`

The `noindex` option will suppress the generation of a separate document file containing an alphabetic index of all the names.

`-notree`

The `notree` option will suppress the generation of a separate file containing the class hierarchy information.

`-sourcepath path`

Using `sourcepath` is the same as using `classpath`.

`-verbose`

The verbose option will cause javadoc to list every class definition it loads and how long it takes it to process it.

`-version`

Any `@version` tags found will be ignored unless the `version` option is specified.

Java Utility Classes

A group of utility classes is included in the `java.util` package, waiting for you to put them to use in your programs. The following sections outline what each of them does.

Date

The `java.util.Date` class can be used by a Java program to handle clock and calendar arithmetic with one-second accuracy. An object of this class can be created for a specific time or, by using the default constructor, one can be created for the current time. (This is not a running clock. Whenever you want the current time you will need to create another object.) Various methods can be used to set and retrieve temporal information by year, month, day, hour, minute, or second.

There are Date comparison methods as well as methods to do conversions to and from the Java long date format.

TIP **The Date class is only as accurate as the clock in your computer. If that's wrong, the Date object will be wrong. Do you want to set your clock? Look at http://tycho.usno.navy.mil or http://homepage.twd.net/common/time. These sites will both give you accurate running clocks for the current time. Hint: Do this when the Internet is not very busy.**

Listing 11-1 is a simple program creating a Date object and displaying the three string formats the Date object is capable of generating.

Listing 11-1 DateShow.java

```
import java.util.*;

public class DateShow {
  static public void main(String arg[]) {
   Date date = new Date();
   System.out.println("GMT:    " + date.toGMTString());
   System.out.println("LOCALE: " + date.toLocaleString());
   System.out.println("LOCAL:  " + date.toString());
  }
}
```

Output from the program looks like the following:

```
GMT:    17 Apr 1997 16:07:38 GMT
LOCALE: 04/17/97 11:07:38
LOCAL:  Thu Apr 17 11:07:38  1997
```

Random

There comes a time in every programmer's life when he or she has a sudden craving for a random number. To satisfy this urge, we have the java.util.Random class. You can create a Random object by supplying its constructor with a seed value. The resulting numbers are what is known as pseudorandom: any given seed value will always generate the same sequence of numbers. The random number sequence can be generated in any of the fundamental numeric types. The float and double values will be in the range of 0.0 to 1.0, while the values of int and long will be any value throughout their range.

TIP **If you want to make sure you get a different sequence of numbers every time (randomize the randomness, so to speak), use the Java internal clock as the seed when creating a Random object. This technique is demonstrated in listing 11-2.**

Listing 11-2 RandomShow.java

```
import java.util.*;

public class RandomShow {
  public static void main(String arg[]) {
   Random r = new Random(new Date().getTime());
   for(int i=1; i<4; i++)
         System.out.println(i +  :   + r.nextFloat());
  }
}
```


Because the example in Listing 11-2 uses the Java clock as the seed to `Random`, a different sequence of values will be generated every time the program is run. Following is a sequence from one run:

```
1: 0.765793
2: 0.014353
3: 0.725361
```

And this is the output from a second run made immediately after the first:

```
1: 0.156374
2: 0.447174
3: 0.759984
```

TIP **If your random number requirements are simple, take a look at the `random()` method in `java.lang.Math`. It's a bit easier to use, but you have less control.**

BitSet

This class is an array of an infinite number of `boolean` values — sort of. (OK, it's not really infinite, but it seems that way when you use it.) It is a variable-length array of bits that are all initially set to `false`. Each bit is addressed by its zero-based index into the array. The action of setting a bit to `true` will, if necessary, automatically extend the array of bits to accommodate the new indexed location. If any bit has not been explicitly set to `true` it will be returned as `false`, even if its index is beyond the end of the array of bits.

You can get a good idea of how this works from Listing 11-3.

Listing 11-3 BitSetShow.java

```
import java.util.*;

public class BitSetShow {
  static public void main(String arg[]) {
```

```
        BitSet bit = new BitSet();
        bit.set(12);
        show_settings(bit);
        bit.set(90);
        show_settings(bit);
        bit.clear(12);
        bit.set(13);
        bit.set(542);
        show_settings(bit);
        bit.clear(90);
        bit.clear(542);
        show_settings(bit);
        if(bit.get(90))
              System.out.println( Bit 12 is on );
       }

       static void show_settings(BitSet bit) {
        System.out.println( size=  + bit.size() +
                bits (  + bit.size()/8 +   bytes)   +
                bits set:   + bit);
       }
    }
```

This program sets and clears some bits. The method `show_settings()` prints the number of bits — and bytes it takes to hold them — that have been allocated in the array. It also prints the index of the bits set to `true`. Bits are made to be `true` with `set()` and made to be `false` with `clear()`. The method to read a bit is `get()`. The output looks as follows:

```
size=64 bits (8 bytes)  bits set: {12}
size=128 bits (16 bytes)  bits set: {12, 90}
size=576 bits (72 bytes)  bits set: {13, 90, 542}
size=576 bits (72 bytes)  bits set: {13}
```

From this we can conclude that eight bytes are initially allocated. Setting bit 90 required the allocation of another eight bytes. When we went and set bit 576, the array expanded to 72 bytes so it could reach far enough to include the one we set. Note that as we cleared the bits, the size of the array was not reduced — once you ask for it, you've got it.

Among the other methods that can be used as logical operators on two `BitSet` objects are `and()`, `or()`, and `xor()`; they operate on the entire array.

Hashtable

A `Hashtable` object is a container. It will take any number of objects and file them away for later retrieval with a key.

TIP **Inside the `Hashtable` the objects are stored and retrieved by the value returned from their `hashCode()` methods — which is where the class got its name — but you will not have to deal with any hashing unless you just want to. All objects have a `hashCode()` method because they all inherit one from the `Object` class. All you need to do is shove 'em in and pull 'em out whenever you want to.**

Listing 11-4 demonstrates a very simple way to use a `Hashtable` object. We stuck some `Color` objects into a table using a `String` object as the key.

Listing 11-4 HashtableShow.java

```
import java.util.*;

import java.awt.*;

public class HashtableShow {
  public static void main(String arg[]) {
   Hashtable table = new Hashtable();
   table.put( red ,Color.red);
   table.put( green ,Color.green);
   table.put( blue ,Color.blue);

   // Extract one element by its key.
   Color color = (Color)table.get( green );
   System.out.println( green=  + color);

   // Extract all elements.
   Enumeration enum = table.elements();
   while(enum.hasMoreElements()) {
         color = (Color)enum.nextElement();
         System.out.println(color);
   }
  }
}
```

The `Color` objects are each put into the table using a character string description of their names as the key. As you can see, it is possible to retrieve a single object by using its key. It is also possible to retrieve all the objects by creating an `Enumeration` object and reading each one in turn. Following is the resulting output:

```
green=java.awt.Color[r=0,g=255,b=0]
java.awt.Color[r=0,g=255,b=0]
java.awt.Color[r=0,g=0,b=255]
java.awt.Color[r=255,g=0,b=0]
```

Comparing the code to the output, you can see they came out in an order different from the one they went in with. This is characteristic of hashing — the order is always guaranteed to be entirely random. If you have to have things in order, see the `Vector` class in this same section. If you need both, use both; it's a bit more code, but it's no more overhead than any other form of double indexing because all that is stored are the references.

StringTokenizer

If you have written much C code, you have probably developed some sort of relationship with `strtok()`. The `StringTokenizer` class does everything `strtok()` does, but with a bit more flair and style. For one thing, it doesn't destroy the string you pass to it. For another, it can give you a count of the number of tokens you are going to get before you actually get them. An example of how it can be used in shown in Listing 11-5.

Listing 11-5 StringTokenizerShow.java

```
import java.util.*;

public class StringTokenizerShow {
  public static void main(String arg[]) {
   String string =
          You can t roller-skate, in a buffalo herd. ;
   System.out.println( Start:   + string);
   StringTokenizer st =
         new StringTokenizer(string, ,. \t\n\r );
   int count = st.countTokens();
   System.out.println( This string contains   +
         count +   tokens. );
   for(int i=0; i<count; i++)
         System.out.println(        +
               st.nextToken());
   System.out.println( Finish:   + string);
  }
}
```

The `StringTokenizer` object is constructed using the string to be tokenized and the list of characters that will delimit the tokens. The list in the example includes comma, period, space, tab, newline, and carriage return; these characters are the ones that will separate tokens and be discarded. Following is the output from the example:

```
Start: You can t roller-skate, in a buffalo herd.
This string contains 7 tokens.
     You
```

```
        can't
        roller-skate
        in
        a
        buffalo
        herd
Finish: You can't roller-skate, in a buffalo herd.
```

As you can see, only the characters in the list of delimiters were used as token separators. Also, the tokenized `String` came through entirely unmolested.

TIP **You can do some pretty fancy stuff with delimiters. For one, the `nextToken()` method allows you to change them on the fly. Also, we could have chosen to use the constructor that, instead of discarding the delimiting characters, would cause the delimiters to be returned as tokens.**

Vector

The `Vector` class is a container that maintains an ordered list of objects. You can put objects in at the beginning, middle, or end of the list and it will adjust itself to accommodate them. Isn't that nice of it?

There are a lot of things you can do with this ordered list (insert at an index, append to the end, locate by reference, delete by reference, delete by index, and so on) so there are a lot of methods. In Listing 11-6 we use a few methods to demonstrate the basic `Vector` class operations.

Listing 11-6 VectorShow.java

```
import java.util.*;

public class VectorShow {
  public static void main(String arg[]) {
   Vector vec = new Vector();
   vec.addElement("first");
   vec.addElement("second");
   vec.addElement("third");
   listem(vec);
   vec.addElement("fourth");
   listem(vec);
   vec.insertElementAt("first-and-a-half",1);
   listem(vec);
   vec.removeElementAt(2);
   listem(vec);
  }
```

```
  private static void listem(Vector vec) {
   int count = vec.size();
   System.out.print(count + " elements: ");
   for(int i=0; i<count; i++)
         System.out.print((String)vec.elementAt(i) +
               " ");
   System.out.println();
  }
}
```

In this example we add objects, one at a time, to the vector. An object is added to and deleted from the interior of the list. Following is the output from the example:

```
3 elements: first second third
4 elements: first second third fourth
5 elements: first first-and-a-half second third fourth
4 elements: first first-and-a-half third fourth
```

TIP **There is no way to retrieve an object from a `Vector` by using a key. You can't even trust the index — inserting or deleting objects causes index values to be adjusted up and down. If you need to be able to use keys to retrieve an object, use the `Hashtable` discussed earlier in this section. Again, if you need both, use both; it's a bit more code, but it's no more overhead than any other form of double indexing.**

Stack

The `Stack` class is a simple extension of the `Vector` class. It adds the `push()` method to place something on top of the stack and the `pop()` method to retrieve it. Listing 11-7 demonstrates use of the `Stack` class.

Listing 11-7 StackShow.java

```
import java.util.*;

public class StackShow {
  public static void main(String arg[]) {
   Stack stack = new Stack();
   stack.push("first");
   stack.push("second");
   System.out.println((String)stack.pop());
   stack.push("third");
   stack.push("fourth");
```

```
    while(!stack.empty())
            System.out.println((String)stack.pop());
  }
}
```

Listing 11-7 pushes some `String` objects onto the stack and then pops them off. In every case, the string popped off the stack is the youngest one still on the stack. The output from this example looks like the following:

```
second
fourth
third
first
```

11

BONUS

The Properties Class

The `Properties` class is used to store information that some programs will need to have every time they run. A set of system properties is always available for reading, and you can establish your own set of persistent properties for reading and writing. Let's look at the system properties first.

A property is made up of a pair of strings. One is the key, or *name*, of the property, and the other is its value. For example, the property key "java.version" could have the value "1.0.2" or "1.1" — or whatever the current version happens to be.

System Properties

Listing 11-8 reads through all the system properties and prints them out.

Listing 11-8 PropertiesShow.java

```
import java.util.*;

public class PropertiesShow {
  static public void main(String arg[]) {
   Properties p = System.getProperties();
   Enumeration enum = p.propertyNames();
   while(enum.hasMoreElements()) {
         String property_name =
```

```
                (String)enum.nextElement();
            String property =
                p.getProperty(property_name);
            System.out.println(property_name +
                ": " + property);
        }
    }
}
```

Following is the output it generated when run. Your mileage will vary in some of the specifics, but the names of the entries should be the same. The list shown here gives the standard properties specified in every Java interpreter.

```
java.home: C:\JAVA\BIN\..
awt.toolkit: sun.awt.win32.MToolkit
java.version: 1.0.2
file.separator: \
line.separator:

java.vendor: Sun Microsystems Inc.
user.name: Arthur
os.arch: x86
os.name: Windows 95
java.vendor.url: http://www.sun.com/
user.dir: C:\vcafe\tmp
java.class.path: .;C:\LIB\CLASSES;C:\lib\classes.zip
java.class.version: 45.3
os.version: 4.0
path.separator: ;
user.home: C:\HOME
```

The meanings of each of these should be fairly obvious. In writing portable applications, the `file.separator` and `line.separator` can be quite useful for writing portable file manipulation routines in Java applications. (Notice there is nothing to the right of `line.separator`, but the line following it is blank — that proves it works.)

Persistent Properties

In addition to the system properties, you can build your own property lists and store them on disk. These are configuration files a program will load each time it executes (sort of like the Windows Italian files — `system.ini`, `win.ini`, and so forth). The exact format of the data on disk is controlled by the Properties class; this should make it portable to all systems. Neat, eh? In Listing 11-9 we have created a Configuration class to give you an idea of how this could work.

Listing 11-9 Configuration.java

```
import java.util.*;
import java.io.*;

public class Configuration extends Properties {
  static public void main(String arg[]) {
   Configuration con = new Configuration();
   con.create();
   con.saveAll();
   con.loadAll();
   System.out.println( day 1:   +
         con.getProperty( Monday ));
   System.out.println( day 2:   +
         con.getProperty( Tuesday ));
  }

  public void create() {
   defaults = new Properties();
   defaults.put( Monday , wash day );
   defaults.put( Tuesday , wear clean clothes );
   defaults.put( Wednesday , change clothes );
   defaults.put( Friday , count socks );
  }

  public void saveAll() {
   File file = new File( configuration.data );
   try {
         FileOutputStream fout =
               new FilcOutputStream(file);
         defaults.save(fout,
                The demo configuration information );
         fout.close();
   } catch(IOException e) {
         System.out.println(e);
   }
  }

  public void loadAll() {
   defaults = new Properties();
   File file = new File( configuration.data );
   try {
         FileInputStream fin =
               new FileInputStream(file);
         defaults.load(fin);
```

```
            fin.close();
      } catch(IOException e) {
            System.out.println(e);
      }
    }
  }
```

The `main()` method first calls `create()` to build a RAM-resident form of a `Property` object holding our four properties. The `saveAll()` method is called to create (or perhaps overwrite) the disk file with the new property information. The `loadAll()` method replaces any existing `Properties` object with a new one and then fills it with the values from the disk. The program then acquires a couple of properties by their keys, printing them out as follows:

```
day 1: wash day
day 2: wear clean clothes
```

The disk file looks like this:

```
#The demo configuration information
#Tue Nov 19 08:47:16  1996
Monday=wash day
Tuesday=wear clean clothes
Wednesday=change clothes
Friday=count socks
```

This file has a pretty simple format, but it is bound to be a little different from one system to another. For one thing, it is an ASCII file, and it will most likely need to be maintained in Unicode on some systems.

This may be a very simple example, but you can see how this facility can be used to hold entire application system configurations. By using the directory information found in the system-level properties, it is possible to maintain a separate set of properties for each user.

Summary

This chapter described how to use the javadoc utility to document programs. It has been proven true over the years that no decent documentation ever appears after the code has been written. Using the Java comments and javadoc seems to be an excellent way to have documentation reflect what is really in the code from the outset. Also, whenever changes are made to the code, the documentation is right there to be maintained also.

We also surveyed some utility classes. Not all the capabilities of all the classes were covered, but you now know these things exist and have a good idea of just what they do. These classes can be used as containers to keep things for you, tell you the date and time, and operate at the bit level.

This chapter completes a journey through the Java language that we began in Chapter 2. In these chapters we have attempted to give you a complete overview of the entire Java language and its API. You probably know more about Java than you think you do — a lot of ground was covered. If you grasped the concepts in these chapters, there should be no more mysteries — just refinements to what you already know.

Coming up next: details of Visual Café and how you can use it to unleash your applet and application masterpieces.

PART TWO

PROGRAMMING WITH VISUAL CAFÉ

THIS PART CONTAINS THE FOLLOWING CHAPTERS

In this part, you're introduced to the important parts of Visual Café, starting with the interface design tools, moving on through the Interaction Wizard and the source code editor, and continuing to the Component Library and the customizable parts of Visual Café. At the end of this section, you're introduced to Visual Café Pro and Visual Café Enterprise, Visual Café's big brothers.

REAL LIFE VISUAL CAFÉ: DEV TOOLS

CUPERTINO, Calif. — Symantec Corporation's Internet and Developer Tools division — "Dev Tools" in the employees' lingo — makes its home in a four-story faux-adobe building with horizontal rust-brown bands of windows. In the center of the office compound Symantec shares with Apple and Microsoft, a single turbulent jet of water bursts from the center of a round fountain, surrounded by a courtyard of red brick. Trees and flowers of every description pack the courtyard, and the air blows thick with their moist scent. Maintenance workers with leaf blowers circle the courtyard every fifteen minutes it seems.

Examples of all forms of geek life — a term we use as a high compliment and in the spirit of self-promotion — stroll through the courtyard, past the round fountain. Youthful programmers toting nylon backpacks pass aging gurus sporting sandals and waist-length ponytails.

Dev Tools is growing fast. In the courtyard, a programmer ready to jump ship from another software house sits waiting for an interview — he wants to work on the Visual Café team. Dev Tools was looking to hire some seventy people in the fall of 1996.

He and others converged on Dev Tools — which hired people left and right in the fall of 1996 — to be part of a revolution. It's a revolution that, not long ago, you might not have expected to find at Symantec, of all software companies. After all, as recently as the middle of 1995, Symantec stirred little emotion in the hearts of computer users. Software packages from Symantec were like Hyundai automobiles — entirely competent products that sold well, but nothing to get excited about.

Symantec sold the Norton Utilities, a collection of tools for repairing and souping up personal computers. It also sold Norton Anti-Virus, a respected but decidedly unsexy program that detects malicious software. And it sold ACT!, a contact manager that sold well and won accolades from critics. But it was still a program designed to merely keep track of the names and phone numbers of bunches of people. Most folks thought of Symantec as a utilities company.

On the other hand, Dev Tools had an excellent C++ integrated development environment — a superb product, priced affordably — that raked in awards from all kinds of magazines and industry groups. The trouble was, Symantec C++ had to compete with Microsoft Corporation's Visual C++. Though Symantec C++ was (and is) widely considered technically superior to Visual C++, Microsoft's titanic marketing budget threatened to squash Symantec C++ into a minuscule niche market, just large enough to keep Microsoft out of antitrust trouble.

Then Java came along and changed all the rules.

CHAPTER TWELVE

UNDERSTANDING THE VISUAL CAFÉ INTERFACE

IN THIS CHAPTER YOU LEARN THESE KEY SKILLS

Now it's time to explore the mechanics of the program itself. In this chapter you'll learn what the various parts of Visual Café actually do. You'll learn the function of all those buttons on the Visual Café toolbars and the meaning of all menu commands.

These are the sort of things you'll need to know if you want to do some quick-and-dirty job on a Java application or applet — or if you're in a hurry to impress somebody with a surface knowledge of Visual Café. Not that you'd ever do anything like that, of course.

In later chapters of *Discover Visual Café*, you'll learn the nitty-gritty details of the Visual Café interface — the kinds of things you'll need to know before you attempt to do serious Java coding from the ground up.

TIP **This chapter covers only the menus that appear in Visual Café all the time. Several menus appear only under special circumstances — the Calls menu, for example, appears only when the Call Stack window is active. You'll learn about these menus in the chapters that deal with their specific functions.**

Projects

If you're new to Visual Café, and especially if you're new to visual integrated development environments in general, it's a good bet that you're wondering what exactly a "project" is. Visual Café organizes the work you do with it in terms of projects.

Think of projects as wrappers. A project contains all the material — source code, library references, everything — related to what ultimately will be a Java applet or application. In traditional programming terms, a project is the logical equivalent of a makefile — the file you use to send source information to the linker and compiler.

Visual Café saves projects with a .VPJ filename extension.

TIP **Visual Café calls the project to be compiled the main project. When you issue the Run or Build command, only the main project gets compiled. Perhaps contrary to intuition, the main project is not the logical equivalent of what your word processor might call the active document. It's the project to be compiled.**

Workspaces

All of the work you do with Visual Café is done in a *workspace,* a collection of programming and debugging tools arranged on your screen. Visual Café has two standard workspaces: the Edit workspace and the Debug workspace.It also allows you to create your own custom workspaces. You can switch among your Visual Café workspaces with the drop-down list box in the Workspaces toolbar (covered later in this chapter), by choosing Window → Workspaces from the menu bar (also covered in subsequent sections of this chapter), or by choosing a workspace from the Workspaces box on the toolbar.

TIP **The following descriptions list the most important parts of each workspace. Remember, though, that you're not limited to the tools listed. If you want to open the Class Browser in the Debug workspace, you can do that. You can also save a collection of open windows as a workspace. You'll learn more about that later in this chapter and in Chapter 21, "Customizing Visual Café."**

Edit

The Edit workspace is where you'll do most of your work in Visual Café. Here you write new code and revise old code. The most important parts of the Edit workspace include the following:

* The Form Editor, which you use to design the interface of your applet or application.
* The Code Editor, in which Java source code appears.
* The Property List, which lists the characteristics of objects such as buttons, text boxes, and entire classes.
* The Project Manager, which helps you keep track of all files relating to your current Java programming project.

The Edit workspace appears in Figure 12-1.

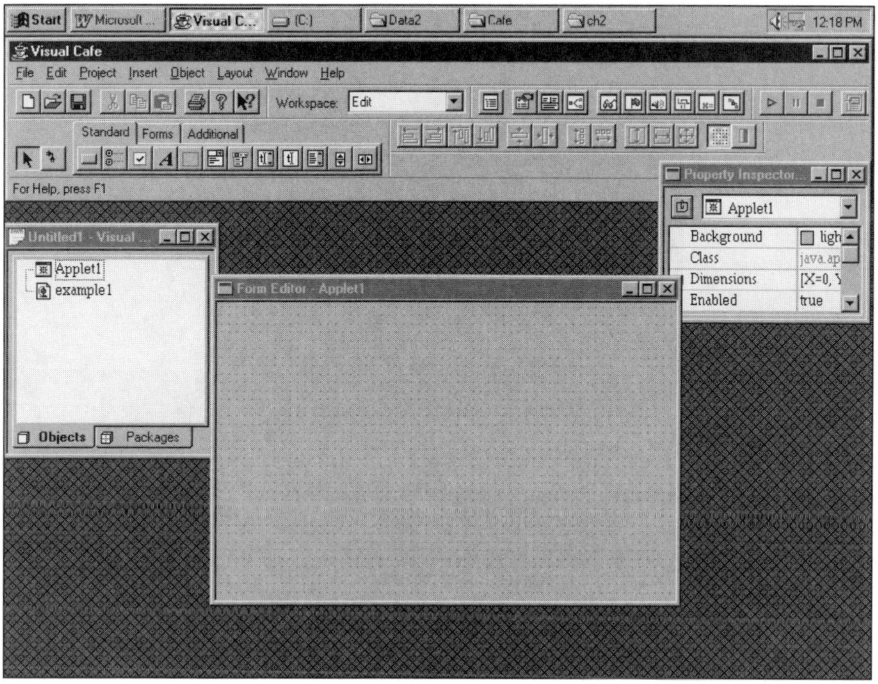

Figure 12-1 The Visual Café Edit workspace is where you'll write code.

Debug

You'll test your programs in the Visual Café Debug workspace. The Debug workspace provides you with several tools for figuring out what your applets and applications are doing and how to make them stop misbehaving. The most important parts of the Debug workspace include the following:

* The Applet Viewer, which shows your Java applets executing (or trying to).
* The Variables window, which lists the values of each of your code's variables as execution progresses.
* The Call window, which shows a list of running classes.

* The Breakpoints window, which list breakpoints (places where execution is stopped) you've inserted to aid error tracing.
* The Project Manager, which keeps track of all the classes in a project.

The Debug workspace appears in Figure 12-2.

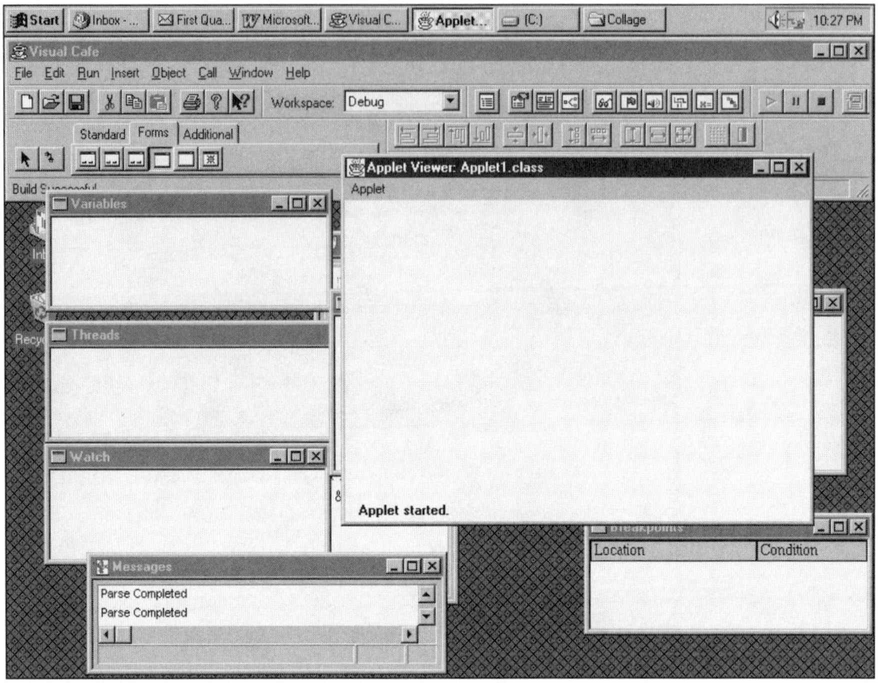

Figure 12-2 The Visual Café Debug workspace gives you access to error-finding tools.

Custom Workspaces

You can modify the two standard workspaces to suit your tastes or the particular needs of an unusual problem you're facing. You can, for example, open the Class Editor in the Debug workspace to keep track of the meaning of the statements in the Call window. Or you might want to have your Breakpoints window open in the Edit workspace so you can see exactly where you're placing diagnostic breakpoints in your code.

If you find a configuration of development tools that you like, you can save it and give it a workspace name. That way you'll have additional workspace names from which to choose in your Workspace toolbar or in the Window → Workspaces menu item.

You might name your workspace after yourself, if many people use your copy of Visual Café, or for a particular purpose, if your custom workspace helps solve a certain kind of problem.

You'll learn more details of creating custom workspaces in Chapter 21, "Customizing Visual Café."

The Menu Bar

Like practically all graphical programs, Visual Café features a menu bar right below its title bar. You can use your mouse — or keyboard shortcuts — to access features built into the menu bar.

The various Visual Café toolbars duplicate many of the functions of the menu bar. If you prefer your mouse to your keyboard, or if you are just learning Visual Café, you may find it easier to click the appropriate toolbar button than to dig the needed command out of the menu bar.

TIP **Remember, too, that many menu bar commands have keyboard shortcuts. For example, you can save the current project by pressing Alt+F+S or by pressing Ctrl+S. Taking the Save toolbar button and the Save menu bar entry into account, that's four separate ways to save a project.**

In the text, keyboard shortcuts are shown by underlined characters. When you read about the Object menu, for instance, you should know that you can open the Object menu by pressing Alt+O.

File

At the far left end of the menu bar you'll find the good old File menu. As in every other program that features a File menu (and that's a lot of programs), you should look here for file manipulation commands, such as New, Save, and Close. The File menu appears in Figure 12-3.

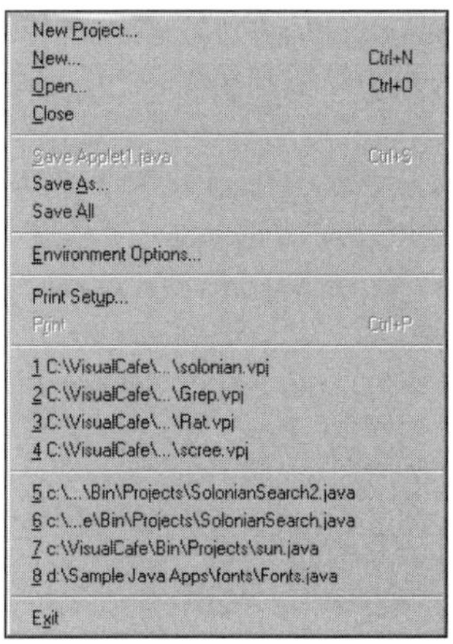

Figure 12-3 The File menu holds file manipulation commands.

NEW PROJECT

Use **File** → **New Project** to open a new Visual Café project — a Java applet or application complete with source code and debugging information.

When you use the **New Project** command, you'll see the New Project dialog box, in which you can choose a template on which to base your coding work. By default, you can choose from the following:

- Empty Project. This is exactly what it sounds like — a clear slate on which to start writing anything you like.
- Basic Application. A template for writing stand-alone applications in Java, complete with a basic menu bar already coded.
- Basic Applet. A template for writing Java code to be embedded in an HTML page — a nearly clean slate.

You can also create your own templates and include them in the New Project dialog box. You'll learn how to do that in Chapter 21, "Customizing Visual Café."

The New Project dialog box appears in Figure 12-4.

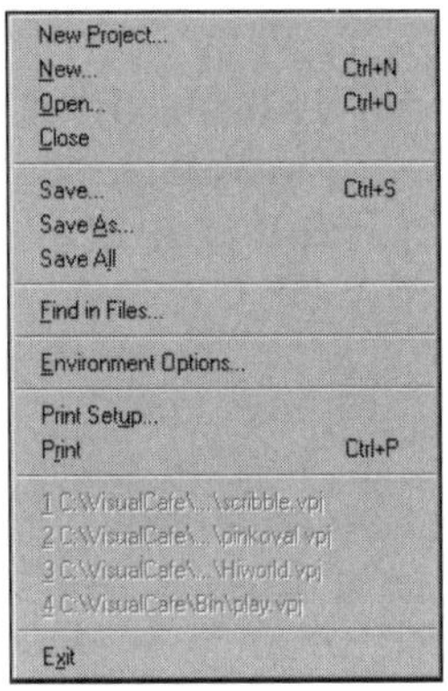

Figure 12-4 The New Project dialog box opens a new program template.

NEW

The **File** → **New** command, like the **File** → **New Project** command, can be used to generate the bare bones of a programming project. You can also use **New** to create a new text file, which you may want to keep open during development for making notes to yourself (or to your sweetie, for that matter), or for building a `README.TXT` file to accompany your software.

The New dialog box appears when you choose the New command. In it you can choose Visual, which brings up the template-packed New Project dialog box, or Text, which starts a new text file.

The New dialog box, which you can see in Figure 12-5, also appears when you press Ctrl+N or click the New button on the toolbar.

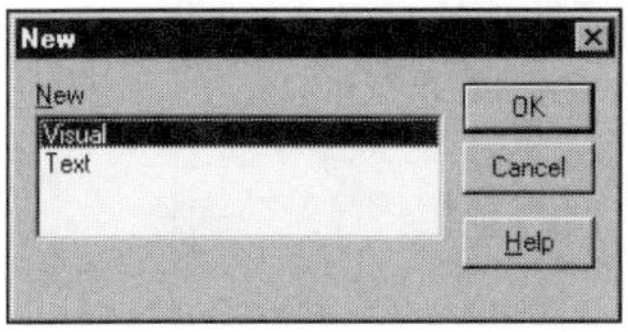

Figure 12-5 The New dialog box gives you the option of opening a project or a text file.

OPEN

Choosing File → Open — the equivalent of the Ctrl+O shortcut and the Open toolbar button — calls the standard File Open dialog box. You can use File → Open to retrieve saved projects.

CLOSE

The File → Close command is what you use when you're done playing with a project and want to move on to a new toy. File → Close shuts down only the current project — if you have several projects going, it will only close the active one. If you haven't saved the active project before you choose File → Close command, Visual Café will prompt you to save your work before closing.

SAVE

The File → Save command writes the active project — and only the active project — to disk. You should save frequently — you can do the job quickly with the Ctrl+S shortcut or the Save toolbar button — to protect your work. The first time you save a project, File → Save has the same effect as File → Save As.

SAVE AS

The File → Save As command enables you to save the active project under a new name via the standard Save As dialog box.

SAVE ALL

With the File → Save All command, you can quickly write all open projects to disk. This is handy if you happen to note an approaching thunderstorm or your network administrator announces impending server doom. If any of the open projects haven't been saved before you choose the File → Save All command, you'll see a Save As dialog box for those projects.

ENVIRONMENT OPTIONS

The File → Environment Options command displays the Environment Options dialog box — shown in Figure 12-6 — that you can use to adjust the behavior of Visual Café to your liking. With the multitabbed dialog box, you can exercise your whim over such things as what font Visual Café uses to display source code, which keys have special hot key functions, and how often the development environment saves your work automatically.

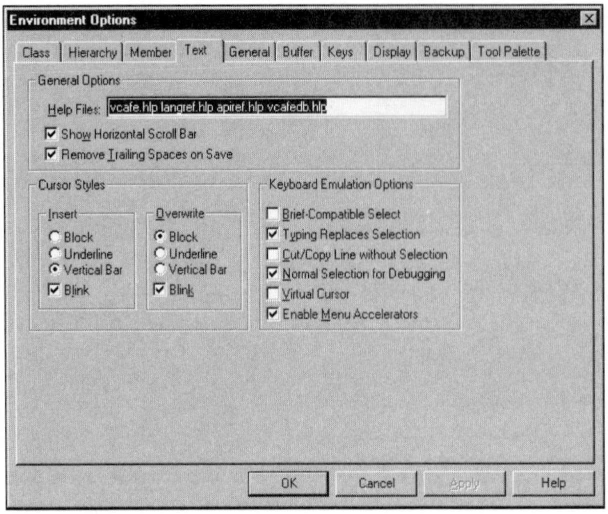

Figure 12-6 The Environment Options dialog box lets you configure Visual Café.

PRINT SETUP

The File→Print Setup command calls up the standard Print Setup dialog box, which you can use to select and adjust your printer.

PRINT

The File→Print command displays the standard Print dialog box in preparation for sending the contents of the active window to the printer. In the Print dialog box you can specify how many copies to print and call the Print Setup dialog box, if needed. The shortcut Ctrl+P is equivalent to the Print menu command, while the Print toolbar button prints directly, without showing the Print dialog box.

RECENT PROJECTS

The numbered recent projects provide you with a quick way to access the files you've had open most recently. You can select with your mouse the project you want from the File menu or enter the number of the file you want to open.

RECENT SOURCE CODE REFERENCES

Below the listing of recent project files used, you'll see some more numbered file listings. These are files containing Java source code that you've accessed recently. To reopen a source file in the menu, you can either select it with your mouse or enter its number.

EXIT

The File → Exit command bids *adiós* to Visual Café. If you haven't saved one or more open files before choosing this command, the development environment will prompt you to save them first.

Edit

The Edit menu, like the File menu, appears everywhere in the graphical user interface universe. It contains a collection of familiar tools for manipulating text. The Edit menu appears in Figure 12-7.

TIP **Only the Delete and Select All commands appear in the Edit menu in the Debug workspace. In order to use the others you have to be in the Edit workspace.**

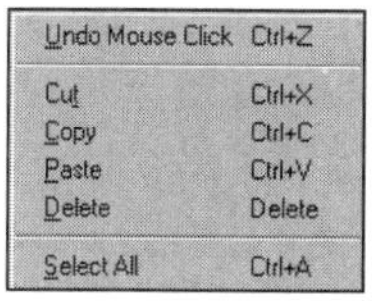

Figure 12-7 The Edit menu contains commands for cutting, pasting, and correcting mistakes.

UNDO

The Edit → Undo command cancels the last operation made. You may want to use Undo if you accidentally copy something to the clipboard, for instance. Ctrl+Z is the keyboard shortcut for Undo.

REDO

The Edit → Redo command is an undo command for the Undo command. Redo redoes whatever action you last canceled with the Edit → Undo. Ctrl+Y is the keyboard shortcut for Redo.

CUT

The Edit → Cut command removes a selected item from your screen and stores it in the Clipboard. You can reinsert it anywhere you like with the Edit → Paste command. Ctrl+X is the keyboard shortcut for Cut and, as you can see, there's a Cut toolbar button, too.

COPY

The Edit → Copy command stores a selected item in the Clipboard, but does not remove it from your screen. You can reinsert the copied item anywhere you like with the Edit → Paste command. Ctrl+C is the keyboard shortcut for Copy, and there's a toolbar button, too.

PASTE

The Edit → Paste command inserts the contents of the Clipboard at the cursor location or other insertion point. Use Ctrl+V or the Paste toolbar button to access Paste quickly.

DELETE

The Edit → Delete command removes a selected item without copying it to the Clipboard. The Delete key has the same function as the Edit → Delete menu command. You can only undo a deletion with the Edit → Undo command or, if the deletion was your most recent action, with the Undo button on the toolbar.

SELECT ALL

The Edit → Select All command, which you can invoke easily with the Ctrl+A shortcut, highlights or selects every editable object in the active window. In the source code editor, for example, the Select All command highlights all the code for easy manipulation, such as copying to an electronic mail message.

Search

The Search menu contains commands for locating things in Java programs. The Search menu appears in Figure 12-8.

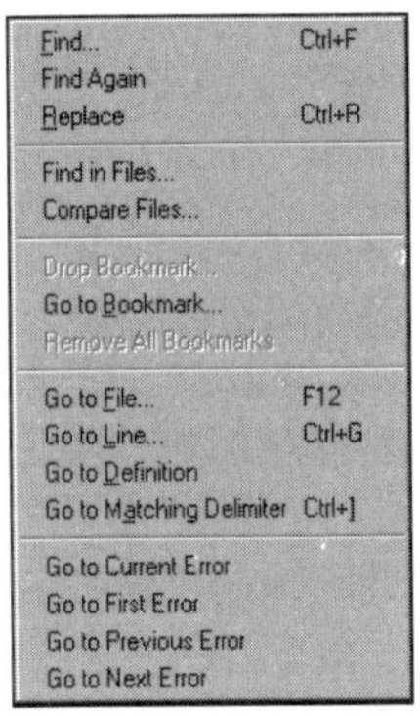

Figure 12-8 The Search menu offers your choices for finding what you need quickly.

FIND

The Search → Find command displays the Find dialog box, shown in Figure 12-9. Use the Find dialog box to specify a series of characters for the program to locate. You can also press Ctrl+F to invoke the Find command.

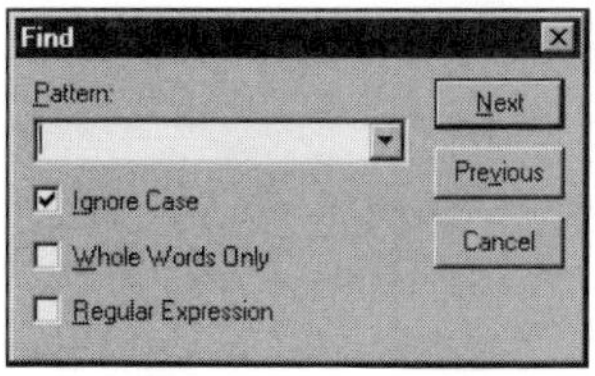

Figure 12-9 The Find dialog box lets you specify text to locate.

FIND AGAIN

Use the Search→Find Again command to search again for the pattern you specified in the Find dialog box.

REPLACE

The Search→Replace command displays a dialog box (shown in Figure 12-10) that allows you to find all instances of a specified pattern (such as a word or series of words) and replace them all with another pattern. Use Ctrl+R as a keyboard shortcut to the Replace dialog box.

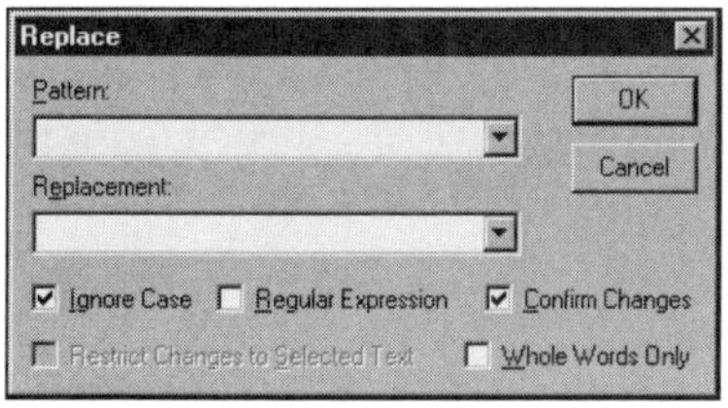

Figure 12-10 The Replace dialog box lets you specify text that needs to be replaced — and the new text that will replace it.

FIND IN FILES

This handy feature of Visual Café helps you find the &*!$% snippet of code you saw last week — somewhere — and need right bloody now! With the Global Find dialog box, shown in Figure 12-11, you can specify search terms that include:

- What a file is named
- When it was modified last
- What specific strings it contains

You can also narrow your search by limiting second and third searches to the results of earlier searches.

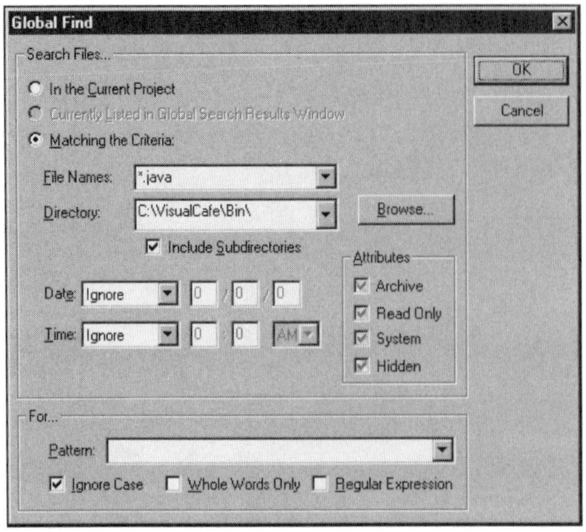

Figure 12-11 The Global Find dialog box tells the search engine what to find.

COMPARE FILES

Choosing **Search** → **Compare Files** opens the Compare Files dialog box, in which you can specify two source code files for comparison. Visual Café tells you if the two files are identical or not.

DROP BOOKMARK

The **Search** → **Drop Bookmark** command inserts a bookmark — a marked place that you can find again easily — at the location of the cursor. Bookmarks come in handy in very large source code files, in which scrolling up and down can quickly become a serious pain.

GO TO BOOKMARK

The **Search** → **Go To Bookmark** command displays a dialog box containing all the bookmarks in place in the current project. You can choose one from the list and the source code editor will home in on the bookmarked location.

REMOVE ALL BOOKMARKS

The **Search** → **Remove All Bookmarks** command does exactly what you'd expect — it clears all bookmarks you've set in the active project.

GO TO FILE

The **Search** → **Go To File** command displays any of the files involved in the current project.

GO TO LINE

The Search → Go To Line command takes you to a line number you specify in the open source code file.

GO TO DEFINITION

The Search → Go To Definition command opens the Class Browser to the definition of the class or method you've highlighted in the source code editor. The class can be part of the Java API or a class defined elsewhere.

GO TO MATCHING DELIMITER

The Search → Go To Matching Delimiter command works only when you have the cursor on a parenthesis, bracket, or brace in the source code editor. The command takes you to the complementary delimiter — the "}" that matches the "{", or the "(" that matches the ")".

GO TO CURRENT ERROR

The Search → Go To Current Error command takes you to the point in the source code at which the current error is happening. 12

GO TO FIRST ERROR

The Search → Go To First Error command takes you to the point in the source code at which the first error listed in the Messages window is happening.

GO TO PREVIOUS ERROR

The Search → Go To Previous Error command takes you to the point in the source code at which the error before the current one is happening.

GO TO NEXT ERROR

The Search → Go To Next Error command takes you to the point in the source code at which the error after the current one is happening.

Project

The Project menu contains all commands relating to Visual Café projects generally — commands that have to do with turning source code into interpretable files. Figure 12-12 shows the Project menu.

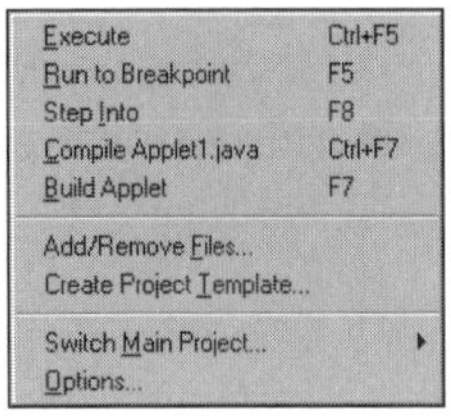

Figure 12-12 The Project menu contains commands that affect the project as a whole.

EXECUTE

The Project→Execute command (also accessible via its keyboard shortcut, Ctrl+F5) compiles your applet or application and begins running it in the Applet Viewer window, as shown in Figure 12-13. Run executes your program without stopping (unless you've set breakpoints or have made a programming error).

Compare the Project→Execute command to the Step Into and Build commands in the next sections. You can also run, pause, and stop your code with the corresponding toolbar buttons, which look like the controls for a tape deck or CD player.

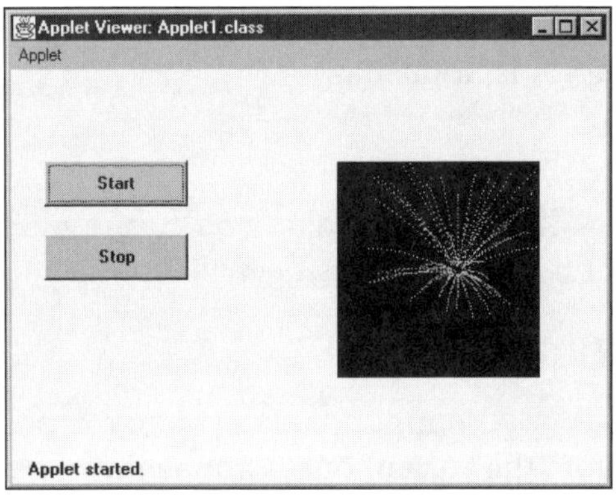

Figure 12-13 The Applet Viewer window displays applets without a complete Web browser.

RUN TO BREAKPOINT

The Project→Run To Breakpoint command tells your program to compile and run until it encounters a breakpoint. You'll learn a lot more about this command and Visual Café's related tools in Chapter 18, "Using the Visual Debugging Tools."

STEP INTO

Like the Project→Execute command, Project→Step Into compiles your source code. Instead of executing the compiled program straight through, however, Step Into runs the program one line at a time so you can see what's going on and catch errors. You also can use the Step Into toolbar button.

COMPILE

The **Project** → **Compile** command creates a .class file for the current source code file only, not for the entire project.

BUILD APPLET/APPLICATION

The **Project** → **Build Applet/Application** command (it shows up as **Compile Applet** when a Java applet is the current project and as **Compile Application** when a Java application is the current project) compiles your project, but doesn't execute it. You might use **Build** in order to test your work outside the Visual Café environment, or to generate a final release of your work.

ADD/REMOVE FILES

The **Project** → **Add/Remove Files** command calls up the Add/Remove Files dialog box, shown in Figure 12-14. With the dialog box you can define which files are part of the main project.

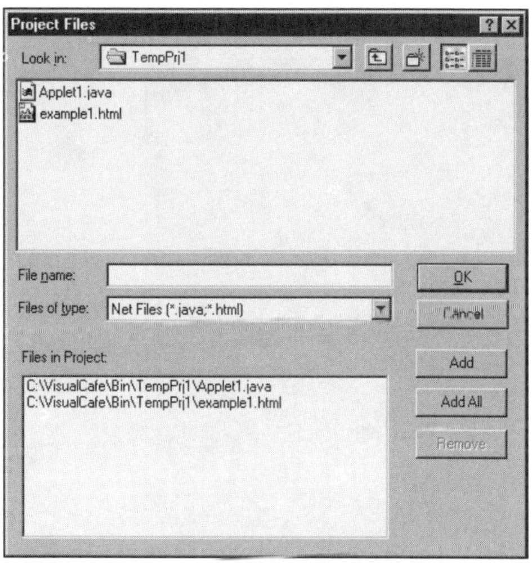

Figure 12-14 Use the Add/Remove Files dialog box to add source code files to your project.

CREATE PROJECT TEMPLATE

The **Project** → **Create Project Template** command saves the main project as a new template file, which, if you want, can be made to appear in the New Project dialog box you learned about earlier in this chapter.

SWITCH MAIN PROJECT

The **Project** → **Switch Main Project** command lets you choose which open project gets compiled and run by the **Project** menu commands. When you let your mouse pointer linger on the Switch Main Project command, a list of open projects will appear to the right of the **Project** menu, with a bullet next to the current main project. Select the project you want to make the main project.

TIP **Remember, the main project is the project that compiles when you issue the Run or Build command.**

OPTIONS

This **Project** → **Options** command, which you should be careful not to confuse with the **File** → **Environment Options** command, deals with options that relate only to the main project. Environment Options, you may recall, deals with global Visual Café settings. Through the tabbed Options dialog box, shown in Figure 12-15, you can define such things as:

* Whether Visual Café should compile for debugging or release purposes
* Whether Visual Café should use its own compiler or the standard Sun Microsystems Java compiler
* How Visual Café deals with compiler error messages
* Where Visual Café saves files

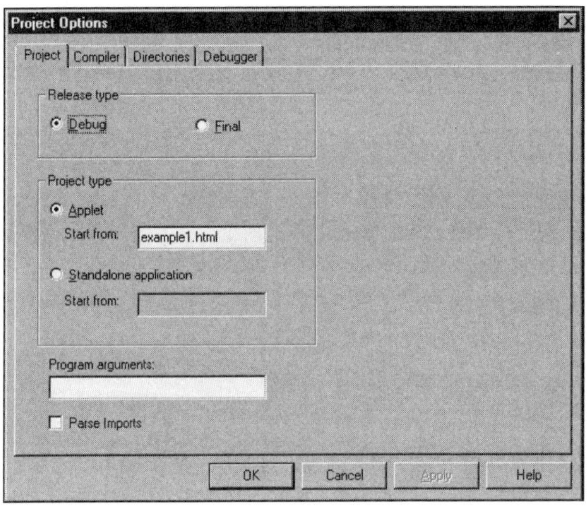

Figure 12-15 The Options dialog box helps you set preferences that relate to the main project.

Insert

The **Insert** menu contains commands you use to add items to the current project. With the **Insert** menu, you can insert the framework for an applet, an organizational folder in the Project Window or the Component Library, or a form, which is a piece of screen real estate — such as a dialog box — on which you can place buttons, text boxes, and other controls.

The Insert menu appears in Figure 12-16.

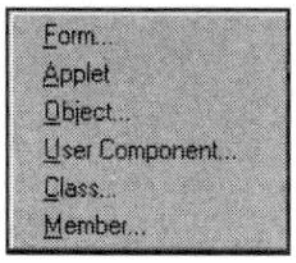

Figure 12-16 The Insert menu makes it easy to add elements to your project.

FORM

The Insert→Form command displays the Form Templates dialog box, shown in Figure 12-17, with which you can insert a new form — such as a dialog box or window — into the main project. You can then make reference to the form from the application or applet you're coding.

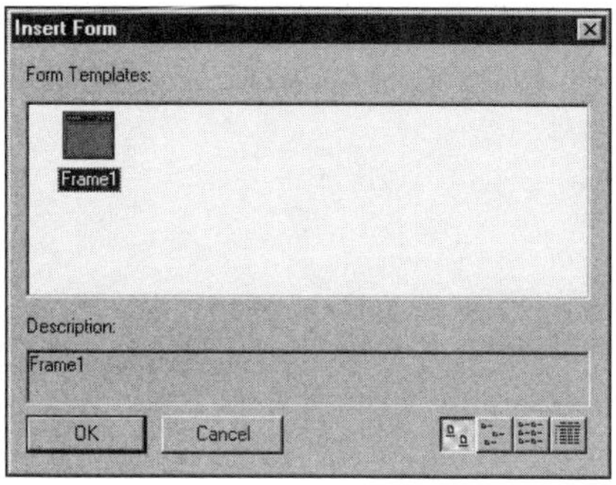

Figure 12-17 The Form Templates dialog box can assist you in adding windows to a project.

APPLET

The Insert→Applet command displays the Applet Templates dialog box, shown in Figure 12-18, with which you can insert an applet into the main project. You can then make reference to the applet and its contents from the application or applet you're coding.

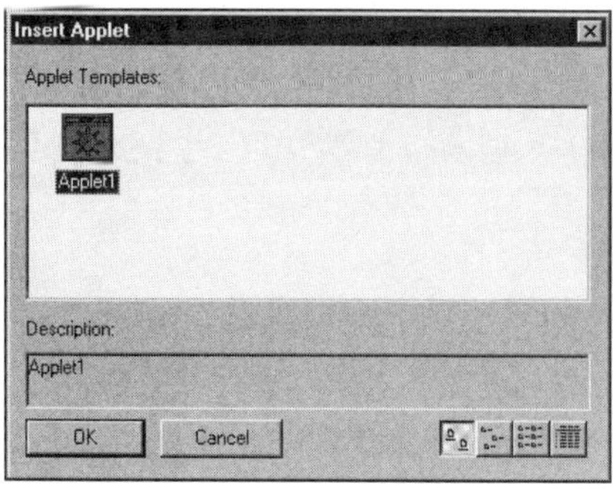

Figure 12-18 The Applet Templates dialog box lets you insert a complete applet into your project.

OBJECT

Because Java is an object-oriented language, and forms and applets are kinds of objects, the Insert→Object command is a sort of catch-all insertion command.

Via the Insert Object dialog box, shown in Figure 12-19, you can add any object — including forms and applets — to the main project.

TIP **If you don't want to use the Interaction Wizard — a Visual Café feature you'll learn about in Chapter 15, "Using the Interaction Wizard" — you may find the Object command especially handy for inserting event handlers.**

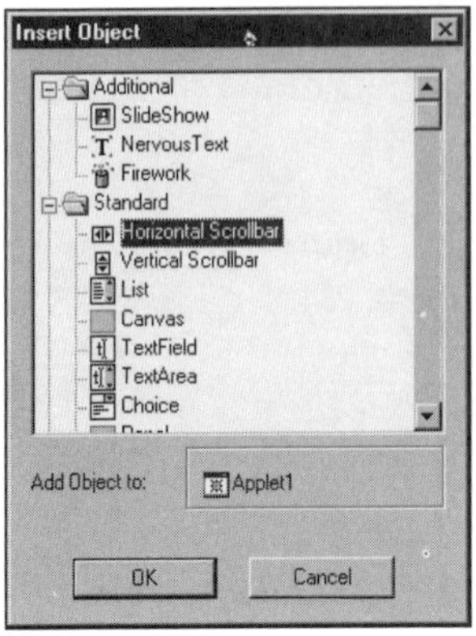

Figure 12-19 The Insert Object dialog box is a general-purpose insertion command.

USER COMPONENT

The Insert → User Component command lets you insert a Java component — such as a Java Bean-compliant piece of code — into the current project.

CLASS

The Insert → Class command inserts a Java class into the current project, so you can call it from other classes.

MEMBER

The Insert → Member command adds a new method or data item to a class that's displayed in the Class Browser.

Object

The Object menu, shown in Figure 12-20, contains all commands that relate to manipulating objects. When you want to work with the guts of one of your project's component objects, head for the Object menu.

TIP **Most of the Object menu commands also appear when you right-click (or long-click, for Mac users) an object. This way of accessing commands is often faster than going through the menu bar.**

Figure 12-20 The **Object** menu gives you access to the Form Editor, the source code editor, and the Interaction Wizard.

EDIT APPLET

The **Object** → **Edit Applet** command brings forward the Form Editor, enabling you to work with the objects it contains.

EDIT SOURCE

Also accessible via the Ctrl+Shift+S keyboard shortcut, the **Object** → **Edit Source** command brings up an editor window that contains the source code for the selected object. The editing window, shown in Figure 12-21, is where you'll do your manual code writing in Visual Café.

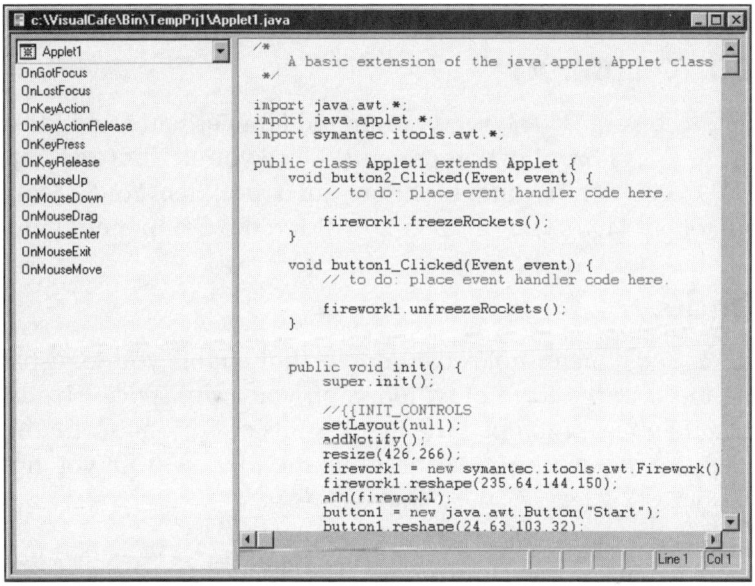

Figure 12-21 The Visual Café source code editor is where you'll do most of your Visual Café work.

ADD INTERACTION

The **Object** → **Add Interaction** command conjures up the Interaction Wizard, a handy, time-saving feature of Visual Café that you can see for yourself in Figure 12-22. The Interaction Wizard automates the process of defining how objects interact with one another. More specifically, it's useful for defining the behaviors you want to occur in the case of certain events, such as a mouse click.

You'll learn all about the Interaction Wizard in Chapter 15, "Using the Interaction Wizard."

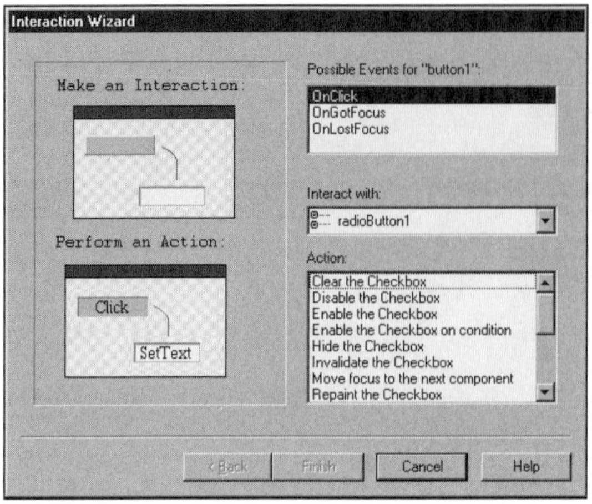

Figure 12-22 The Interaction Wizard makes creating simple event handlers even easier.

ADD TO LIBRARY

The Object → Add To Library command enables you to add the selected component to your library of components. Once you do that the object will be available to you for adding to future Java projects. You'll learn all about the Component Library in Chapter 20, "Using the Component Library."

Window

The Window menu holds commands that enable you to display certain Visual Café tools, in the form of windows, in your workspace. Head for the Window menu if you want to open the Breakpoints or Variables windows, or if you want to define a new workspace containing the windows that you have opened.

Figure 12-23 shows the Window menu.

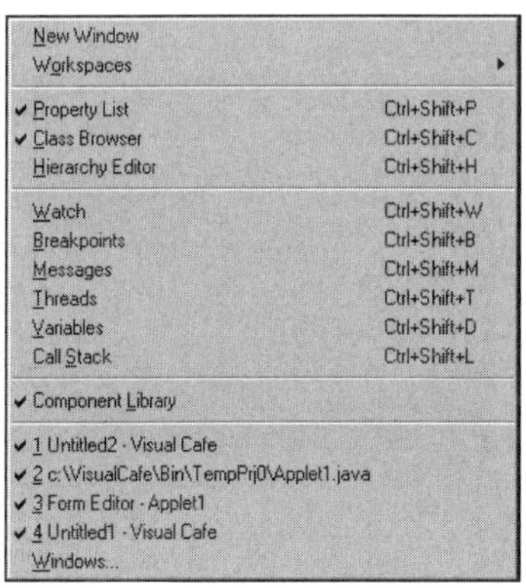

Figure 12-23 The Window menu is one way to open many of Visual Café's debugging windows.

NEW WINDOW

The Window → New Window command creates a new instance of the active window.

WORKSPACES

The commands that fly out to the right of the Workspaces menu item allow you to switch among workspaces to create, rename, and delete workspaces.

EDIT

By selecting Window → Workspaces → Edit, you switch to the Edit workspace.

DEBUG

By selecting Window → Workspaces → Debug, you switch to the Debug workspace.

NEW

Selecting Window → Workspaces → New enables you to define the current workspace — all the windows you have open at the time you select Workspaces New — as a workspace to be added to the list. Visual Café prompts you for a name for the new workspace with the New Workspace dialog box, shown in Figure 12-24.

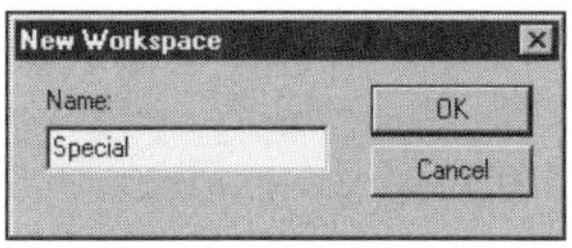

Figure 12-24 The New Workspace dialog box is where you give a name to a newly defined workspace.

RENAME

Selecting Window → Workspaces → Rename calls up the Rename Workspace dialog box. This dialog box looks just like the New Workspace dialog box and prompts you for a new name for the current workspace.

DELETE

Selecting Window → Workspaces → Delete removes the current workspace from Visual Café's list of workspaces.

TIP **Be aware that Visual Café doesn't prompt you before deleting the current workspace — it just does the job.**

PROPERTY LIST

The Window → Property List command displays the Property List window, shown in Figure 12-25. Use the Property List to examine and modify the properties of the selected item — in this case, an item is anything that can be displayed in a window. For example, you might select a list box and use the Property List to define what items appear in the list. You can also call up the Property List with its toolbar button or with the Ctrl+Shift+P keyboard shortcut.

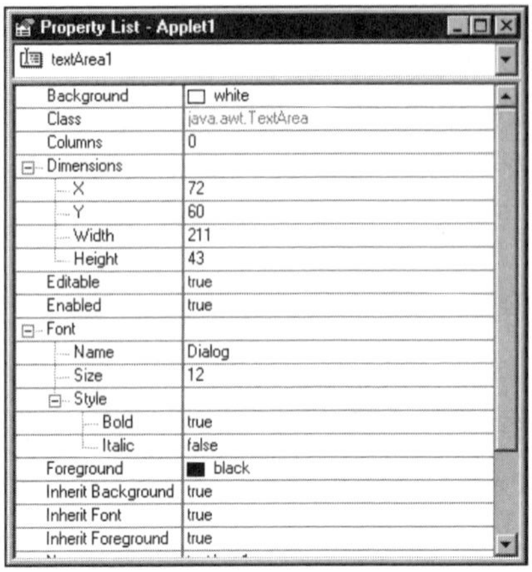

Figure 12-25 The Property List tells the whole truth about the selected object.

CLASS BROWSER

The Window → Class Browser command displays the Class Browser window, shown in Figure 12-26. Use the Class Browser to see the classes contained in an applet, application, or library file, then drag the needed class names into your source code editor. It's an easy way to insert classes without worrying about typing mistakes. You can also call up the Class Browser with its toolbar button or with the Ctrl+Shift+C keyboard shortcut.

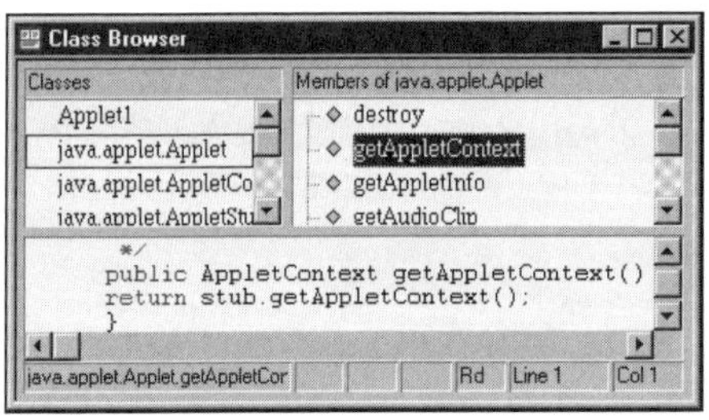

Figure 12-26 The Class Browser shows all the classes involved in a project.

HIERARCHY EDITOR

Use the Window → Hierarchy Editor command to open the Hierarchy Editor, shown in Figure 12-27. The Hierarchy Editor gives you a flowchart-like look at the classes in the current applet or application, and allows you to modify the relationships of classes you've created with your mouse. You can also call up the Hierarchy Editor with its toolbar button or with the Ctrl+Shift+H keyboard shortcut.

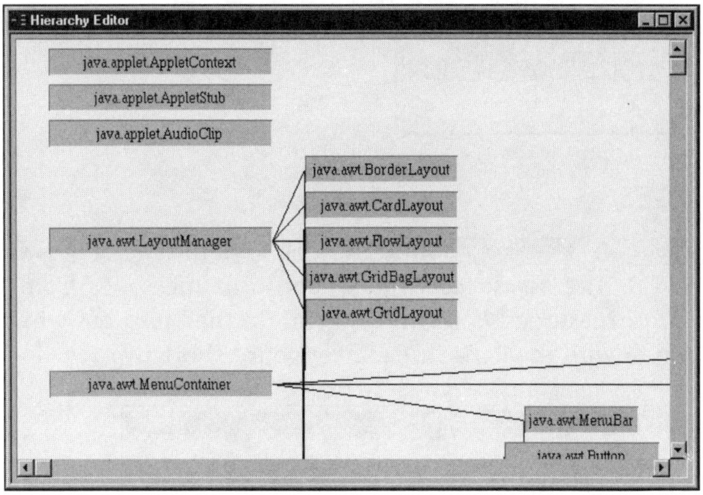

Figure 12-27 The Hierarchy Editor shows the structure of a Java program.

WATCH

The Window → Watch command opens the Watch window, shown in Figure 12-28. With the Watch window, you can monitor the contents of variables as your program executes. Usually, you'll use the Watch window in conjunction with breakpoints, so you can see what your variables are doing at critical points in your program's execution. You can also call up the Watch window with its toolbar button or with the Ctrl+Shift+W keyboard shortcut.

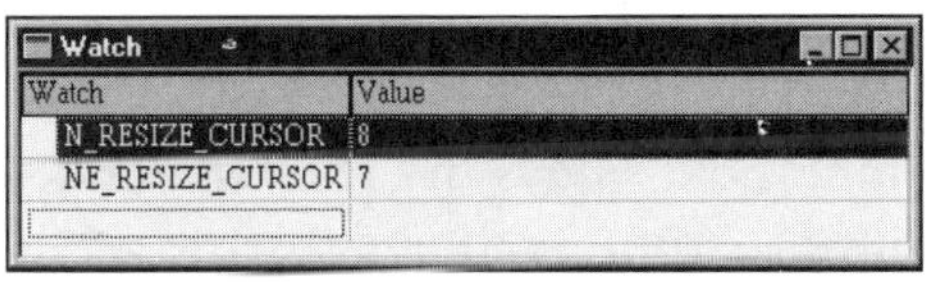

Figure 12-28 The Watch window monitors specific variables in an executing program.

BREAKPOINTS

The Window → Breakpoints command displays the Breakpoints window, shown in Figure 12-29, which lists the breakpoints you've established. Breakpoints are places at which program execution stops to allow you to examine what's going on. You can also call up the Breakpoints window with the toolbar button featuring a waving flag or with the Ctrl+Shift+B keyboard shortcut. You'll learn all about breakpoints and other debugging tools in Chapter 18, "Using the Visual Debugging Tools."

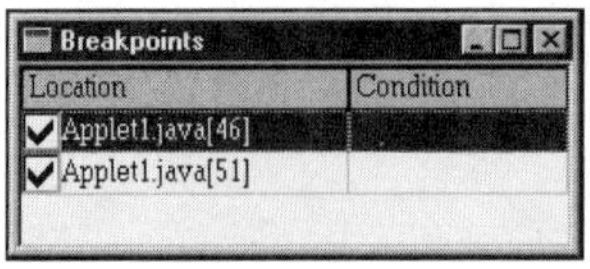

Figure 12-29 The Breakpoints window lists the pause points in a project.

MESSAGES

The Window → Messages command displays the Messages window, shown in Figure 12-30. The Messages window contains messages from the compiler — notably error messages. You can also call up the Messages window with its toolbar button or with the Ctrl+Shift+M keyboard shortcut.

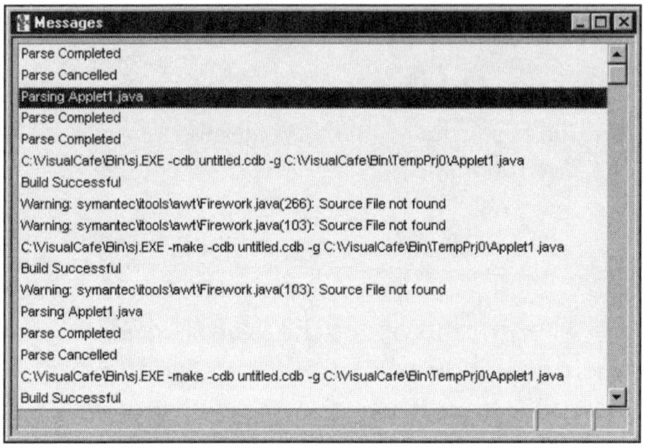

Figure 12-30 The compiler communicates with you via the Messages window.

THREADS

The Window → Threads command displays the Threads window, which lists all the threads executing in your program. A thread, by the way, is a sequence of execution — you might have two threads going simultaneously, such as one saving a file and one handling mouse events. The Threads window appears in Figure 12-31. You can also call up the Threads window with its toolbar button or with the Ctrl+Shift+T keyboard shortcut.

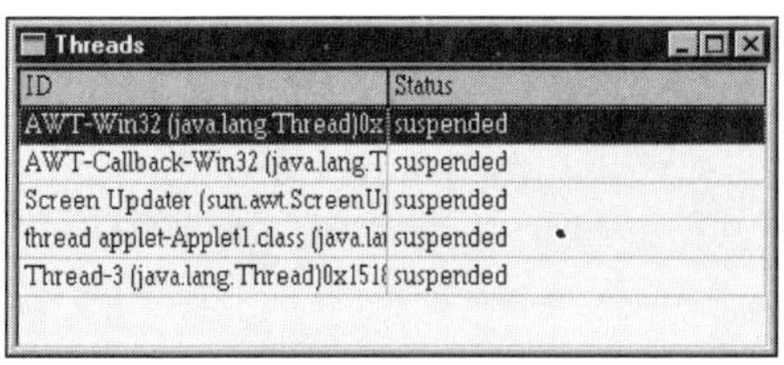

Figure 12-31 The Threads window tracks several paths of execution for debugging purposes.

VARIABLES

The **Window** → **Variables** command displays the Variables window, which displays the contents of specified variables in real time. The Variables window, which appears in Figure 12-32, is often best used with Visual Café's Breakpoints feature. You can also call up the Variables window with its toolbar button or with the Ctrl+Shift+D keyboard shortcut.

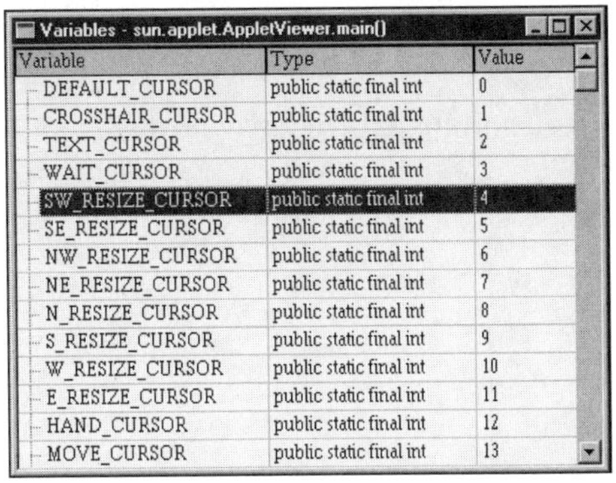

Figure 12-32 The Variables window displays all active variables.

TIP **The Watch window and the Variables window are two different animals, yet you use the Watch Variables command to add a variable to the Variables window.**

What's the difference between the Watch window and the Variables window? It's an issue of selectivity. The Watch window displays the name and value of all variables that the executing program is using at the moment. The Variables window displays only the values of the variables you specify with the Watch Variables command.

CALL STACK

The **Window** → **Call Stack** command displays the Call window, shown in Figure 12-33. In the Call window you can monitor which methods are being executed at the moment. You can also call up the Call window with its toolbar button or with the Ctrl+Shift+L keyboard shortcut.

Figure 12-33 The Call window shows which objects are referring to other objects at run time.

COMPONENT LIBRARY

The Window → Component Library command displays the Component Library window, from which you can drag archived forms (a form, remember, is a piece of screen real estate, such as a window) or components (such as buttons and list boxes) into your current coding project. The Component Library serves as a handy way to organize the bits and pieces you assemble into applications and applets.

Because you can add your own contributions to the Component Library, it becomes a repository of things you've created with Java — making it that much easier to expand upon past work.

Figure 12-34 shows the Component Library window.

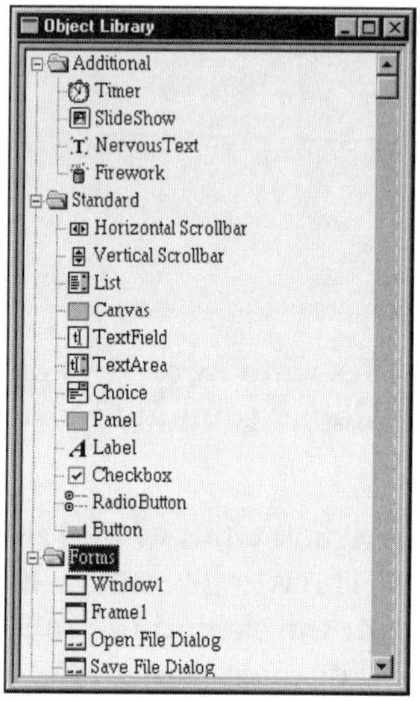

Figure 12-34 The Component Library window shows pieces of Java you've stored for later use.

Help

Turn to the Help menu if you're stuck with a Visual Café problem...but only if you don't have *Discover Visual Café* handy, of course! Figure 12-35 shows the Help menu.

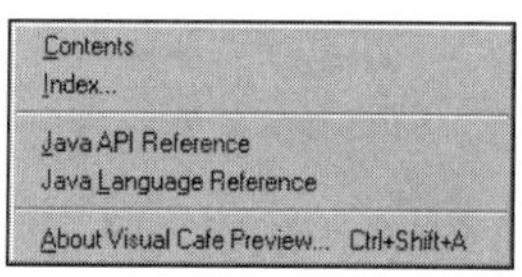

Figure 12-35 The Help menu is where you turn for assistance.

CONTENTS

The Help → Contents command displays in outline form the topics covered by the Visual Café help files. You can type search terms in the text box at the top of the window or you can scroll through the list in search of the help you need.

INDEX

The Help → Index command calls up a utility that searches the Visual Café help files for a keyword you specify. You also can click the Help toolbar button and then click an on-screen item whose purpose you don't understand.

JAVA API REFERENCE

The Help → Java API Reference command displays documentation on the Java Application Program Interface — the Java language itself — in hyperlinked form.

JAVA LANGUAGE REFERENCE

The Help → Java Language Reference command opens a hypertext tutorial in Java syntax and structure.

ABOUT VISUAL CAFÉ

The Help → About Visual Café command displays Visual Café's About dialog box, which gives you information about your version of Visual Café and Symantec. You can also open the About dialog box by clicking the About toolbar button or with the Ctrl+Shift+A keyboard shortcut.

BONUS

Other Toolbar Buttons

There are still other buttons on the toolbar, all of which relate to objects you can attach to forms. This section describes those buttons and their functions.

All of the remaining buttons reside on the Palette toolbar, which has six tabbed sections.

TIP **You can add buttons to and remove buttons from the various tabs by right-clicking (or long-clicking, if you're on a Mac) and choosing Customize Palette from the pop-up menu.**

Standard Tab

The Standard tab holds all the objects you expect to find in a standard graphical user interface, including list boxes, radio buttons, text areas, and buttons. To use the objects, click the button corresponding to the object you want, then drag out a region for the object in the Form Editor. Don't worry about precise sizing and alignment — you can adjust that later. Figure 12-36 shows the Standard tab.

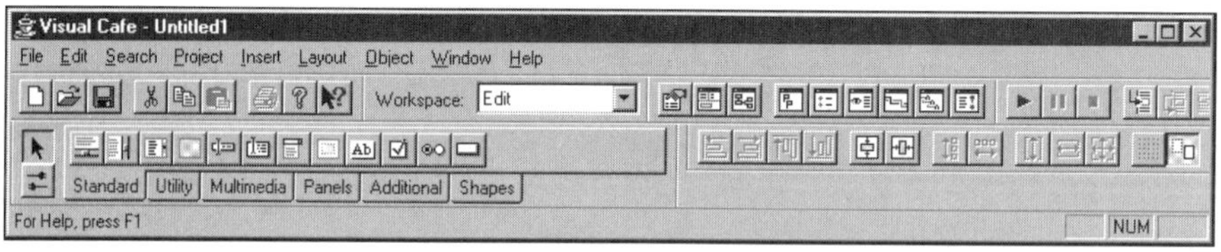

Figure 12-36 The Palette toolbar's Standard tab contains popular interface elements.

Utility Tab

The Utility tab contains things that aren't standard controls, but which give information to the user. The Utility tab contains a calendar component, a timer component and a status bar. Figure 12-37 shows the Utility tab.

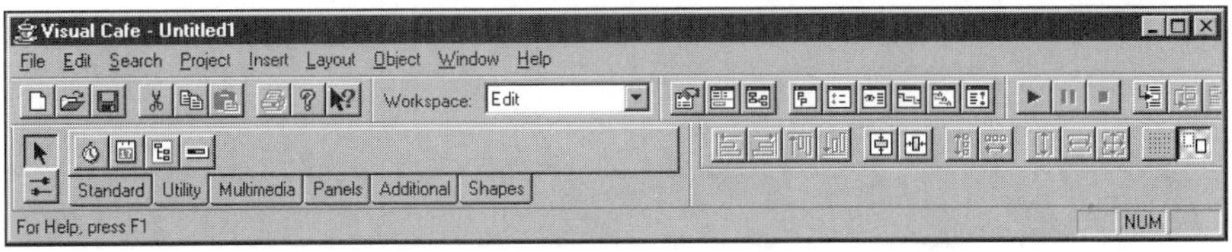

Figure 12-37 The Palette toolbar's Utility tab contains such coolness as a calendar and a timer.

Multimedia Tab

The Multimedia tab contains tools that bring animation to your applets. Here, you'll find the Slide Show component, which rotates through a series of images, and the Sound Player component, which does exactly what you'd think. Figure 12-38 shows the Multimedia tab.

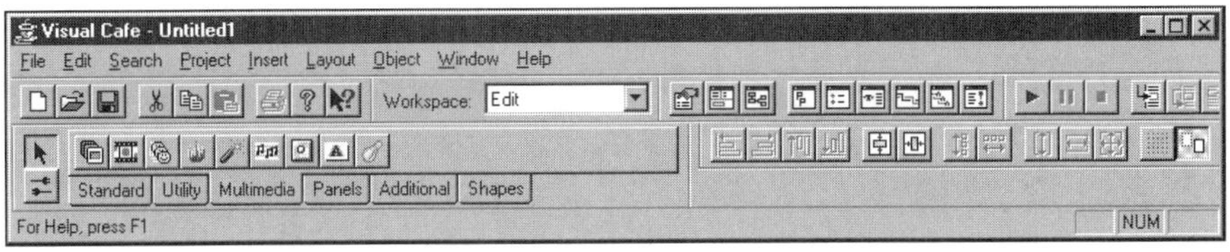

Figure 12-38 The Palette toolbar's Multimedia tab helps you add motion to your applets and applications.

Panels Tab

The Panels tab contains all sorts of layout patterns on which you can arrange components. You'll find a Tabs panel, which will organize your components into tabbed "pages," and a Toolbar panel, which will organize buttons into an easy-to-use toolbar. The Panels tab appears in Figure 12-39.

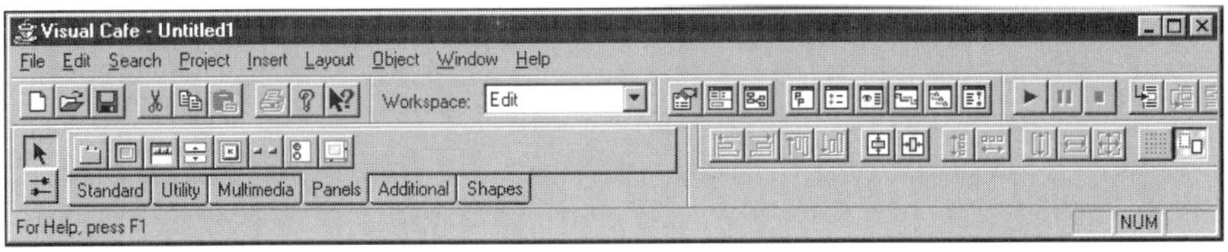

Figure 12-39 The Panels tab contains frames you can use to organize components.

Additional Tab

The Additional tab holds miscellaneous stuff — objects you may need to use now and then, but not as frequently as items on the other tabs. The Additional tab is loaded with spinners, special buttons and a component that embeds an invisible HTML link in your document. Figure 12-40 shows the Additional tab.

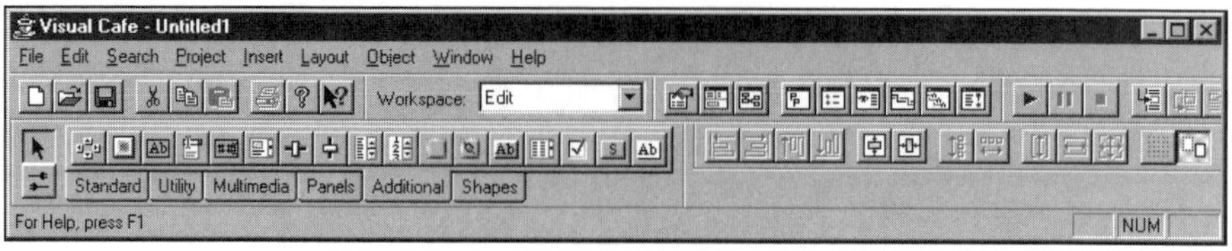

Figure 12-40 The Palette toolbar's Additional tab contains dials, spinners, and miscellaneous goodies.

Shapes Tab

Often, you'll want to surround components with borders, such as an engraved rectangle or an embossed oval. The Shapes tab contains several borders you can use to organize your components. On the Shapes tab, you'll find squares, rectangles, circles, and lines, all of which can be made to appear embossed or recessed by adjusting properties with the Property List.

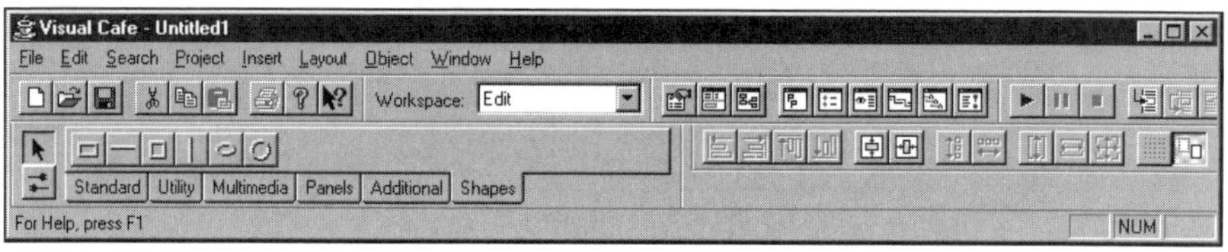

Figure 12-41 The Shapes tab lets you surround components with attractive borders.

Summary

Now you know that Visual Café has lots of menu commands and toolbar buttons, each of which serves a specific purpose. In addition, you know that often there's both a toolbar button and a menu command for a given purpose. You're also familiar with the various Visual Café windows — those that are used for writing programs as well as those used to find and correct problems in programs you've written.

This chapter introduced you to all the major commands in the Visual Café interface, but there's much more information to come. In Chapter 13, "Building a User Interface," you'll get the complete scoop on the Form Editor. In Chapter 14, "Tweaking Components with the Property List," you'll learn how to adjust components in the Form Editor with the Property List. Subsequent chapters will explain how to use the Interaction Wizard and source code editor to make those components do exactly what you want.

CHAPTER THIRTEEN

BUILDING A USER INTERFACE

IN THIS CHAPTER YOU LEARN THESE KEY SKILLS

One of Visual Café's most intuitive features is the Form Designer, the programming tool you use to arrange text boxes, buttons, check boxes, and other components on the user's screen. Using the Form Designer you can define your interface graphically, with your mouse, without having to diddle with code (although Visual Café allows you easy access to the code behind your interface, if you want to work with it).

In conjunction with the Form Designer, you'll use the Property List to set the characteristics of the components you create. With the Property List, you can do such things as determine the text that appears on the face of a button, the items that appear in a list box, or the color of a text area. Though using the Property List is a little bit less intuitive than using the Form Designer, you can quickly learn to make it do your bidding. *Discover Visual Café* will help you.

This chapter walks you through the process of creating a user interface with the Form Designer — but only on the surface. You'll learn all about fine-tuning your interface components with the Property List in the next chapter. In Chapter 15, "Using the Interaction Wizard," you'll get your components to actually do things with the help of the truly outstanding Interaction Wizard.

Understanding Containers and Components

Before you get going, madly creating the interface for your Java applet or application with Visual Café's outstanding design tools, you need to gain some familiarity with the generalities of Java interfaces. More specifically, you need to gain an understanding of the terminology Java uses to describe the things that it causes to appear on computer screens.

The user interfaces of Java programs consist of *components* (such as buttons and text fields) that reside in *containers* — pieces of screen real estate. All containers have the parent class `Container`. There are four major containers:

* Panels
* Applets
* Windows
* Frames

Additionally, Java has a Dialog container and a FileDialog container.

Note that an application is not a container. That's because an application isn't visible, and if it's a command-line application, it doesn't need to be. Every application that uses windowing, however, has at least one frame, and frames are containers.

TIP **Like the plastic canisters in which you keep your leftovers, certain Java containers can nest within one another. That's handy when you want different portions of a given piece of screen to behave in different ways. You'll learn more about this in the upcoming sections.**

You'll learn about the four main containers in this section, then move on to the many components that Java supports.

Panels

A *panel* — a member of the `Panel` class — is an area to which special layout rules apply. You'll learn about the details of layout after you familiarize yourself with components, but understand for now that you can have a set of layout rules in an applet or frame in general and another set for the components inside a frame.

Applets

The `Applet` class is a subclass of the `Panel` class.

Applets are panels designed to be embedded in larger frames or Web pages.

That's all they are — just fixed-sized square or rectangular pieces of screen onto which you can place components. You can also nest other panels inside your applet, or cause windows to appear in response to user actions in the applet.

Windows

Members of the `Window` class, *windows* are pieces of screen real estate. Unlike instances of the `Panel` and `Applet` classes, instances of the `Window` class and its subclasses can be made to change size during the execution of an application or applet.

Frames

Frames, members of Java's `Frame` class, which is a subclass of the `Window` class, are the basic containers for components that make up graphical Java applications. Frames are containers that include a title bar and, often, a menu bar. Sometimes, as in the case of frames that contain an entire program, frames can be minimized, maximized, and adjusted to all sizes in between.

TIP **The `Frame` is the only container that can accept a menu bar.**

Creating Components in the Form Designer

To make components appear on the Form Designer — and subsequently on your program's completed user interface — you use your mouse to choose components from the toolbar, then drag out areas for the components to occupy. After getting components to appear on the Form Designer, you can use various sizing and alignment commands to make the components look the way you want. Use the Property List to adjust their details.

The basic steps for installing a component on the Form Designer are as follows:

1. Click the button of the component you want on the toolbar. In this example, we'll click the List Box button. Take a look at Figure 13-1.

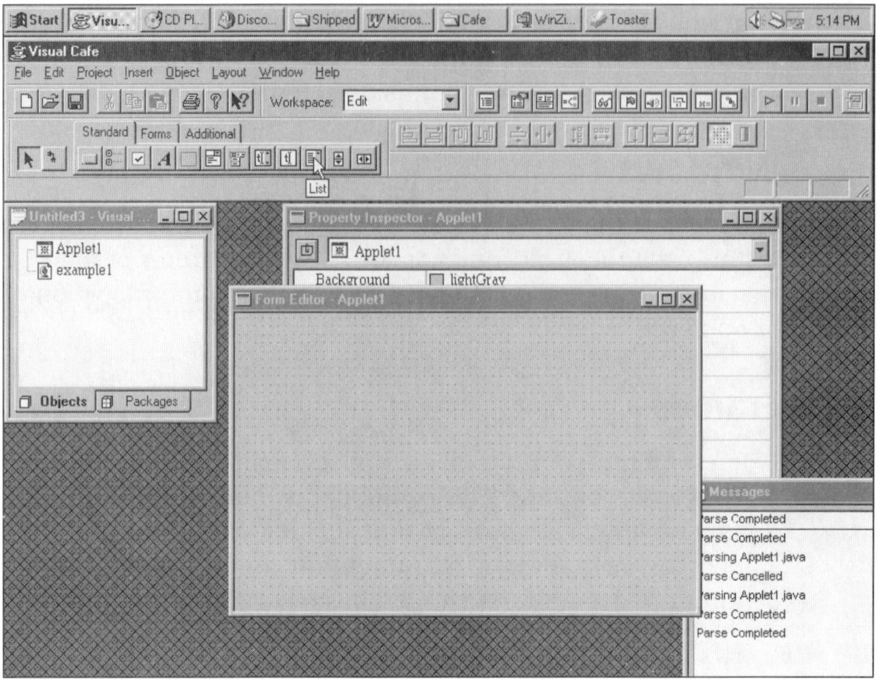

Figure 13-1 To create a list box, click the List Box button on the toolbar.

2. Move your mouse pointer to one of the corners of the component you want to create. Drag the pointer to the opposite corner — from the top-left corner to the bottom-right corner, for example. Your component will appear, as shown in Figure 13-2.

TIP **Don't worry if the component isn't in exactly the right place or isn't precisely the size you want. You'll fine-tune the appearance of your component later. For now, you're just roughing them into place.**

TIP **The Form Designer can display a grid of dots over itself. These dots can help you align components in complex patterns, and most interface designers leave the grid on all the time. Unless you specify otherwise, components will conform to the imaginary lines formed by the grid to help you line things up accurately.**

To adjust the spacing of the dots in the grid, choose Layout → Grid Options from the menu bar. Adjust the horizontal and vertical spacing and click OK.

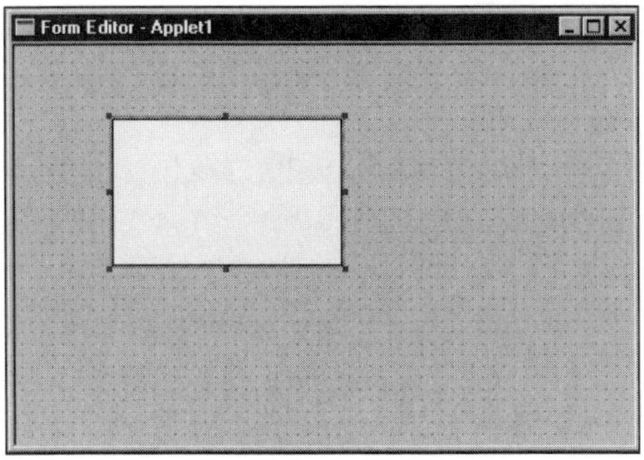

Figure 13-2 Your list box appears in place on the Form Designer.

Understanding Components

You know how to install components, but what in the world are they, anyway? You're probably familiar with buttons and check boxes, but the vagaries of radio buttons and the function of panels may escape you. This section details all the components that Visual Café makes available to you on the toolbar and explains their functions.

Components fall into three categories:

* Controls and displays: Components such as text boxes and buttons.
* Forms: Specially prepared frames, such as those already arranged as familiar dialog boxes.
* Other classes: Individual, utilitarian modules of code that do specific things.

In this chapter you'll learn about the first two kinds of components. The samples of code that come with Visual Café and the reuseable components you create and store in the Component Library fall into the final category.

Controls and Displays

Users will interact with your programs via controls, such as radio buttons and list boxes, while your programs will pass information back to your users by means of displays, such as text fields. Here you'll learn how to use the handiest controls and displays.

TIP **All of the components covered in this section appear on the Standard tab of the Palette toolbar, which you learned about in Chapter 2, "The Java Nickel Tour."**

You'll find out more about the various properties of each of these components in the next chapter. This chapter deals only with the appearance and basic functions of each interface component.

You'll learn about the events that can involve each component — and what we mean by "the events that can involve each component" — in Chapter 15, "Using the Interaction Wizard."

BUTTONS

Ah, the dear old button — the interface component we use most frequently. The most basic dialog boxes have an OK button that you click to make the dialog box go away. Use a button when you want something to happen immediately after the user clicks. Usually, a button makes a dialog box appear or disappear, or causes a calculation or other computer action to take place.

TIP **Creating a button with the Form Designer is the same as creating a new instance of the Button class by entering:**

```
Button1= new java.awt.Button ( ) ;
```

in your code, where Button1 is the variable name of the new instance of the `Button` **class.**

Figure 13-3 shows a button.

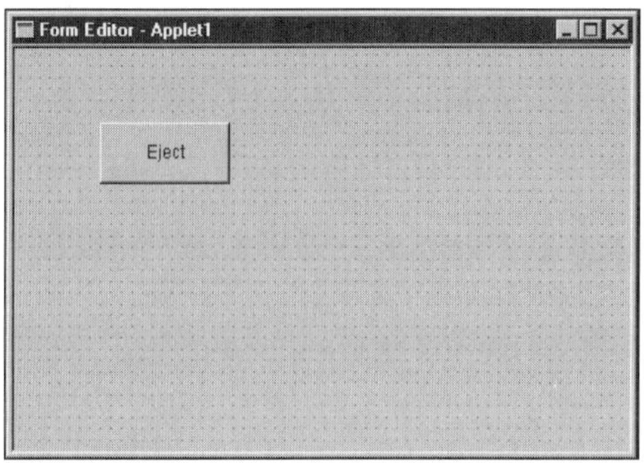

Figure 13-3 A button can be used to initiate actions.

OPTION SELECTORS

This section covers check boxes and their cousins, radio buttons. You'll use these two kinds of components to enable your programs' users to make decisions about the way your applets and applications perform tasks.

Check Boxes

Your users will use check boxes, like radio buttons, to make choices. The difference is that check boxes are not mutually exclusive — you can check more than one check box at a given time. Check boxes usually set a single boolean variable, as in the case of a "Match Case" check box, in which a single check box is either checked or unchecked. Sometimes check boxes swim in schools, but in those situations, each check box operates independently of the others.

TIP **Creating a check box with the Form Designer is the same as creating a new instance of the `Checkbox` class by entering:**

```
checkbox1 = new java.awt.Checkbox ( ) ;
```

in your code, where `checkbox1` is the variable name of the new instance of the `Checkbox` class. You can adjust the details of the check box's implementation with the Property List.

Figure 13-4 shows a check box.

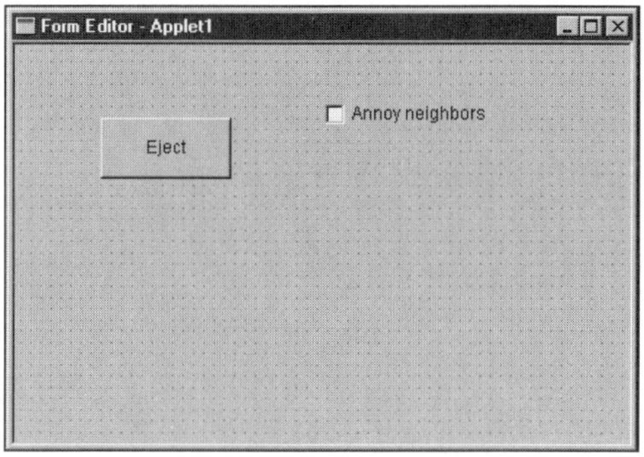

Figure 13-4 Check boxes enable the user to select several options.

Radio Buttons

Radio buttons are those circles that, when selected, contain a dot. Like wolves, radio buttons come in packs. Only one of the radio buttons in a cluster can be on at a particular time; when the user selects one radio button, the others are automatically de-selected. You should use groups of radio buttons for situations in which only one option of several can be chosen, such as whether a document is to print in landscape or portrait mode (it can't do both simultaneously) or whether a search engine is to return 25, 50, 100, or 200 hits.

TIP **Creating a new radio button is just like creating a new check box, except for the details. The code looks like the following:**

```
radioButton1 = new java.awt.Checkbox (label, Group1, false ) ;
```

TIP **In this example,** `radioButton1` **is the variable name of the new** `Checkbox`, `label` **is the radio button's label (which you can set in the Property List),** `Group1` **is the name of the cluster to which the radio button belongs (the group in which only one button can be selected at one time), and** `false` **indicates that this radio button initially isn't selected. You can adjust all of these values in the Property List.**

A cluster of radio buttons appears in Figure 13-5.

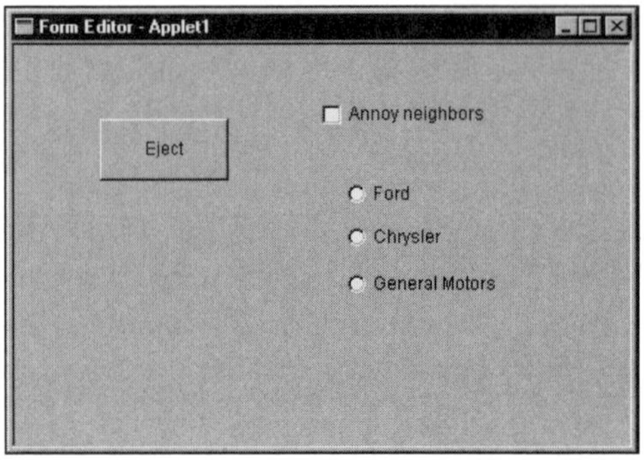

Figure 13-5 A series of radio buttons allows the user to select only one of several options.

LABELS

A label is uneditable text that appears on your interface. You might use a label to describe a collection of controls with phrases such as "Image Options" or "Print Controls."

TIP **Don't confuse the Label component with the Label properties of many other components. The text that appears on the face of a button is also called a label, but it's something totally different from the Label component. You'll learn how to adjust components' properties — including the Label property — in the next chapter.**

Without resorting to extreme measures, you can't adjust the contents of a label while a program is executing. Therefore, labels aren't suitable for displaying output from your programs. To show output, use either a Text Area (for multiple lines of text) or a Text Field (for single lines of text). You'll learn about both of these in a moment.

TIP **Creating a label with the Form Designer is the same as creating a new instance of the `Label` class by entering:**

```
label1 = new java.awt.Label ( ) ;
```

in your code, where `label1` is the variable name of the new `Label`. Using the Property List you can adjust the implementation of the label, including the words it displays.

Figure 13-6 shows a label.

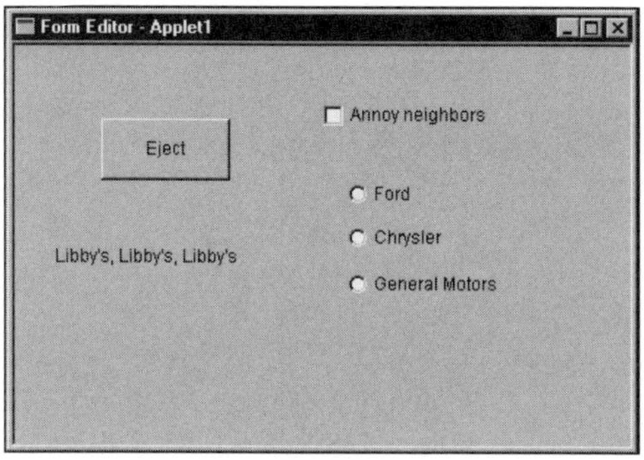

Figure 13-6 A label can be used to indicate the functions of other components.

13

PANELS

In the introduction to components and containers earlier in this chapter, you discovered that a panel is a special kind of container that allows the components it contains to have a layout different from that of components outside the panel.

Take a look at Figure 13-7, which shows a panel in the Form Designer. With the Property List — which is covered in the next chapter — you can define the layout of the components that fill the panel. Figure 13-8 shows the interface running. Note that the frame isn't visible at all in run mode.

TIP **Creating a panel with the Form Designer is the same as creating a new instance of the `Panel` class by entering:**

```
Panel1= new java.awt.Panel ( ) ;
```

in your code, where `Panel1` is the variable name of the new `Panel`.

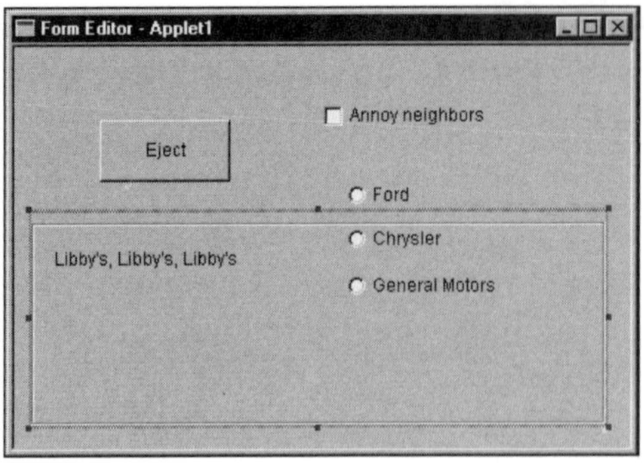

Figure 13-7 A panel in the Form Designer shows up as a rectangle.

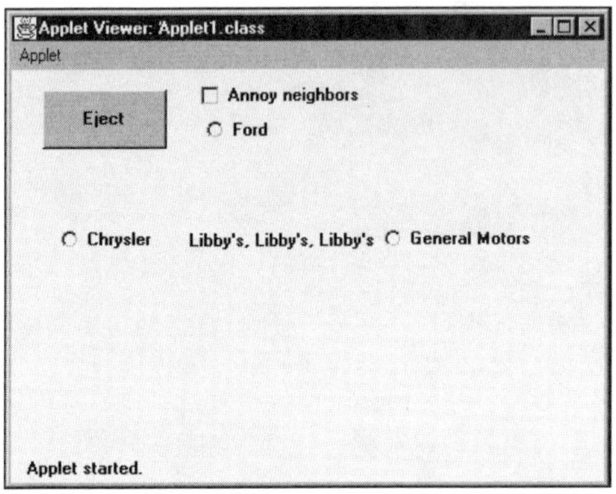

Figure 13-8 The panel itself is not visible in a finished layout that incorporates a panel.

PICK AN ITEM — ANY ITEM

Sometimes you'll want the users of your programs to be able to choose from a list of options. Java provides two handy ways to do this: the choice box and the list box. Which one you use depends mostly upon your interface's design characteristics.

CHOICE BOXES

A choice box in Java is the equivalent of what Windows (in other words, the Microsoft Foundation Class specification) calls a "combo box." The users of your programs will use choice boxes to select one item from a pop-up list of several items.

TIP **Creating a choice box with the Form Designer is the same as creating a new instance of the `Choice` class by entering:**

```
choice1 = new java.awt.Choice ( ) ;
```

in your code, where `choice1` is the variable name of the new `Choice`. You'll use the Property List to set the details of your choice box, including the contents of the list it displays.

Figure 13-9 shows a choice box, in both its normal and extended states.

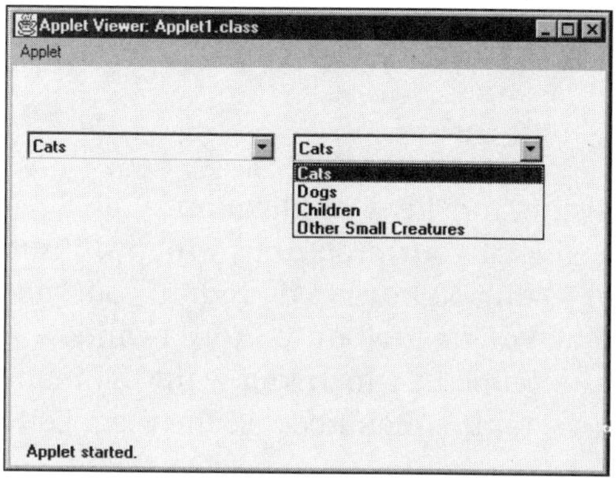

Figure 13-9 Users can manipulate a choice box, normally (left) and extended (right), to pick an item from a list.

LIST BOXES

A list box is similar in function to a choice box, but different in appearance. List boxes don't extend when the user clicks them; they're always the same size and, if needed, the user uses a scrollbar to peruse the contents of the list.

TIP **Creating a list box with the Form Designer is the same as creating a new instance of the `List` class by entering:**

```
list1 = new java.awt.List ( ) ;
```

in your code, where `list1` is the variable name of the `List`. You'll use the Property List to set the details of your choice box, including the contents of the list it displays and whether users can select more than one list item at a time.

Figure 13-10 shows a list box.

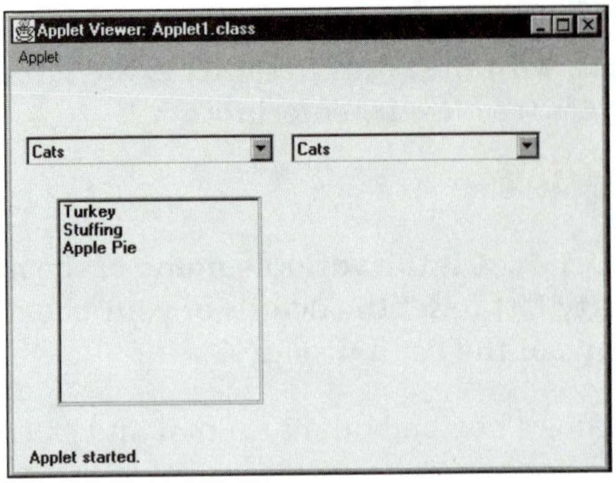

Figure 13-10 Your list box will never change size.

MENU BARS

If you're creating a free-standing Java application, you'll need to include a menu bar across the top edge of your program's window. Visual Café makes it easy to install a menu bar — all you have to do is drag your mouse pointer from the Menu Bar button on the Palette toolbar to Project window — specifically, to the icon that represents the frame in which you want the menu bar to appear. You can't just drag out space for the menu bar on the Form Editor.

TIP **So, what, exactly, is included in a "basic" menu bar? Here's the list:**

- File, containing Open, Save, Save As, and Exit
- Edit, containing Cut, Copy, and Paste
- Help, containing About

You can also add to these slim menus.

TIP **You shouldn't often have to create menu bars manually. When you start a new project, and specify in the New Project dialog box (which you learned about in the Visual Café Quick Tour that opened this book) that you want to start with the Basic Application template, the main frame comes factory-equipped with a basic toolbar, which you can expand as needed.**

To add menus to the basic toolbar, right-click (or long-click, if you're running a Macintosh) one of the menu bar commands (such as File) in the Project window. From the pop-up menu, select Insert Menu. After a copy of the menu you right- or long-clicked appears, give it a new name by clicking on it in the Project window and typing the new name.

TIP **Creating a choice box with the Form Designer is the same as creating a new instance of the `MenuBar` class by entering:**

```
mb = new java.awt.MenuBar ( ) ;
```

in your code, where `mb` is the variable name of the new `MenuBar`.

Figure 13-11 shows a basic menu bar in a Java application.

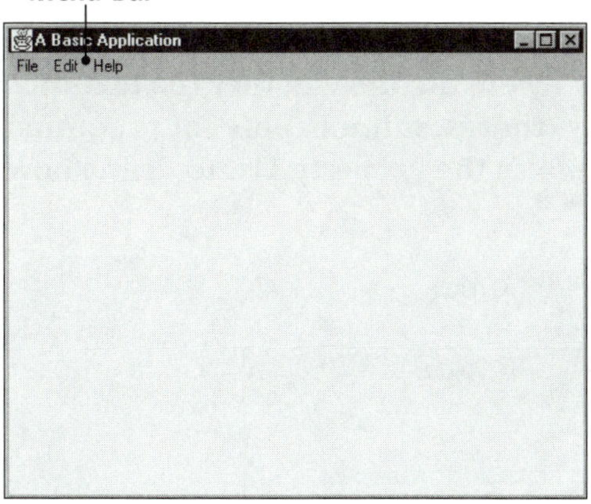

Figure 13-11 The basic menu bar appears in every Java application.

TEXT HANDLERS

Much of what we do with computers has to do with text. We often need to make our programs read text input from the user, or display text for him or her to read.

Java provides two components that facilitate the input and output of characters, including text and numbers. These components are the text area, which can handle multiple lines of text, and the text field, which can accommodate only one line.

Both of these components are subclasses of the `TextComponent` class.

TIP **The thing to remember about text areas and text fields is that they can read and display only data of the string type. In order to do calculations with numbers read in from a text area or text field, you must convert them to the proper data type — `int`, `long`, `float` or whatever. You read about converting among data types in Chapter 3, "Data Types."**

Text Areas

Text areas handle multiline passages of text. You may want to use a text area for explanatory text that varies according to conditions in your program, for reading multiple-line search strings, or as the editing window in a word processing application.

TIP **Creating a text area with the Form Designer is the same as creating a new instance of the `TextArea` class by entering:**

```
text1 = new java.awt.TextArea ( ) ;
```

in your code, where `text1` is the variable name of the new `TextArea`. You can use the Property List to dictate whether the text area is user-editable or read-only (that is, suitable only for program output). Additionally, you can use the Property List to define how much text fits into the text area.

Figure 13-12 shows a text area.

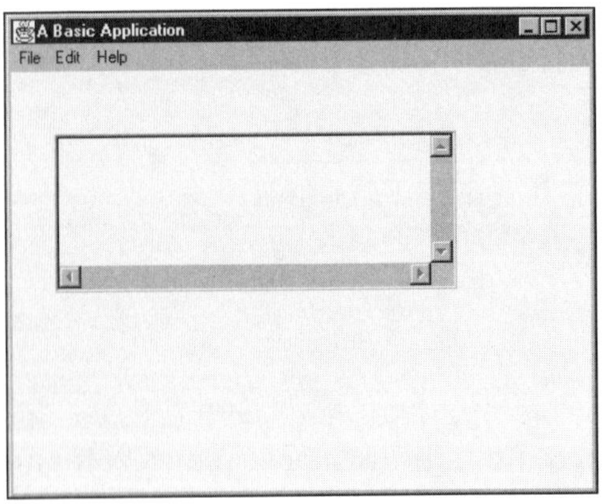

Figure 13-12 A text area can handle several lines of text as input or output.

Text Fields

Text fields are like text areas, but can handle only a single line of text. Often, you'll use text fields for reading in and writing out numbers. When you do that, you'll have to convert the numbers to strings — a process covered in Chapter 4, "Strings."

TIP **Creating a text field with the Form Designer is the same as creating a new instance of the TextField class by entering:**

```
text1 = new java.awt.TextField ( ) ;
```

in your code, where `text1` is the variable name of the new `TextField`. You can use the Property List to dictate whether the text area is user-editable or read-only (that is, suitable only for program output). Additionally, you can use the Property List to define the length of the text field.

Figure 13-13 shows a text field.

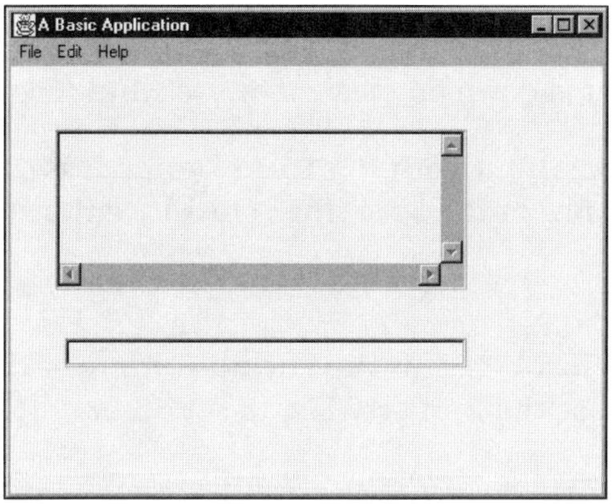

Figure 13-13 Use a text field for single lines of text.

SCROLLBARS

Everybody loves scrollbars. They're so cute! And they make great gifts for the holidays.

Seriously (and what could be more grave than a scrollbar?), scrollbars make it easy for users of your programs to choose from among a range of values. They're especially handy in applications in which precision isn't critical, but the ability to change values quickly is important. A volume control is an example of such an application.

That said, scrollbars rarely find application as separate components. List boxes and choice boxes incorporate scrollbars; you'll rarely need to use them outside these contexts.

Visual Café makes it easy to create both vertical and horizontal scrollbars.

TIP A geek factoid for you: The little thingy you slide back and forth (or up and down) in a scrollbar has a name. It's called the scrollbar *thumb*. The Java specification calls it a *bubble*, while elsewhere you may see it called a *slider*.

TIP The value of a scrollbar depends upon the position of the thumb in relation to the two ends of the scrollbar. You set the minimum and maximum values of the scrollbar with the Property List. Remember: The scrollbar has its minimum value when the thumb is at the bottom (in the case of a vertical scrollbar) or far-right (in the case of a horizontal scrollbar) extreme of the scrollbar.

VERTICAL SCROLLBARS

Vertical scrollbars run up and down on the windows to which they're attached.

TIP Creating a vertical scrollbar with the Form Designer is the same as creating a new instance of the `Scrollbar` class by entering:

```
scrollbar1 = new java.awt.Scrollbar (1) ;
```

in your code, where `scrollbar1` is the variable name of the new `Scrollbar`. You can use the Property List to set other options for your scrollbar.

A vertical scrollbar is illustrated in Figure 13-14.

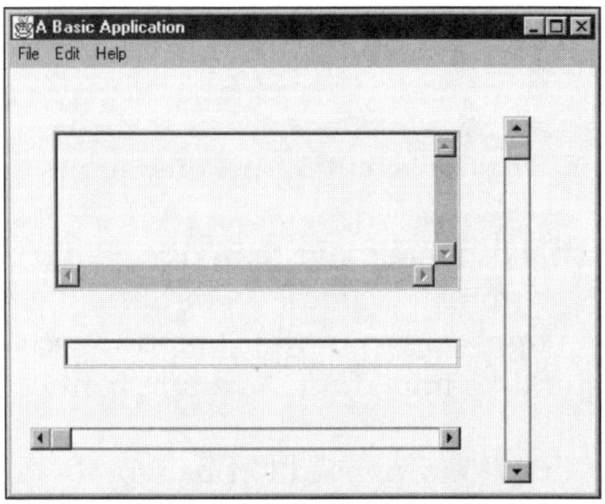

Figure 13-14 Vertical and horizontal scrollbars rarely get used on their own.

Horizontal Scrollbars

Horizontal scrollbars run left and right on the windows to which they're attached.

TIP **Creating a list box with the Form Designer is the same as creating a new instance of the `Scrollbar` class by entering:**

```
scrollbar1 = new java.awt.Scrollbar (0)  ;
```

in your code, where `scrollbar1` is the variable name of the new `Scrollbar`. You can use the Property List to set other options for your scrollbar.

A horizontal scrollbar is also illustrated in Figure 13-14.

13

BONUS

Placing Components in Containers

One of the most important functions of the Form Designer is to enable you to arrange components inside containers — and containers inside containers — easily. This section is a guide to laying out components in the Form Designer.

Standard Layout Managers

Java programs run on any computer for which there is a Java interpreter. This is a blessing most of the time, as it saves software engineers the hassles of having to develop separate programs for separate systems. But in the area of interface layouts, Java's multi-platform nature can be a bit of a headache.

You see, there are almost as many ways of implementing user interface components as there are operating systems. A button looks one way on a Macintosh, another way on an X-windowing system, and yet another way on a computer running Windows NT. To compound the problem, a given operating system probably runs on machines with video displays of vastly different sizes and resolutions.

To combat this problem, Java containers come with Layout properties. You'll learn how to set Layout properties (and lots of other properties) in the next chapter. For now, just understand what a component's layout property does.

The Layout property gives Java the authority to arrange components in a container in a way suitable to the platform your program encounters when it's time to run. The various values for the Layout property — called *layout managers* — define the rules under which Java automatically arranges components.

There are five standard values for the Layout property. In addition, you can opt to specify no layout rules.

TIP **Remember: You can use a panel if you want part of a container to have one layout manager while the rest of the container has another.**

NO LAYOUT

You can build interfaces without specifying a layout manager, but you run the risk of having your components arranged in a weird way on a machine on which you didn't do any testing.

BORDERLAYOUT

BorderLayout is a layout manager that looks at the Place property of each component in a container and locates and sizes it accordingly. The five components get Place property values of North, South, East, West, and Center. The layout manager moves the East and West components to the left and right edges of the container and stretches them vertically. It then moves the North and South components to the top and bottom edges of the container and stretches them horizontally. Finally it places the Center component in any space left in the middle.

CARDLAYOUT

The CardLayout layout manager facilitates the creation of a multi-tabbed interface that enables the user to click the tab he or she wants and manipulate only the components on that card, without distraction from the contents of other cards. CardLayout comes in handy when fitting several components into a small dialog box.

FLOWLAYOUT

FlowLayout arranges components in horizontal rows. It first fits as many components as it can onto the first line, then centers the components that fit onto that line. It repeats the process until no more components remain.

GRIDLAYOUT

The GridLayout layout manager defines a grid for a group of components in a container and fits the components into the grid.

GRIDBAGLAYOUT

GridBagLayout is a complex and confusing layout manager that relies on values specified in the GridBagConstraints property of each component.

Summary

In this chapter you learned how to create good-looking user interfaces with Visual Café's Form Designer. Now you're ready to go beyond the surface and start adjusting the attributes of your containers and components with the Property List. Then, when you get to Chapter 15, it'll be time to make your components do things — with the aid of the Interaction Wizard. Read on.

CHAPTER FOURTEEN

TWEAKING COMPONENTS WITH THE PROPERTY LIST

IN THIS CHAPTER YOU LEARN THESE KEY SKILLS

DISCOVER WHAT COMPONENTS' PROPERTIES DO PAGE 239

LEARN HOW TO USE THE PROPERTY LIST PAGE 240

FIND OUT ABOUT THE COMPONENT PROPERTY GUIDE ON THE CD-ROM PAGE 241

In Chapter 13, "Building a User Interface," you learned the mechanics of locating components in a user interface. Now it's time to adjust the details of the components you created in the previous chapter.

The "details" of Java user interface components are called *properties*. They determine such things as the following:

- The color of components
- The label text that appears on or near components
- The contents of choice and list boxes
- The size and position of components

To make components look the way you want, you have to adjust the components' properties. You can do this in code by specifying certain arguments when you declare an interface component. But that requires lots of diddling with program instructions and demands that you, the programmer, remember lots of obtuse verbiage.

Visual Café makes the process of adjusting properties reasonably painless. By providing a programming tool called the Property List, Visual Café makes it easy for you to see and adjust all the properties of a component. This chapter explains properties and the Property List.

Using the Property List

This section provides you with a brief introduction to the Property List, the tool Visual Café provides to help you view and edit the properties of the various parts of your Java applets and applications.

The Property List appears in Figure 14-1.

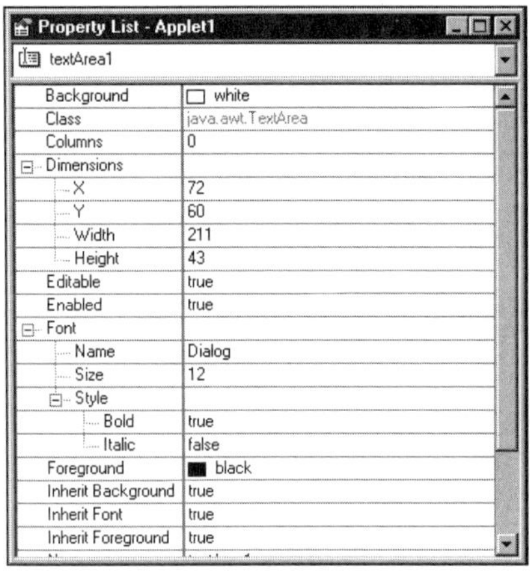

Figure 14-1 The Property List displays components' characteristics.

Starting the Property List

The Property List should be open any time you're in the Edit workspace (if you've forgotten what that is, refer back to Chapter 2). If you've closed the Property List and want to open it again, use one of the following procedures:

* Choose **Window** → **Property List** from the menu bar.
* Press Ctrl+Shift+P.
* Press F4.
* Click the Property List button on the toolbar.

TIP **The most important thing to remember is that the Property List displays the properties of the selected components. If you see components in the Property List that puzzle you, make sure you've selected the right component, and only the right component.**

Editing Properties

In the Property List, you will adjust the values of various properties in two ways.

The most common way is just to type a value into the box to the right of the property name. This is how you enter values for Label, Name, and other properties.

Some properties can accept only a limited range of values, and for these properties the Property List contains pop-up menus with the acceptable values. You can choose the value you want from the pop-up menu, as shown in Figure 14-2.

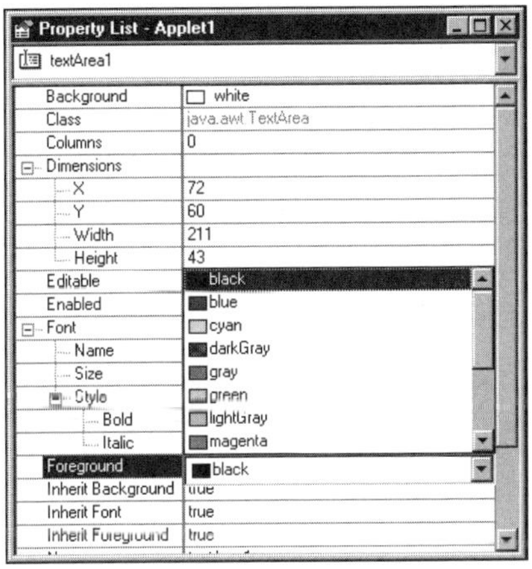

Figure 14-2 You can select a value from a pop-up menu in the Property List.

Using the Component Property Guide

To save space, the complete guide to the properties you can adjust on the various Java components appears in an HTML file that accompanies *Discover Visual Café*. The HTML file contains the Component Property Guide, shown in Figure 14-3.

You may find the contents of the Component Property Guide repetitive, particularly if you read it from beginning to end. Many Java components share properties, and each property appears under each component to which it applies.

The Component Property Guide was designed to be used as a reference. If you want to know what a panel's properties do, scroll right to the panel section. You'll see something that looks like what appears in Figure 14-4.

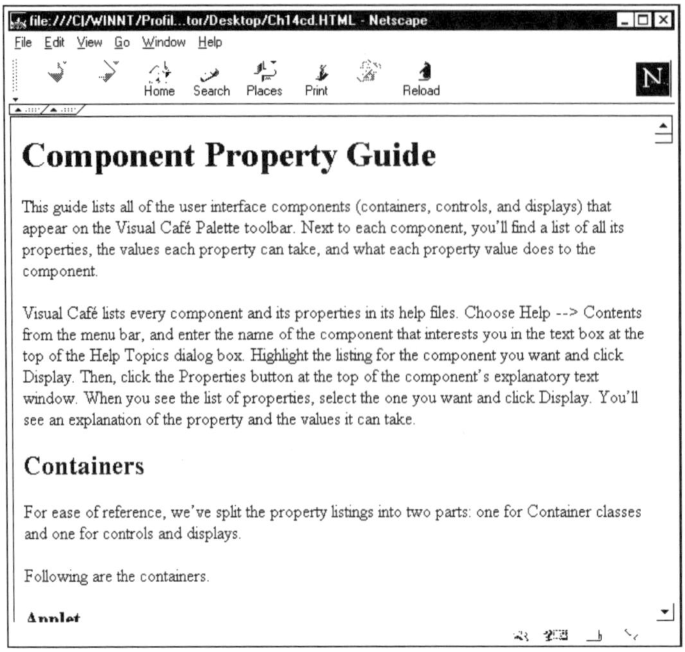

Figure 14-3 The Component Property Guide appears on the CD-ROM.

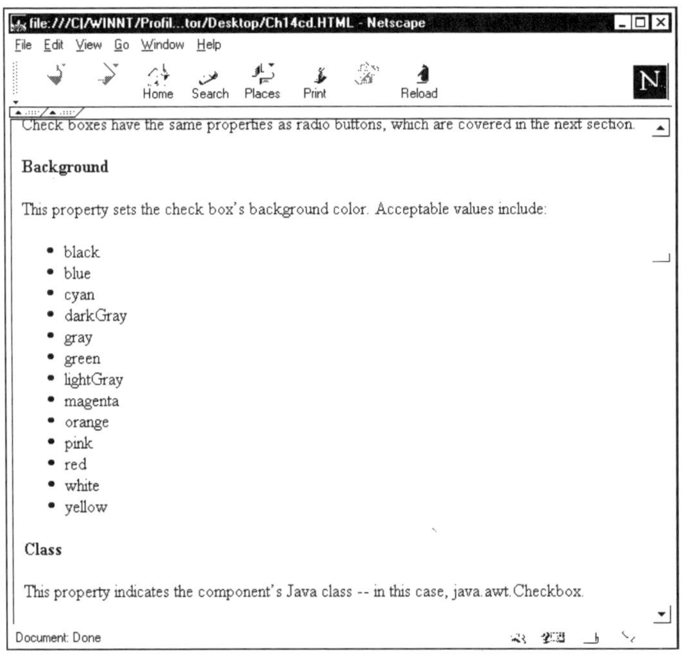

Figure 14-4 The Component Property Guide displays components' characteristics.

BONUS

Other Components' Properties

So far in this chapter, we've learned only about some of the components that appear on the various tabs of the Palette toolbar and a few containers into which you can put those components. Every component contains properties that can be viewed with the Property List, though — including those components you define yourself. But what is a property, really? Here's a guide.

Extending Other Classes

Most of the components discussed in this chapter contain the following line in their class definitions:

```
public class Whatever extends Component {
```

That means that the class, called `Whatever`, has all the properties of `java.awt.Component`, plus whatever properties are defined within the local class definition. That's why most of the components covered here have Inherit Font and Background Color properties.

Adding New Properties

You can add more properties to those defined by whatever class you're extending. Let's look at `java.awt.Scrollbar` as an example.

In addition to the following line:

```
public class Scrollbar extends Component {
```

the Scrollbar class definition contains several lines like this:

```
public int getPageIncrement
```

Note that Page Increment is a property displayed by the Property List in Visual Café. You can add all of the properties you want by defining them as methods in your class definitions.

Summary

In this chapter, you learned how to tailor components to precisely fit your needs. Now that you have a properly tuned user interface, you're ready to step into the breech and start making your customized components *do* things. Visual Café provides several ways to bring your components to life, but the fastest and easiest way to add interactions among components is with the Interaction Wizard. Chapter 15 covers interactions and the Interaction Wizard in depth.

CHAPTER FIFTEEN

USING THE INTERACTION WIZARD

IN THIS CHAPTER YOU LEARN THESE KEY SKILLS

You learned in Chapter 1, "The Story of Java and Visual Café," that the Interaction Wizard is Visual Café's most powerful feature for the novice programmer. With it you can quickly build attractive interfaces and designate the functions of each of their components.

The Interaction Wizard works by automating the process of creating relationships among various modules of Java code. It tells you what you can do to a component — a button, for example — and what another class — such as a calculator — can do in response. You can use the Interaction Wizard to specify that when the user of your program clicks a button, the contents of a text box should be inserted into a drop-down list box.

Figure 15-1 shows the Interaction Wizard.

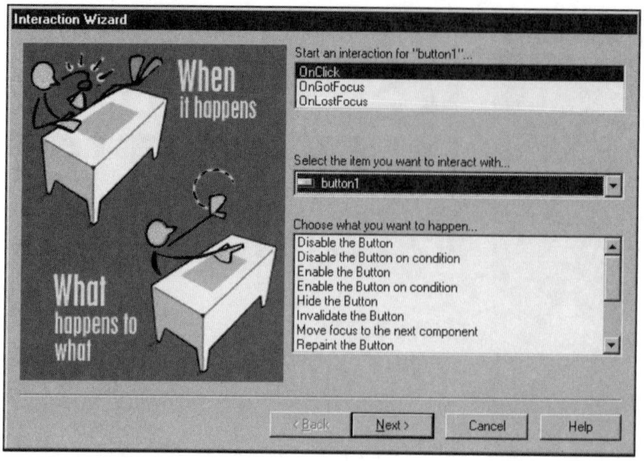

Figure 15-1 The Interaction Wizard makes many programming tasks faster.

What the Interaction Wizard Does

The Interaction Wizard automates the process of making various components do certain things in response to specific events that occur during the execution of a Java program. You can use the Interaction Wizard, for example, to specify that a certain dialog box should appear when the user clicks a certain button, or that a set of radio buttons should be enabled only when a specific check box has been clicked.

The Interaction Wizard does its work with *events* and *behaviors,* automatically writing Java code that specifies which behaviors are to occur in response to which events.

Events

Events are things that can happen to components. A button, for example, has only three events that can befall it:

* The user can click the button
* The button can gain the focus
* The button can lose the focus

You'll learn all the events that apply to each of the commonly used components in Chapter 20, "Using the Component Library." For now, understand that events are the "input side" of what the Interaction Wizard orchestrates. Events are the triggers that set off behaviors.

Behaviors

Behaviors are things that components can do. Take the Timer component, which comes with Visual Café, as an example. It can start timing and it can stop timing. "Start Timer" and "Stop Timer" are behaviors that the Timer can perform.

Conjuring the Interaction Wizard

First, look around in your basement for an old coffee urn. Carry it to a well-ventilated area and begin to rub it. No wizard appeared? Of course not — but now you're ready to make a big batch of coffee to keep you awake while you brew Java. Ah, the synchronicity of it all.

You can call up the Interaction Wizard in any of three ways — four ways, really, if you count the keyboard hot keys for the menu bar command. This section explains both the best way to run the wizard and the other ways, so you know how to start the Interaction Wizard in any situation.

The Mouse and the Wizard

Recall the Sorcerer's Apprentice segment in Disney's *Fantasia*, in which Mickey Mouse plays with the magical implements of his master and gets into real trouble as a result. Visual Café is similar to *Fantasia* in that it involves a mouse and a wizard — but you'll find that your results are much happier than Mickey's.

TIP **If you *do* see dancing broomsticks after using the Interaction Wizard for a while, you probably didn't clean the coffee urn well enough.**

You can start the Interaction Wizard in any of three ways:

- You can use menu bar commands, or their keyboard shortcuts
- You can right-click (or long-click) with the mouse
- You can click the toolbar button and drag connections between components

Each of these means of starting the Interaction Wizard has its place. Let's explore each procedure.

15

Using the Menu Bar

To start the Interaction Wizard via the commands on the menu bar, choose Object → Add Interaction. You'll see the Interaction Wizard window, as shown in Figure 15-1. If you don't want to use your mouse to open the menu bar, you can press Alt+O, then select Add Interaction with your arrow keys and press Enter.

Using the Mouse

You can also start the Interaction Wizard by right-clicking (or, in the case of the Macintosh, long-clicking) the component in the Form Editor to which you want to add an interaction. When you right-click or long-click a component, you'll get a pop-up menu that looks like the one in Figure 15-2.

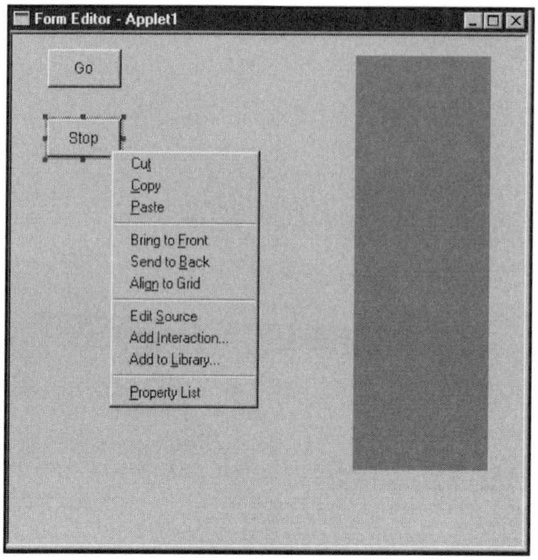

Figure 15-2 You can start the Interaction Wizard with the pop-up menu.

If you choose **Add Interaction** from the menu, you'll get the Interaction Wizard window, configured to add an interaction to the component you right- or long-clicked.

For example, you might create a button in the Form Editor and right-click (or long-click) that button to get the pop-up menu. If you choose **Add Interaction** from the pop-up menu, you'll get the Interaction Wizard, with the button you right- or long-clicked already specified in the "Start an interaction for" label at the top. Take a look at Figure 15-3 to see what we mean.

Right-clicked (or long-clicked) component already specified here

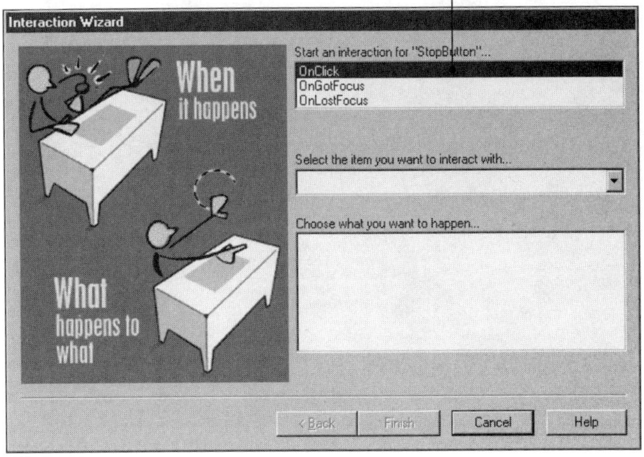

Figure 15-3 Here's an Interaction Wizard that resulted from a right- or long-click.

Using the Toolbar Button

The third way to start the Interaction Wizard is with the toolbar button.

Here's how:

1. Select the component to which you want to add an interaction.
2. Click the **Interaction Wizard** on the toolbar.
3. Drag your mouse pointer from the component that will experience an event (such as a mouse click) to the component you want to react to the event.

You'll see the Interaction Wizard window, configured to add an interaction between the selected components. Here's an example:

If you click the toolbar button and drag a connection between two components you want to interact, you'll get an Interaction Wizard in which the "Start an interaction for" label contains the name of the component you dragged *from*, while the "Select the item you want to interact with" box contains the name of the component you dragged *to*. Figure 15-4 shows an Interaction Wizard that was started by dragging a connection between two components.

15

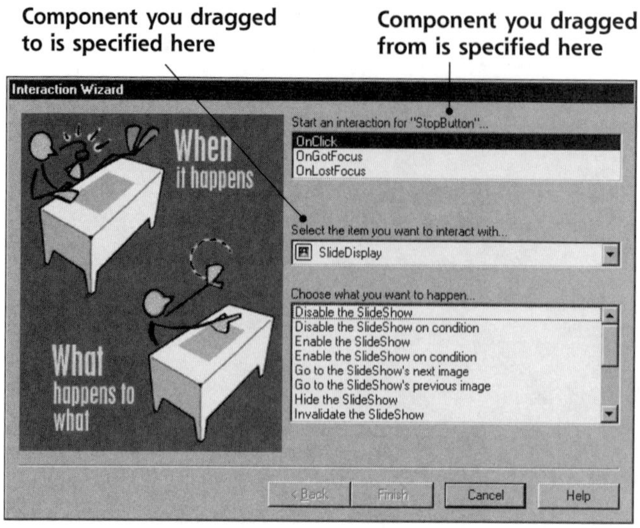

Figure 15-4 This Interaction Wizard resulted from dragging a connection between components.

Using the Interaction Wizard with Other Tools

The first step in creating an interaction with the Interaction Wizard is to create those things you want to interact. Usually you'll do that by dragging components, such as buttons and text boxes, onto the Form Editor. You learned all about the Form Editor and how to use it in Chapter 13, "Building a User Interface."

Other times, though, you'll want to create interactions with components that don't have an on-screen presence and, therefore, don't appear in the Form Editor. In those situations, you'll want to drag components into the Project window directly. You learned how — and why — to do this in Chapter 14, "Tweaking Components with the Property List."

Once you've created components for the Interaction Wizard to work with, you can select them and start the Interaction Wizard in any of the ways you learned in the last section.

Creating Simple Interactions

Let's walk through the process of creating a simple interaction with the Interaction Wizard. Imagine you want a check box on your user interface to be disabled ("grayed out") when the user clicks a button.

Here is the procedure to follow:

1. Create a button and a check box (as you learned in Chapter 16).
2. Click the **Interaction Wizard** button.
3. Drag a line from the button to the check box. When you release your mouse button, you'll see the Interaction Wizard, as shown in Figure 15-5.

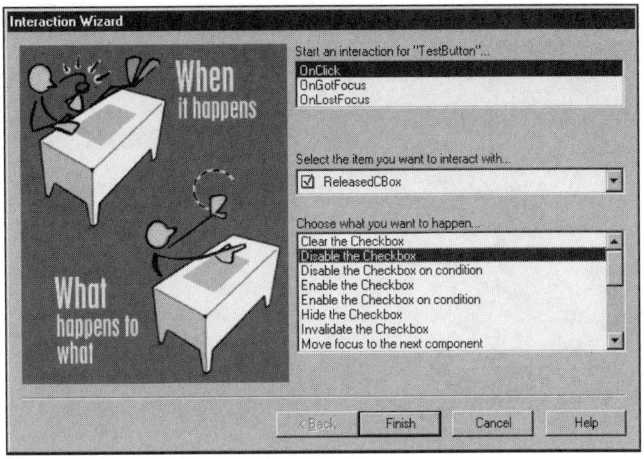

Figure 15-5 This Interaction Wizard is creating an interaction between a button and a check box.

4. Specify the event you want: "OnClick."
5. Specify the behavior you want: "Disable the Checkbox."
6. Click the Finish button.

The Interaction Wizard will insert code into your applet or application specifying that when the user clicks the button, the check box should be grayed out.

Creating More Complex Interactions

Sometimes you'll want to build more complex event-behavior relationships with the Interaction Wizard. For these situations, the Interaction Wizard supports a two-step interaction creation process. For this example, assume you want to take the selected item from a list box and place it in a text area when the user clicks a button.

Here's the procedure to follow:

1. Create a list box, text area, and button in the Form Editor, as you learned in Chapter 13.
2. Click the **Interaction Wizard** button on the toolbar.

3. Drag a line from the button to the text area.
4. Specify the button event you want: "OnClick."
5. When someone clicks the button, you want to add text to the text area, so choose "Append string in TextArea."
6. Click the Next button. You'll see the Interaction Wizard's second "page," shown in Figure 15-6.

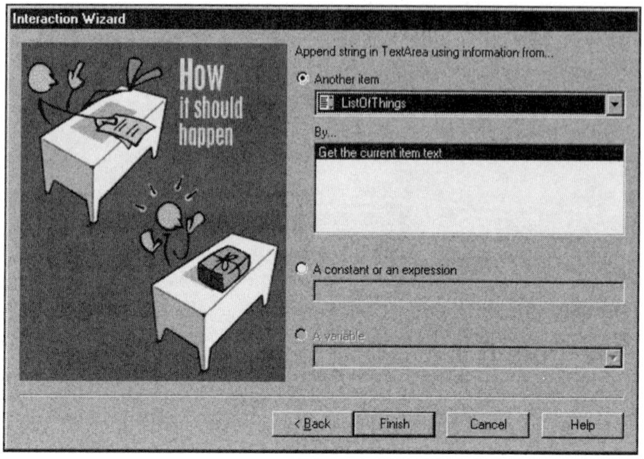

Figure 15-6 The second "page" of the Interaction Wizard lets you configure complex interactions.

7. Click the radio button next to "Another item," and select the list box from the components listed in the choice box. The only behavior a list box can perform, "Get the current item text," will appear in the "By" box.
8. Make sure "Get the current item text" is selected.
9. Click the Finish button.

TIP **Remember, when you're creating an interaction that will involve more than two components, drag your line from the component that will experience the initial triggering event to the component that will ultimately do something. You can specify the third contributing component later, in the Interaction Wizard.**

TIP **In this situation, you could have specified a constant or a variable to insert in the text area by clicking one of the other radio buttons on the second "page" of the Interaction Wizard. If you wanted to use a constant or expression, you'd have to enter it in the "A constant or an expression" text field. If you wanted to insert the value of a variable, you'd have to choose the name of the variable from the "A variable" choice box at the bottom of the Interaction Wizard window.**

BONUS

Using the Interaction Wizard's Choice Boxes

Earlier in this chapter you learned the most common way to specify components to be manipulated by the Interaction Wizard. What happens if you start the Interaction Wizard with a right-click (or long-click) on a single component, or if you start the Interaction Wizard via the menu bar?

You have to specify the second component (the one that executes a behavior in response to an event) by choosing it from the "Select the item you want to interact with" choice box. Figure 15-7 shows the choice box extended.

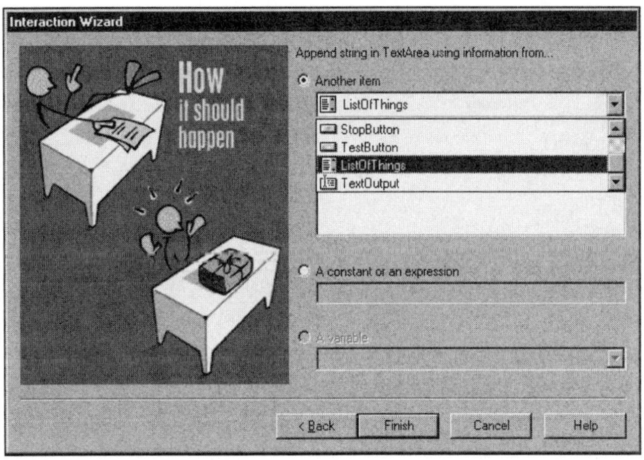

Figure 15-7 Here's how to select a component in the Interaction Wizard.

Summary

In this chapter, you learned that the Interaction Wizard speeds the process of building Java applications in Visual Café by allowing you to specify events, and the behaviors that result from those events, in more or less plain English. Now you're ready to delve into the world beyond the reach of the Interaction Wizard: the source code of your programs. Visual Café provides an excellent source code editor. Let's get moving!

CHAPTER SIXTEEN

EDITING SOURCE CODE

IN THIS CHAPTER YOU LEARN THESE KEY SKILLS

The Interaction Wizard represents Visual Café's single most powerful programming tool, especially for those who have only a passing understanding of Java programming. Still, it's limited in power: Java can do lots of things that the Interaction Wizard cannot.

When the Interaction Wizard fails you (or when you grow weary of its handholding and want to work with the undisguised Java code itself), you have to work with Visual Café's source code editor. This is the tool with which you can write raw Java program instructions. It's an eminently flexible tool — as flexible as the Java language itself — but it's not as forgiving to those who are less familiar with the ins and outs of Java programming.

This chapter introduces you to Visual Café's source code editor. You'll gain familiarity with its features and see how it interacts with other parts of the Visual Café Java programming toolkit.

16

Java Source Code in Visual Café

If you remember only one thing about source code, remember this: A single Visual Café project file (with a .VPJ filename extension) doesn't necessarily correspond to a single .java source code file. You can, and often will, have several different source code files wrapped into a single project file.

TIP **You learned in the Visual Café Quick Tour that Visual Café projects get filenames with .VPJ filename extensions. Java source code files get filenames with the extension .java. Visual Café doesn't save source code files unless you tell it to do so (by choosing File → Save As when the source code editor is open). If you haven't specifically saved a .java file, then your source code is still integrated into the corresponding project's .VPJ file.**

Using the Source Code Editor

Now that you understand what source code is and how Visual Café integrates it into project files, you're ready to explore the mechanism by which Visual Café lets you write and revise Java source code: the source code editor, shown in Figure 16-1.

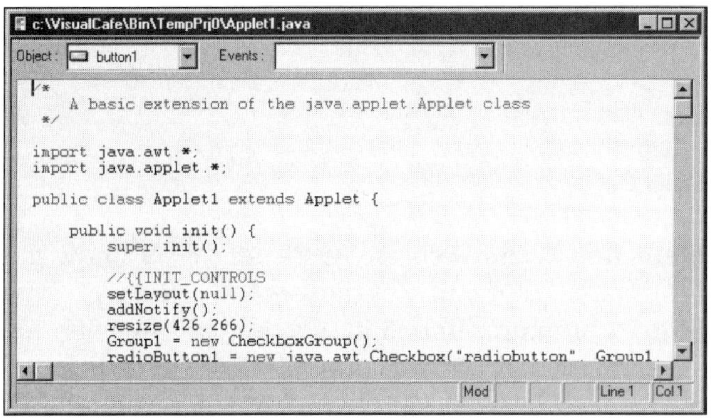

Figure 16-1 The source code editor helps you with low-level programming tasks.

Think of the source code editor as a sort of word processor for source code (the original word processing programs derived their designs from source code editors, but that's a different story). The source code editor is a collection of tools that make programming easier. Let's see how to use it.

Starting the Source Code Editor

You can start the source code editor in any of three ways:

1. Double-click a component in the Form Editor or the Form Editor window itself.
2. Right-click (or long-click, if you're using a Macintosh) in the Form Editor and choose **Edit Source** from the pop-up menu.
3. Choose **Object** → **Edit Source** from the menu bar or use the keyboard shortcut Ctrl+Shift+S.

Reserved Words and Comment Highlighting

As you type Java instructions in the source code editor, you'll notice that Java reserved words — such as `null`, `new`, `this`, and `super` appear in blue type. Comments — lines defined by "//" and "/*...*/" and "/**...*/" — appear in green. This feature of the Visual Café source code editor helps you remember not to use reserved words as variable names, and helps you get a better idea of what is commented out and what is not. Figure 16-2 illustrates some Java source code with blue reserved words and green comments.

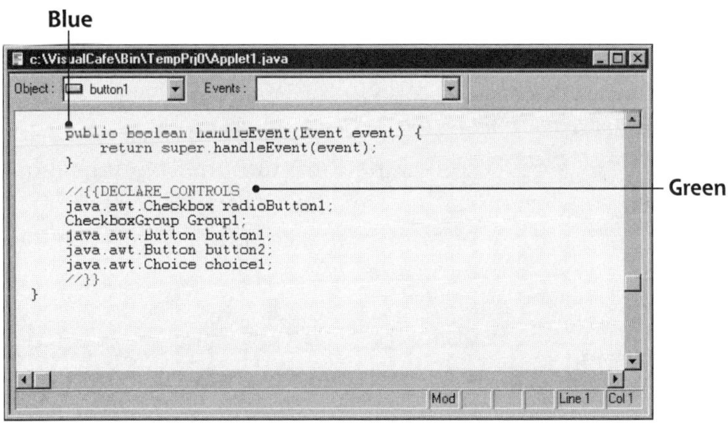

Figure 16-2 Visual Café makes reserved words blue and comments green, by default.

> TIP **If you don't like the blue and green keyword colors you can change them. Take a look at Chapter 21, "Customizing Visual Café," for instructions.**

The Source Menu

When the source code editor is on the screen, you'll see the **Source** menu on the menu bar. The Source menu contains commands that relate to the appearance and presentation of Java source code. Commands on the **Source** menu include the following:

- **Watch Variable** Adds a variable to the Watch window for debugging purposes. You'll learn more about the Watch window in Chapter 18, "Using the Visual Debugging Tools."
- **Toggle Breakpoint** Turns breakpoints — places at which execution of your program pauses for debugging purposes — on and off. The keyboard shortcut for **Toggle Breakpoint** is F9.
- **Set Conditional Breakpoint** Establishes a conditional breakpoint — a breakpoint that applies only under certain conditions.
- **Indent** Indents the current line one tab more.
- **Unindent** Indents the current line one tab less.
- **Upper** Changes the selected text to ALL UPPERCASE LETTERS.
- **Lower** Changes the selected text to all lowercase letters.
- **Tabs to Spaces** Converts tab characters to a number of spaces (you can set the exact number via the **Format Options** command; the default is four spaces to the tab).
- **Spaces to Tabs** Converts spaces to tab characters (you can set the exact number of spaces per tab via the **Format Options** command; the default is four spaces to the tab).
- **Format Options** Displays the Current Buffer Options dialog box, with which you can adjust several source code editor settings. You'll learn more about these settings in this chapter's Bonus Section.

Programming at the Source-code Level

Java applets, and many Java applications, are event-driven. They wait for certain events (defined by the programmer) to take place, then react to them in the way the programmer specified in the source code. The Interaction Wizard, which you learned about in the previous chapter, had everything to do with events and reactions to them.

The source code editor is very much event-driven, too.

Take a look at Figure 16-3, which shows the source code editor. Note the two choice boxes at the top. The one on the left contains all the objects in the current project (in this situation, an *object* is any component). The right-hand choice box contains two things: the events that can befall the component specified in the left-hand dialog box and a list of all the classes defined in the current project.

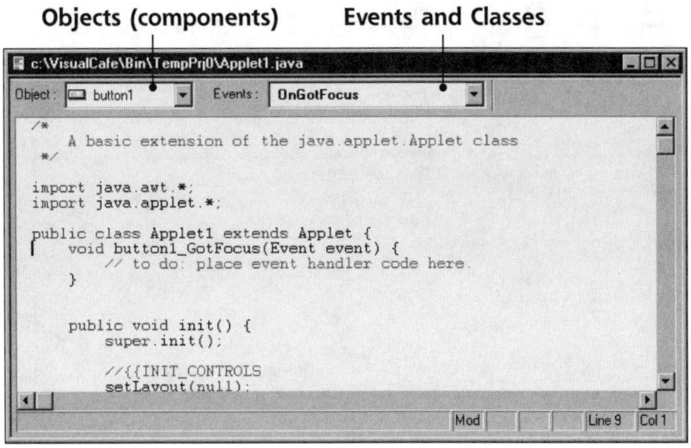

Figure 16-3 The source code editor has two choice boxes.

Objects

In the choice box on the left side of the source code editor — the one labeled "Object" — you'll find a list of components in the current project. Figure 16-4 shows the Object choice box extended.

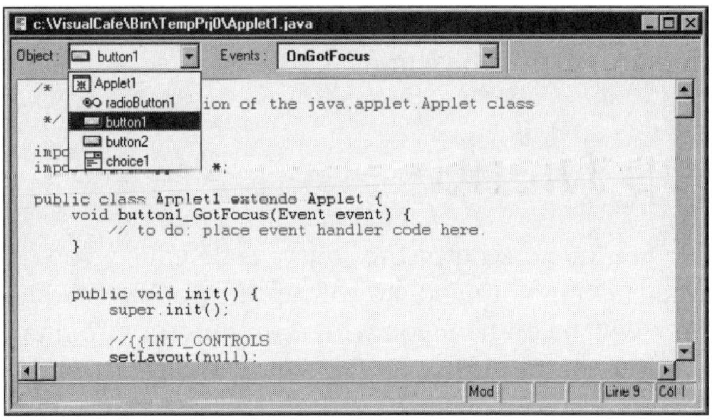

Figure 16-4 The Object choice box extends to show all components.

When you select a component from the Object choice box, you're determining what appears in the Events choice box.

Events

Let's say, for example, that you chose a button with the variable name "GoButton" from the Object choice box. In that case, the Events choice box would look like the one shown in Figure 16-5.

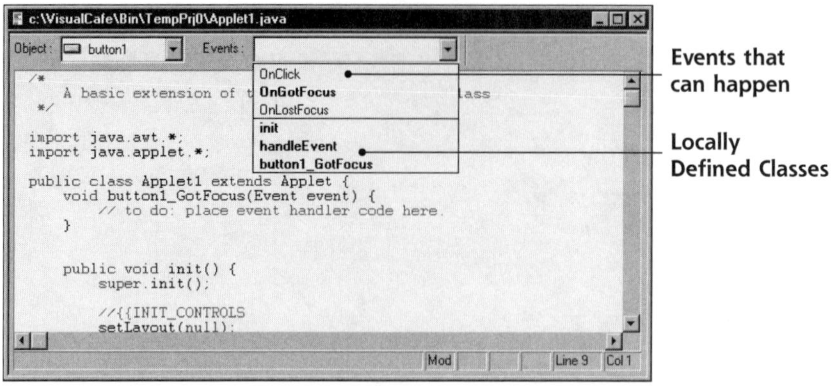

Figure 16-5 The Events choice box extends to show classes and events.

There are two groups of listings in the Events choice box. The upper group, above the divider bar, is a list of events that can happen to the component you selected in the Object choice box. If you select an event from the upper portion of the Events choice box, the cursor in the source code editor will move to the class that deals with the selected event, if one exists. If one doesn't exist, Visual Café will create a bare-bones event-handler class, ready for you to insert code into.

The lower portion of the Events choice box lists the classes defined in the current source code file. If you select one of these, the cursor moves to that class. This feature of the source code editor is especially handy when you're working with long programs that involve many classes.

The Pop-up Menu

While you're working in the source code editor, you can right-click (or long-click) in your code to call up the pop-up menu, shown in Figure 16-6, which can help you with many programming tasks. The pop-up menu contains six commands:

- Cut
- Copy
- Paste
- Go to Definition
- Watch Variable
- Toggle Breakpoint

You're familiar with all of these commands except one: Go to Definition. Go to Definition serves as the link between the source code editor and the Class Browser, which is the subject of the next chapter. In brief, the Go to Definition command shows the class (probably made available to your program by an import statement) that you've used in your program. For example, right- or long-clicking the command resize and choosing **Go to Definition** shows the five Java classes (two from java.applet and two from java.awt) that implement the resize command.

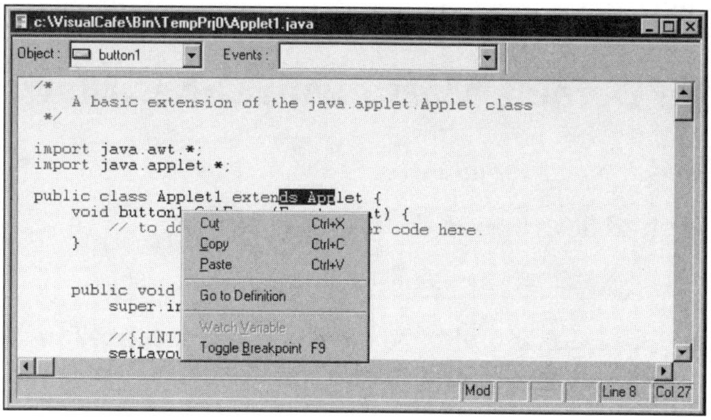

Figure 16-6 The source code editor's pop-up menu gives you quick access to some commands.

Macros

The Visual Café source code editor comes with a macro facility — a simple means of automating repetitive tasks. You might want to write macros to do such things as enter a comment block at the top of your source code files, identifying them as your copyrighted property.

TIP **The Macro menu, used in creating and playing macros, appears when the source code editor, Class Browser, or Hierarchy Editor is on the screen. It's covered here because macros come in handiest in the source code editor.**

Recording and Playing the Default Macro

The Visual Café macro feature makes it easy to record a single macro and then use it repeatedly without fooling with dialog boxes and macro names. This one easily recorded and easily accessed macro is called the *default macro.*

To record the default macro:

1. Choose **Macro** → **Record Macros**.
2. Perform whatever action you want to automate. Visual Café will record your actions.

3. When you're done with the task you want to record, choose Macro → Stop Recording.

To play the default macro, choose Macro → Play.

The default macro isn't automatically saved when you shut down Visual Café. You can save it though, and that's the subject of the next section.

Using the Default Macro with Other Macros

To save the default macro for future use:

1. Record it as described in the previous section.
2. Choose Macro → ScriptMaker.
3. In the ScriptMaker dialog box, shown in Figure 16-7, make sure the `<default>` entry is highlighted.

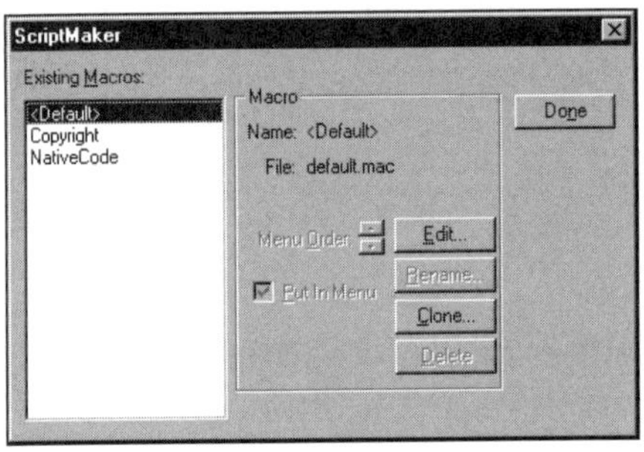

Figure 16-7 The ScriptMaker dialog box catalogs macros.

4. Click the Clone button.
5. In the Rename/Clone script dialog box, shown in Figure 16-8, enter a name for the macro and a filename.

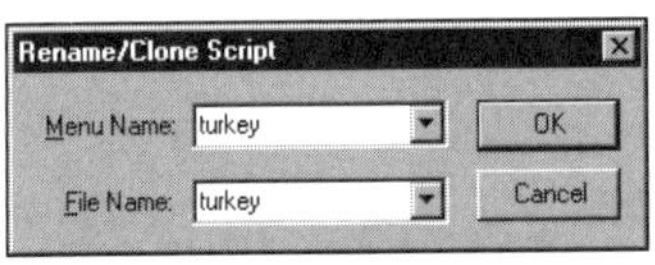

Figure 16-8 The Rename/Clone dialog box takes the default macro and renames it.

6. Click the OK button.

TIP **You can use the "Put in Menu" check box in the ScriptMaker dialog box to put a macro's name in the Macros menu.**

To run a macro other than the default macro, open the Macro menu and select the macro you want to run from the menu.

BONUS

Using an External Source Code Editor

Many Java programmers like to work with a source code editor other than the one that comes with Visual Café. Whether they prefer vi, emacs, or another editor, some programmers just like to write code in a certain environment. Happily, Visual Café accommodates these folks by making it possible to import .java source code files.

TIP **This also applies to .java files that you don't write, such as those you download from Web sites.**

Here's how to import an existing source code file:

1. Create a .java file, either with a text editor or by downloading it from another source. If the `public` class in the file is called ImaHogg, make sure the file is saved as ImaHogg.java. Capitalization matters.
2. If the source code corresponds to an applet, create an HTML file with your text editor. Save it with any filename you like.
3. In Visual Café, choose File → New Project.
4. In the New Project dialog box, choose to create an empty project.
5. Choose File → Save As and save the project in the same directory as the .java and .html files you created.
6. Choose Project → Add/Remove Files.
7. Highlight the .java and .html files by holding down the Ctrl key and clicking them.
8. Click Add.

16

Summary

In this chapter you saw that Visual Café is more than a dumbed-down programming environment suitable only for building simple applications in a hurry. Here, you learned that Visual Café includes a full-featured source code editor, complete with choice boxes that can take you to any portion of a .java file promptly, and a Macro facility that can automate repetitive tasks.

If you don't like the Visual Café source code editor — and lots of people don't, particularly those who learned to write code on a text editor such as vi or emacs — you can import source code files into a Visual Café project.

Now you're ready to move on to some of Visual Café's more exotic programming aids — the Hierarchy Editor and Class Browser. The Hierarchy Editor helps you see your program in a larger context, while the Class Browser helps you zoom in on the details of classes.

CHAPTER SEVENTEEN

USING THE HIERARCHY EDITOR AND CLASS BROWSER

IN THIS CHAPTER YOU LEARN THESE KEY SKILLS

GET AN IDEA OF WHAT THE HIERARCHY EDITOR DOES PAGE 266

LEARN THE FUNCTIONS OF THE CLASS BROWSER PAGE 270

FIND OUT HOW TO USE BOTH THE HIERARCHY EDITOR AND THE CLASS BROWSER PAGE 270

Objects, objects everywhere. You thought this object-orientation business was supposed to make your programs easier to understand. Now, you have 800 classes that make up an applet that counts to 15, and you're all befuddled about which classes derive what from which other classes. It's like the old spaghetti code you used to write in BASIC — except now, there are no line numbers, and most of the spaghetti is not visible.

For better or for worse, the Hierarchy Editor and Class Browser in Visual Café make the spaghetti spring into view again. These tools may contain a lot of faults, but they can help you see and alter the relationships among the classes that make up a Java program.

This chapter shows you what the Hierarchy Editor and Class Browser do, and explains how you can use them.

Using the Hierarchy Editor

Every Java class, except `java.lang.Object`, extends another class. Recall that `java.awt.Component` inherits the properties of `java.lang.Object`, and several classes, such as `java.awt.Label` and `java.awt.Container`, inherit the properties of `java.awt.Component`. Furthermore, a class can implement several interfaces, and an interface can be implemented in several classes. The `java.awt.MenuContainer` interface is implemented by three classes: `java.awt.MenuBar`, `java.awt.Menu`, and `java.awt.Frame`. On the other hand, the `java.io.RandomAccessFile` class implements two interfaces: `java.io.DataInput` and `java.io.DataOutput`.

The Hierarchy Editor's mission in life is to document the relationships among classes within a Java program. It's pre-loaded with all of the standard class relationships that make up the Java language, and it allows you to add the classes that define your program.

The trouble is, the Hierarchy Editor, at least at this writing, doesn't show you all of the information you need. Take a look at Figure 17-1. All the lines connecting the classes look the same, and all the boxes that represent the classes look the same, too. There's no way to distinguish a regular class from an abstract class, and no way to distinguish an abstract class from one that merely implements the interface of another class.

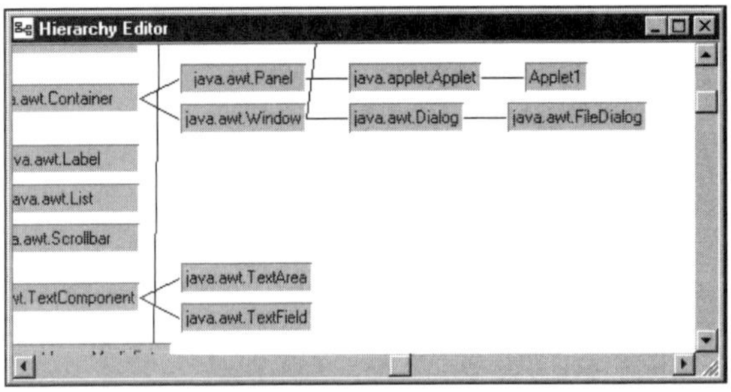

Figure 17-1 The Hierarchy Editor helps you structure your program at the highest levels.

Add to this the fact that on an average-sized computer screen you can see only a handful of classes at a time — far fewer than you might need to see in order to understand the organization of a complex Java program — and you'll see what limited utility the Hierarchy Editor has for most users of Visual Café.

Starting the Hierarchy Editor

You can start the Hierarchy Editor by choosing **Window** → **Hierarchy Editor**. Alternately, you can press Ctrl+Shift+H. You'll see the Hierarchy Editor, as it appears in Figure 17-1.

Adding Hierarchy Relationships

The most appealing part of the Hierarchy Editor is its ability to create classes and automatically make them derive from the proper other classes. When you create a new class in the Hierarchy Editor, Visual Café automatically builds a new .Java source code file, complete with the appropriate `extends` statement and explanatory comments.

To create a new class, right-click (or long-click) the box that represents the existing class (the one to which the new class will relate). You'll see the pop-up menu that is shown in Figure 17-2.

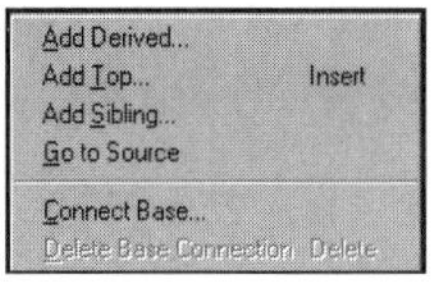

Figure 17-2 The Hierarchy Editor's pop-up menu gives you access to class-creation commands.

You can use commands in this pop-up menu to create each of the following three kinds of class relationships:

* Top classes, which are classes that derive from nothing except `java.lang.object`
* Sibling classes, which are classes that derive from the same class as the class you right- or long-click
* Derived classes, which are classes that derive from the class you right- or long-click

Following are detailed instructions for creating each kind of class relationship.

TOP CLASSES

To create a top class, right- or long-click anywhere (not just on a box) in the Hierarchy Editor and choose **Add Top** from the pop-up menu. You'll see the Add Class dialog box, which appears in Figure 17-3.

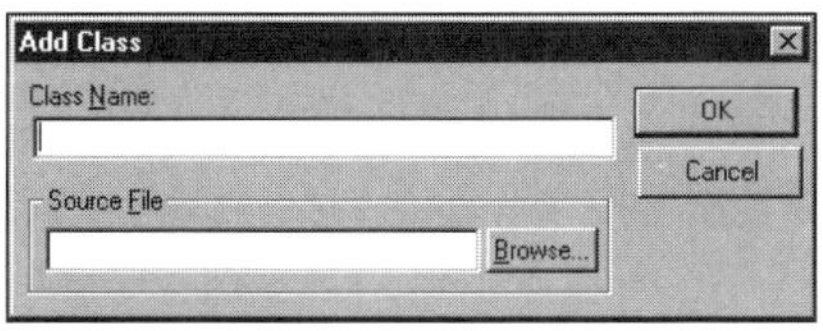

Figure 17-3 The Add Class dialog box is where you specify the details of the class you're inserting.

Type a name in the Class Name text field. Note how Visual Café automatically fills in the appropriate filename for you. Click OK, and Visual Café will parse and save the new source code file in the same directory as the rest of the project's classes.

TIP Alternately, you can press the Insert key while the Hierarchy Editor is active to insert a top class.

SIBLING CLASSES

To create a sibling class, right- or long-click the box that represents the class for which you want to create a sibling. Choose Add Sibling from the pop-up menu. You'll see the Add Class dialog box, which appears in Figure 17-3. Type a name in the Class Name text field. Note how Visual Café automatically fills in the appropriate filename for you. Click OK, and Visual Café will parse and save the new source code file in the same directory as the rest of the project's classes.

DERIVED CLASSES

To create a derived class, right- or long-click the box that represents the class for which you want to create a derived — subsidiary — class. Choose Add Derived from the pop-up menu. You'll see the Add Class dialog box, which appears in Figure 17-3. Type a name in the Class Name text field. Note how Visual Café automatically fills in the appropriate filename for you. Click OK, and Visual Café will parse and save the new source code file in the same directory as the rest of the project's classes.

Base Connections

Base connections are class relationships that connect a class to the classes it implements. In the Visual Café Hierarchy Editor, base connections are depicted as black lines.

ADDING BASE CONNECTIONS

To add a base connection, highlight the box representing the class to which you want to add a base connection. Right- or long-click the box and choose Connect Base from the pop-up menu. You'll see the Add Base dialog box, shown in Figure 17-4.

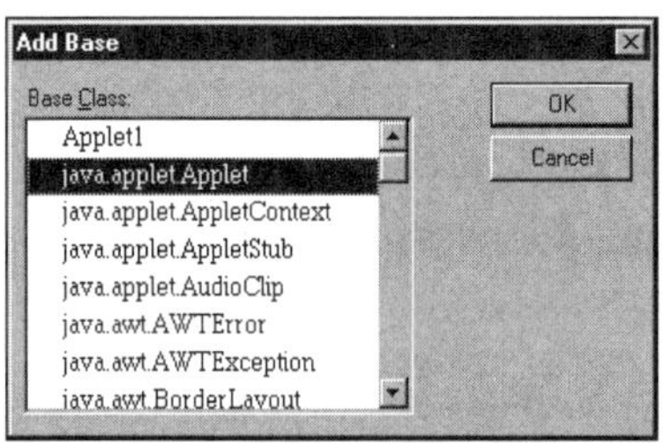

Figure 17-4 The Add Base dialog box lets you specify a class for the implements statement.

Choose the base class from the Base Class list box. Click the OK button, and that class will be added to the `implements` line of the class that was highlighted when you started.

DELETING BASE CONNECTIONS

To eliminate a base connection and remove a class from another class's `implements` line, right- or long-click the line representing the base connection you want to get rid of. Choose Remove Inheritance from the pop-up menu. Alternately, you can click the doomed base connection and press the Delete key.

The Hierarchy Menu

When the Hierarchy Editor is active, the Hierarchy menu appears on the menu bar. The Hierarchy menu contains a command that gives you more information about the class you've highlighted in the Class Editor. The menu also contains a command that determines how the Hierarchy Editor displays information, and offers yet another way to access source code. The Hierarchy menu appears in Figure 17-5.

Figure 17-5 The Hierarchy menu contains commands that relate to the Hierarchy Editor.

CLASS ATTRIBUTES

When you highlight a class box in the Hierarchy Editor and choose Hierarchy → Class Attributes, you'll see a dialog box that displays the full name of the highlighted class and a list of all of its base classes.

GO TO SOURCE

Choosing Hierarchy → Go to Source opens the source code editor with the highlighted class's code in the editing pane.

VIEW IMPORTS

View Imports can be checked or unchecked. When checked, the Hierarchy Editor displays all of the Java classes imported into your program — classes such as `java.awt.FlowLayout` and other rarely altered classes.

TIP **To keep the Hierarchy Editor uncluttered, you should keep View Imports unchecked most of the time.**

Using the Pop-up Menu

The pop-up menu that appears in the Hierarchy Editor includes a **Go to Source** command, which opens the source code for the highlighted class in the source code editor. The pop-up menu also includes a **View Imports** command, which has the same effect as choosing **Hierarchy** → **View Imports**.

Using the Class Browser

The Class Browser complements the Hierarchy Editor by showing you the details of classes — those in Java generally and those in your project in particular. The Class Browser shows you the methods and properties of each class, and provides a handy colored-diamond system that indicates which methods are public, private, and protected. The Class Browser appears in Figure 17-6.

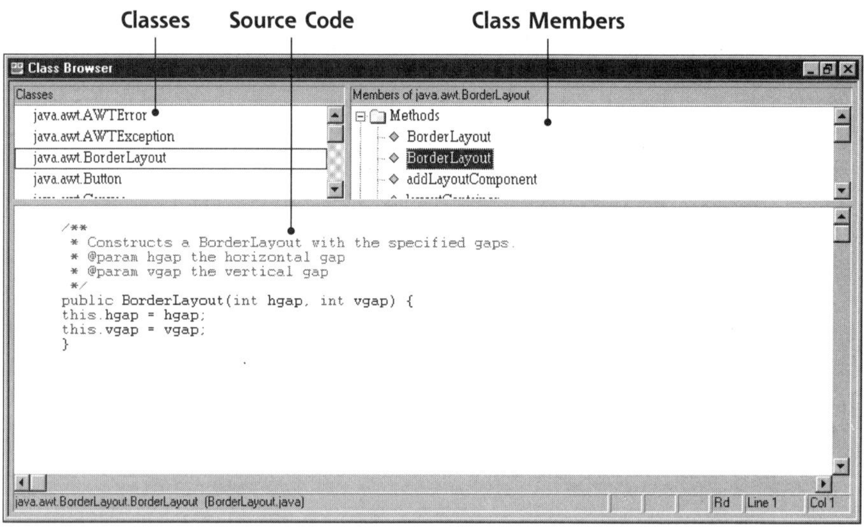

Figure 17-6 The Class Browser gives you critical class information in a hurry.

That said, the Class Browser, like the Hierarchy Editor, doesn't (at least, not as of this writing) tell you which classes are regular, which are abstract, and which merely implement interfaces. The Class Browser won't be one of the Visual Café tools you use frequently.

Starting the Class Browser

To start the Class Browser, choose **Window** → **Class Browser** or press Ctrl+Shift+C. Alternately, you can open the Hierarchy Editor and double-click the class you want to open in the Class Browser, or right-click (or long-click) a class in the Project Manager and choose **Browse Class** from the pop-up menu.

The Panes of the Class Browser

The Class Browser, shown in Figure 17-6, is divided into three panes. Each pane tells something about the classes in your program, and particularly the class you've selected for examination. The following sections describe each of the three panes.

TIP **You can re-size any of the panes by positioning your mouse pointer over the bars that divide the panes so that the mouse pointer turns into a two-headed arrow. Then, click and drag the divider where you want it.**

CLASSES

The Classes pane, in the upper-left corner of the Class Browser, lists the classes in the Java API and in the current project. Clicking or otherwise highlighting a class causes that class's members to be displayed in the Class Members portion of the Class Browser.

If you right- or long-click in the Classes area of the Class Browser, you'll see a pop-up menu containing several commands, including the following:

* **Insert Class** Inserts a top-level class in your project.
* **Class Attributes** Displays the full name of the class and all its base classes.
* **Go to Source** Opens the source code editor with the source code of the selected class.
* **Options** Opens the Window Style dialog box, shown in Figure 17-7. The Window Style dialog box contains options that have to do with which classes appear in the Class Browser, and how classes are displayed there. For example, you can choose to have classes displayed alphabetically by name, or hierarchically.

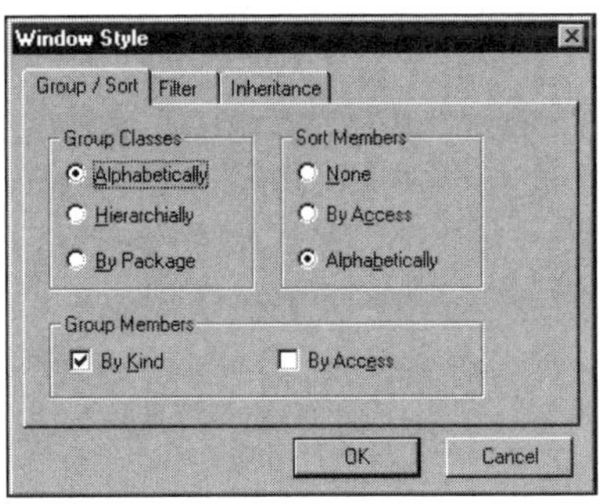

Figure 17-7 The settings in the Window Style dialog box determine how things are displayed in the Class Browser.

CLASS MEMBERS

The top-right pane of the Class Browser window contains the members — methods and data items — in the class you selected in the Class pane. There's a Methods folder and a Data folder; you can click the folder that interests you to see its contents. Note that the methods have colored diamonds next to them that denote their accessibility: Green for `public`, yellow for `protected`, and red for `private`.

If you right- or long-click in the Class members pane, you'll see a pop-up menu that contains the following commands:

* **Insert Member**
* **Delete Member**
* **Member Attributes** Displays the Change Member Attributes dialog box that you can use to change the accessibility of the selected method.
* **Go to Source** Opens the source code editor so that it contains the selected class, open to the selected method.

SOURCE CODE

The source code window, which occupies the entire bottom half of the Class Browser, displays the source code of the selected class and method — but you can't edit it here. You have to open the source code file in the source code editor in order to make modifications.

There's a pop-up menu in the source code pane, too, that contains the following commands:

* **Copy** The standard editing command.
* **Go to Definition** Opens a new Members window, like the one shown in Figure 17-8, containing the methods of the highlighted class.
* **Watch Variable** Adds the highlighted variable to the Watch window, which you'll learn more about in Chapter 18.
* **Toggle Breakpoint** Turns breakpoints on and off. Breakpoints are debugging tools you'll learn more about in the next chapter. Pressing the F9 key is the equivalent of the **Toggle Breakpoint** command.

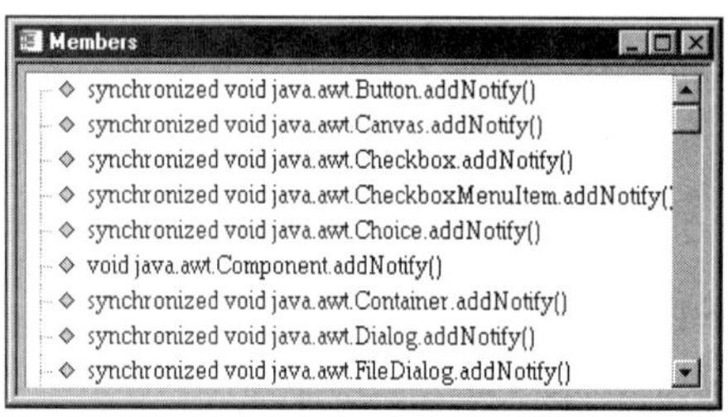

Figure 17-8 When you issue the **Go to Definition** command, you get a list of methods like this one.

The Classes Menu

When the Class Browser is active, the Classes menu appears on the menu bar. Following is a guide to the functions of each of the commands.

CLASS ATTRIBUTES

Choosing Classes → Class Attributes brings up the Class Attributes dialog box, which displays the full name of the highlighted class and lists the base classes from which it derives.

MEMBER ATTRIBUTES

Choosing Classes → Member Attributes calls up the Change Member attributes dialog box, which tells whether a class is `public`, `protected`, or `private`. You can change the attributes in this dialog box, too.

DELETE MEMBER

Choosing Classes → Delete Member does exactly what you'd think — it deletes the highlighted member of the current class. Pressing the Delete key accomplishes the same thing.

TIP **Delete Member only works with classes that are not part of the Java API.**

GO TO SOURCE

Choosing Classes → Go to Source calls up the source code for the highlighted class.

OPTIONS

Choosing Classes → Options opens the Window Style dialog box, which determines which classes appear in the Class Browser, and how they are displayed.

BONUS

Stupid Class Browser and Hierarchy Editor Tricks

The Class Browser has some little-known properties that you may find handy as you create Java applets and applications in Visual Café. For example:

- You can drag a class or method name from the Class Browser to the source code editor.
- If you double-click a method in the Class Browser, a new copy of the Class Browser will appear, with that method in the source code window.
- If you drag a line from a Hierarchy Editor box to a blank space within the Hierarchy Editor window, Visual Café will prompt you for the name and specifications of the connecting class.
- You also can create a new instance of the Class Browser by choosing Window → New Window when the Class browser is active.

Summary

In this chapter, you learned a little bit about the Hierarchy Editor and the Class Browser. You saw that the Hierarchy Editor is of some — not a lot, but some — use in viewing and modifying the overall structure of your Java programs, and learned that the Class Browser is a speedy way to find out what methods and properties are available in a class.

You discovered that with the Hierarchy Editor, you can add superior, equivalent, or subordinate classes to any Java class except `java.lang.Object`, whether you defined the class or not. And you saw that, because you can call up the source code editor quickly from within the Hierarchy Editor, you can use the Hierarchy Editor as a sort of top-level index to your program's parts.

Now, you're ready to move on to test-running your program and finding mistakes in your code. Chapter 18 teaches you about Visual Café's visual debugging tools.

CHAPTER EIGHTEEN

USING THE VISUAL DEBUGGING TOOLS

IN THIS CHAPTER YOU LEARN THESE KEY SKILLS

Visual Café helps you build applications and applets quickly and efficiently, but that's only part of its job. Visual Café also helps you debug your programs — that is, it helps you find and correct errors in order to make your programs do what you want.

This chapter teaches you about debugging in general — what it is and why you will need to do it — and goes into detail about how Visual Café helps you accomplish it. You'll learn about everything from the Messages window, which tells you when an error in your source code prevents it from being compiled: to breakpoints, which can help you localize errors by letting you move through your program a little bit at a time: to the Threads and Call Stacks windows, which can give you a glimpse into what's happening with some complicated aspects of program execution.

Understanding Debugging

Every programmer makes mistakes. You, being a novice Java programmer, will probably make more mistakes than other programmers. That's OK — it's part of the learning process. As you make mistakes and have to correct them, you'll learn what you did wrong and will be less likely to make them again. It's like learning to fly an airplane: Each time you spiral into a flaming ball of death on the ground, you're that much less likely to make future mistakes. Seriously, bugs are really not that bad.

Symantec's Java development tools had an early boost because they were the first to include a graphical debugging tool. Prior to their release, you had to find errors in your code with a command-line debugger from Sun, which was not fun at all. The result for you is that Visual Café has some of the best debugging tools in the Java development industry. These features of Visual Café can help you track down and correct your programming mistakes.

TIP **Why are programming errors called *bugs*, anyway? The term goes back to the ENIAC, the first electronic computer. Once, when the ENIAC was behaving strangely, its attending engineers took off one of its access hatches (the computer filled a room, after all) and found a huge moth shorting out two terminals with its body. The bug in the system had caused the program to misbehave.**

Visual Café has no insect-detection facility.

Before you get to the specifics of bug-hunting, you need to know about the two main kinds of bugs: code bugs and logical bugs.

Code Bugs

As you learned in the first part of this book, Java has very specific rules about how programs must be written. If you deviate from these rules — which include such things as putting a semicolon after instructions and defining blocks of code with pairs of curly braces — Java source code files will not compile. These mistakes in code, therefore, are called *code bugs* or *compile-time bugs*.

Visual Café does an OK job of catching these bugs. When you compile a program whose source code contains a code bug, the Messages window will send you one or more errors and refuse to compile or test-run your program. It will give you a clue about where to look for the bugs, but its hints aren't always much good. So you're stuck with the knowledge that there's a code bug in your program, but you have only limited knowledge about where.

TIP **When the Messages window lists several errors in compiling your program, correct the first one in the list and then try to compile again before trying to troubleshoot any of the others. You may find that the others go away, because one mistake often leads to others in the compiler.**

Logical Bugs

Often you'll compile and test-run an applet or application without incident, but the program will give you unexpected results.

For example — and this is a very simple example — you might have written an applet to take two numbers from the user, multiply them together, and display the result in a text field. You tell Visual Café to run the program and it compiles without incident and starts to run. You give the applet the numbers 4 and 2, expecting the applet to display the numbers' product, 8. But much to your chagrin, the applet gives 2 as its result. This is a *logical bug,* or *run-time bug.*

What happened? Looking at your source code you may discover that instead of multiplying the two variables that hold the input from the user, your code processes them with the / operator instead. Because of a typo, your applet divides the numbers rather than multiplying them.

There's no way Visual Café would catch this error; for all it knows, you wanted to divide the numbers all along. You have to catch logical bugs through careful testing.

Testing for Logical Bugs

To test for a logical bug, find a likely one and ask it, "If one train leaves Denver at 10:00 in the morning, traveling at 60 miles per hour, and another train leaves Houston at 11:00...." No. That won't do, but there are certain procedures you can follow to catch as many run-time errors as possible.

Every program is designed to accept a certain kind of input. The program in the previous example was designed to take numbers — integers or floating-point numbers, we're not sure. A word processor takes characters into its main text window. A database parser might take an array of field names. One thing you should do is test a program with an illegal kind of input, to see how it reacts.

Further, most programs react in special ways to certain kinds of input. Let's say you have a program that does one thing to numbers equal to or less than five, and another thing to numbers greater than five. Your testing sequence ought to include the numbers four, five, and six, even if you don't have time to test every possible input value.

If you test a series of inputs, and your program does indeed generate faulty output, how do you go about finding the place in the code at which the error occurs? At one time, you had to trace through the code by hand, figuring out what each instruction did and, with luck, pinpoint the mistake. Truth be told, that still happens with greater frequency than the makers of graphical development environments would like to admit. But Visual Café gives you some powerful tools for bug detection and if you learn how to use them, you'll get your programs up and running correctly in a hurry.

How Visual Café Makes Debugging Easier

Visual Café speeds the process of finding and correcting errors in programs. It does this in two general ways:

* It allows you to test-run your program in a controlled environment.
* It helps you see what's going on behind the scenes in your program.

Test-Running Your Program

Imagine you're developing an applet. If you didn't have Visual Café to run the applet for you in the Applet Viewer, you'd have to compile the applet into a .class file, create by hand an HTML file that included an <APPLET> tag with a link to the class file, start your Web browser, and load the HTML file into it. Every time you made a change in the Java program, you'd have to restart the browser and load the HTML document again.

Visual Café makes life much easier. With the Applet Viewer available, all you have to do is choose **Project** → **Execute** or one of the other execution commands, and the Applet Viewer takes over the responsibilities of the Web browser and HTML file. Now you can sit back and watch, devoting the saved energy to making the applet work better. Graphical and command-line applications can be test-run equally well, except that there's no need for a viewer program because applications stand alone.

Monitoring What Your Program Does

The other, much more elaborate, debugging function of Visual Café is to tell you what's going on in the depths of your program while it's executing. Visual Café has four major monitoring features:

- The *Watch window* displays the contents of any variable you specify.
- The *Variables window* displays the contents of all the variables your program is using at the moment.
- The *Call Stack window* shows references among classes in your program.
- The *Threads window* lets you follow several strands of execution in your program.

18

In addition to these, Visual Café lets you define *breakpoints,* places in your source code at which program execution halts to allow you to examine what's happening via the four monitor windows; and *conditional breakpoints,* which are breakpoints that take effect only when certain conditions are met. Visual Café also has a Messages window, which displays compile-time error messages.

Test-Running Applets and Applications

To test-run your applets or applications within the controlled environment of Visual Café, use any of three techniques:

- Click the **Run** button.
- Choose **Project**→**Execute**.
- Press Ctrl + F5.

These three methods run your applet or application until they encounter breakpoints.

When you run a program within Visual Café, the way it is displayed depends on what kind of program it is. Applets run in the Applet Viewer; graphical applications run in their own windows; command-line applications run in an MS-DOS window on Windows machines and in a text window on Macintosh computers.

While a program is running, a couple of additional commands, Pause and Stop, are available to you. The Pause command — which appears in several places, including the **Pause** button and the **Run**→**Pause** command — causes the program to stop temporarily, to be restarted where it left off. The Stop command — manifested as the **Stop** button and as the **Run**→**Stop** command, among others — stops the program so that it must be restarted from the beginning.

The Applet Viewer

When you're test-running a Java applet, Visual Café runs it in the Applet Viewer, a handy display program that takes Visual Café's automatically created HTML file and opens it, showing your applet in action (see Figure 18-1).

TIP

You ought to run your applet through your Web browser — several different ones, really — as your debugging process nears its conclusion. It's possible that something that works well in the Applet Viewer won't work well at all in a real browser.

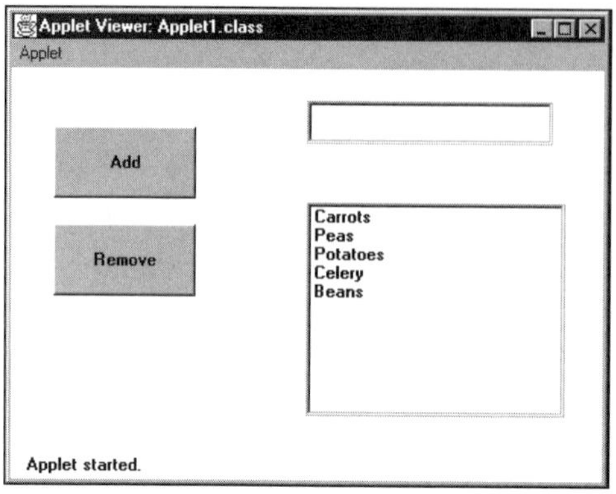

Figure 18-1 The Applet Viewer lets you see what an applet does without loading it into your Web browser.

Running Graphical Applications

Applications, by definition, run by themselves and don't require the aid of the Applet Viewer or a Web browser to exist in an operating environment. Graphical applications — those that employ windowing — can run by themselves in any Windows or Macintosh operating environment.

Figure 18-2 shows a graphical application running. Note that it's a separate program — it even has its own entry on the Windows NT taskbar — but note also that Visual Café is keeping a close eye on what the application is doing.

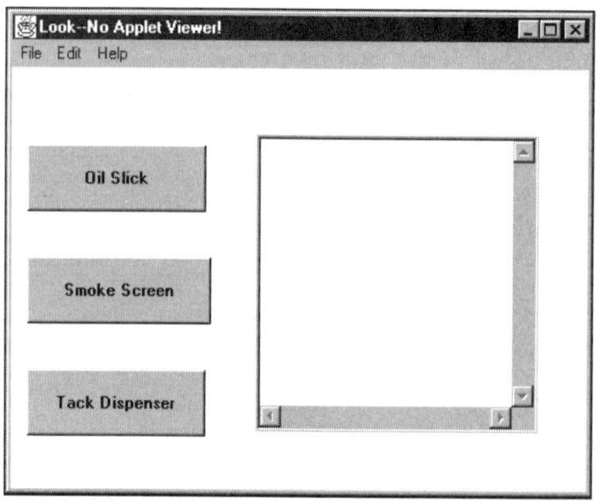

Figure 18-2 Graphical applications run on their own, but under the vigilant eye of the Visual Café debugging tools.

Running Command-line Applications

Java isn't limited to creating graphical applets and applications. Lots of handy Java tools exist that operate from the command line, with no graphical interface at all.

When you run a command-line application in Visual Café, your program is run in the Messages window, as shown in Figure 18-3.

TIP **Running a command-line application this way uses the Symantec Just-in-Time compiler to compile and run your code (that's what `java.exe` is) — unless you specify in the Project Options dialog box (covered in Chapter 21, "Customizing Visual Café") that Visual Café should use the Sun Microsystems compiler.**

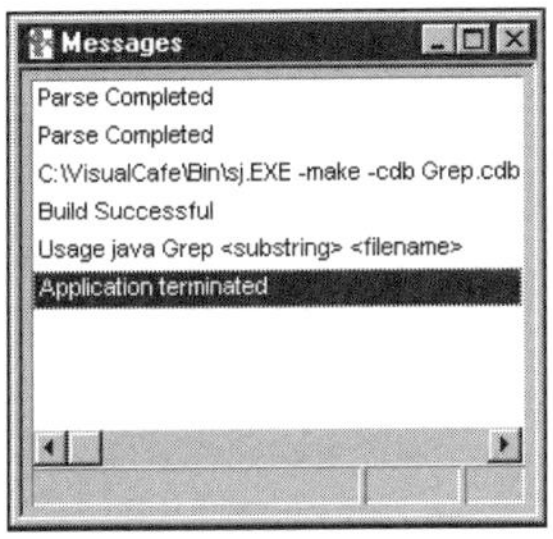

Figure 18-3 Command-line applications run in MS-DOS windows on Windows machines.

Using the Messages Window

When you first try to test-run your program, you may not get it to run at all. Instead, you may get one or more error messages in the Messages window, as shown in Figure 18-4, and the unhappy notice: Build Failed. This is an indication of a compile-time error that must be fixed before you even get around to finding problems that occur during program execution.

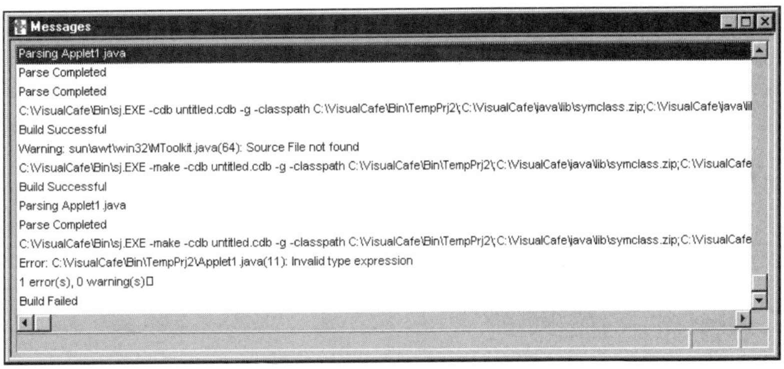

Figure 18-4 The Messages window gives you information about compile-time errors.

CAUTION

A word of warning about things that appear in the Messages window: don't take them literally. Compilers — all compilers, not just Symantec's Java compiler — are pretty brain-dead. If you leave out a closing bracket on line 25 of a program, the compiler might not catch it until it's 150 lines past the site of the initial error. The general rule is to look at the line the compiler says is faulty and then examine every line before that.

Using Breakpoints

Tracy Kidder, writing in *The Soul of a New Machine* about engineers at Data General, describes a team that spent weeks debugging the processor of a new minicomputer. One of the engineers, having worked for months trying to track down tiny faults that appeared for only billionths of a second in the speedy chip, gave up in frustration. "I am going to a commune in Vermont," he wrote in a note he left taped to his terminal, "where I will deal with no period of time shorter than a season."

Programs can do their thing very quickly. If you run a program and find that the end result is not what you want, how do you spot the place where the program is messing up? Wouldn't it be handy to be able to stop your program at key points to see what it's doing?

Breakpoints can prevent you from running off to communes in Vermont. Breakpoints are places — specific lines of code — at which Visual Café halts execution of your program and waits for you to give the go-ahead command. You can use breakpoints in conjunction with Visual Café's various monitoring features, such as the Watch and Variables windows, to see what your code's innards are up to.

Figure 18-5 shows the source code editor with several breakpoints, indicated by diamond markers in the left margin, in place. When this code is compiled and run, the execution will pause before each of the lines marked with a diamond and wait for instructions to go ahead.

TIP

What is a breakpoint in terms of what the computer sees? It's actually a new piece of code, inserted into yours, that tells the program to wait. You don't see the new code in the source code viewer — except as represented by a diamond — but the compiler sees it, and treats it like another part of your program. Breakpoints matter to the compiler only when you're test-running your program; they're ignored when you use Project → Build Applet or Project → Build Application to generate a final .class file.

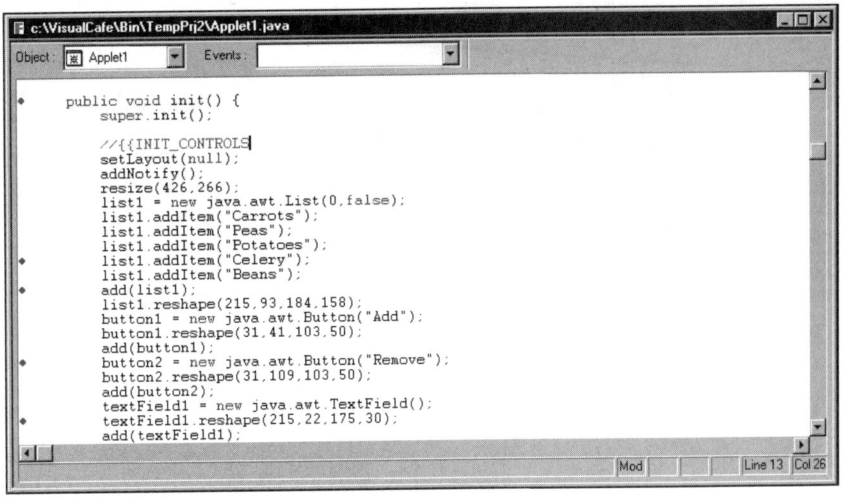

Figure 18-5 Each of the diamond markers at left denotes a breakpoint.

The next section teaches you how to set and release breakpoints, including conditional breakpoints, and how to work with them.

Setting Breakpoints

You can place a breakpoint in your source code in any of four ways. These methods all have the same effect; you can use them interchangeably to suit the situation.

THE F9 KEY

The easiest way to set a breakpoint is with the F9 key. To set a breakpoint this way, just position your cursor on the line of source code before which you want the breakpoint to appear and press the F9 key. You'll see a diamond marker appear in the left margin of the source code editor at the place you inserted the breakpoint.

RIGHT- OR LONG-CLICKING

If you right-click (or long-click, in the case of the Macintosh) in the source code editor, you'll get a pop-up menu like the one shown in Figure 18-6. To set a breakpoint, right- or long-click the line of code at which you want the break to appear, then choose Toggle Breakpoint from the pop-up menu. Again, the diamond marker will appear in the left margin.

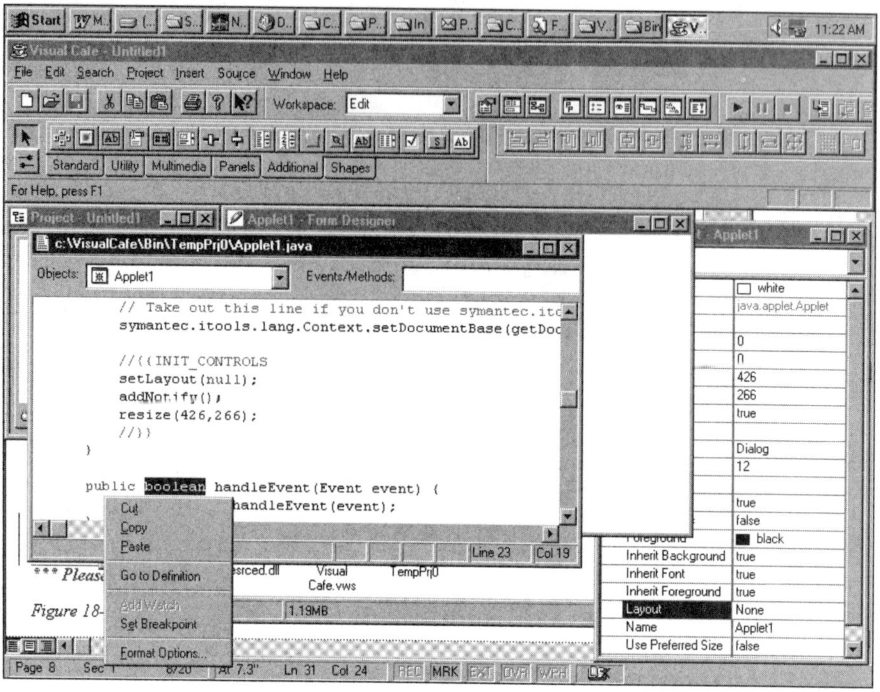

Figure 18-6 The source code editor's pop-up menu can be used to set breakpoints.

THE TOGGLE BREAKPOINT BUTTON

For toolbar fanatics, there's a button for turning on a breakpoint on the toolbar. Place the cursor on the line before which you want the breakpoint to take effect, then click the Toggle Breakpoint button. The breakpoint will be put into place and the red diamond marker will appear to remind you of the breakpoint's presence.

THE MENU BAR

You can also set breakpoints via the menu bar, though this takes longer than the other three methods. To set a breakpoint, position your cursor on the proper line and choose Source → Toggle Breakpoint. The Source menu appears in Figure 18-7. A diamond marker indicates the location of the new breakpoint.

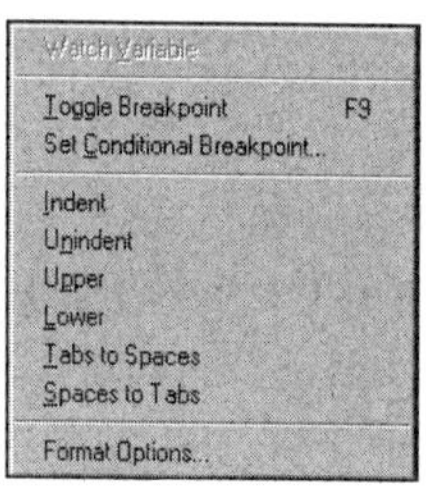

Figure 18-7 You can use the Source menu to set a breakpoint.

The Run Menu

When a program is running — whether as a stand-alone application in a command-line window or in the Applet Viewer — the Run menu appears on the menu bar. It contains commands that start and stop execution of the program in various ways in order to allow you to identify problems and correct them as execution progresses.

Figure 18-8 shows the Run menu. A brief summary of the commands on the Run menu and their functions follows:

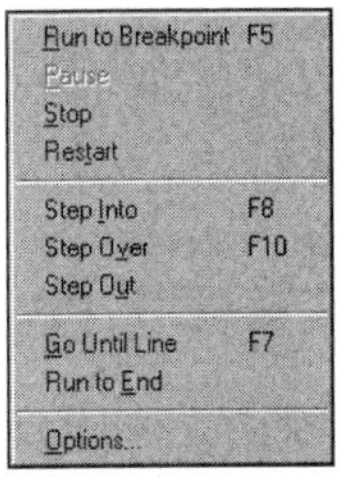

Figure 18-8 The Run menu contains breakpoint-dodging commands.

RUN TO BREAKPOINT

Choosing Run→Run to Breakpoint causes the program to start wherever it's paused — at the beginning, if it isn't at a breakpoint — and execute until it encounters a breakpoint. If there are no breakpoints in the program, this command will run it all the way through.

PAUSE

Choosing Run→Pause temporarily halts execution of the running program wherever it is when you issue the command. Pause is like a breakpoint, except it's harder to place a Pause command with great accuracy.

TIP **If you suspect that your program has gone into an infinite loop, choose Run→Pause. You can examine where your program got into trouble by looking at the contents of the various monitor windows.**

STOP

Choosing Run→Stop halts execution of a running applet or application. You must restart a stopped program at the beginning.

RESTART

The Run→Resume command starts a program from the beginning. Resume differs from Run to Breakpoint in that Resume restarts program execution where a breakpoint stopped it, while Restart begins at the beginning every time.

STEP INTO

The **Run** → **Step Into** command causes your program to execute one line of source code at a time, effectively placing a breakpoint in front of each line of code.

The Step Into button gives you access to the Step Into command from the toolbar.

STEP OVER

The **Run** → **Step Over** command treats function calls as single instructions and does not enter them. If you think you've isolated a problem onto a single function, **Step Over** can help you confirm that you're right.

The Step Over button gives you access to the Step Over command from the toolbar.

STEP OUT

The **Run** → **Step Out** command finishes executing the current function and pauses when execution returns to the calling statement. If the program encounters a breakpoint or exception before it gets back to the calling statement, it will pause there first.

The Step Out button gives you access to the Step Out command from the toolbar.

RUN TO CURSOR

This nifty feature lets you create a temporary breakpoint by placing the text-insertion cursor in the source code editor on the line before which you want execution to pause. Then, when you choose **Run** → **Run to Cursor**, the program executes up to the line on which you had your cursor. This feature comes in handy when you're tracking the progress of a program line by line and don't want to deal with dozens of permanent breakpoints.

RUN TO END

The **Run** → **Run to End** command causes your program to run from the current point to the end, ignoring any breakpoints. The program will, however, pause if it encounters an exception.

OPTIONS

The **Run** → **Options** command is yet another way to open the Project Options window — the home of compiler and debugger options settings that you'll learn about in Chapter 21, "Customizing Visual Café."

The Breakpoints Window

Want to see all the breakpoints in place in the current project? Use the Breakpoints window, which exists for precisely that purpose.

To open the window, choose Window → Breakpoints, or press Ctrl+Shift+B. You'll see the Breakpoints window, as shown in Figure 18-9.

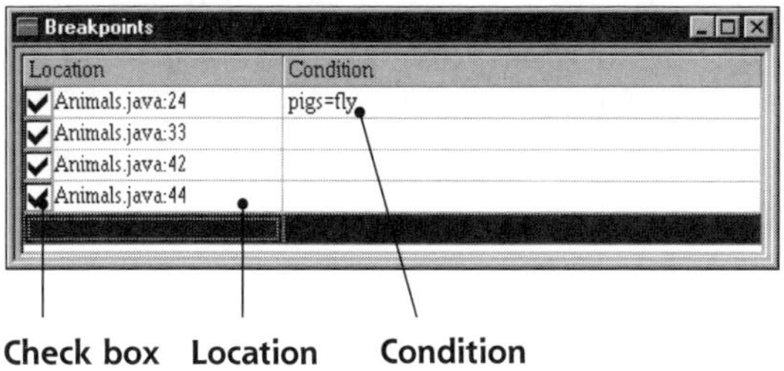

Figure 18-9 The Breakpoints window displays all the breakpoints in the current project.

The Location column, labeled in Figure 18-9, contains the source code file and line number of all the breakpoints in the current project. There's also a check box that indicates whether the breakpoint is enabled.

The Condition column, which shows the circumstances under which a breakpoint takes effect, matters only for conditional breakpoints, which you'll learn about in a moment.

The check box indicates whether the breakpoint is enabled. If the box contains a check mark, program execution will halt at the breakpoint and wait for you to tell it to go ahead. If there is no check mark, the breakpoint won't have any effect on the execution of the program — execution will whiz right by the breakpoint without pausing — but it's easy to reinstate the breakpoint by clicking the check box or using one of the Enable commands.

You can manipulate your project's breakpoints via the Breakpoints menu bar menu or the pop-up menu that appears when you right- or long-click the Breakpoints window.

THE BREAKPOINTS MENU

When the Breakpoints window is active, the Breakpoints menu appears on the menu bar. You can use the Breakpoints menu to work with the breakpoints in all the classes in the current project.

Figure 18-10 shows the Breakpoints menu. Following is a summary of what each of the commands does.

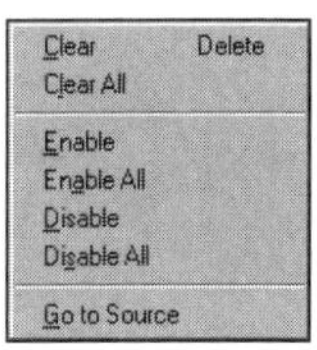

Figure 18-10 The Breakpoints menu appears only when the Breakpoints window is active.

Clear

By choosing Breakpoints → Clear, you remove the selected breakpoint from your project. The diamond marker disappears and you have to go back and re-create the breakpoint if you want it there again.

TIP **You can clear more than one breakpoint at once by clicking one breakpoint in the Breakpoints window and holding down the Ctrl key as you click others. Then, when you've selected all the breakpoints you want to clear, choose Breakpoints → Clear. This multiple-selection procedure works for all commands you can apply to listings in the Breakpoints window.**

Clear All

The Breakpoints → Clear All command removes all the breakpoints listed in the Breakpoints window, regardless of whether they are highlighted.

Enable

The Breakpoints → Enable command re-enables a disabled breakpoint. This command is equivalent to clicking an empty check box in the Breakpoints window.

Enable All

The Breakpoints → Enable All sequence makes active all the breakpoints listed in the Breakpoints window.

Disable

The Breakpoints → Disable sequence turns off all selected breakpoints, but does not clear them. Disabled breakpoints can be turned back on with one of the Enable commands or by clicking check boxes in the Breakpoints window.

Disable All

The Breakpoints → Disable All command turns off all breakpoints, whether they are highlighted or not, but does not clear them.

Go to Source

When you highlight a single breakpoint in the Breakpoints window and choose Breakpoints → Go to Source, the source code editor opens to show the line containing the highlighted breakpoint. This command comes in handy when you've localized an error and want to modify the code to correct it.

THE POP-UP MENU

The Breakpoints window's pop-up menu, shown in Figure 18-11, offers all the commands held in the Breakpoints menu, plus some additions from the Run menu, covered earlier in this chapter. A summary of the extra pop-up menu commands follows:

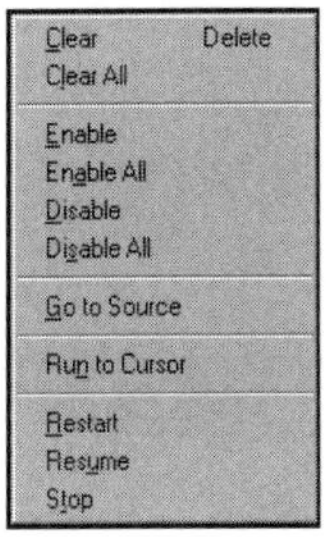

Figure 18-11 The Breakpoints window's pop-up menu gives you access to additional breakpoint-management commands.

From the Breakpoints Menu

These commands have the same functions as those that appear on the Breakpoints menu:

* Clear
* Clear All
* Enable
* Enable All
* Disable
* Disable All
* Go to Source

From the Run Menu

These commands have the same functions as those that appear on the Run menu:

* Run to Cursor
* Restart
* Stop

Resume

In addition to the commands from the Breakpoints and Run menus, the Breakpoints window's pop-up menu includes the Resume command. The Resume command restarts program execution at the point where a breakpoint stopped it.

Releasing Breakpoints

All of the methods for setting a breakpoint work in reverse, too — you can use them to turn off breakpoints after they're no longer useful. By placing your cursor on a line with a breakpoint diamond and pressing F9, choosing Toggle Breakpoint from the pop-up menu, clicking the Toggle Breakpoint button toolbar button, or choosing Source→Toggle Breakpoint, you can turn off breakpoints you inserted previously.

TIP **The methods of toggling breakpoints are interchangeable. You can use one method to set a breakpoint and another to release it.**

To temporarily turn off a breakpoint, open the Breakpoints window and click the check box of the breakpoint you want to turn off so that it is no longer checked. Alternately, highlight the breakpoint or breakpoints you want to disable and choose Breakpoints → Disable or pick Disable from the pop-up menu.

Using Conditional Breakpoints

Sometimes you'll want a breakpoint to be enabled only when certain conditions are met. Often this will be the case when you want to place a breakpoint in a recursive function but don't want to restart execution every time the function runs, as that could be hundreds of times.

For these occasions, Visual Café supports *conditional breakpoints*. Conditional breakpoints pause execution of a program only when certain conditions, such as a variable having a certain value, are met.

To set a conditional breakpoint:

1. Open the source code editor.
2. Position the cursor on the line before which you want to set a conditional breakpoint.
3. Choose Source → Set Conditional Breakpoint. The Conditional Breakpoint dialog box, shown in Figure 18-12, will appear.

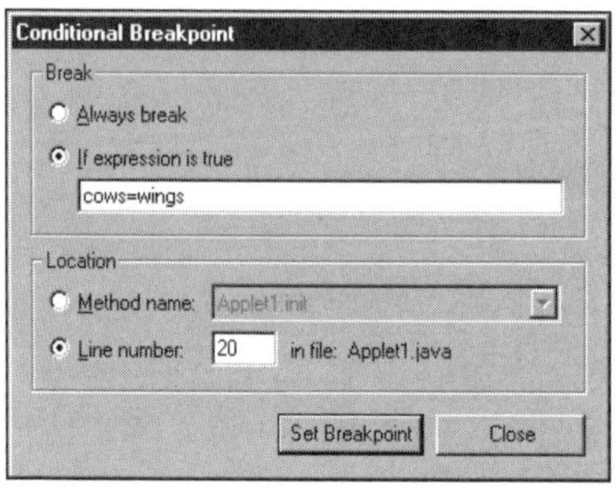

Figure 18-12 The Conditional Breakpoint dialog box helps you set breakpoints that execute only in certain cases.

4. Fill in the conditional expression in the "If expression is true" text field. For example, you might want to enter "RabbitCount = 5" if you want the breakpoint to be enabled only when the variable RabbitCount is equal to five.

Other options are available in the Conditional Breakpoint dialog box. If you select the Always Break radio button, the breakpoint isn't conditional at all; it will act like a regular breakpoint and stop execution every time the program reaches that line — unless you also click the Method name radio button, in which case the program will pause every time a particular method is called. Normally, the Line number radio button is selected and the text field is filled in with the line number of your cursor's location when you opened the Conditional Breakpoint dialog box.

Keeping an Eye on Variables

As you're stepping through your program, pausing at breakpoints and other stopping places, you'll want to know what's going on with your program behind the interface. Two main tools for this purpose are incorporated into Visual Café: the Watch window and the Variables window. This section teaches you what each window does and explains how to use them.

Using the Variables Window

The Variables window displays all the variables your program is working with at the moment. If you open the Variables window by choosing **Window** → **Variables** or pressing Ctrl+Shift+D, you'll see a display of many variables, their datatypes, and their values. You'll find the Variables window useful for spotting errors that occur when your program passes parameters to methods.

The Variables window has *context*, which is the particular portion of the program, if any, it focuses on. In the sections on the Threads and Call Stack windows, you'll learn how to tell the Variables window to display only the variables relevant to a particular thread or call.

The Variables window appears in Figure 18-13.

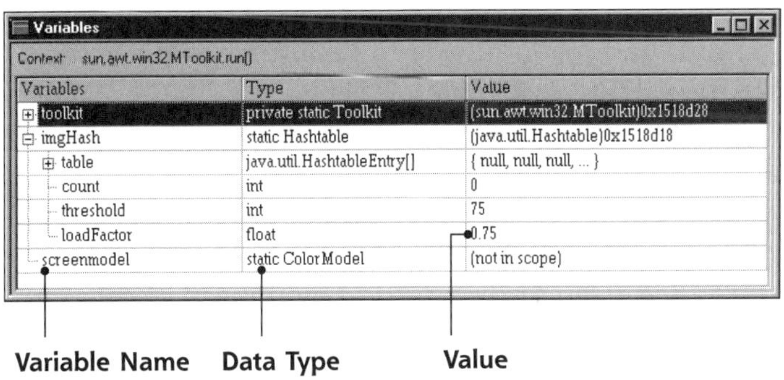

Figure 18-13 The Variables window displays all the variables active at the moment.

TIP **In an effort to troubleshoot, you can also use the Variables window to change the values of variables at breakpoints. To do so, highlight the variable whose value you want to change, then click the value in the "Value" column. Enter the new value in the text field that appears and press Enter.**

THE VARIABLES MENU

The Variables menu, which appears on the menu bar only when the Variables window is active, contains only one command. Choosing Variables → Watch Variable adds the variable highlighted in the Variables window to the Watch window, where it will be monitored regardless of whether it's active at the moment.

Using the Watch Window

The Watch window displays the values of variables and expressions at breaks in program execution. Unlike the Variables window, the Watch window monitors only the variables and expressions you specify, rather than all variables the program is working with at the moment.

For example, you may have an expression in your program that triggers a set of consequences when it reaches a certain value — `WheelRotation + 5`, for example. If you enter `WheelRotation + 5` in the Watch window, whenever you pause your program (or when it pauses automatically when it encounters an enabled breakpoint), the value of that expression will be displayed.

TIP **The Watch window displays its contents only when a program has been started and paused, such as at a breakpoint. At other times, the window is visible but its contents are not.**

You can put variable names into the Watch window, too, so it will display the values held by those variables. Enter `Counter` in the Watch window, and the value of Counter, `5` or `2904`, for example, will be displayed each time your program pauses.

For variables that contain more than one piece of data, such as hashtables and arrays, the Watch window displays the name of the top-level variable with a plus marker to the left of the listing. When you click the plus marker, the listing expands to show an indented list of the contents of the multipart variables. This works on any number of levels, so you can display all the contents of multidimensional arrays in the Watch window if you need to do so.

Figure 18-14 shows the Watch windows, with its two columns and a multipart variable labeled.

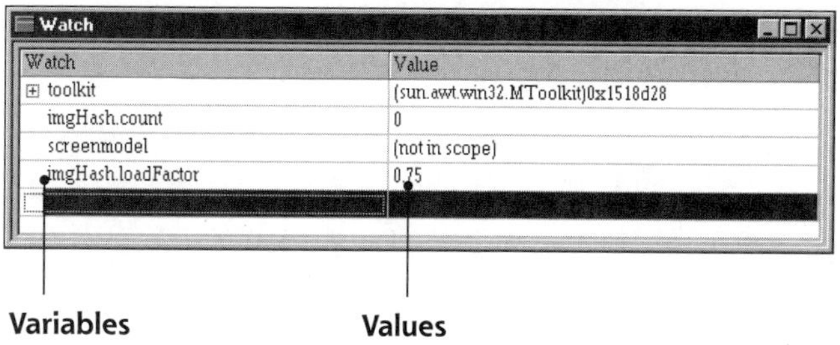

Figure 18-14 The Watch window displays the values of specified variables.

ADDING A VARIABLE TO THE WATCH WINDOW

To add a value to the Watch window, test-run your program and wait for it to pause, either at a breakpoint or when you issue a Pause command.

When execution is halted temporarily, follow this procedure:

1. Open the Watch window by choosing **Window** → **Watch** or pressing Ctrl+Shift+W.
2. Click the left column (the one labeled "Watch").
3. When the text-editing box appears, type the name of the variable you want to watch or type out the expression you want the window to evaluate.
4. Press Enter.

Alternatively, you can add a variable to the Watch window via the Variables window:

1. Open the Variables window by choosing **Window** → **Variables** or pressing Ctrl+Shift+D.
2. Select the variable you want to add to the Watch window.
3. Right-click or long-click the selected variable and choose **Watch Variable** from the pop-up menu, or choose **Variables** → **Watch Variable** from the menu bar.

REMOVING A VARIABLE FROM THE WATCH WINDOW

To remove a variable from the Watch window, use the following procedure:

1. In the Watch window, click the variable you want to delete.
2. Press the Delete key, or right-click (or long-click) the variable and choose **Delete** from the pop-up menu.

Following Threads and Calls

Java is multithreaded (it can have more than one sequence of execution going at one time) and object-oriented (pieces of code call other pieces of code). These attributes make Java eminently powerful and adaptable, but they can raise hob with your debugging efforts.

Visual Café provides the Threads window to help you track the various threads that are executing at a given moment and the Call Stack window to show you which classes and methods are executing in response to calls from other pieces of code.

The following section provides you with an introduction to the Threads and Call Stack windows.

Using the Threads Window

Much of what you do with Java involves individual paths of execution within a program — threads. You might use threads to enable your programs to talk across the network to more than one client at one time or to animate more than one sprite within an applet's display space.

The trouble with threads is that they make it harder to spot errors as they appear. Rather than having to watch a single path of execution, as is the case with programs written in languages that do not support threads, Java makes you keep track of several different threads, all running concurrently. Sometimes synchronized threads will wait for certain mutually incompatible conditions to arise before proceeding, and your program will be in a state of *deadlock*.

Visual Café offers you the Threads window, which lists all the threads in existence at any breakpoint (the program has to be paused in order for the Threads window to work; otherwise, threads would come and go so too fast to make the contents of the window legible). You also can use the Threads window to adjust the focus of the Variables window — that is, make it display only those variables associated with a particular thread and ignore others.

To open the Threads window, which appears in Figure 18-15, choose **Window** → **Threads** or press Ctrl+Shift+T.

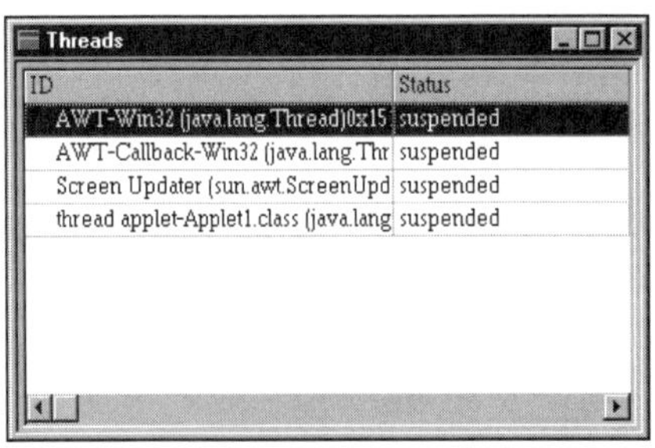

Figure 18-15 The Threads window displays all threads executing at a single point in time.

THE THREADS MENU

When the Threads window is active, the **Threads** menu appears on the menu bar. The **Threads** menu, which appears in Figure 18-16, contains commands that affect the contents of the Threads window. Following are summaries of the functions of each of the commands.

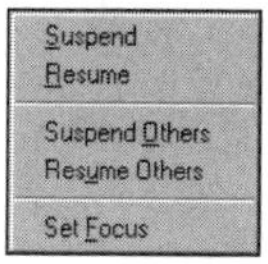

Figure 18-16 The **Threads** menu contains commands that control the contents of the Threads window.

SUSPEND

Choosing **Threads** → **Suspend** causes the thread selected in the Threads window to pause execution until you restart it with the **Threads** → **Resume** command. Suspending a thread can help you figure out in which thread an error is occurring. You can suspend several threads at once by selecting several in the Threads window with the Ctrl key and your mouse.

RESUME

The **Threads** → **Resume** command unfreezes any threads halted by the **Threads** → **Suspend** command.

SUSPEND OTHERS

The **Threads** → **Suspend Others** command suspends all threads but those selected in the Threads window.

RESUME OTHERS

The **Threads** → **Resume Others** command unfreezes the execution of all suspended threads not selected in the Threads window.

SET FOCUS

Choosing **Threads** → **Set Focus** applies the Variables window's watchful eye to the variables involved in the thread selected in the Threads window. When you've selected a thread to focus on, the Variables window displays the name of that thread below its title bar.

THE POP-UP MENU

The Threads window's pop-up menu contains all the commands in the **Threads** menu, plus some commands from the **Run** menu:

- Restart
- Resume
- Stop

All of these commands have the same functions as they do on the {Run} menu, covered earlier in this chapter.

Using the Call Stack Window

The Call Stack window displays active calls — references made from one class to methods in another. You can use the Call Stack window to keep track of what methods your program is referencing and, with the help of the Watch and Variables windows, figure out which method calls are causing errors in your program.

To open the Call Stack window, which appears in Figure 18-17, choose **Window** → **Call Stack** or press Ctrl+Shift+L.

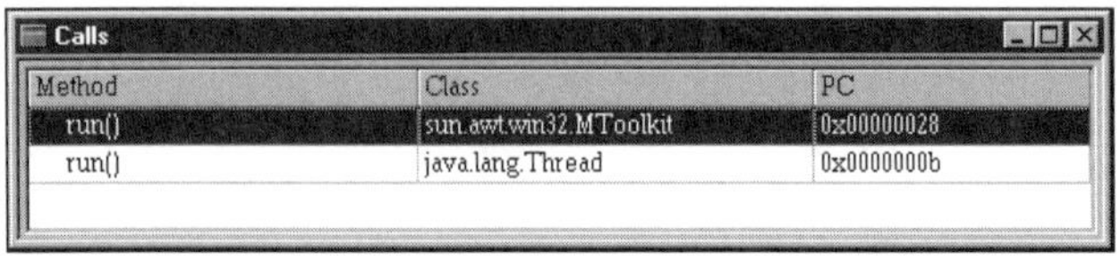

Figure 18-17 The Call Stack window lists references from one class to another.

THE CALLS MENU

Whenever the Call Stack Window is active, the **Calls** menu appears on the menu bar. The **Calls** menu, which appears in Figure 18-18, contains commands that relate to the way information is displayed in the Call Stack window and how that information relates to the contents of other windows.

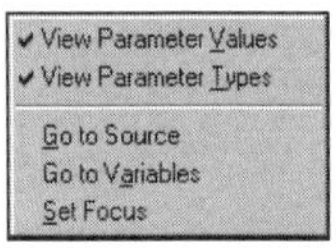

Figure 18-18 The **Calls** menu contains commands that affect the contents of the Call Stack window.

VIEW PARAMETER VALUES

When you choose **Calls** → **View Parameter Values**, the values of parameters sent along with each call appear in the Calls window.

VIEW PARAMETER TYPES

Choosing **Calls** → **View Parameter Types** causes the parameters' data types to appear in the Calls window.

GO TO SOURCE

Choosing **Calls** → **Go to Source** opens the source code editor to the class selected in the Call Stack window.

Go to Variables

Choosing Calls→Go to Variables causes the Variables window to be displayed. You might want to use this command after choosing Calls→Set Focus (covered next) to make sure the Variables window is displaying the right information.

Set Focus

Choosing Calls→Set Focus causes the Variables window's attention to be placed on the variables involved in the class selected in the Call Stack window.

18

THE POP-UP MENU

In addition to providing an alternate means of accessing the commands on the Calls menu, the Call Stack window's pop-up menu includes commands from the Run menu:

* Run to Cursor
* Restart
* Resume
* Stop

All these commands have the same functions they have in the Run menu, covered earlier in this chapter.

BONUS

Using Visual Café's Help Files

What, you still have questions after studying *Discover Visual Café*? Unbelievable. Fortunately for you, Visual Café comes with a complete complement of hypertext help files that can answer your questions about Java and Visual Café.

Getting Help with Visual Café Itself

If you have a question about how to use some feature of Visual Café, choose **Help** → **Contents**. Enter the topic that confuses you in the text field at the top of the window. As you type, the lower window will home in on an entry that matches your typing alphabetically, as closely as possible. Use the arrow keys, if needed, to highlight the entry that you want and press Enter. You'll see a help file entry explaining the topic, often with hyperlink references to other related topics.

A typical help entry appears in Figure 18-19.

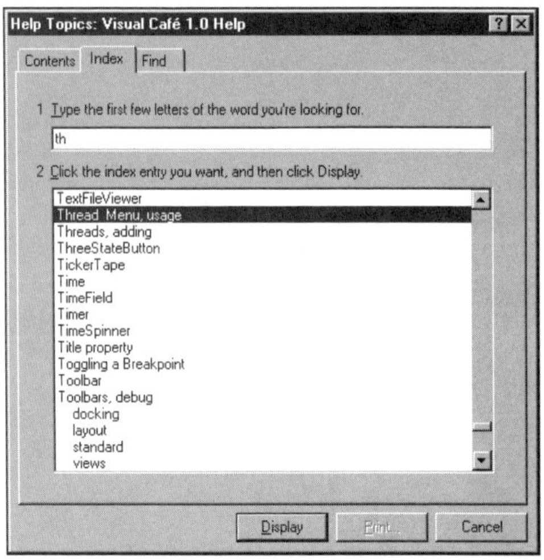

Figure 18-19 Visual Café comes with a complete set of Help files for questions about Visual Café itself, as well as Java.

Using the Java API Reference

The Visual Café Java API documentation can help you find information about particular Java packages, the classes contained in those packages, and the methods those classes support.

To access the Java API reference, choose **Help** → **Java API Reference**. You'll see a window full of instructions, as shown in Figure 18-20. Read them, then click the All Packages button.

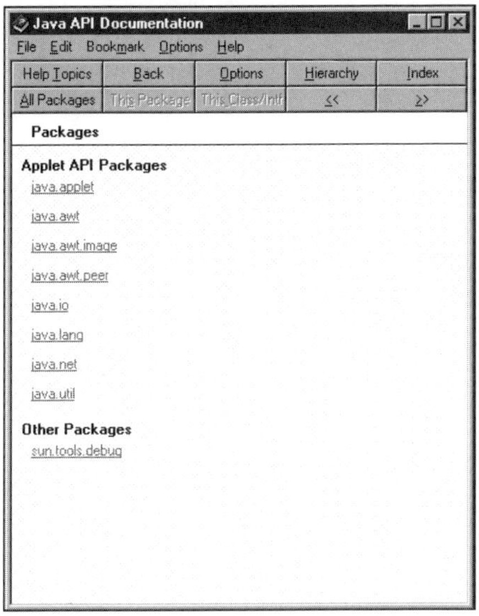

Figure 18-20 Visual Café comes with a complete set of Java API Help files.

You'll see a window containing all the Java packages — `java.applet`, `java.awt`, `java.io`, and the rest. Each of the package names is hyperlinked to a list of classes in that package, each of which is in turn linked to a description page, with links to all the constructors and methods available.

Consulting the Java Language Reference

For questions about the Java language that don't relate specifically to packages and the packages they comprise, such as questions of syntax, refer to Visual Café's Java Language Reference. Choose **Help** → **Java Language Reference**. You'll see that the Java Language Reference takes the form of an outline with general topics that, when clicked, expand to list subtopics.

For example, if you want to know about array indexing in Java, click the top-level entry for "Arrays" to see all the related subtopics, then click "Array Indexing" to get the scoop on how to index arrays. Figure 18-21 shows the outline organization of the Java Language Reference.

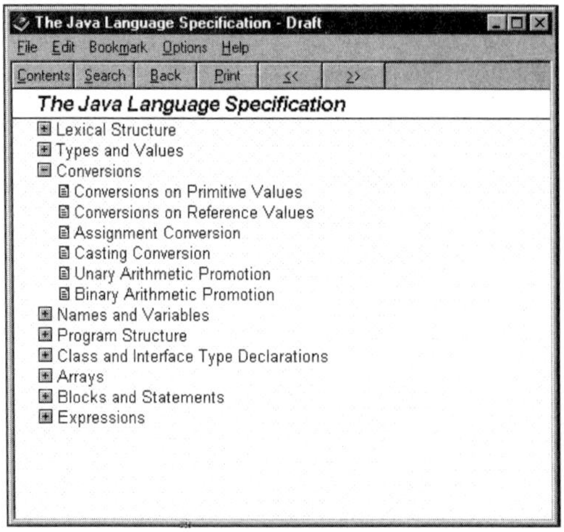

Figure 18-21 The Java Language Reference takes the form of a hyperlinked outline.

Summary

In this chapter you learned some techniques for tracking down errors in your Java programs — basic errors that prevent your code from compiling and trickier errors that allow your programs to run, but prevent them from working properly. You learned that testing for errors is a matter of giving your programs input that's likely to cause malfunction, such as data that the program is not designed to handle, or data that should yield a result different from similar input data.

You saw that Visual Café makes debugging less of a chore by providing you with tools that give you insight — literally — into the inner workings of programs as they execute. You learned how to set breakpoints, including conditional breakpoints, that pause program execution at points you define and wait for your go-ahead command. You also learned about the various Visual Café windows, including Watch, Variables, Threads, and Call Stack, that let you see what your variables and other program components are up to.

Now that you have an idea of how to find errors in your Java programs, you're ready to move on to the next step: compiling your debugged source code into .class files, ready for embedding in Web pages or use as stand-alone applications.

CHAPTER NINETEEN

COMPILING YOUR CODE

IN THIS CHAPTER YOU LEARN THESE KEY SKILLS

Now that you've carefully worked all the bugs out of your Java programming project and have verified that it does what you want, you're ready to generate a .class file, which you can embed in a Web page (in the case of an applet) or run as a stand-alone application (on machines with Java interpreters). This chapter shows you how Visual Café builds .class files.

Understanding the Compiler

Let's strip away all the luxuries Visual Café provides and look at Java in terms of its essential files. First there's a source code file, with the extension .java. You learned about source code and Visual Café's means of dealing with it in Chapter 16, "Editing Source Code." Then there's a file with the extension .class. These files are the ones that actually get interpreted and run by Java-wise computers. Files with the extension .class contain *bytecodes* — pieces of hexadecimal data that Java interpreters understand.

The compiler translates .java files into .class files. You can then take the .class file and use the <APPLET> tag to attach it to a Web page, or you can treat it like an executable file on machines designed to execute Java applications.

Using the Build Commands

The key to compiling Visual Café Java applets and applications is the Build command. Actually, there are two Build commands — Project → Build Applet for applets and Project → Build Application for stand-alone applications — but they're functionally the same; the difference is a cosmetic one. Only one of the two commands appears at a time; if an application's Project window is active, the Build Application command will appear in the Project menu; otherwise the Build Applet command will show up there.

Following is the procedure for compiling applets and applications:

1. Make sure the Project window for the project you want to compile is active.
2. Choose Project → Build Applet (if you're working with an applet) or Project → Build Application (if you're working with an application).
3. Watch the Messages window for information about compiler errors.
4. When the Message window says "Build Successful," look in the PROJECTS folder in your Visual Café folder for a file with a filename that corresponds to the name of the applet or top-level frame of the application — editable in the Property List — with the .class extension.

TIP **An applet named Hero, even if it existed in a project named TUESDAY.VPJ, would compile into a file named** `Hero.class`.

Comparing Build to the Visual Debugging Tools

Visual Café creates a .class file anytime you click Run or Step Into — but it starts to run your applet or application, too. That's not what you want when you've debugged your work and just want a .class file to run somewhere other than in the Visual Café development environment. Use one of the Build commands to create a final version of your applet or application. Use the debugging tools before you're ready to release your program to other people.

Using the Messages Window

When you issue one of the **Build** commands, the Messages window will come forward. If everything goes well, you'll see a line that ends with the name of the compiled .class file, such as `Hero.class` in the previous example. After that you'll see the words "Build Successful." This means that your code compiled properly, and you can retrieve the .class file from the Project folder. Figure 19-1 shows the Messages window after a successful build.

TIP **If `Hero.java` compiled successfully, you'd have a working class — Hero.**

Figure 19-1 The Messages window says "Build Successful" after successfully compiling.

If the Messages window doesn't show the words "Build Successful," and perhaps lists some errors and warnings, you need to go back and debug your code. The compiler wasn't able to create a working .class file from your source code. Figure 19-2 shows the Messages window after a failed build attempt.

Figure 19-2 The Messages window says "Build Failed" after unsuccessful compiling.

Setting Compiler Options

Visual Café lets you adjust the way it builds .class files. By choosing **Project** → **Options** and choosing the Compiler tab in the Project Options dialog box, shown in Figure 19-3, you can control the way the compiler does its work. The advantages of each option are outlined in the following list:

- **Show compiler warnings.** When checked, Visual Café puts warnings — notices of code that isn't necessarily faulty, but may misbehave — in the Messages window as it compiles files.

* **Show debug messages.** When checked, Visual Café displays debugging in the messages window.
* **Show all Java messages.** When checked, the messages window displays lots of extra — and generally unnecessary — compiler messages.
* **Use Java optimizations.** When checked, Visual Café builds .class files that contain smaller, more efficient Java bytecodes. You can't use this option during development and testing because it confuses the debugger, but you should use it when you generate a final .class file. Test it, however, as optimizers sometimes hold bugs.
* **Use Sun's Java compiler.** When this is checked, Visual Café compiles code with Sun Microsystems' Java compiler, rather than Symantec's. Symantec's compiler is generally faster than Sun's, but if you're encountering a seemingly inexplicable problem, you may want to try the Sun compiler to verify whether the mistake is in Symantec's compiler code.

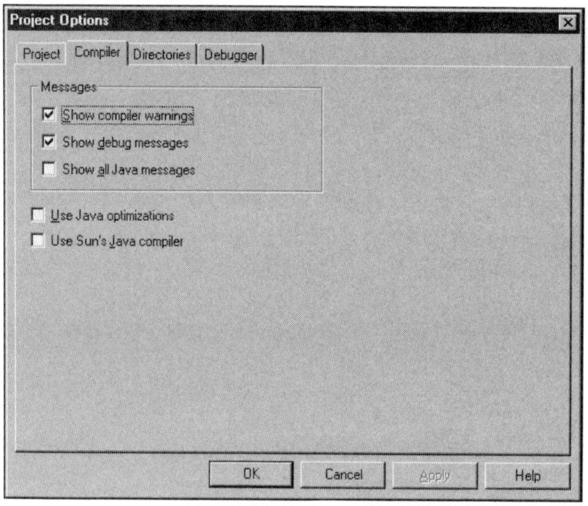

Figure 19-3 The Project Options dialog box, with the Compiler tab selected, contains many handy settings controls.

BONUS

The Just-In-Time Compiler

One of the most innovative aspects of Visual Café is its incorporation of Symantec's own Java interpreter — the gizmo that actually handles the task of converting generic Java bytecodes to platform-specific executable code. Symantec calls its interpreter the Just-In-Time Compiler.

The Just-In-Time Compiler, sometimes called the JIT or JITC, takes a .class file and compiles it for the local platform just before it's run. The net effect is that Java classes execute much faster than with the original Sun interpreter.

Can you get the JIT to work with your Web browser? Not yet, but Netscape Communications has licensed the Symantec JIT for inclusion in the next version of its Web browser. When Netscape teams up with the JIT, applets will run much more speedily.

For now you're limited to using the JIT with Visual Café programs and other Java programs that exist on your local machine.

WEB PATH **Visit `http://cafe.symantec.com` for information about the JIT and how to replace your Sun JDK interpreter with it.**

Summary

Compiling source code with the Build Applet or Build Application command yields a .class file, ready for embedding in a Web page or executing as a stand-alone application on machines with Java interpreters. In this chapter you learned the procedure for compiling your source code and the options that you have for customizing the way that Visual Café builds your .class files.

The Component Library, which you'll learn about in the next chapter, stores components of your programs so that you can reuse them again later without having to code them all over again. You'll find that most of the programs you write in Java will have certain components in common, and the Component Library comes in handy.

CHAPTER TWENTY

USING THE COMPONENT LIBRARY

20

IN THIS CHAPTER YOU LEARN THESE KEY SKILLS

Maybe you've heard the story about the man who complained to a railroad about the bedbugs that infested his bunk during a long rail trip. He received in reply a very apologetic letter from the president of the railroad, expressing the company's sincere regret. The man was somewhat pleased by the personal response from the railroad president — until he looked at a message penciled faintly on the outside of the envelope. "Send this clown the bedbug letter," the note said.

What does this have to do with Java and Visual Café? Use boilerplate — flexible, reusable modules — wherever possible.

Object-oriented languages such as Java represent the epitome of boilerplate. A class — such as one that runs several inputs through a series of equations — might be used to calculate mortgage interest in one application, then modified slightly to calculate the return on a mutual fund investment for another application.

You'll find that most of the programs you write will have certain components in common. Every graphical program uses an OK button, for example.

Later, as you program more in Java, you'll collect a group of classes for use in various programming projects.

Visual Café provides a place for you to store and organize these pieces of code: the Component Library. You can store components in the Component Library, organized in any way that suits you, and drag them into projects as you need them. Or, you can look around in the Component Library for components you want to add to the Palette toolbar.

This chapter teaches you all about the Component Library.

Understanding the Component Library

The Component Library serves as a place to store and organize classes. Shown in Figure 20-1, the Component Library takes the form of a group of folders and their contents, but it's important to know that the folders in the Component Library don't correspond to any folders or directories on your hard disk. The folders in the Component Library are purely organizational tools — they have nothing to do with file structure.

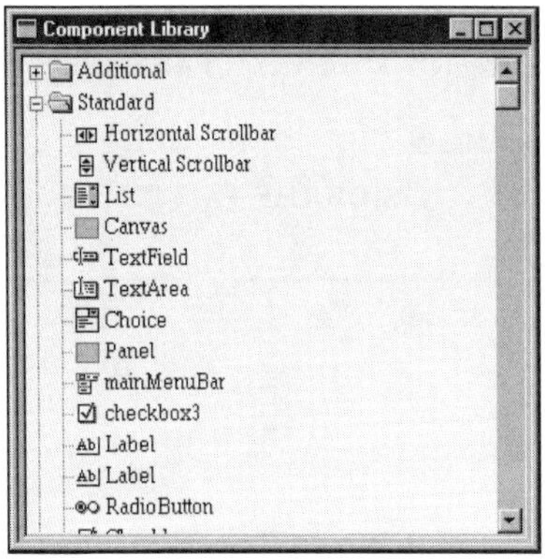

Figure 20-1 The Component Library holds reusable components.

Starting the Component Library

There are several ways to start the Component Library, though most of them are part of a specific procedure, such as adding components to the Component Library, and you'll get the scoop on them soon. For now you should know that you can open the Component Library by choosing Window → Component Library.

Closing the Component Library

To get rid of the Component Library window when it's on your screen, you have two options: You can click the close button in the upper-right corner of the Component Library window or you can make the Component Library window your active window, then choose Window → Component Library to uncheck the Component Library listing in the Window menu and thereby make it disappear from your workspace.

Using the Component Library

Now that you know how to start the Component Library and shut it down, let's explore what the Component Library does in relation to other Visual Café tools. In this section you'll learn how to use the Property List with the Component Library and how to move components contained in the Component Library into projects.

The Component Library and the Property List

Anytime you highlight a component in the Component Library, that component's properties appear in the Property List, if you have it open. This feature of Visual Café comes in handy when you want to know exactly what a component does and how you'll have to adjust it to fit your needs at the moment. Figure 20-2 shows the Property List displaying the characteristics of a highlighted Component Library component.

TIP **The Property List can do more than just display the properties of Component Library contents — it can adjust (most of) them! This is handy for creating similar but slightly different components, such as a series of identically sized buttons: one that says "Go," one that says "Stop," and so on.**

Here's how:

1. Highlight the basic component — the one you want to modify — in the Component Library.
2. Choose Edit → Copy.
3. Choose Edit → Paste. A copy of the basic component will appear just below it in the Component Library.
4. Change whichever attributes you want.

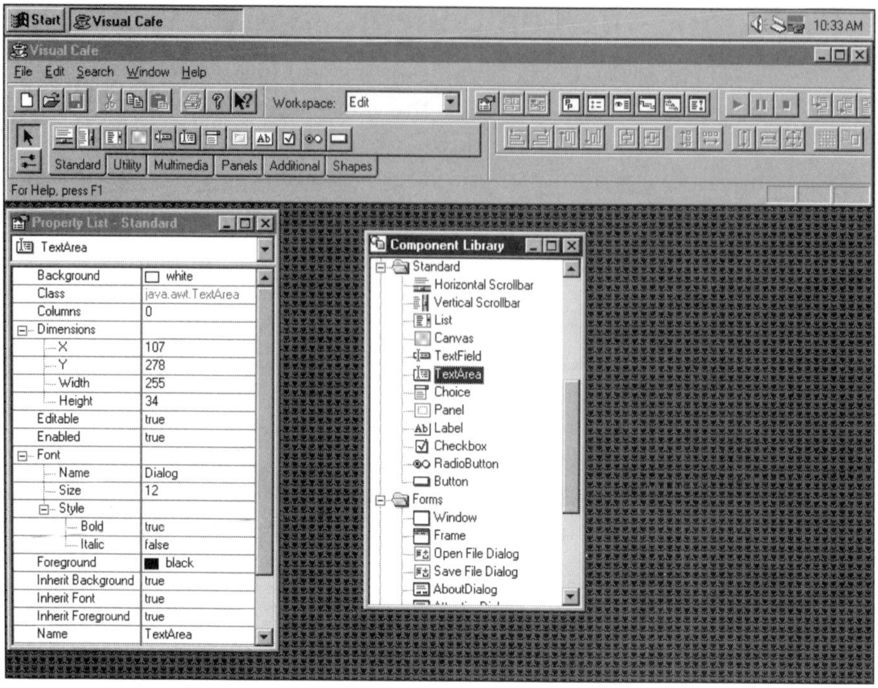

Figure 20-2 The Property List reflects what's highlighted in the Component Library.

Dragging Components into Projects

The whole purpose of having a Component Library is to enable you to add saved components to projects, saving you from having to recode classes you've already written. This section teaches you how to take the contents of the Component Library and incorporate them into the Java programming projects you're working on.

To add a *visible component* — a user interface component or a class with some kind of display — to the current project, it is easiest to click the component and drag it (a copy of it, really, since the component remains listed in the Component Library) to its new home in the Form Editor. The Form Editor automatically records the size specifications of the component and makes the new copy that size when you drop it into place. Once you've dragged a visible component out of the Component Library and into the Form Editor, you can manipulate and align the component just as you would any other component.

To add an *invisible component* — a behind-the-scenes class that isn't visible to the user of your program — drag the component from the Component Library to the Project window rather than to the Form Editor. Drop it into the Project window as a subclass of the appropriate superclass by moving the insertion marker, shown in Figure 20-3, to the right place, then releasing the mouse button.

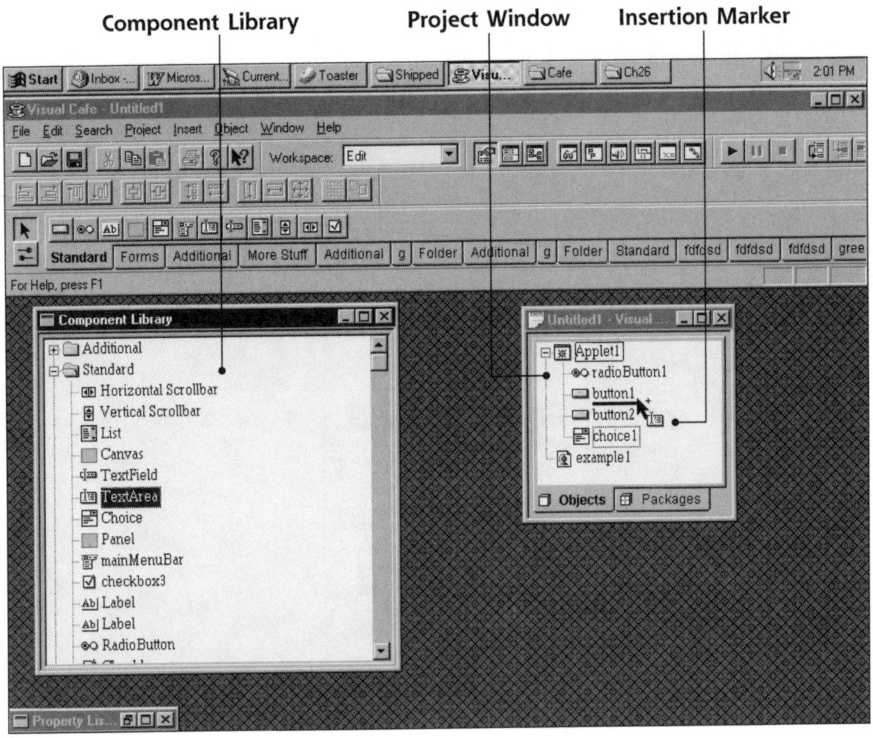

Figure 20-3 You can drag a component from the Component Library to the Project window.

Managing the Component Library

The Component Library isn't a static thing. Symantec designed it to grow and shrink at your command — you can add and subtract Component Library contents at will. Here you'll find a guide to adding components to the Component Library, adding new groups (folders) in which to organize your components, and deleting components and groups you no longer want.

Adding Components

You can add components to the Component Library in any of three ways. The method you use in a particular instance has, most of all, to do with the location of the component you want to add to the Component Library.

If the component is in the Project window, you must open the Component Library and drag the component from the Project window to the Component Library, using the insertion marker, shown in Figure 20-3, to position the component in the list.

If the component is in the Form Editor, you have two options. You can right-click (or long-click, if you're running a Mac) something in the Form Editor and choose **Add to Library** from the pop-up menu. Alternately, you can highlight something in the Form Editor and Choose **Object** → **Add to Library**. Either way, the Add to Library dialog box, shown in Figure 20-4, appears.

In the Add to Library dialog box, highlight the group (folder) into which you want the component to go and click the OK button. Don't type anything in the Name box — Visual Café doesn't use the information you put there.

TIP **You can move Component Library entries around by dragging them from one location to another, using the insertion marker as an indicator of where the component will go.**

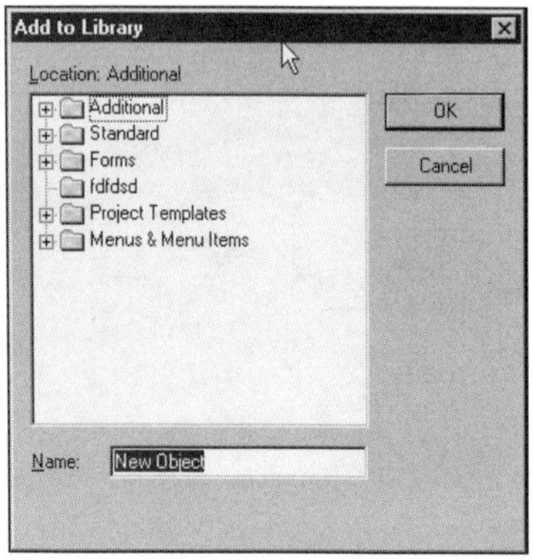

Figure 20-4 The Add to Library dialog box appears when you're expanding the Component Library.

Adding Groups

You've seen that components in the Component Library are organized into groups, and each group is denoted by a labeled folder. Visual Café allows you to create your own folders — both at the top level and nested inside other folders — to organize your Component Library the way you want.

To create a new group:

1. Open the Component Library.
2. Highlight a group or component.
3. Right- or long-click the highlighted component. You'll see the Component Library pop-up menu, shown in Figure 20-5.
4. Choose **Insert Group** from the pop-up menu. You'll see a new group icon with the word "Folder" highlighted next to it.
5. Replace the highlighted "Folder" with a more descriptive label.
6. Press Enter.

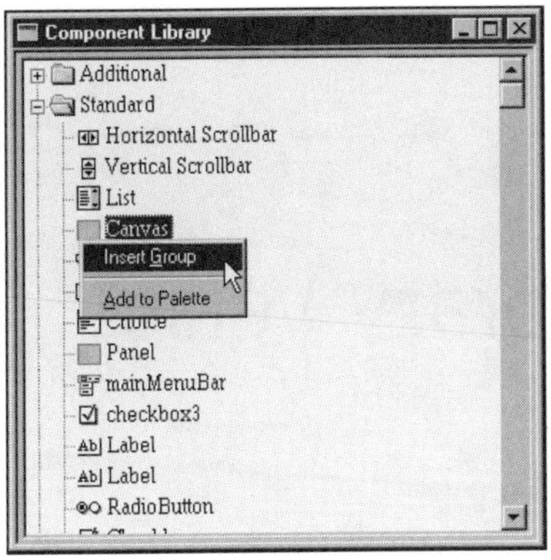

Figure 20-5 The Component Library pop-up menu helps you manage components.

Removing Groups and Components

To remove a group or component from the Component Library:

1. Open the Component Library.
2. Highlight the item you want to delete.
3. Press the Delete key or choose Edit → Delete.

20

TIP **If you're running Visual Café on a Windows 95 or Windows NT system, and you've mangled the Component Library beyond recognition, there's a fast way to return it to the factory default arrangement. Shut down Visual Café, go into your computer's /VisualCafe/bin directory, and delete all files that have .RPS and .REG extensions. Now restart Visual Café — the Component Library will contain only the original components.**

BONUS

The Component Library Versus The Palette Toolbar

The relationship between the Component Library and the superficially similar Palette toolbar is one of the weakest points in the entire Visual Café environment. These features, though they have similar functions — both serve to make it easier for programmers to recycle existing classes into new projects — have different nuances of operation, and their dissimilarities can cause some real frustration. Let's hope this problem gets better with later versions of Visual Café, but for now let's try to understand the relationships between the Component Library and the Palette toolbar.

Similarities and Differences

Both the Palette toolbar and the Component Library hold components for use in programming projects. The Component Library takes the form of a special window you must open; the Palette toolbar is always present on your screen (unless you go out of your way to close it, as you'll learn to do in Chapter 21, "Customizing Visual Café"). The Component Library can comfortably hold and organize hundreds of components, while the Palette toolbar gets cramped after you add only a few dozen components to it.

Think of the Component Library as a place to store every component you have, while the Palette toolbar is a place to keep components you use often. It's the difference between your wallet and your file cabinet: You wouldn't keep your driver's license in your archives, and you wouldn't carry the deed to your house with you at all times.

Adding to the Palette Toolbar via the Component Library

It is possible to add components to the Palette toolbar via the Component Library, but the process is not intuitive and doesn't always yield predictable results. You're much better off if you add components to the Palette toolbar with the procedure outlined in Chapter 21, "Customizing Visual Café."

Here's a glimpse at how to add Component Library components to the Palette toolbar directly from the Component Library:

1. Highlight the component you want to add to the Palette toolbar.
2. Right- or long-click the component. You'll see the Component Library pop-up menu, shown in Figure 20-6.

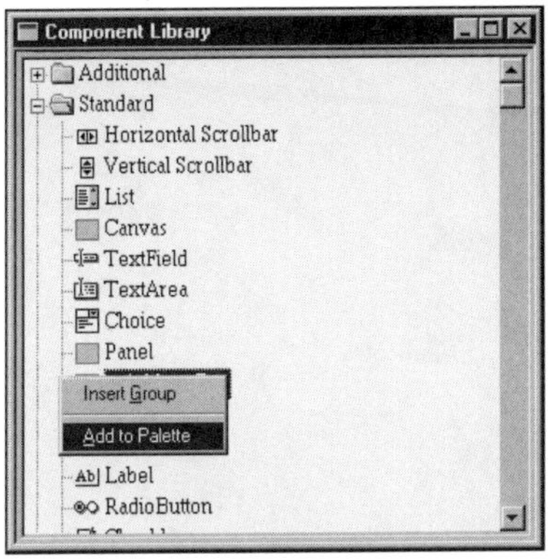

Figure 20-6 Use the Add to Palette command in the pop-up menu to make a Component Library item appear on the Palette toolbar.

3. Choose **Add to Palette** from the pop-up menu. The component will appear on the far-right end of the Palette toolbar tab that bears the same name as its Component Library group, or if the Component Library group doesn't have a corresponding Palette toolbar tab, the component will appear on the Palette toolbar on a new tab with its Component Library group name.

Again, you're better advised to add components to the Palette toolbar with the Environment Options dialog box.

Summary

In this chapter you learned that Visual Café provides you with a handy place to keep classes filed away until you need them — the Component Library. You learned how to open the Component Library, how to close it, how to drag components from it into the projects you're working on, how to add more components to it, and how to organize those components into logical groups. As you reach the end of this chapter, you've learned practically everything there is to know about Visual Café, as it comes from Symantec.

But there's more to it. You can customize various features of Visual Café to suit your personal tastes and style of working. Read on to see how to tailor Visual Café to fit you exactly.

CHAPTER TWENTY-ONE

CUSTOMIZING VISUAL CAFÉ

IN THIS CHAPTER YOU LEARN THESE KEY SKILLS

Look around your desk. Unless you happen to be a model for an office furniture catalog, you probably don't see a work surface that's bare except for a carefully aligned monitor, a blank desk pad, a group of books arranged alphabetically by author, and some tasteful artwork. Chances are, your desk features your favorite books within easy reach, your coffee cup, a collection of tapes or CDs and lots (and lots and lots) of marked-up paper. Your workspace reflects who you are and the work you do.

Visual Café works the same way — it's customizable. This chapter teaches you how to make the Visual Café environment look and function in a way that best suits *you*.

Manipulating Toolbars

Much of the work you carry out in Visual Café involves buttons on one of the toolbars. Some of the toolbars, however, are used more frequently than others, and sometimes the toolbar you need is not readily accessible from the place you're working.

Visual Café takes care of this problem by making it possible for you to dictate which, if any, toolbars appear on-screen, and whether they are attached below the menu bar or float freely in their own windows. Use the following guidelines to make toolbars do what you want.

Selecting Which Toolbars to Display

Visual Café has six toolbars:

* **Standard.** Contains buttons for saving a file, cutting, pasting, and other common functions.
* **Workspace.** Contains a choice box that lets you switch among Visual Café workspaces.
* **Views.** Contains buttons that call up many of Visual Café's most useful windows, such as the Property List and Watch windows.
* **Debug.** Contains buttons relating to test-running your applet or application and working with breakpoints.
* **Palette.** Contains the buttons that set the mouse pointer for standard and Interaction Wizard modes, as well as the tabs that hold component buttons.
* **Form Editor.** Contains layout buttons, including alignment and centering buttons.

You probably use the Views, Palette, and Form Editor toolbars a fair amount, while you use the buttons on the other toolbars less frequently. Why let the little-used toolbars take up valuable screen real estate when you don't use them much?

To get rid of unwanted toolbars, right-click (or, on a Macintosh, long-click) the status bar — the bar below the toolbars that usually says, "For Help, Press F1." The status bar appears in Figure 21-1.

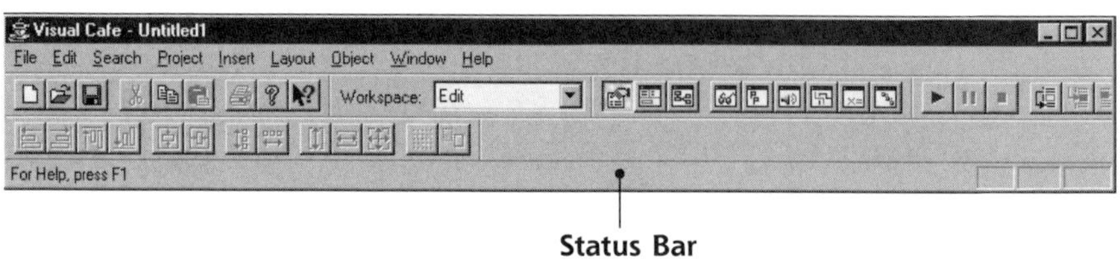

Figure 21-1 Right-click the Status Bar to turn toolbars on and off.

STATUS BAR

When you right- or long-click the Status Bar, you'll get a pop-up menu like the one in Figure 21-2. The toolbars with check marks next to them appear on the screen; those without check marks do not. To change a toolbar's status, click its entry on the pop-up menu. If you want to change the status of more than one toolbar, you'll have to open the pop-up menu several times.

Figure 21-2 The pop-up menu turns toolbars on and off.

Tear-away Toolbars

You've made toolbars disappear. Now, for your next trick, you can make them magically relocate from one place to another!

The trick really isn't terribly magical after all. You can rearrange toolbars under the menu bar or have them float in their own windows on your screen, very easily, thanks to a Visual Café feature called *tear-away toolbars.*

Moving Toolbars to Another Fixed Position

If you've shut off certain toolbars and want to reclaim the newly available space, or if you just don't like the standard arrangement of toolbars, you'll want to move toolbars around in the area just below the menu bar.

Follow these steps:

1. Click the toolbar you want to move in a blank area (not on a button), and hold down the mouse button.
2. Drag the toolbar to the new location. Don't worry if it doesn't fit exactly, or even if there's no room at all. Visual Café will make room.
3. Release the mouse button.

CAUTION **Sometimes Visual Café won't redraw a newly relocated toolbar properly. If this happens to you, switch to another application, then switch back to Visual Café. This gives the program a chance to redraw its window.**

Figure 21-3 shows rearranged toolbars.

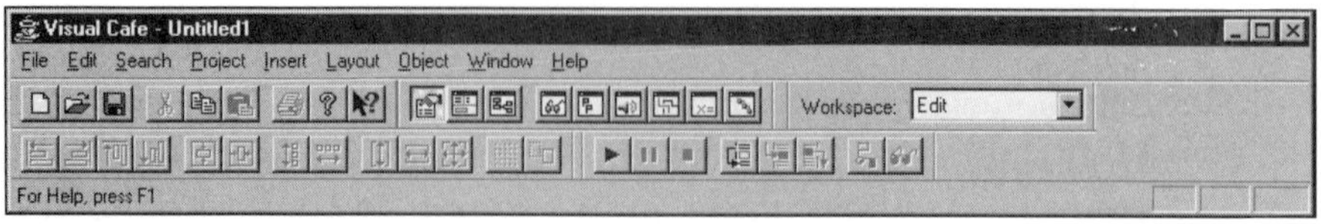

Figure 21-3 These toolbars are fixed in place, but not in the standard positions.

Making Toolbars Free-floating Windows

If you don't want a toolbar locked to the top of your workspace at all, and would rather move it closer to where you're working, you can make it into a free-floating window that you can relocate or close at will.

Follow these steps:

1. Click the toolbar you want to move in a blank area (not on a button), and hold down the mouse button.
2. Drag the toolbar down, away from the menu bar.
3. Release the mouse button.

You can close a free-floating toolbar, like the one in Figure 21-4, whenever you want by clicking the "X" button in its upper right-hand corner, or by right-clicking the Status bar and unchecking its menu entry the old-fashioned way.

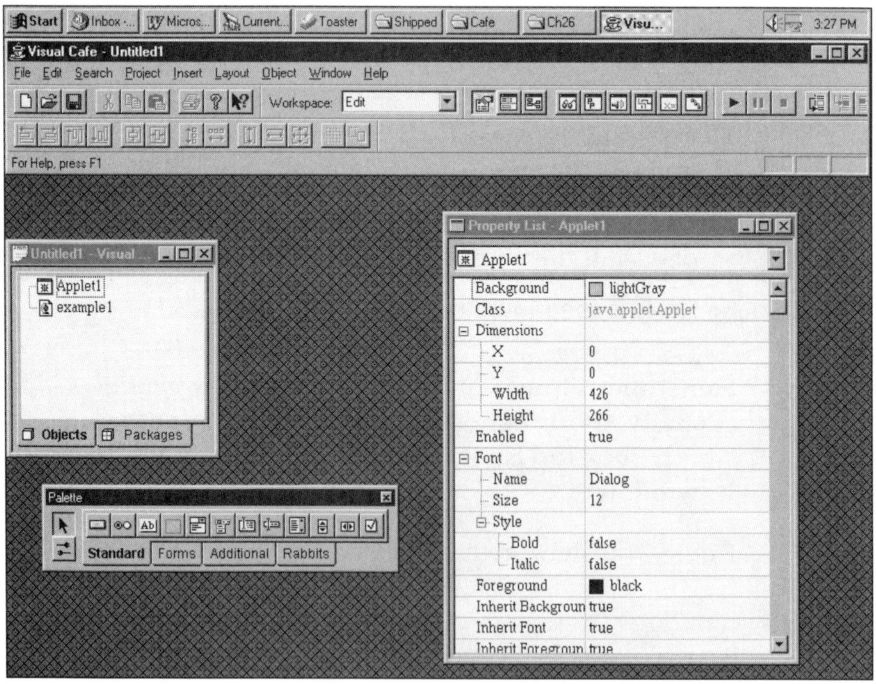

Figure 21-4 This Palette toolbar has slipped its moorings and floats freely as its own window.

Modifying the Palette Toolbar

You'll use the Palette toolbar more frequently than any of the others. Its three standard tabs get quite a workout as you drag components from them into the Project window and Form Editor. But soon you'll find that you want to use components that aren't on the Palette toolbar.

With Visual Café, you can add your own component buttons to the toolbar — and even add more tabs to fit them on. Figure 21-5 shows a modified Palette toolbar, with a new tab called Rabbits. Let's see how to make your own.

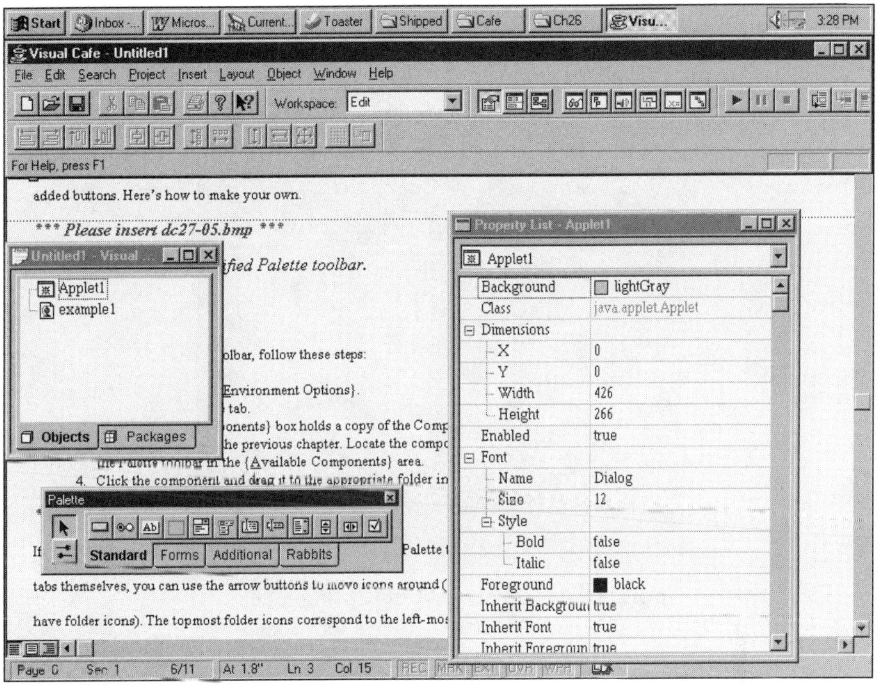

Figure 21-5 A modified Palette toolbar

Adding Buttons

To add a button to the Palette toolbar, follow these steps:

1. Choose **File** → **Environment Options**.
2. Click the Tool Palette tab.
3. The **Available Components** box holds a copy of the Component Library, which you learned about in the previous chapter. Locate the component you want to add to the Palette toolbar in the **Available Components** area.

4. Click the component and drag it to the appropriate folder in the Palette area on the right side of the Environment Options dialog box.

TIP **If you want to change the sequence of component buttons on a Palette toolbar tab, or the sequence of the tabs themselves, you can use the arrow buttons to move icons around (components have various icons; tabs have folder icons). The topmost folder icons correspond to the leftmost tabs, and the topmost components will appear on the left end of their tabs.**

Take a look at Figure 21-6 for an idea of where the important buttons are.

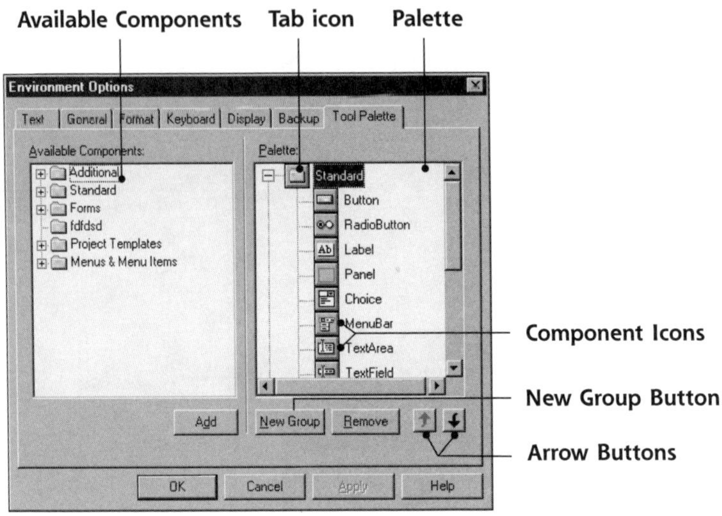

Figure 21-6 Key parts of the Environment Options window's Tool Palette tab

Adding Tabs

You can add your own tabs with even more ease than you can add components to tabs:

1. Position the cursor anywhere in the Palette portion of the Environment Options dialog box's Tool Palette tab.
2. Click the **New Group** button, which is labeled in Figure 21-6.
3. A new folder icon, corresponding to the new tab, will appear at the bottom of the list of tabs.
4. Type a name for the tab in the box next to it and press Enter.
5. To rearrange the sequence of tabs use the arrow buttons.

If you add more tabs than the Palette toolbar space will allow, the space won't expand and scrollbars won't appear. Instead, the tabs will shrink, so size your labels accordingly.

Working with Workspaces

Workspaces are combinations of windows — such as the Form Editor, Property List, Project window, and Watch window — that are well-suited to a task and that can be called up quickly via the Workspaces toolbar choice box or the Window → Workspaces command. Visual Café comes with two standard workspaces — Edit and Debug — already configured, but you can add, remove, or rename workspaces any way you like.

Adding a Workspace

To add a workspace to your copy of Visual Café:

1. Configure Visual Café the way you want the new workspace to be. Open all the windows you want open in the new workspace.
2. Choose Window → Workspaces → New. You'll see the New Workspace dialog box, shown in Figure 21-7.

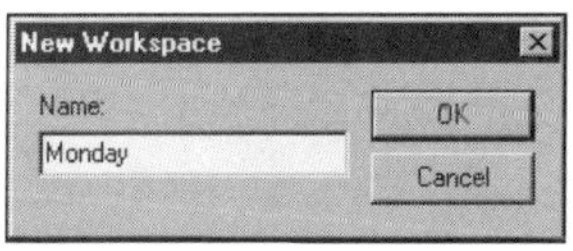

Figure 21-7 The New Workspace dialog box

3. Type the name of the new workspace in the New Workspace dialog box.
4. Click OK.

Deleting a Workspace

To remove a workspace:

1. Open the workspace you want to delete.
2. Choose Window → Workspaces → Delete.

Renaming a Workspace

To change the name of a workspace:

1. Open the workspace you want to rename.
2. Choose Window → Workspaces → Rename. You'll see the Rename Workspace dialog box, shown in Figure 21-8.

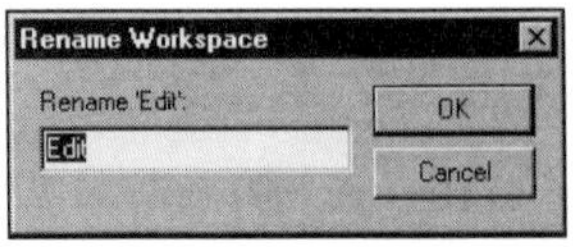

Figure 21-8 The Rename Workspace dialog box changes the name of the current workspace.

3. Enter the workspace's new name in the Rename Workspace dialog box.
4. Click OK.

Environment Options

You've already worked with the Environment Options dialog box to adjust the contents of the Palette toolbar. This section introduces you to the many other functions of this catch-all dialog box that controls the way Visual Café looks and acts. The Environment Options dialog box has seven tabs:

* Text
* General
* Format
* Keyboard
* Display
* Backup
* Tool Palette

Remember, to open the Environment Options dialog box, which appears in Figure 21-9, choose File → Environment Options.

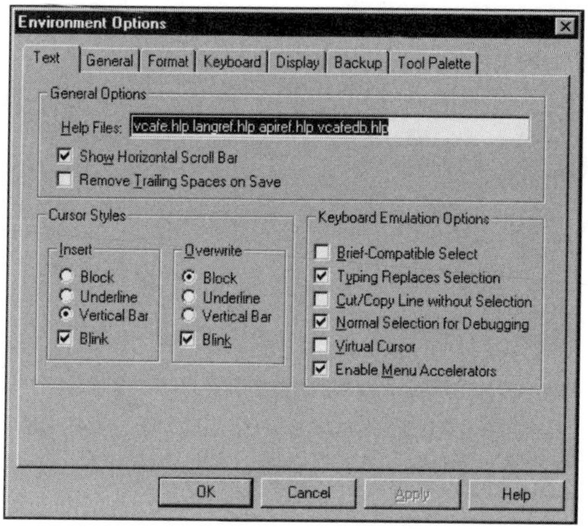

Figure 21-9 The seven tabs of the Environment Options dialog box contain many adjustment controls.

Text

The Text tab holds several options, not all of them related to text (the important text options are on the Display tab). Here you can set everything from the help files Visual Café uses to the style of cursor on the Text tab.

General

The General tab includes adjustments for the number of procedures you can undo with the Edit→Undo command and whether Visual Café asks you to confirm the actions you take in the Hierarchy Editor.

Format

The options on the Format tab determine how text appears in the source code editor (some of these options overlap those in the Current Buffer Settings dialog box, which you learned about in Chapter 17, "Using the Hierarchy Editor and Class Browser") — including whether it makes Java and HTML keywords a special color.

TIP **You can define your own keywords for highlighting by clicking the Edit Custom button. If future versions of Java have new keywords, you can add them here and keep your copy of Visual Café up-to-date.**

You also can use keyword highlighting to assign a special color to classes you use a lot. This way, they only change color when you spell them right.

Keyboard

The Keyboard tab, shown in Figure 21-10, lets you define keyboard shortcuts for Visual Café operations. For example, you might want to make the F2 key the equivalent of the Search → Go to Next Error command. You can make your work in Visual Café go much faster with a set of easy-to-use and easy-to-remember keyboard shortcuts.

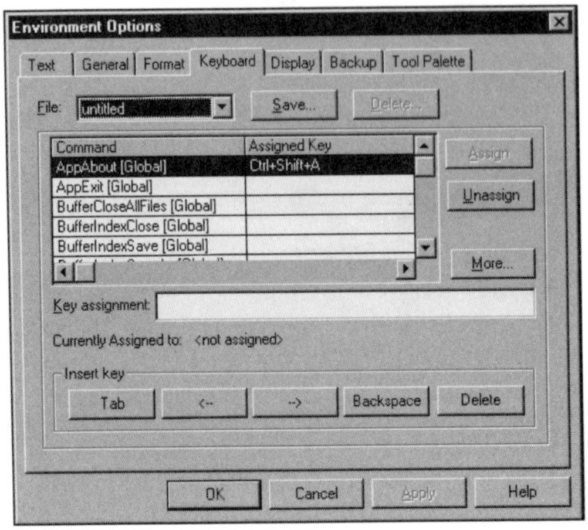

Figure 21-10 The Keyboard tab of the Environment Options dialog box lets you map commands to keystrokes.

Display

The Display tab lets you set the appearance of text in various Visual Café windows. Here you can change the color of comment text in the source code editor or choose the font in which search results are displayed. Choose the window from the list box in the upper-left corner, and the specific kind of text in the list box in the lower-left corner.

Backup

The Backup tab contains options related to automatic saving. Here you can choose to have the computer save your work every so many minutes, or have it save a .BAK file containing the previous version of your project each time you save.

TIP **If you've heard it once, you've heard it a thousand times: save often. Autosave isn't enabled by default, so head to the Backup tab and turn it on right away.**

Tool Palette

For complete instructions on this tab, see the "Modifying the Palette Toolbar" section, earlier in this chapter.

BONUS

Creating a Project Template

When you choose **File** → **New Project**, you will see the New Project dialog box, which contains the templates available to you when you're starting a project. Visual Café comes with three templates: a bare-bones applet, a bare-bones application, and a totally empty project. But what if you do a lot of applets with similar interfaces, or if you always call certain methods and want them included in all your Java applications?

Visual Café makes it possible for you to add your own templates to the New Project dialog box. All you have to do is set up a project the way you want the template to be, then define that project as a template.

Here's the procedure:

1. Set up a project with everything you want in your new template.
2. Choose **Project** → **Create Project Template**. The Create Project Template dialog box, shown in Figure 21-11, will appear.

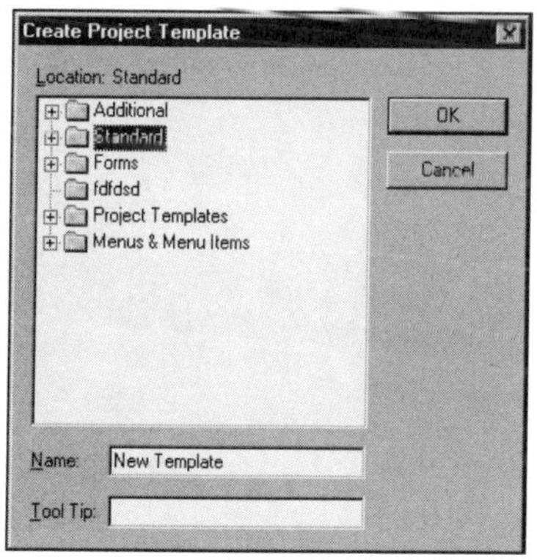

Figure 21-11 The Create Project Template dialog box allows you to define the contents of a project template.

3. Type a name for your template in the text field labeled "Name."
4. If you want to, type some text that explains the purpose of the new template in the text field labeled "Tool Tip."
5. Ideally you should highlight the Project Templates folder before you click OK. That way, all your templates will be in one place. If you don't highlight the Project Templates folder, however, your new template will still appear in the New Project dialog box.
6. Click OK.

Visual Café automatically decides which icon accompanies your template in the New Project dialog box (there's one for applets and one for everything else) based on the contents of the template's source code.

Summary

In this chapter you learned how to make Visual Café look and act the way that best suits you. You adjusted the program to enable you to work (and play) even faster and more effectively.

Congratulations! You've read all this book has to offer on the subjects of Java and Visual Café. Now move on and learn about Visual Café's database-wise brother and business-savvy sister: Visual Café Pro and Visual Café Enterprise.

CHAPTER TWENTY-TWO

DISCOVER VISUAL CAFÉ PRO AND VISUAL CAFÉ ENTERPRISE

IN THIS CHAPTER YOU LEARN THESE KEY SKILLS

So now you're an expert on Visual Café. It's been said that the mark of an expert is the ability to point out the limits and shortcomings of a subject — and by now, you may have started to pick up on the limitations of Visual Café.

What happens if you want to create a database-centric application with Visual Café — say, one that looks in an SQL database for information, then performs Java operations on that information? You're in for a long stretch of custom-code writing. And what happens if you're the MIS manager of a chain of several stores, and you want to create a networked point-of-sale inventory management program? You're pretty much up a creek.

Symantec, in its ongoing quest to dominate the Java rapid application development environment market, has two products that do everything that Visual Café does, plus some additional features. Visual Café Pro adds database-management programming tools to Visual Café, and Visual Café Enterprise adds tools for creating programs that handle many transactions across a network.

This chapter gives you an introduction to Visual Café Pro and Visual Café Enterprise.

NOTE **At this writing, Visual Café Enterprise is still deep in development, and only sketchy details about it are available. This book contains the best information we could get — but it's likely that the details of the program will have changed by the time it actually becomes available. That's the software industry for you.**

Visual Café Pro

Designed to appeal to the Java programmer whose main interests lie in giving people access to databases via the Internet or an intranet, Visual Café Pro keeps the look and feel — and all of the features — of Visual Café and supplements them with programming tools that speed the design and implementation of database interfaces.

Visual Café Pro has a suggested retail price of $499, in contrast to $199 for the standard version of Visual Café.

The two main additional features of Visual Café Pro are dbANYWHERE and an intelligent agent code-named Merlin.

dbANYWHERE

The dbANYWHERE feature of Visual Café Pro allows a person using a TCP/IP network, such as the Internet, to access a database of practically any kind without having to first install client-side database software on the same computer as his or her Web browser. All the client-side database drivers reside with dbANYWHERE, insulated from the browser on the server.

Here's how it will work in real life: A person surfing the Web wants to find out when flights leave from Salt Lake City bound for Dallas. It so happens, in this example, that a database containing departure information for Salt Lake City International Airport exists on a Web server you created with Visual Café Pro. The person enters the URL of your site in his or her browser and gets a form — more about how Visual Café Pro helps you design forms in a moment — that asks for query information, such as the date, destination city, and airline.

So the Web surfer — whose computer holds no database drivers, by the way, just a Java-wise browser — enters the requested information in the form and submits it to the server. When it arrives at the server, dbANYWHERE takes over and translates the raw data from the user into whatever format the database prefers — whether it is a Microsoft Access database, an Oracle Server 7.*x* database, or any of about 30 other kinds of databases that dbANYWHERE supports is irrelevant. Then, dbANYWHERE sends the translated query to the database, gets a reply, and translates the reply into a format that can be incorporated into a Java applet running on the client machine. The whole exchange is fast, secure, and doesn't require database drivers on the client machine.

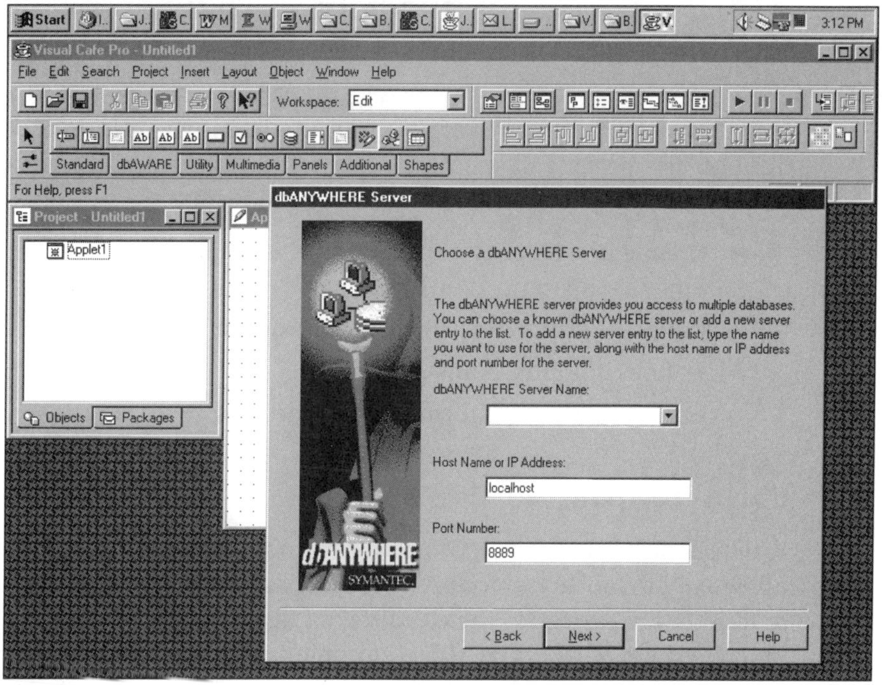

Figure 22-1 Visual Café Pro features a database-aware interaction wizard that works with Symantec's dbANYWHERE servers.

What databases does dbANYWHERE support? Quite a few, including the following:

* Microsoft Access 2.0 and 7.0
* Microsoft SQL Server 4.*x* and 6.*x*
* Oracle Server 7.*x*
* Sybase SQL Anywhere 5.0 (Watcom SQL 4.0) using ODBC
* Sybase SQL Server Systems 4.*x*, 10.*x*, and 11.*x* using DB-Library
* Other ODBC databases

Additionally, dbANYWHERE supports JDBC, Sun Microsystems' standard for Java-based database queries and the Visual Café Pro API, an enhanced version of JDBC that includes more flexible query commands.

Merlin

Merlin, the code name for the enhancements to the Visual Café programming environment that distinguish Visual Café Pro from Visual Café, includes three main parts: the wizards, dbNAVIGATOR, and dbAWARE components.

WIZARDS

Visual Café Pro comes with four semi-intelligent wizards designed to guide you through the process of creating Java forms that interface with databases via dbANYWHERE. The wizards do all of the following:

* Creates a form that corresponds to fields in a database (This Wizard appears in Figure 22-1.)
* Connects an existing form to a database
* Defines database joins
* Creates tables and forms from templates

dbNAVIGATOR

A real boon to developers of networked database applications, dbNAVIGATOR allows you to look at your dbANYWHERE server across the network and see what databases it can access. You can then examine the data fields in those databases and use them with dbAWARE components, which are covered in the following section, to build database applications.

The greatest thing about dbNAVIGATOR is its facility to graphically display the fields in a database and to allow you to drag those graphical representations into the Java forms you're designing.

dbAWARE COMPONENTS

Visual Café Pro comes with all of the components found in Visual Café, such as buttons and check boxes, plus additional components that make database access more automatic. These additional components, called dbAWARE components, include the following:

* **Session.** Creates and maintains a socket connection across a TCP/IP network to a dbANYWHERE server.
* **TextArea.** Different from the regular TextArea component, the dbAWARE TextArea displays a view of a database and keeps it updated in real time. Similarly featured dbAWARE versions of TextField, ListBox, and CheckBox are available, too.
* **ImageViewer.** Similar to the dbAWARE TextArea, ImageViewer supports the display of images from a database.

Visual Café Enterprise

Even deeper in development than Visual Café Pro is Visual Café Enterprise. This super-high-end version of Visual Café will incorporate all of the features of Visual Café and Visual Café Pro, plus features designed to aid the creation of large-scale networked Java applications. Visual Café Enterprise will most likely carry a price tag of $999 or so.

Visual Café Enterprise will also most likely facilitate the creation of Java applications used by geographically distributed companies that are linked by a network, in situations where many people need to access and modify a database more or less simultaneously. Visual Café Enterprise will probably feature a version of dbANYWHERE that allows extensive monitoring and management of queries to the database by clients on the network. It will also probably include more advanced security features than Visual Café and Visual Café Pro. Wait and see.

BONUS

Keeping Up With Symantec News

The best way to keep up with news about your Java programming tools is to keep an eye on several online resources.

WEB PATH **Visit** `http://cafe.symantec.com` **for the latest dirt on Visual Café, Visual Café Pro, Visual Café Enterprise, and every other Symantec product.**

The Symantec Web site is so up-to-date even Symantec employees use it to get the latest copies of their company's software.

You may also want to scan such print publications as *Macworld, PC World, Java Report, Internet World, Mac User,* and *PC Magazine* for news about Java development environments.

Summary

In this chapter, you learned a little bit about Visual Café's big siblings: Visual Café Pro and Visual Café Enterprise. You saw that these relatively high-end integrated development environments fill in the gaps left by Visual Café.

- Visual Café Pro adds programming tools that make database connectivity easier.
- Visual Café Enterprise adds database-connectivity tools and features that facilitate the creation of programs that will handle many transactions over a network, as in the case of a centralized inventory-management system.

You also got the scoop on the Symantec Web site — `http://cafe.symantec.com` — where you can get up-to-the minute information about new products in the Visual Café family.

DISCOVERY CENTER

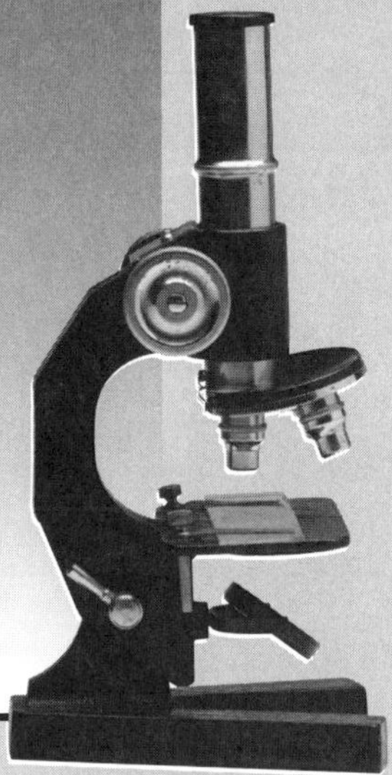

In this section, you'll discover many of the important steps for how to accomplish tasks in Visual Café. The Discovery Center serves as a handy reference to the most important tasks in the chapters. These quick summaries include page references referring you back to the chapters if you need more information.

CHAPTER 1

What's Java Good For? (page 10)

You can create a calculator that's embedded in a Web page for the world to access...

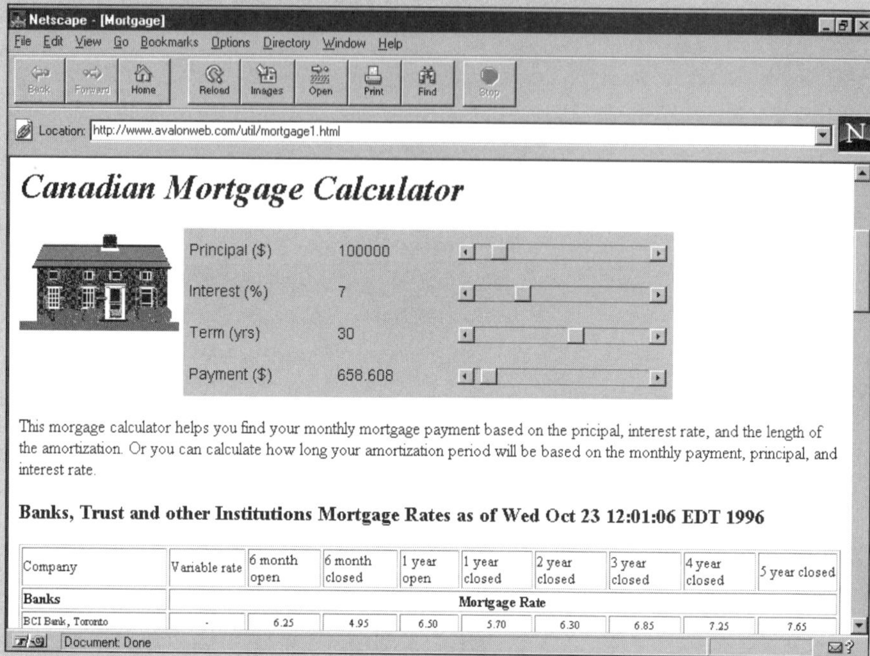

or build a complete, stand-alone Java application that demonstrates the effects of gravity, muzzle velocity, and launch angle on the flight of a cannonball...

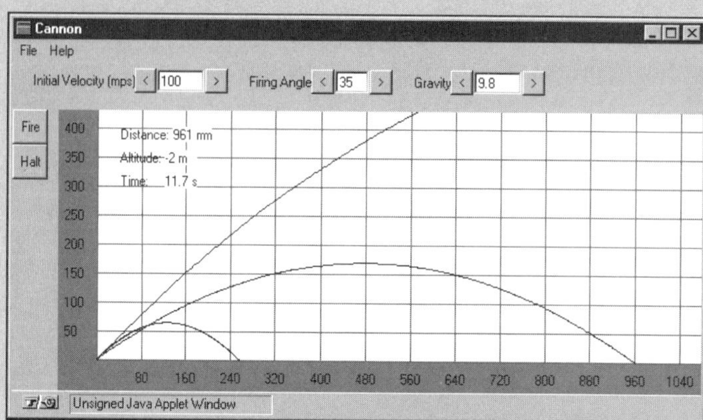

or put an animated, graphical representation of the Bay Area Rapid Transit system on the Web!

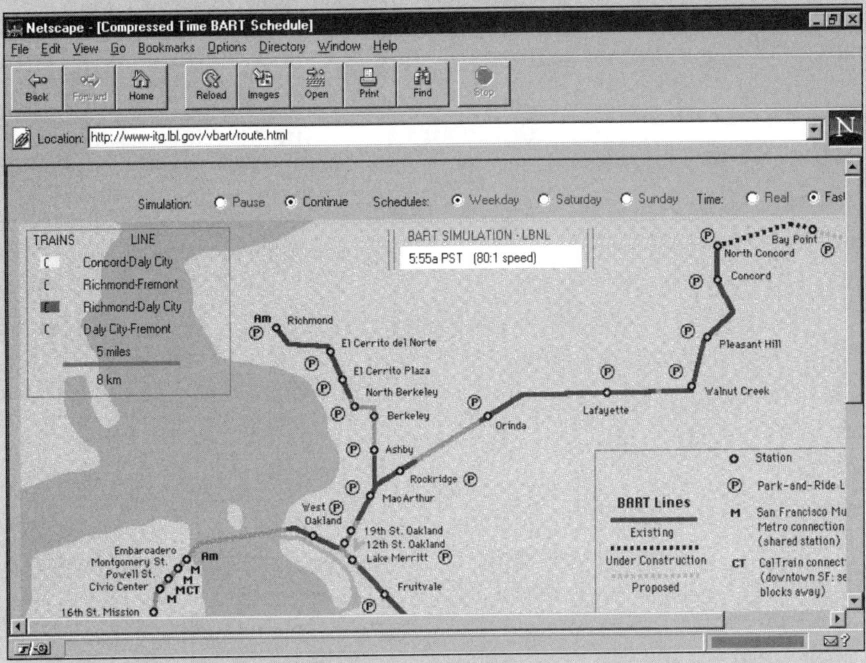

CHAPTER 2

At the lowest level — arithmetic and looping and such — C and Java are very much alike. As you move up to the function-call level, some substantial differences start to show up. Once you get up to the level of the API, they no longer have any kinship — Java has an enormous API that is all objects.

Let's make some comparisons. The following two programs do exactly the same thing — one in C and one in Java. Each reads its own source code file, character by character, and prints it to standard-out. They are written to be as much alike as possible to demonstrate both similarities and differences.

In order to read the notes on the comparison, there is one terminology difference you will need to be aware of: Java doesn't have functions. Instead, it has something very similar called *methods*.

```
#include <stdio.h>
#include <stdlib.h>

void main(int argc,char *argv[])
{
    FILE *fd;
    int character;

    fd = fopen("SeeMe.c","r");
    if(fd == NULL) {
        perror("Unable to open SeeMe.c");
        exit(1);
    }

    while((character = fgetc(fd)) != EOF)
        printf("%c",character);

    fclose(fd);
}
```

Designation of C input and output — `#include <stdio.h>`

C execution starts with main() — `void main(int argc,char *argv[])`

Open the C file — `fd = fopen("SeeMe.c","r");`

Test for failure to open the C file — `if(fd == NULL) {`

Report failure to open the C file — `perror("Unable to open SeeMe.c");`

Read a C input character — `while((character = fgetc(fd)) != EOF)`

Write a C output character — `printf("%c",character);`

Close the C file — `fclose(fd);`

1. Designation of C input and output. The `#include` statement directs the compilation process to read the named source file and make it a part of this source file.
2. C execution starts with `main()`. The function `main()` has a count of the number of command line arguments, and an array of pointers to them.
3. Open the C file. The file is opened with a call to `fopen()` using the name of the file and "r" to specify read-only. The result of the `fopen()` is a pointer to a `FILE struct`.
4. Test for failure to open the C file. If the file fails to open, `fopen()` returns a `NULL` pointer.
5. Report failure to open the C file. The function `perror()` is called with a descriptive string. The `perror()` function will combine the string with a description of the reason for the error and write it all to standard-error.
6. Read a C input character. The function `fgetc()` reads one character from the file as an `int`. It returns the predefined constant value `EOF` at the end of the file.
7. Write a C output character. The `printf()` function is used to convert an `int` into a single ASCII character and direct it to standard-out.
8. Close the C file. A call is made to the function `fclose()` with the `FILE` pointer.

Designation of Java input and output · **Open the Java file** · **Close the Java file** · **Report failure to open the Java file** · **Java execution starts with main()** · **Test for failure to open the Java file** · **Read a Java input character** · **Write a Java output character**

```
import java.io.*;

public class SeeMe {
    public static void main(String arg[]) {
        File file = new File("SeeMe.java");
        try {
            FileInputStream filein = new FileInputStream(file);
            while(true) {
                int character = filein.read();
                if(character == -1) {
                    filein.close();
                    return;
                }
                System.out.print((char)character);
            }
        } catch(IOException e) {
            System.err.println(e);
        }
    }
}
```

1. Designation of Java input and output. The `import` statement directs the compiler to search the named set of classes for unresolved references.
2. Java execution starts with `main()`. The method `main()` has a single argument that is an array of `String` objects containing command line arguments.
3. Open the Java file. A `File` object is created — it contains all the descriptive information about the file. A `FileInputStream` object is created using the `File` object.

4. Test for failure to open the Java file. The attempt to open the file is inside a `try` block, which will automatically test for success or failure.

5. Report failure to open the Java file. The `IOException` contains all the information about the error. A descriptive string will be written to standard-error with a call to the method `System.err.println()`.

6. Read a Java input character. The method `read()` gets one character from the file as an `int`. It returns minus one at the end of the file.

7. Write a Java output character. The `System.out.print()` method is used to convert an `int` to a single ASCII character and then direct it to standard-out.

8. Close the Java file. A call is made to the method `filein.close()`.

CHAPTER 3

As you can see from the diagram, the fundamental data types are derived from the ones in C — but there are enough differences to cause a little confusion until you get the hang of them. One major difference is that the Java fundamental types do not vary in size from one computer to another — they are always exactly as shown in the diagram.

Primitive Data Types (page 30)

Java is a strongly typed language. This means that the primitive types all have exact definitions and there are exact rules on how to go about converting data from one type to another. You can't directly convert certain types to certain other types.

With your knowledge of C, you may know most of the material in this chapter, but Java has some special characteristics with which you still need to be familiar. Some of this will be repetitive, so if you're very good and read the entire chapter, we'll give you a cookie.

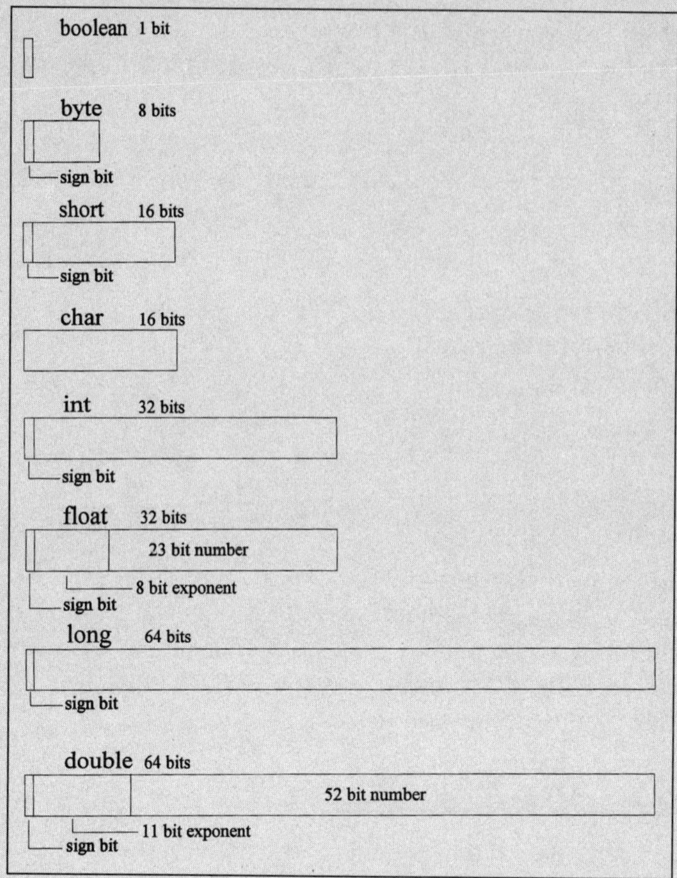

CHAPTER 4

The String Class (page 39)

The Java String class utilizes a number of methods that can be used to manipulate character strings. The following figure illustrates a sample Java program showing how some of these methods work.

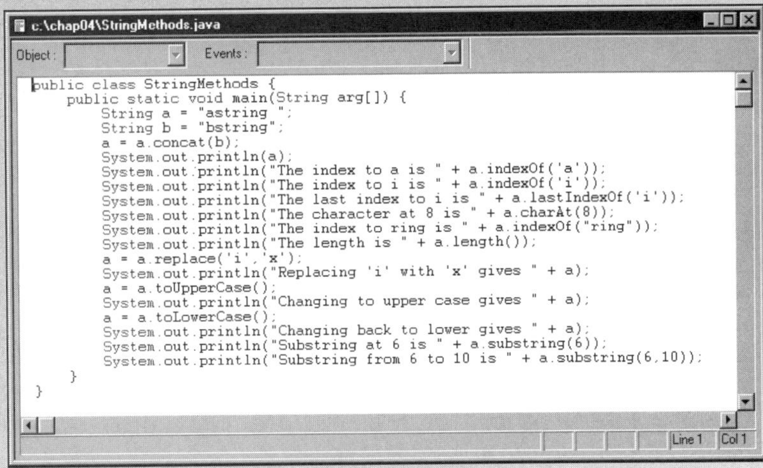

At the beginning of `main()`, a pair `String` objects — `a` and `b` — are declared and both are assigned initial values. The two are concatenated together to create a new `String` named `a` that has the contents of `b` tacked onto it. When displayed — with a call to `System.out.println()` — we discover the following concatenated string:

```
astring bstring
```

The `indexOf()` method can be used to find the first occurrence of a character. Because the index values are zero based, the output from the two calls to `indexOf()` look like the following:

```
The index to a is 0The index to a is 0The index to a is 0The index
  to a is 0
The index to i is 4
```

Not only can we find the first occurrence of a letter, but we can also find the last occurrence, by making a call to `lastIndexOf()`:

```
The last index to i is 12
```

The reverse is also possible. Given an index, we can find what letter is there by calling `charAt()`:

```
The character at 8 is b
```

The `indexOf()` method is overloaded and can be used to locate an entire substring. In our example, we locate the index to the first letter of the substring "ring":

```
The index to ring is 3
```

We can discover the number of characters in a string with a call to `length()`. The output from our example looks like the following:

```
The length is 15
```

But we can do more than just inquire into the contents of a string; we can also make modifications to it. Look what happens when we call `replace()`. All occurrences of the letter "i" are replaced by the letter "x":

```
Replacing 'i' with 'x' gives astrxng bstrxng
```

The entire string can be converted to uppercase:

```
Changing to upper case gives ASTRXNG BSTRXNG
```

And it can be converted back to lowercase again:

```
Changing back to lower gives astrxng bstrxng
```

It is possible to extract a substring by specifying a beginning offset in a call to `substring()`. The substring will start at the specified index and continue to the end of the string:

```
Substring at 6 is g bstrxng
```

The `substring()` method is also overloaded. It is also possible to generate a substring by specifying both the beginning and ending indexes:

```
Substring from 6 to 10 is g bs
```

That is all we do in our example, but it is not all that can be done with the `String` class. Other methods are also part of the `String` class, and the special Java operators of '+' and '+=' can be used on strings.

CHAPTER 5

What we are dealing with here are the nuts and bolts used to construct Java programs. Except for the ones that deal with pointers, Java inherited all the operators from C and added a few new ones.

Unary Operators (page 61)

The arithmetic unary operators include the post- and pre-increment and decrement operators. The leading unary minus (for negation) and the leading tilde (for one's complement) were inherited from C. The unary plus is new in Java. It doesn't really do anything because all numbers default to positive, but it does add a nice touch of symmetry to things.

Arithmetic unary operators

`++  --  +  -  ~`

Arithmetic binary operators

`+  -  *  /  %  <<  >>  >>>`

Logical operators

`!  &  |  &&  ||`

Comparison operators

`<  >  <=  >=  !=  ==`

Assignment operators

`=  +=  -=  <<=  >>=  >>>=`

`*=  /=  %=  &=  |=  ^=`

String operators

`+  +=`

The ternary operator

`?  :`

Binary Operators (page 58)

The arithmetic binary operators add, subtract, multiply, divide, and modulo are the same as in C — but there has been a change in the shifters. The regular old shift-left and shift-right operators are the same, but there is a new one. The unsigned shift (that's the triple >>>) can be used to a right shift of a signed number as if it were an unsigned number — no sign extension.

The logical operators are the same as the ones in C, but there are some subtle differences in the way they work. The rules are more strict because only boolean data types can be used in boolean expressions. This means, for example, there is no way to use the exclamation point on an integer value — it only works for booleans.

All Java comparison operators result in a boolean data type. Other than that, they are the same as their predecessors in C.

Assignment Operators (page 59)

The assignment operators work the same as they do in C. A new one performs the unsigned shifting of a signed value It's the long one — the one that's four characters long. Is that a record?

The string operators were discussed in the previous chapter.

The ternary operator works just as you would expect. The leftmost of the three expressions must be a boolean expression.

The grouping operators work the same as they do in C.

Methods (page 63)

Dot referencing is used to locate things that are located in objects other than the object being executed. The list in the following diagram shows some typical examples of referencing. A reference in the form of `vname` is the address of a local variable (local in the sense that it is inside the class or method being executed). The reference to `mname()` is to a local method. The way that `bar` is referenced implies that it is a variable inside an object that has the name `clname` — just as the reference to `fred()` is to a method in the `clname` class. The reference to `labno` implies that `fred()` returns a reference to an object of a class that contains the public variable named `labno`. In like fashion, the reference returned by `fred()` must be to the object of a class that contains the method `sam()`.

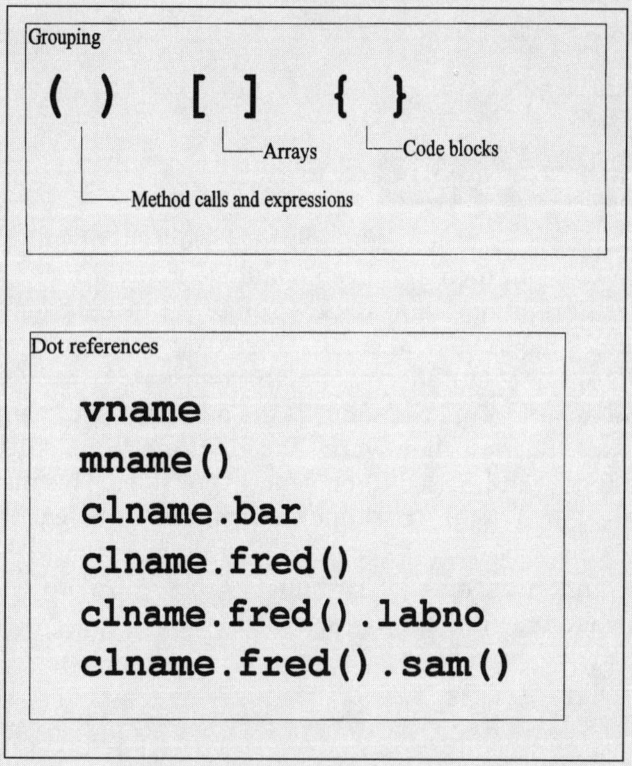

CHAPTER 6

A Class Named Gus (page 76)

Gus is a single class that is also a complete program. It doesn't do much — it just takes a couple of numbers, multiplies them together, and prints out the results to brag about what it has done. Our Gus is a single class that is a complete applet — and a complete application. The source of Gus looks like the following in the Visual Café source edit window:

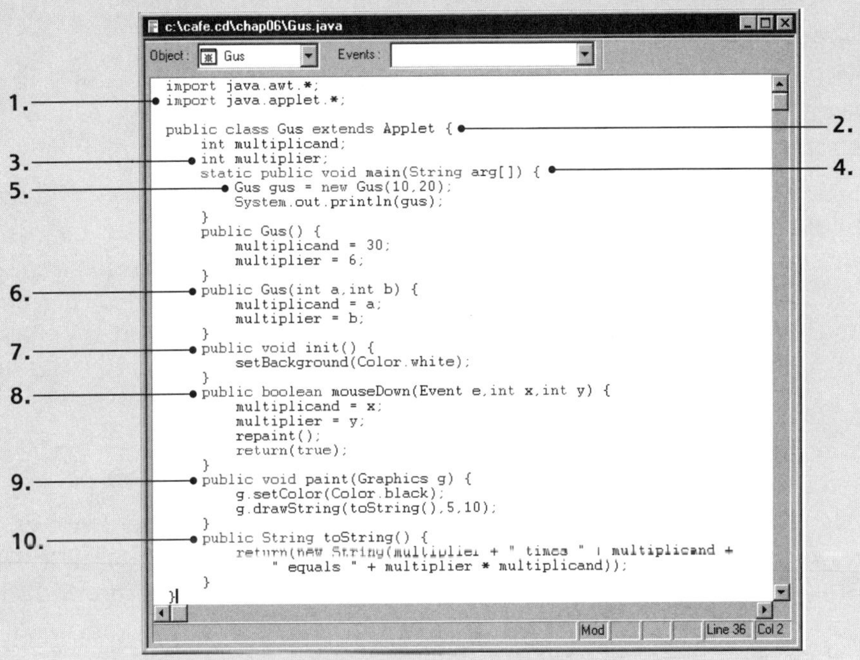

Figure Callout 1: import java.applet*

Gus does two things that makes use of some Java API calls: It can be run as an applet (requiring it to import the java.applet package) and it does a little graphics (requiring it to import the java.awt package).

Figure Callout 2: Gus extends Applet

In order for Gus to be an applet, it must extend the Applet class (the full name of which is `java.applet.Applet`). Because the immediate parent of Gus is Applet, Gus is also an Applet, with all the rights and privileges thereof. This is known as *inheritance*.

Figure Callout 3: private int multiplier

This class contains two data items: the two numbers that will be multiplied together. These are declared as `private`, which means they can be accessed only by methods inside this class. There is no way any other class can ever directly address `multiplicand` or `multiplier`. This is called *encapsulation*.

Figure Callout 4: main

This class can be executed as a stand-alone application in the Java interpreter. Whenever the Java interpreter is asked to execute a class, it loads the class from disk and calls the method named `main()`. When `main()` returns, the application has finished running. The `main()` in `Gus` uses `new` to create an instance of `Gus` with the values 10 and 20. It then uses `System.out.println()` — which causes an automatic call `gus.toString()` — to print the results of the multiplication. It comes out as follows:

```
20 times 10 equals 200
```

Figure Callout 5: Gus()

This method has the same name as the class that makes it a constructor. Every time a class is created, one of its constructors is called. Its primary job is to initialize everything — in this case, it sets our two numbers to some initial values.

Figure Callout 6: Gus(int a,int b)

This method is also a constructor because it has the same name as the class. However, it has arguments, so it is not the default constructor — it has to be specially called. It is the one used by the `main()` method to create a new `Gus` object. Two methods having the same name but a different set of arguments is called *overloading*.

Figure Callout 7: void init()

Because this class is also an applet, it contains an `init()` method. This is the first method called by the Web browser's Java interpreter whenever the browser has loaded the applet and wants to start it running. The Web browser (with explicit sizing instructions from HTML) has kindly allocated our `Gus` with an area on the display — the `init()` gets things started by setting the background to white.

Figure Callout 8: mouseDown()

When run as an applet, `Gus` will respond to the mouse. Every time a mouse button is pressed — `Gus` doesn't care which mouse button — the `mouseDown()` method is called. Inside the `mouseDown()` method, the two internal values are set to the coordinates of the mouse pointer and a call is made to `repaint()` where a call to `paint()` is scheduled. There is a `mouseDown()` method in the parent `Applet` class, but because there is one defined as a part of `Gus`, this one will be used instead. This is called *overriding*.

Figure Callout 9: paint()

Whenever the Web browser wants to have the applet drawn on the display, it makes a call to `paint()`. This happens whenever the applet is first loaded. It also happens whenever the applet reappears (by being scrolled into view or something). It also will happen pretty soon after there has been a call to `repaint()`, as `Gus` does in `mouseDown()`.

Figure Callout 10: toString()

This is another case of overriding. A `toString()` method somewhere in Gus' heritage is being overridden. We know there is one in the family tree because there is a `toString()` method in a class named `Object`, and every class in Java can trace its heritage back to `Object`. Every `toString()` method in every class does the same thing — it returns a `String` that contains a description of itself.

The following figure shows what `Gus` looks like when being run as an applet:

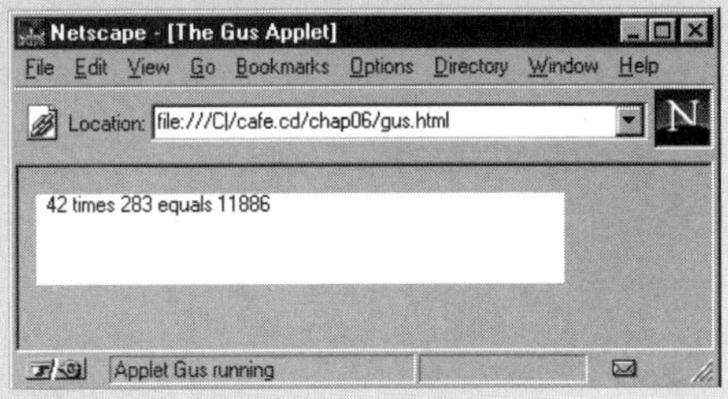

CHAPTER 7

We are all familiar with the logic flow in computer programs — one line of code at a time, with each line executed one after the other. Whenever one statement finishes, the statement right below it takes over. Sometimes an occasional `if` statement, or call to another method, or a loop of some sort will vary the pattern. With exceptions and threads, the flow of execution can leap around your program — the point of execution can even be in several places at once.

A Java program can split into multiple directions by simultaneously following different threads. The following diagram of a simple program is doing two things at once:

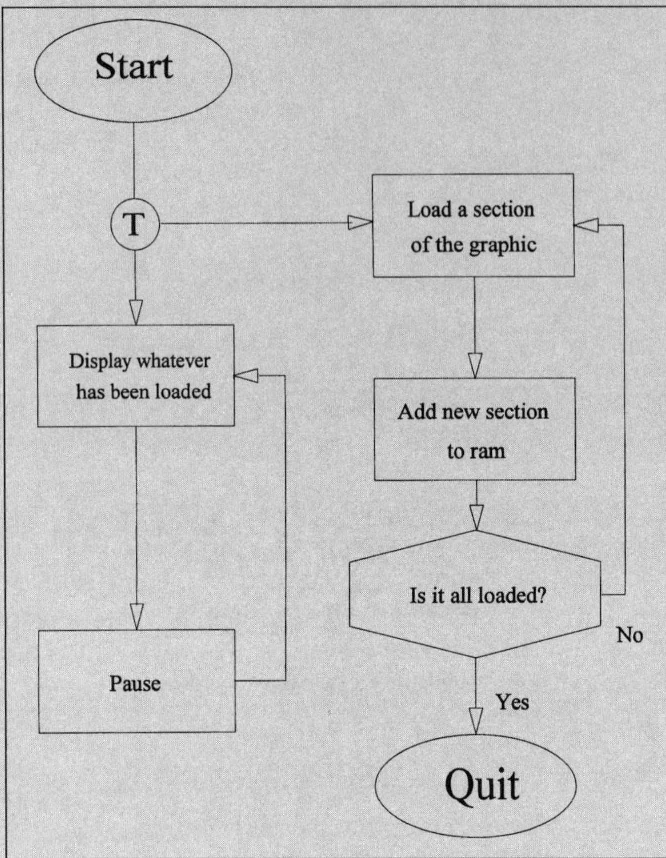

The program's purpose is to load some sort of graphic and display it. It has one method that will display any and all portions of the RAM-resident graphic, and another method that will load the graphic into RAM. The program starts running and, by creating a new thread, goes in both directions at once. The display portion will constantly update the screen (after short pauses) with whatever graphic data has been loaded. The other thread begins loading the graphic file into RAM. Each time a chunk of the graphic is loaded, it is added to the RAM location that will eventually hold the entire picture. The loading continues until the entire graphic is loaded into RAM and, because there is no more loading to be done, the thread goes out of existence. Once the picture is loaded, the program does nothing but continue to show it.

The following diagram shows another form of nonlinear execution:

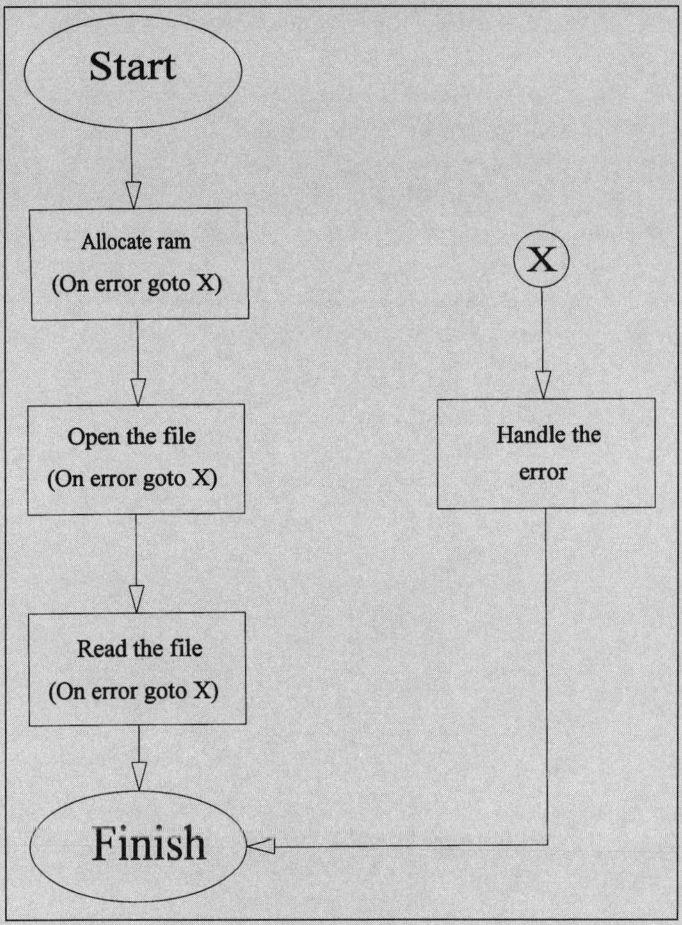

In this case, the program makes every attempt to execute linearly. It wants to allocate some RAM and then read some data from a file into the RAM — one step at a time, one after the other. However (in case you haven't heard about this), there are times when things go wrong — when a program does not run right because of some sort of error. Any one of the three steps in the diagrammed process can go wrong (and in a real program, this "go wrong" can happen way off in some other class in some obscure method that someone wrote the day before leaving for vacation. By having an *exception handler* take over whenever something goes wrong, the program flow is dynamically switched to some friendly place in the code where the problem can be dealt with. This isn't just some blind `goto` or `longjmp` — this beauty tidies up everything behind it. There are no dangling objects or stray stack pieces lying around to cause problems — it is a clean exit to a special place in the program where your own personal, brilliant error-handling code can take care of things for you.

There are two sides to this event story — the system side and the Java side. On the system side, there is some hardware (the mouse, keyboard, and their interfaces) and an operating system. Whenever something noteworthy happens — a key is pressed on the keyboard, for example — this fact is passed to the window that currently has focus and from there into the Java Virtual Machine that has the responsibility of running your program. There is a special part of the Java Virtual Machine that snuggles right up to the border between it and the system — the *event handler*. Its entire purpose in life is to wait for incoming system events.

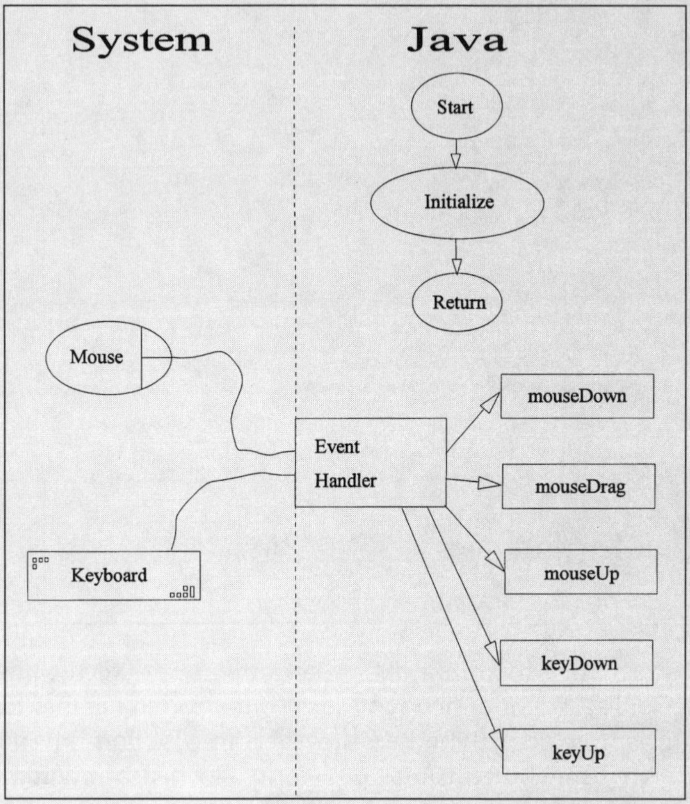

The Java event handler takes raw information from the system and uses it to create *event objects* that are passed on to your program.

There are two basic kinds of event objects: those from the mouse and those from the keyboard. The events from the keyboard identify the key, whether the key is being pressed or released, and whether any meta keys were involved. (The meta keys are shift, alt, and control — any of which can be held down while the reported key action takes place.) The event objects from the mouse include the position of the mouse, whether a button is pressed, and whether a button is being held down while the mouse is moved. There are also events that report when a mouse leaves or enters the window.

All the event handler does is construct events and pass them on to the appropriate method; nothing else will happen unless you program it.

Java programs that accept input from the user are event-driven. This means they have a special form. The diagram shows the general layout of an event-driven program. Whenever the program starts execution, it does only the things it has to do to get itself started (display the window and stuff like that). The program then just sits and waits for the user to do something — it waits for an event from the mouse or the keyboard. When an event finally arrives, the program springs into action and amazes the user with its graphics, its correctness, and its overall intuitive feel. Once it performs this simple chore, it goes back to sleep and waits for another event.

CHAPTER 9

You can do two things in Java to generate pictures that will move. Figures can be drawn dynamically at run-time using the drawing tools available in the java.awt.Graphics object, or a series of stored images can be loaded from disk and flashed on the screen one after the other.

Java has built-in mechanisms that enable you to write code that runs continuously without having to bother with such things as checking for mouse events or watching the keyboard. By implementing methods in the Runnable interface, an applet can execute itself as a separate thread.

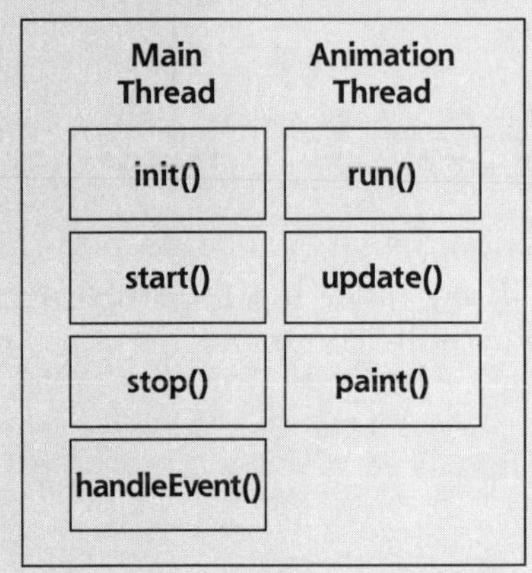

You may already be familiar with `init()` and `handleEvent()` in the diagram from previous chapters, but the other methods are new. The `start()` method is called by Java to kick off the thread, and the `stop()` method is used to make it quit running. Java puts a thread into action by calling its `run()` method. The `run()` method causes calls to be made to `update()` and `paint()`. The thread stays in operation until the `run()` method returns.

This is a handy trick because if your program were to run a continuous animation stream without checking for the mouse and keyboard there would be no user interface. This is where threads come in. If you wanted to do it the hard way, you could do animation without threads. There is nothing to stop you, but because the threads are already there to do exactly what you want them to do, why not use them?

```java
import java.awt.*;
import java.applet.*;

public class Skeleton extends Applet implements Runnable {
    public void init() {
        // Do all the one-time setups.
    }

    public void start() {
        if(thread == null) {
            thread = new Thread(this);
            thread.start();
        }
    }

    public void run() {
        try {
            while(true) {
                repaint();
                Thread.sleep(PAUSE);
            }
        } finally {
            return;
        }
    }

    public void stop() {
        if(thread != null) {
            thread.stop();
            thread = null;
        }
    }

    public void update(Graphics g) {
        if(thread.isAlive()) {
            // Prepare to draw the next frame.
            paint(g);
        }
    }

    public void paint(Graphics g) {
        // Draw the entire frame
        g.dispose();
    }
}
```

The basic structure of an animation applet is laid out in the Skeleton class. This applet doesn't actually do anything, but it has the structure of an animation applet. Just fill in the blanks (where the comments are) and away we go to the land of moving pictures.

CHAPTER 10

Java input and output is performed, like everything else in Java, using classes.

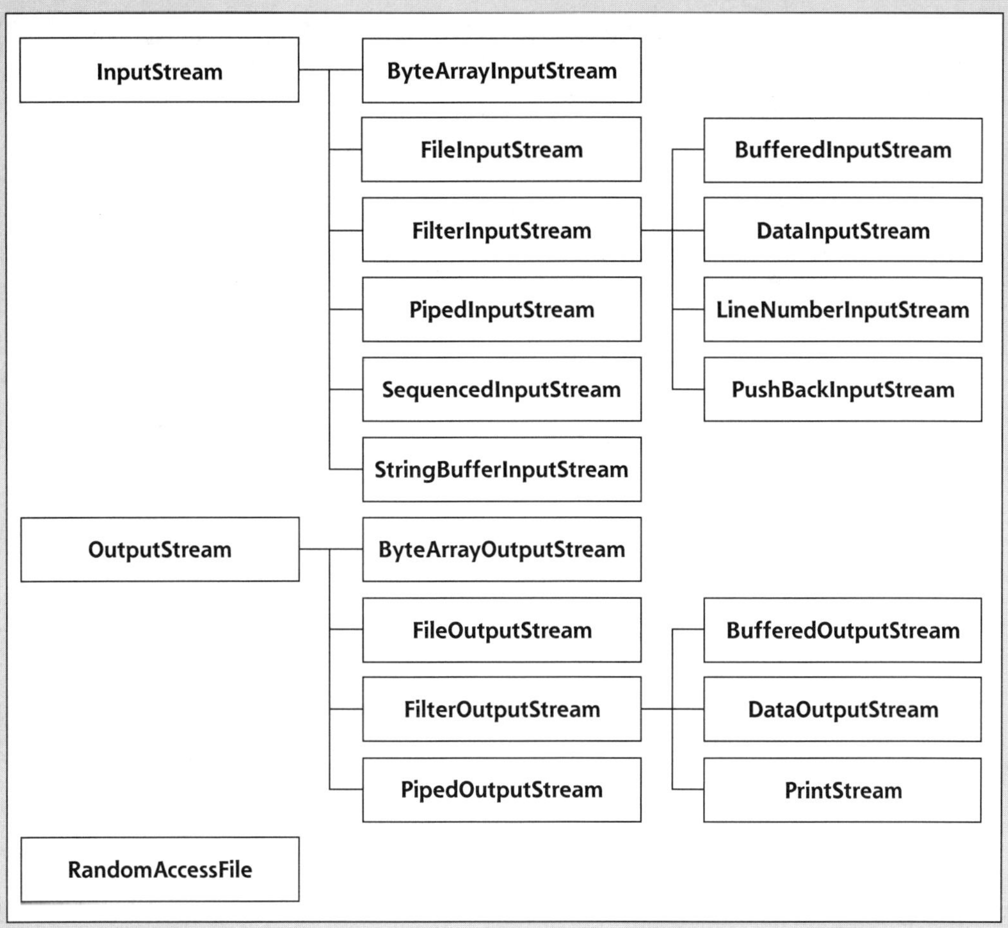

On the left of the diagram you can see the three major classes. The `InputStream` class is the superclass of all input classes, the `OutputStream` class is the parent of all output classes, and the `RandomAccessFile` is the (one and only!) class that handles both input and output.

Input (page 161)

There are different types of input. The `ByteInputStream` is for input from an array of bytes somewhere in RAM. The `FileInputStream` is capable of reading bytes from a file. The `PipedInputStream` can read information from another thread running in the same program. Several different input streams can be combined together by using the `SequenceInputStream` class, which makes it appear as if the input from several sources is all coming from a single source. Each time the end of a file is reached on one input, the sequencer will switch to the next one. The `StringBufferInputStream` reads incoming data as a stream of 8-bit bytes. (Even though it has the word *String* in its name, it does not read Unicode.)

The `FilterInputStream` class is the superclass of a group of classes that can be used to format data coming in through the other classes. The `BufferedInputStream` class performs input data buffering while reading. The `DataInputStream` class is capable of reading fundamental data types such as `double` and `int`. The `LineNumberInputStream` reads and enumerates lines of text. The `PushBackInputStream` class provides space for the most recently read byte to be pushed back to as if it had not been read.

Output (page 162)

The output classes are all extensions of the `OutputStream` class. The `ByteArrayOutputStream` class is capable of writing a stream of 8-bit bytes. The `FileOutputStream` class is capable of writing bytes to a file. A `PipedOutputStream` object is capable of sending data to another thread running in the same application.

The `FilterOutputStream` is the superclass of several classes that can be used to control output formatting. The `BufferedOutputStream` will perform output buffering and write blocks of data whenever the buffers become full. The `DataOutputStream` is capable of writing data in the binary form of the various fundamental types, such as `double` and `int`. The `PrintStream` class is used to write strings of 8-bit character data — ASCII strings, not Unicode.

Input/Output (page 163)

Only one class is capable of both input and output — the `RandomAccessFile` class. As its name implies, you can move its current read-write pointer to any position in the file. It doesn't have the flexibility of operating on streams like the other classes do.

CHAPTER 11

Javadoc extracts information from source files and generates documentation. You write the code and the comments; javadoc writes the documentation. Well, it doesn't really write the documentation, but it does take the information you give it and hook it all together in a very usable form. Consider this simple class:

```
import java.applet.*;

/** This is a complete bug-free applet. There are several
  tricks that we use to prevent bugs from ever occurring.
  Mainly, because it does nothing at all, there is no
  possibility of anything going wrong. */
public class BugFree extends Applet {
  /** Total number of bugs. This is a running count of
   the total number of bugs that have been found so
   far in the class.
```

```
   It is never actually incremented, which keeps the
   whole class completely bug free. */
  public int bug_count;

  /** Do the one-time initialization. To keep the bug
   count to a minimum, we actually don't do anything
   but make sure the counter is zero. */
  public void init() {
   bug_count = 0;
  }

  /** Return the current count of the number of bugs.
   This is just as pointless as the rest of the class
   because, even though the count of bugs is
   returned, it is always going to be zero. */
  public int getCount() {
   return(bug_count);
  }
}
```

As you can see, it doesn't do anything — but it is well commented. Javadoc is able to read the names of the methods and their associated comments to generate HTML documentation. The top portion of the Web page names the class and lists its superclasses all the way back to the `Object` class. Hypertext links are included for the entire hierarchy of the class.

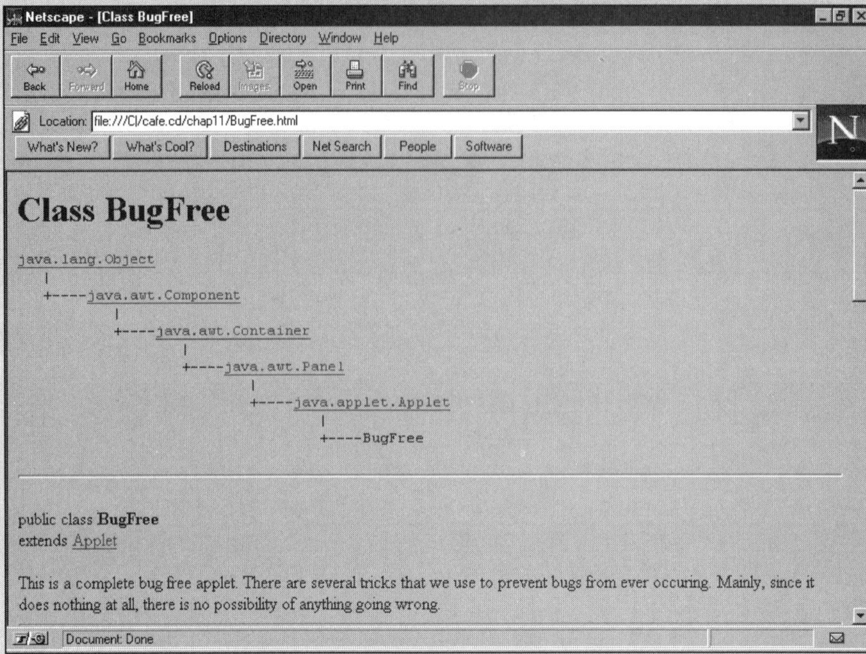

The comment block — the one right before the class definition in the source file — is assumed to be the text of a general description of the class. Scrolling down to the middle section of the page exposes the indexes to the various parts of the class.

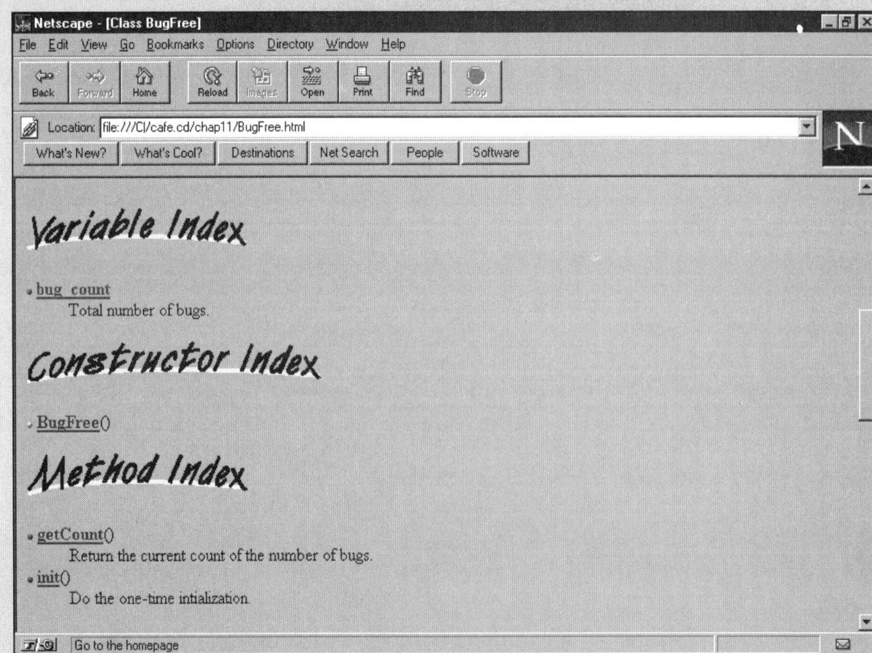

Every nonprivate variable and method is included in the list, and each is tagged with the first sentence of the description found in the source file. There is also a link to the full description information lower down on the page. The full description information includes declaration syntax and the complete text of the comment from the source file.

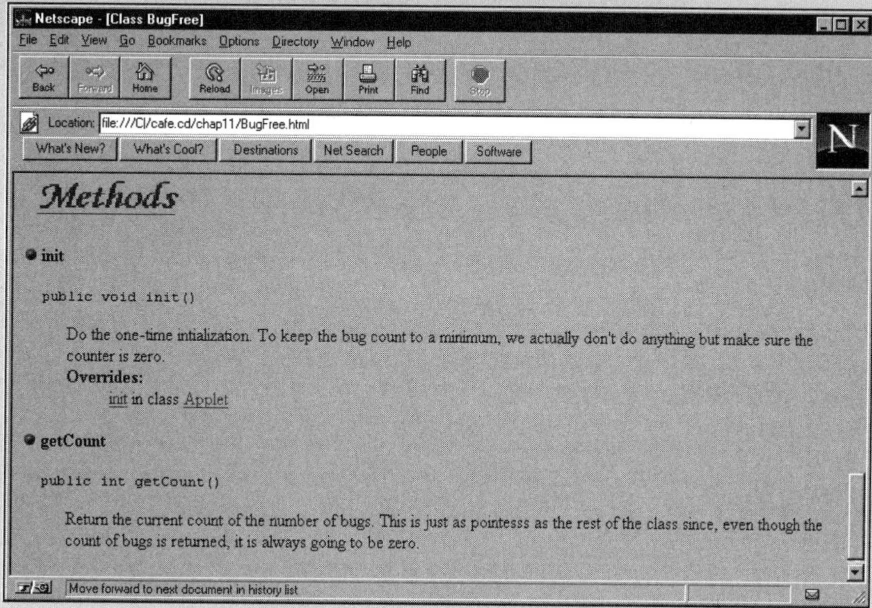

Of course, javadoc can only generate descriptions using the words you give it in the comments in the code. Historically, that has been the crucial limiting factor.

CHAPTER 12

This chapter describes many of the commands available in Visual Café. Following is a table summarizing them.

Command	Hot Key	Toolbar Button	Menu Command
CREATE A NEW PROJECT	Ctrl+N		File → New Project
CREATE A NEW PROJECT OR TEXT FILE	None	None	File → New
OPEN A PROJECT	Ctrl+O		File → Open
CLOSE A PROJECT	None	None	File → Close
SAVE THE CURRENT PROJECT	Ctrl+S		File → Save
SAVE THE CURRENT PROJECT WITH A NEW NAME	None	None	File → Save As
SAVE ALL OPEN PROJECTS	None	None	File → Save All
CONFIGURE THE APPEARANCE AND BEHAVIOR OF VISUAL CAFÉ	None	None	File → Environment Options
CONFIGURE PRINTING	None	None	File → Print Setup
PRINT	Ctrl+P		File → Print
QUIT VISUAL CAFÉ	None	None	File → Exit
UNDO THE LAST	Ctrl+Z	None	Edit → Undo
REDO THE COMMAND YOU JUST UNDID	Ctrl+Y	None	Edit → Redo
CUT THE HIGHLIGHTED ITEM TO THE CLIPBOARD	Ctrl+X		Edit → Cut
COPY THE HIGHLIGHTED ITEM TO THE CLIPBOARD	Ctrl+C		Edit → Copy
PASTE THE CONTENTS OF THE CLIPBOARD	Ctrl+V		Edit → Paste
DELETE THE HIGHLIGHTED ITEM	Delete	None	Edit → Delete

Command	Hot Key	Toolbar Button	Menu Command
SELECT ALL THE SELECTABLE ITEMS IN THE ACTIVE WINDOW	Ctrl+A	None	Edit → Select All
FIND A SEQUENCE OF CHARACTERS	Ctrl+F	None	Search → Find
FIND THE NEXT INSTANCE OF THE SPECIFIED SEQUENCE OF CHARACTERS	None	None	Search → Find Again
REPLACE THE SPECIFIED SEQUENCE OF CHARACTERS WITH SOMETHING ELSE	Ctrl+R	None	Search → Replace
FIND A PIECE OF CODE IN AN UNKNOWN FILE	None	None	Search → Find in Files
DETERMINE THE SIMILARITY OF TWO SOURCE CODE FILES	None	None	Search → Compare Files
INSERT A BOOKMARK	None	None	Search → Drop Bookmark
GO TO A BOOKMARK	None	None	Search → Go to Bookmark
REMOVE BOOKMARKS	None	None	Search → Remove all Bookmarks
OPEN A FILE IN THE CURRENT PROJECT	F12	None	Search → Go to File
GO TO A LINE IN THE CURRENT SOURCECODE FILE	Ctrl+G	None	Search → Go to Line
GO TO THE SOURCE CODE THAT DEFINES THE SELECTED CLASS OR METHOD	None	None	Search → Go to Definition
FIND THE PARENTHESIS, BRACKET OR BRACE THAT MATCHES THE CURRENTLY SELECTED ONE	Ctrl+]	None	Search → Go to Matching Delimiter
GO TO THE CURRENT ERROR IN A PROJECT THAT'S FAILED TO COMPILE	None	None	Search → Go to Current Error

(continued)

Command	Hot Key	Toolbar Button	Menu Command
GO TO THE FIRST ERROR IN A PROJECT THAT'S FAILED TO COMPILE	None	None	Search → Go to First Error
GO TO THE PREVIOUS ERROR IN A PROJECT THAT'S FAILED TO COMPILE	None	None	Search → Go to Previous Error
GO TO THE NEXT ERROR IN A PROJECT THAT'S FAILED TO COMPILE	None	None	Search → Go to Next Error
COMPILE AND RUN YOUR PROGRAM	Ctrl+F5		Project → Execute
RUN YOUR PROGRAM UNTIL IT ENCOUNTERS A BREAKPOINT	F5	None	Project → Run to Breakpoint
RUN YOUR PROGRAM ONE LINE AT A TIME	F8		Project → Step Into
COMPILE A SINGLE SOURCE CODE FILE	Ctrl+F7	None	Project → Compile
COMPILE AN ENTIRE PROGRAM	F7	None	Project → Build Applet/Application
ADD A FILE, SUCH AS A .JAVA OR .HTML FILE, TO THE CURRENT PROJECT	None	None	Project → Add/Remove Files
MAKE THE CURRENT PROJECT A TEMPLATE	None	None	Project → Create Project Template
DEFINE THE PROJECT THAT COMPILES	None	None	Project → Switch Main Project
SET PROJECT PREFERENCES	None	None	Project → Options
INSERT A FORM INTO THE CURRENT PROJECT	None	None	Insert → Form
INSERT AN APPLET INTO THE CURRENT PROJECT	None	None	Insert → Applet
INSERT AN OBJECT INTO THE CURRENT PROJECT	None	None	Insert → Object
INSERT A COMPONENT INTO THE CURRENT PROJECT	None	None	Insert → User Component

Command	Hot Key	Toolbar Button	Menu Command
INSERT A .CLASS FILE INTO THE CURRENT PROJECT	None	None	Insert → Class
INSERT A METHOD OR DATA ITEM INTO THE CURRENT CLASS	None	None	Insert → Member
BRING FORWARD THE FORM EDITOR	None	None	Object → Edit Applet
OPEN THE SOURCE CODE EDITOR	Ctrl+Shift+S	None	Object → Edit Source
RUN THE INTERACTION WIZARD	None		Object → Add Interaction
ADD THE SELECTED OBJECT TO THE COMPONENT LIBRARY	None	None	Object → Add to Library
CREATE ANOTHER INSTANCE OF THE ACTIVE WINDOW	None	None	Window → New Window
SWITCH AMONG WORKSPACES	None		Window → Workspaces
OPEN THE PROPERTY LIST	Ctrl+Shift+P		Window → Property List
OPEN THE CLASS BROWSER	Ctrl+Shift+C		Window → Class Browser
OPEN THE HIERARCHY EDITOR	Ctrl+Shift+H		Window → Hierarchy Editor
OPEN THE WATCH WINDOW	Ctrl+Shift+W		Window → Watch
OPEN THE BREAKPOINTS WINDOW	Ctrl+Shift+B		Window → Breakpoints
OPEN THE MESSAGES WINDOW	Ctrl+Shift+M		Window → Messages
OPEN THE THREADS WINDOW	Ctrl+Shift+T		Window → Threads
OPEN THE VARIABLES WINDOW	Ctrl+Shift+D		Window → Variables
OPEN THE CALL STACK WINDOW	Ctrl+Shift+L		Window → Call Stack

(continued)

Command	Hot Key	Toolbar Button	Menu Command
OPEN THE COMPONENT LIBRARY	None	None	Window → Component Library
SWITCH AMONG OPEN WINDOWS	None	None	Window → Windows
OPEN THE GENERAL VISUAL CAFÉ HELP FILE	None		Help → Contents
OPEN A SEARCHABLE INDEX TO THE GENERAL VISUAL CAFÉ HELP FILES	None	None	Help → Index
GET HELP WITH THE JAVA API	None	None	Help → Java API
GET HELP WITH JAVA SYNTAX AND STRUCTURE	None	None	Help → Java Language Reference
VIEW THE ABOUT VISUAL CAFÉ WINDOW	Ctrl+ Shift+A		Help → About Visual Café

CHAPTER 13

Identifying Java Components (page 223)

(page 223)

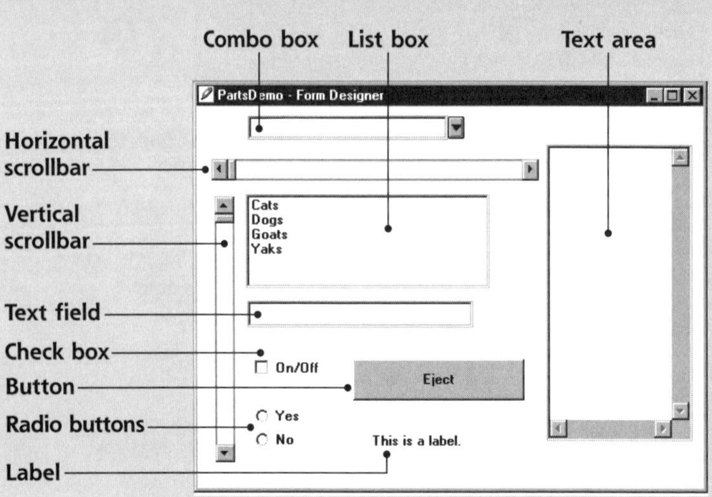

Visual Café makes it easy for you to use many different components. Some of the most common ones include the following:

- **Combo Box.** Used to list several items, the combo box expands when clicked.
- **Horizontal Scrollbar.** Rarely used, the horizontal scrollbar can be used to set values.
- **Vertical Scrollbar.** Similar to the horizontal scrollbar, with one critical difference.
- **Text Area.** Used to handle multiline passages of text.
- **List Box.** Used to list several items, list boxes never change size.
- **Text Field.** Used to handle single-line passages of text.
- **Check Box.** Used to indicate a yes/no or on/off condition.
- **Radio Buttons.** Used to select options when only one of several options may be chosen.
- **Button.** Initiates an action.
- **Label.** Indicates the purpose of other components.

CHAPTER 14

Starting the Property List (page 240)

To start the Property List, perform one of the following:

- Choose Window → Property List from the menu bar.
- Press Ctrl+Shift+P.
- Press F4.
- Click the Property List button the toolbar.

Using the Property List (page 240)

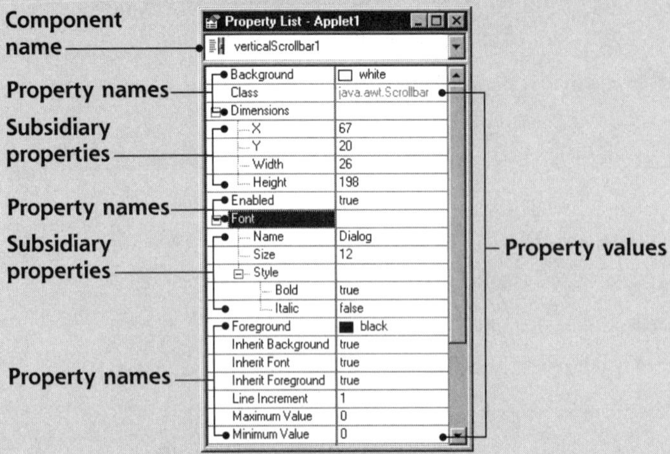

Here's how you use the Property List:

1. In the Form Editor, highlight the component you want to inspect.
2. Open the Property List.
3. Find the name of the property that interests you in the left column.
4. Set its value in the right column, either by choosing from a list or typing in a value.
5. The property you're adjusting, if it's a visible property, will be adjusted in real-time in the Form Editor.

Adjusting properties in the Property List (page 241)

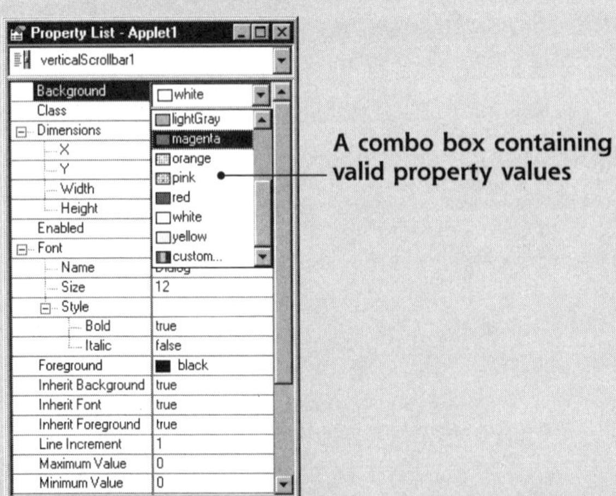

There are two main ways of adjusting the value of a component's property:

- You can type in a value, as you do with Label properties.
- You can choose a value from a combo box, as you do with `True/False` properties and color properties.

CHAPTER 15

To Start the Interaction Wizard (page 247)

There are three ways to start the Interaction Wizard:

- Click the **Interaction Wizard** button on the toolbar, then drag the component that will experience an event to the component that will perform a behavior in response to the event.
- Select **Object** → **Add Interaction**.
- Right-click (or, in the case of Macintoshes, long-click) the component that is to experience a triggering event.

Usually it's most convenient to use the first method.

To Create a Simple Interaction (page 250)

1. Start the Interaction Wizard.
2. Specify the triggering event in the "Start an interaction for..." list box.
3. Specify a resultant behavior in the "Choose what you want to happen" list box.
4. Click the Finish button.

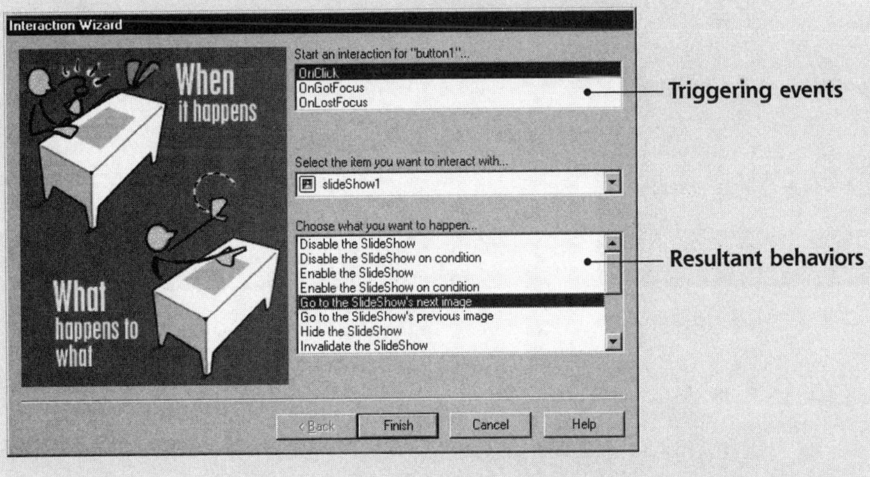

To Create a More Complex Interaction (page 251)

1. Start the Interaction Wizard.
2. Specify the triggering event in the "Start an interaction for..." list box.
3. Specify a resultant behavior in the "Choose what you want to happen" list box.
4. Click the Next button.
5. On the second page of the Interaction Wizard, specify any of the following:
   a. Another component to supply needed data and the means by which it should supply it.
   b. A constant or expression.
   c. A variable.
6. Click the Finish button.

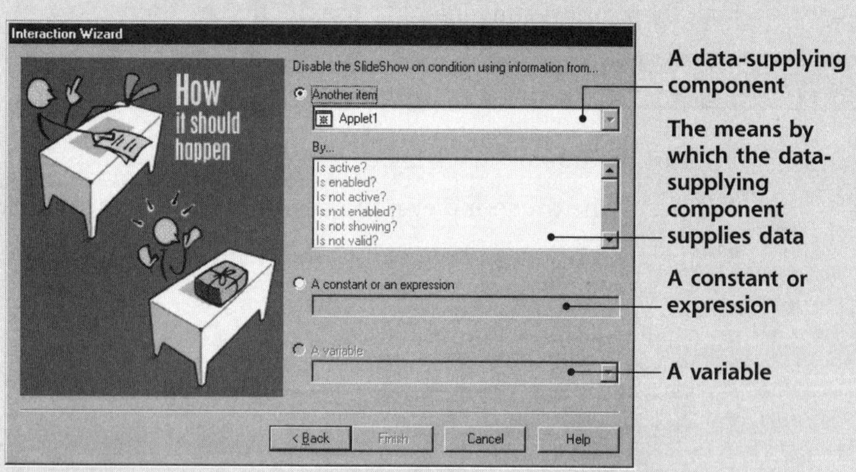

CHAPTER 16

To Start the Source Code Editor (page 257)

There are three ways to start the source code editor:

* Double-click a component in the Form Editor or the Form Editor window itself.
* Right-click (or long-click, if you're using a Macintosh) in the Form Editor and choose **Edit Souce** from the pop-up menu.

* Choose **Object** → **Edit Souce** from the menu bar or use the keyboard shortcut Ctrl+Shift+S.

To Specify a Component (page 259)

1. Start the source code editor.
2. Open the left-hand ("Objects") choice box.
3. Select the component you want.

To Specify an Event (page 259)

1. Make sure you've selected the component to which the desired event applies (see "To Specify a Component").
2. Open the right-hand ("Events") choice box.
3. Choose the event for which you want to write an event handler from the top part of the extended choice box (above the divider).

To Go to a Class (page 259)

1. Open the Events choice box.
2. From the bottom part of the extended choice box (below the divider), choose the class with which you want to work. Visual Café will move the cursor to that class.

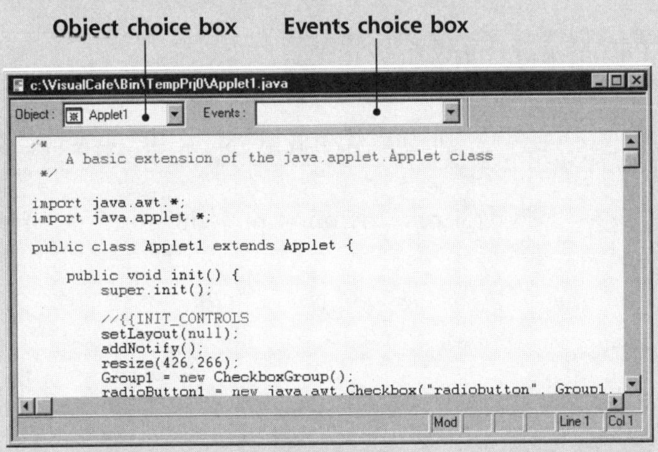

CHAPTER 17

Using the Hierarchy Editor (page 266)

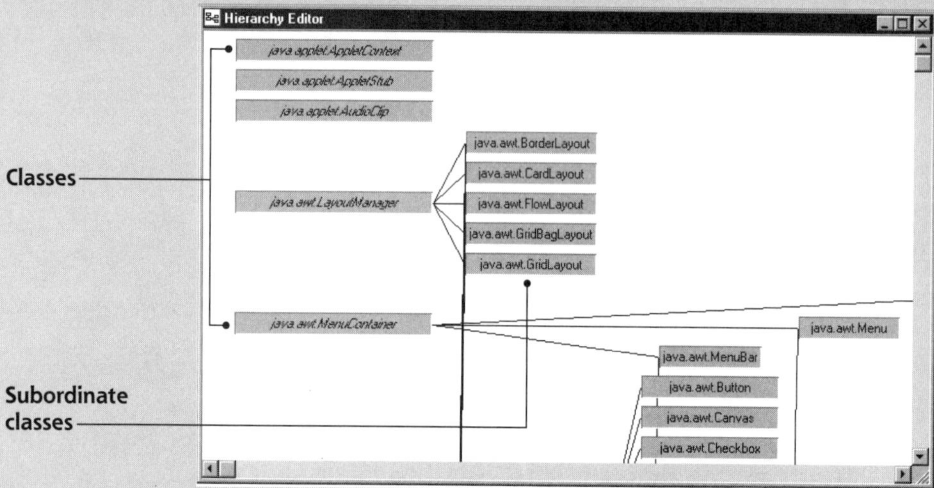

To start the Hierarchy Editor, choose Window → Hierarchy Editor. Or press Ctrl+Shift+H

Adding a Top-Level Class (page 267)

1. Right- or long-click anywhere in the Hierarchy Editor.
2. Choose Add Top from the pop-up menu.

Adding a Sibling Class (page 268)

1. Right- or long-click the box that represents the class for which you want to add a sibling class.
2. Choose Add Sibling from the pop-up menu. You'll see the Add Class dialog box.
3. Type a name in the Class Name text field.
4. Click OK.

Adding a Derived Class (page 268)

1. Right- or long-click the box that represents the class for which you want to add a derived class.

2. Choose **Add Derived** from the pop-up menu. You'll see the Add Class dialog box.

3. Type a name in the Class Name text field.

4. Click OK.

Using the Class Browser (page 270)

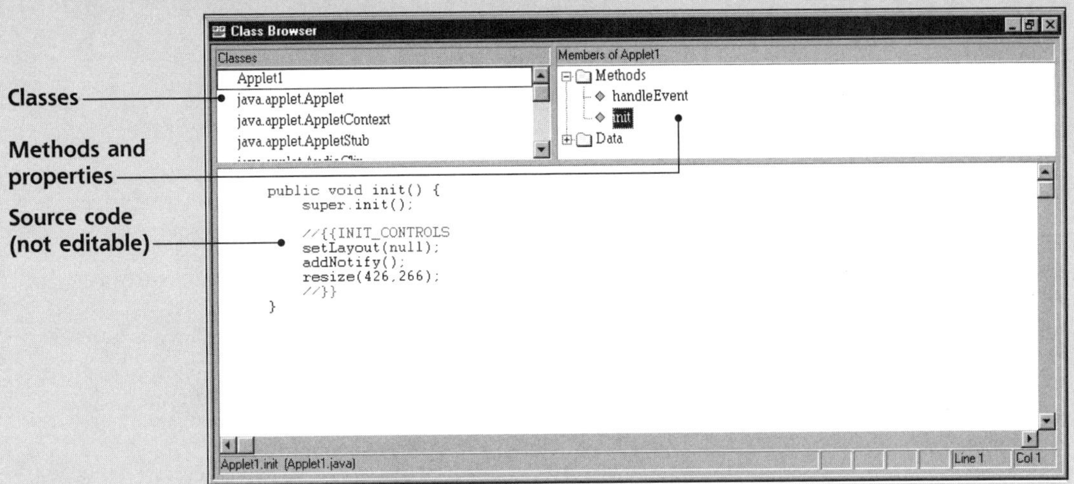

Understanding Member Attributes (page 272)

- Red diamond `Private`
- Yellow diamond `Protected`
- Green Diamond `Public`

Changing Member Attributes (page 273)

1. Choose **Classes** → **Member Attributes**. You'll see the Change Member attributes dialog box.

2. Select the attribute you want.

3. Click OK.

Deleting a Member (page 273)

This procedure works only for members that are not part of the Java API.

1. Highlight the member you want to delete.
2. Press the Delete key.

CHAPTER 18

Understanding Debugging (page 276)

* Most developing programs have errors, called *bugs*.
* Syntax errors and other errors that prevent your program from compiling are called *compile-time bugs* or *code bugs*.
* Errors that allow your program to run but cause it to give faulty results, are called *run-time bugs* or *logical bugs*.
* The best way top catch bugs is to torture-test your programs.
* Visual Café provides many tools for finding and fixing bugs.

Test-Running Your Programs (page 278)

To run your applet or application under the watchful eyes of the Visual Café debugging tools, choose one of the following procedures:

* Click the Run button.
* Choose Project → Execute.
* Press Ctrl + F5.

Using Breakpoints (page 282)

Breakpoints are places in your program's code at which execution pauses to allow you to examine what's going on — and catch mistakes. To set breakpoints, open the source code editor, position your cursor on the line before which you want the breakpoint to occur, and do one of the following:

* Press F9.
* Choose Source → Toggle Breakpoint.
* Right-click or long-click the line and choose Toggle Breakpoint from the pop-up menu.

You can also set conditional breakpoints — breakpoints that take effect only when certain program conditions are met — by positioning your cursor in the source code and choosing Source → Set Conditional Breakpoint.

The Breakpoints Window (page 287)

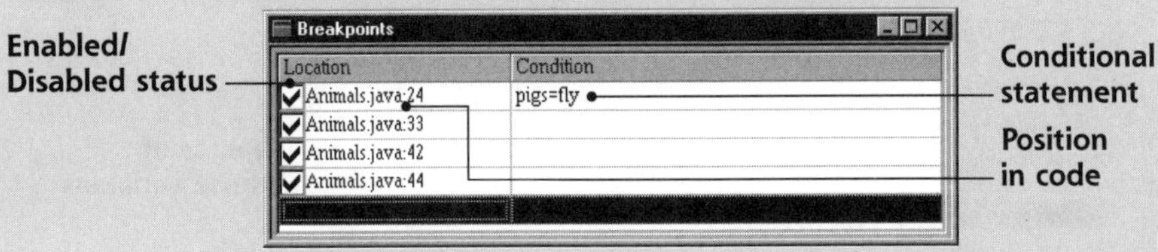

The Breakpoints window lists all the breakpoints in place in the current project and makes it easy for you to enable and disable them (disabled breakpoints are in place in your source code but have been "turned off" temporarily; enabled breakpoints are both present and active).

To open the Breakpoints window, choose **Window** → **Breakpoints** or press Ctrl+Shift+B.

The Variables Window (page 291)

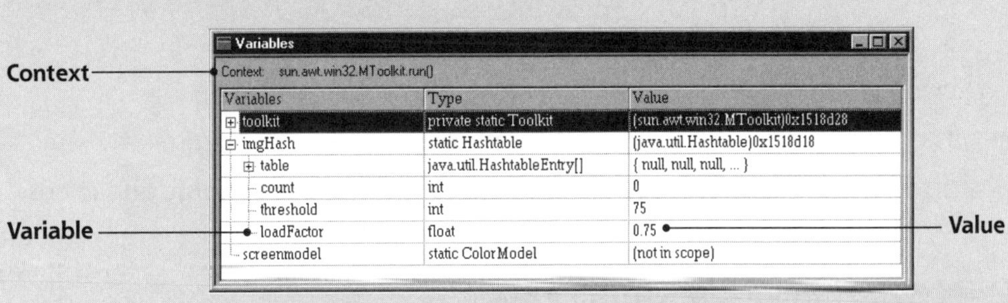

The Variables window lists all the variables your program is using at the moment, along with their values. You can use the Variables window to see where your program is saving data and to get a general picture of what your program is up to at the moment. The Variables window can have *context*, which is the particular class or thread for which it's displaying variables and values. You can adjust the context via the **Calls** → **Set Focus** command when the Call Stack window is active, or via the **Threads** → **Set Focus** command when the Threads window is active.

The Watch Window (page 292)

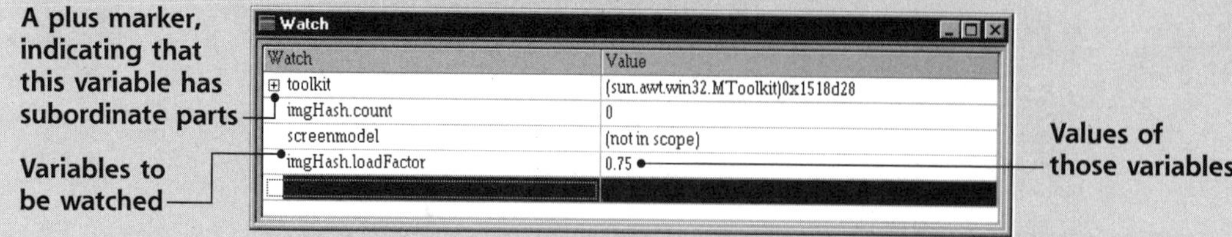

The Watch window lets you monitor the values of variables and expressions you specify, not just those that are presently active. Open the Watch window by choosing **Window** → **Watch** or pressing Ctrl+Shift+W.

To add a variable or expression to the Watch window:

1. Click the left column (the one labeled "Watch").
2. When the text-editing box appears, type the name of the variable you want to watch or type out the expression you want the window to evaluate.
3. Press Enter.

To Remove a variable from the Watch window:

1. In the Watch window, click the variable you want to delete.
2. Press the Delete key or right-click (or long-click) the variable and choose **Delete** from the pop-up menu.

The Threads Window (page 294)

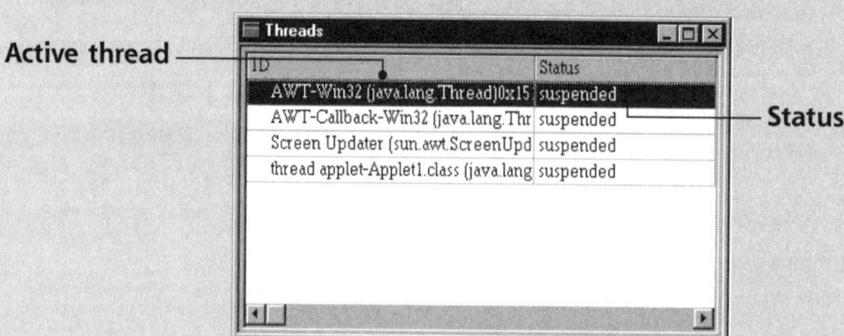

Java lets you create programs that are multithreaded; that is, programs that have several sets of program instructions running simultaneously. Visual Café's Threads window lets you monitor what threads exist at the moment and what those threads are doing.

Open the Threads window by choosing **Window** → **Threads** or pressing Ctrl+Shift+T.

The Call Stack Window (page 296)

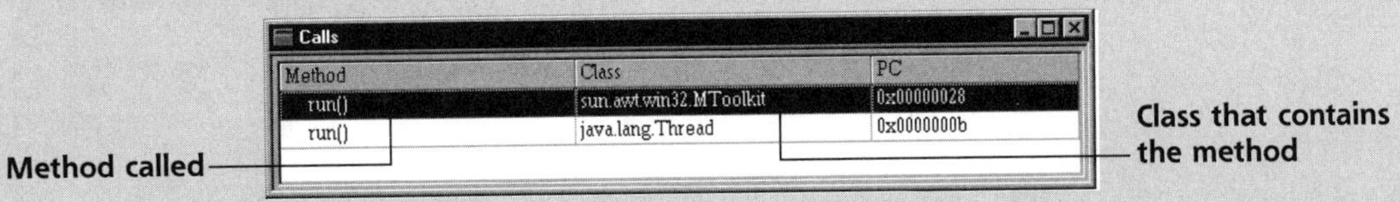

Java, as an object-oriented programming language, is used to create programs in which some pieces of code refer to other pieces of code. These references are termed *calls*, and Visual Café provides you with the Call Stack window to track what calls are underway at a particular breakpoint in your program.

To open the Call Stack window, choose **Window** → **Call Stack** or press Ctrl+Shift+L.

CHAPTER 19

To Compile Source Code (Generate a .class File) (page 302)

1. Make sure the Project window for the project you want to compile is active.
2. Choose **Project** → **Build Applet** (if you're working with an applet) or **Project** → **Build Application** (if you're working with an application).
3. Watch the Messages window for information about compiler errors. If you get one, you have to debug your program before it will do what you want.
4. When the Message window says "Build Successful," look in the PROJECTS folder in your Visual Café folder for your file with the .class extension.

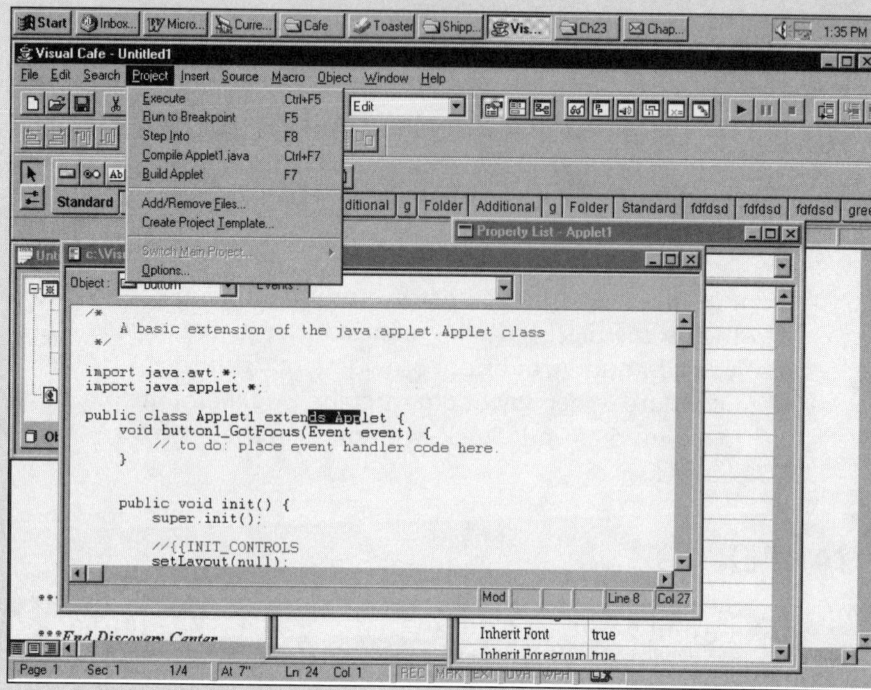

CHAPTER 20

To Open or Close the Component Library (page 308)

1. To open the Component Library, choose **Window** → **Component Library**.
2. To close the Component Library, click the close button in the upper-right corner of the Component Library window or make the Component Library window your active window, then choose **Window** → **Component Library** to uncheck the Component Library listing in the **Window** menu.

To Create a Series of Similar Components with the Component Library and the Property List (page 309)

1. Highlight the basic component you want to modify in the Component Library.
2. Choose **Edit** → **Copy**.
3. Choose **Edit** → **Paste**.
4. Change whichever attributes you want — except the Name property. You'll see that Visual Café won't let you change this property, at least as of this writing.

To Add to the Component Library (page 311)

If the component is in the Project window:

1. Open the Component Library.
2. Drag the component from the Project window to the Component Library.

If the component is in the Form Editor:

1. Right-click (or long-click, if you're running a Mac) something in the Form Editor.
2. Choose **Add to Library** from the pop-up menu.
3. Highlight the group (folder) into which you want the component to go.
4. Click the OK button.

or

1. Highlight something in the Form Editor.
2. Choose **Object** → **Add to Library**.
3. Highlight the group (folder) in which you want the component to go.
4. Click the OK button.

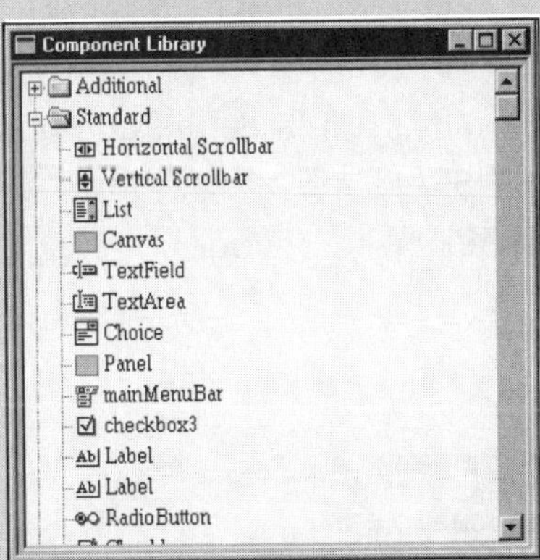

To Add Groups in the Component Library (page 312)

1. Open the Component Library.
2. Highlight a group or component.
3. Right- or long-click the highlighted component. You'll see the Component Library pop-up menu shown later in Figure 20-5.

4. Choose Insert Group from the pop-up menu. You'll see a new group icon, with the word "Folder" highlighted next to it.
5. Replace the highlighted "Folder" with a more descriptive label.
6. Press Enter.

To Delete Groups and Components from the Component Library (page 313)

1. Open the Component Library.
2. Highlight the item you want to delete.
3. Press the Delete key or choose Edit → Delete.

To Add a Component Library Component to the Palette Toolbar (page 314)

This is the method for adding Component Library-resident components to the Palette toolbar directly from the Component Library window. It is included here because this chapter is about the Component Library, but you're best advised to modify the Palette toolbar in the Environment Options dialog box. That procedure is outlined in Chapter 21, "Customizing Visual Cafe."

1. Highlight the component you want to add to the Palette toolbar.
2. Right- or long-click the component. You'll see the Component Library pop-up menu shown later in Figure 20-6.
3. Choose Add to Palette from the pop-up menu.

CHAPTER 21

To Turn Toolbars On or Off (page 318)

1. Right- or long-click the Status Bar.
2. Choose from the pop-up menu the name of the toolbar whose status you want to change.

To Make Toolbars Appear in Free-Floating Windows (page 320)

1. Click the toolbar you want to move in a blank area (not on a button), and hold down the mouse button.

2. Drag the toolbar to the new location. Don't worry if it doesn't fit exactly, or even if there's no room at all. Visual Café will make room.

3. Release the mouse button.

To Add a Button to the Palette Toolbar (page 321)

1. Choose File → Environment Options.
2. Click the Tool Palette tab.
3. The Available Components box holds a copy of the Component Library, which you learned about in the previous chapter. Locate the component you want to add to the Palette toolbar in the Available Components area.
4. Click the component and drag it to the appropriate folder in the Palette area on the right side of the Environment Options dialog box.

To Add a Tab to the Palette Toolbar (page 322)

1. Position the cursor anywhere in the Palette portion of the Environment Options dialog box's Tool Palette tab.
2. Click the New Group button, which is labeled in Figure 21-6.
3. A new folder icon, corresponding to the new tab, will appear at the bottom of the list of tabs.
4. Type a name for the tab in the box next to it and press Enter.
5. To rearrange the sequence of tabs, use the arrow buttons.

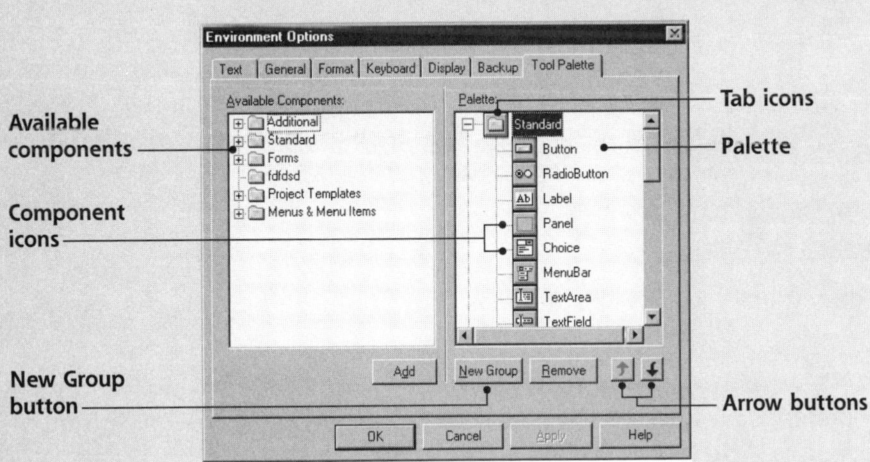

To Add a Workspace (page 323)

1. Configure Visual Café the way you want the new workspace to be. Open all the windows you want open in the new workspace.
2. Choose Window → Workspaces → New. You'll see the New Workspace dialog box, shown in Figure 21-7.
3. Type the name of the new workspace in the New Workspace dialog box.
4. Click OK.

To Delete a Workspace (page 323)

1. Open the workspace you want to delete.
2. Choose Window → Workspaces → Delete.

To Rename a Workspace (page 324)

1. Open the workspace you want to rename.
2. Choose Window → Workspaces → Rename. You'll see the Rename Workspace dialog box, shown in Figure 21-8.
3. Enter the workspace's new name in the Rename Workspace dialog box.
4. Click OK.

CHAPTER 22

Symantec plans to release — and may in fact have released by the time you read this — two products in the Visual Café family: Visual Café Pro and Visual Café Enterprise. These two products will keep the friendly Visual Café user interface, but include advanced programming capabilities.

Visual Café Pro (page 330)

Visual Café Pro will keep the Visual Café look and feel, but add the following features:

* **dbANYWHERE.** Symantec calls dbANYWHERE "middleware" because it operates as an intermediary between databases on Internet or intranet servers and client-side Web browsers that need information. The main advantage of dbANYWHERE is that it eliminates the need for special database-access software on the client side — all that is handled at the middleware level on the server.

* **Merlin.** Merlin, as in the Arthurian legend, is, among other things, a wizard. In this case, Merlin uses his powers to help you construct a database-access scheme. With Merlin, you can drag-and-drop to create Web forms, then connect form fields (which will be sent out to Web browsers) to dbANYWHERE and, ultimately, information in a database.

Visual Café Enterprise (page 333)

Visual Café enterprise — still deep in the planning stages as of this writing — will have all the features of Visual Café and Visual Café Pro, plus additional tools for managing large databases that are updated frequently by many people on a network. Visual Café Enterprise might be used to create a point-of-sale accounting system for a chain of stores, each of which has five cashiers who must be able to access and alter inventory and sales databases at about the same time.

VISUAL INDEX

Insert Buttons in a User Interface

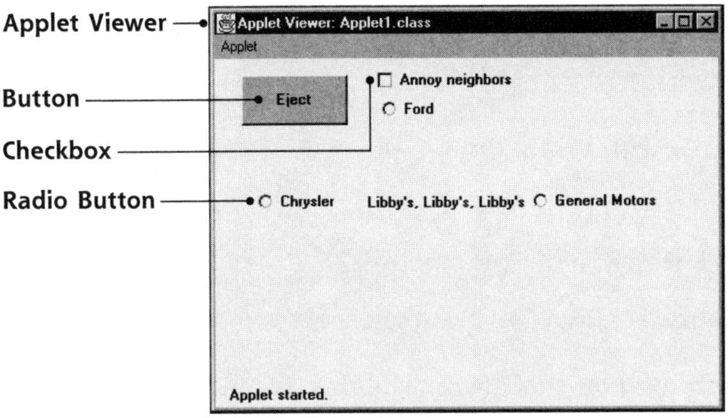

Create Text Areas in a User Interface

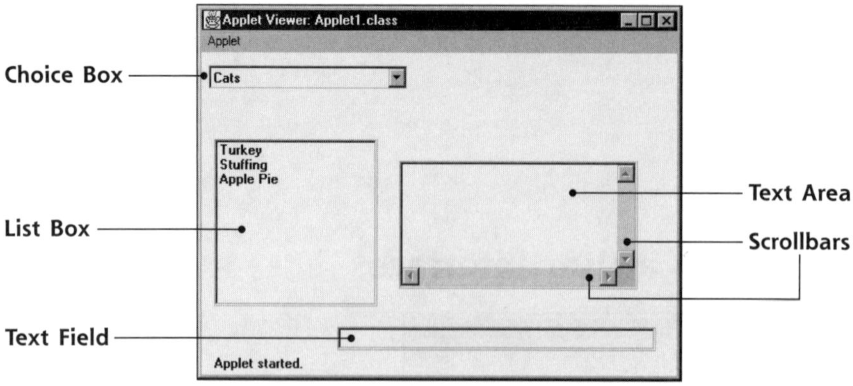

NOTE **Scrollbars rarely get created on their own. They're usually part of Text Areas or other components.**

Tweak Components with the Property List

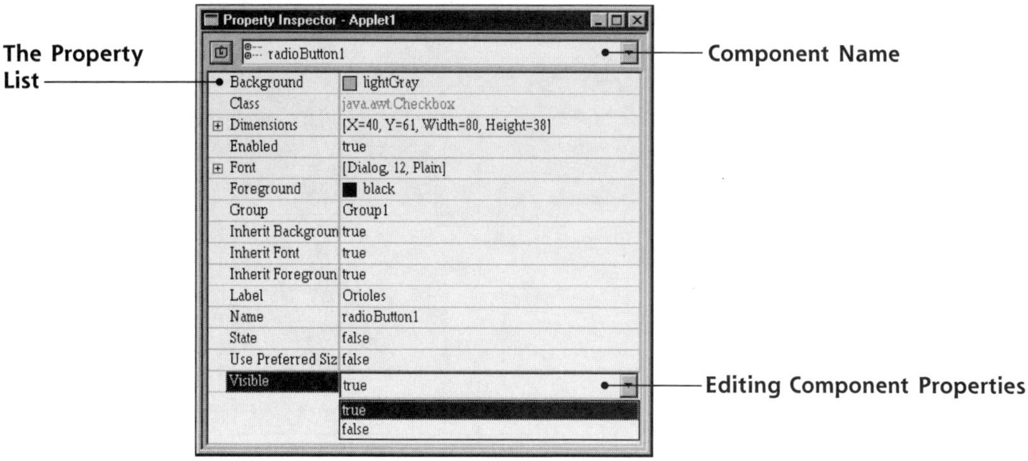

Conjure the Interaction Wizard

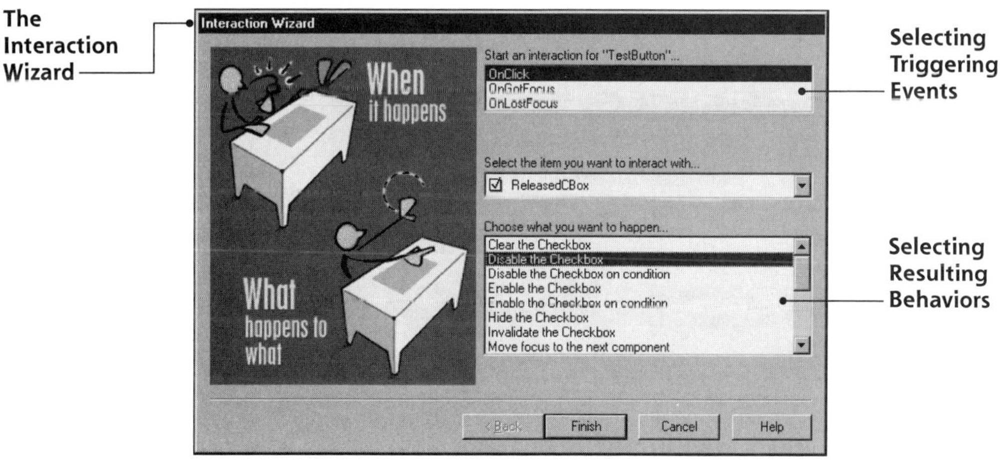

Edit Source Code in Visual Café

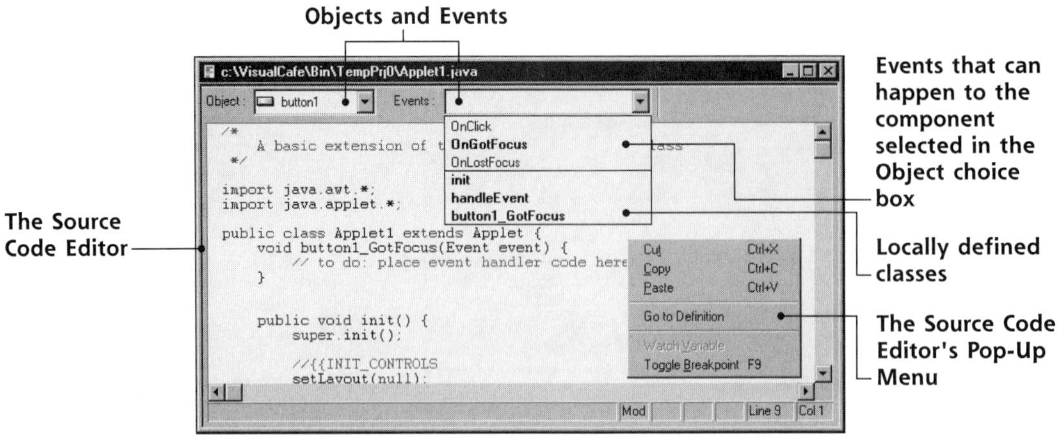

Use Visual Café's Hierarchy Editor

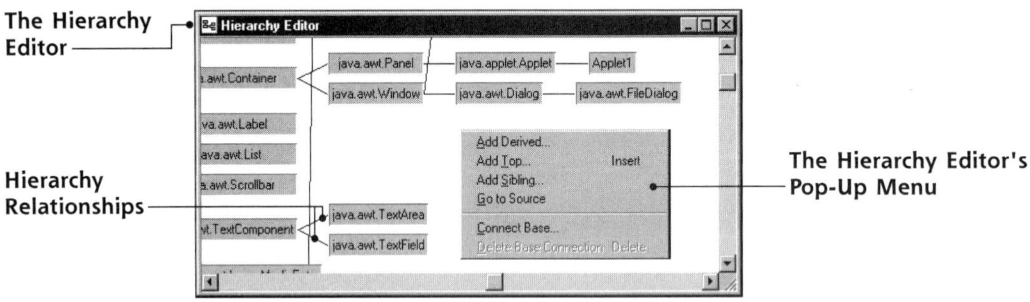

Use Visual Café's Class Browser

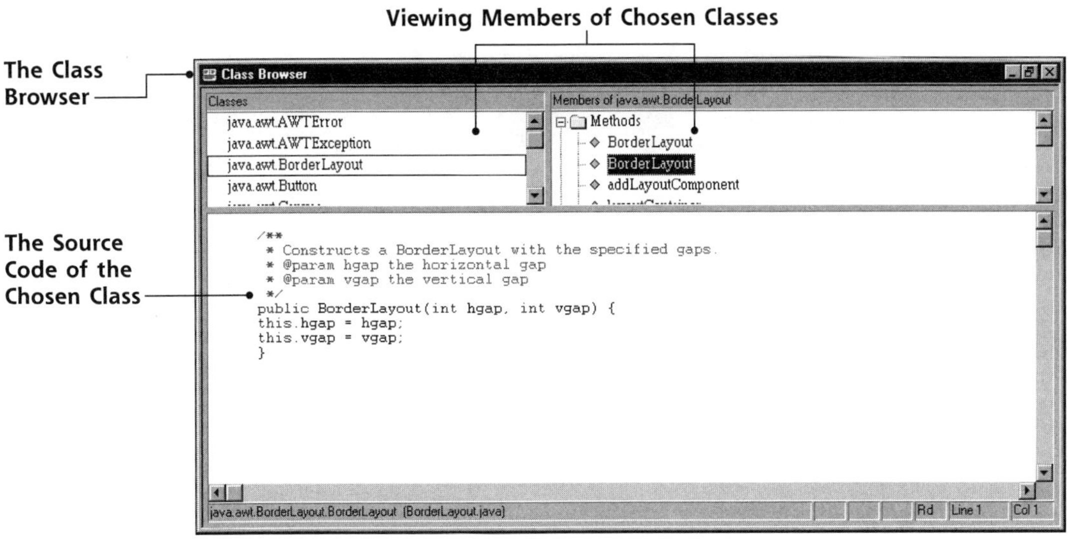

Debug a Program

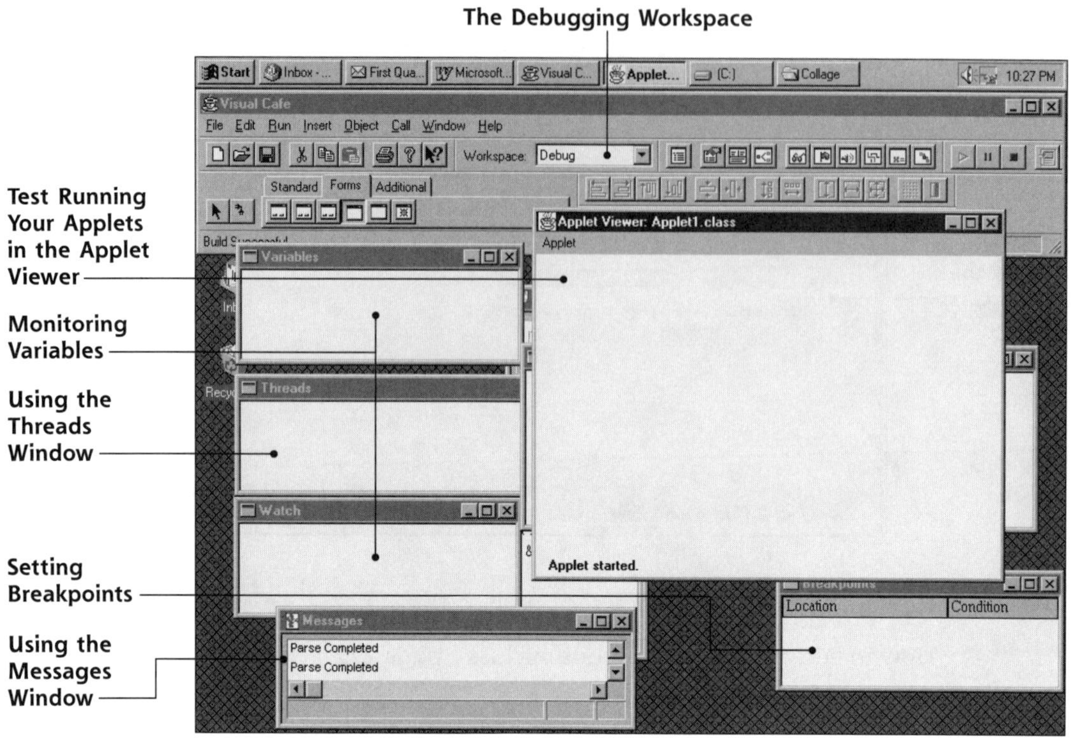

Customize the Palette Toolbar

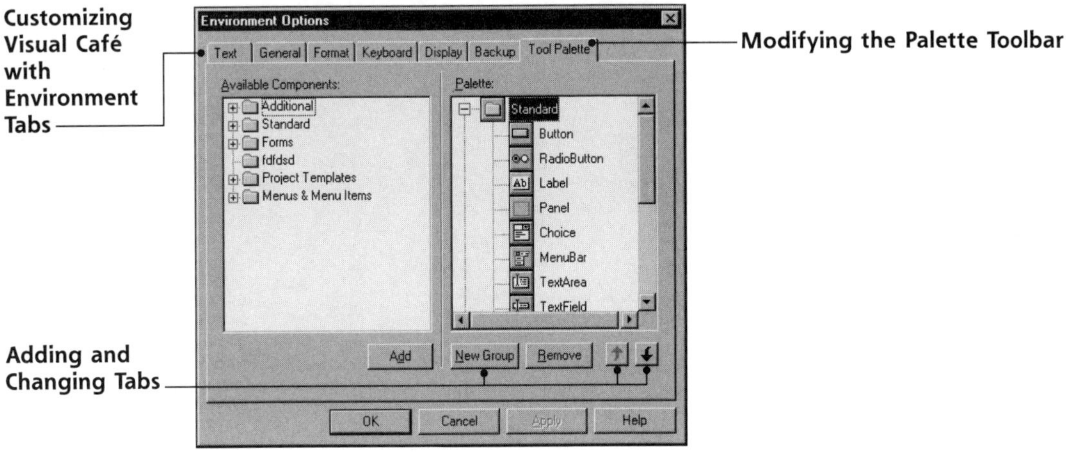

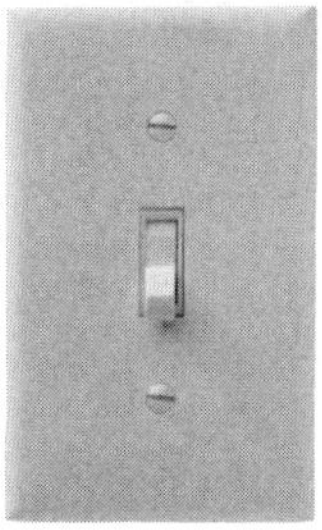

GLOSSARY

.class file — A file containing Java *bytecodes* — that is, a compiled Java file that's ready to be interpreted.

.java file — A file containing Java source code.

.vpj file — A Visual Café project file. Project files are wrappers that can contain several .java, .class, and other files for easy organization.

File menu — A menu on the Visual Café toolbar that contains commands that pertain to files. You can open, close, and save Visual Café projects via the File menu.

Help menu — A Visual Café menu that lists the three help files: one for Visual Café, one for Java structure and syntax, and one for the Java API.

Insert menu — A Visual Café menu that contains commands that add items — such as applets or JavaBeans — to the current project.

Macros menu — A menu that appears on the menu bar only when the source code editor is active. The Macros menu contains commands that enable you to create programs — macros — that can do such things as insert boilerplate text into your programs.

Object menu — An oddly named Visual Café menu that you can use to access the Form Editor or the source code editor, or to unleash the Interaction Wizard on a component.

Project menu — A Visual Café menu that contains commands related to test-running your programs.

Search menu — A Visual Café menu that contains, appropriately, search commands. Various commands on the Search menu will help you find text in source code files and compare the contents of two files for you.

Source menu — A menu that appears on the menu bar only when the source code editor is active. You can use the Source menu to insert breakpoints and conditional breakpoints and to adjust the appearance of code in the source code editor.

Threads menu — A Visual Café menu that appears only when the Threads window is active. You can use commands in the Threads window to pause execution of certain threads or to change the context of the Variables window.

Variables menu — A menu that appears on the menu bar only when the Variables window is active, and that contains only one command. The command adds the variable selected in the Variables menu to the list of watched variables and expressions in the Watch window.

Window menu — A menu that contains commands that display the various Visual Café windows, including the Watch window, the Variables window, the Form Editor, and the Property List.

abstract class — A class that cannot be instantiated. It can only be used as a superclass.

API — Applications Programming Interface. This is the family of objects that are supplied as part of a development environment. The Java API is composed entirely of classes.

Applet Viewer — A Visual Café debugging tool that lets you view Java applets without running them in your Web browser.

applet — A Java program designed to be executed by an HTML page loaded into a browser. The term Applet is also the name of a Java class that is capable of controlling a rectangular area of the display for an applet program. Also see application.

appletviewer — An executable supplied as a part of the Sun Microsystems Java system that has the ability to display applets via simple HTML files.

application — A Java program designed to be executed from the command line by a Java interpreter. It may or may not have windowing capability. Also see applet.

ASCII — American Standard Code for Information Interchange. The character set represented by the Unicode values \u0000 through \u007F.

AWT — Abstract Windowing Toolkit. This is the name often used when referring to the standard package java.awt. It is the graphics package that is used by Java applets.

block — A sequence of executable statements and local variable declarations set off by a pair of opening and closing braces.

breakpint — What a Java programmer drinks when he or she is not programming.

breakpoint — A debugging tool that you place on a line of source code to instruct Visual Café to pause execution at that place. Breakpoints are handy when used in conjunction with the Watch window and Variables window, so you can see what your program is really up to at various points in its execution. Also see conditional breakpoint.

Breakpoints menu — A menu that appears on the Visual Café menu bar only when the Breakpoints window is active. The Breakpoints menu contains commands that have to do with setting and releasing breakpoints.

Breakpoints window — A Visual Café debugging window that lists all of the breakpoints you've placed in the current project. You can enable, disable, set, or clear breakpoints from the Breakpoints window.

browser — A program that can be used to explore sites on the World Wide Web by copying HTML files from the Web site and interpreting it graphically on the screen. The term browser comes from the fact that it is easy to move from one site to another.

bytecode — The form of object code generated by the Java compiler. It can be executed directly by a Java interpreter. It is in a file with the extension class.

cache — Storage used by a Web browser to hold the most recently used Web pages and applets so that they can be loaded again locally. This speeds things up because local access is normally much quicker than access over an Internet link.

caching — The act of using a cache.

Call Stack window — A Visual Café debugging window that lists references from one class to another as your program executes. It's best to use the Call Stack window in conjunction with breakpoints, as calls tend to go by quickly.

Calls menu — A menu that appears on the menu bar only when the Call Stack window is active. You can use the Calls menu to change the context of the Variables window, or to adjust what information appears in the Call Stack window. Also see context.

casting — Forcing the conversion of data from one type to another by placing the desired type in parentheses directly before the data to be converted.

choice box — A component that contains a list of items, of which it displays only one at a time — unless the user clicks the choice box. Then, the list appears in a menu that drops down from the choice box. Microsoft Foundation Class programmers call choice boxes "combo boxes." Compare with list box.

Class Browser — A semi-useful Visual Café programming tool that displays the methods and data items associated with a particular class and the source code that defines a particular method or data item.

class — A collection of encapsulated data items and a group of methods to operate on the data.

code bug — See compile-time error.

compile-time error — An error that shows up when you try to compile your program and that prevents the compilation from taking place. Syntax errors are among the most common compile-time errors. You're told of compile-time errors in the Messages window. Compare with run-time error.

Component Library — A Visual Café feature used to store components. Though it comes filled with lots of often-used components, such as scroll bars and list boxes, you can add your own components to the Component Library, thereby making it easier for you to use them again in future programming projects. Reusable code is perhaps the greatest benefit of programming languages such as Java.

component — A vague term that can mean "a class" or "something that appears on the screen, such as a button or a dialog box." Discover Visual Café sticks to the second definition, but some documentation you'll see will use the first.

concatenate — To combine two character strings into one by connecting them end to end.

conditional breakpoint — A breakpoint that pauses the execution of a program only when certain conditions are met. For example, you might want to use a conditional breakpoint to stop a program only when a counter variable has reached a certain value, so as not to pause on each of hundreds of recursions. The condition Counter=100 might be the one to use in such a situation.

constructor — The method in a class that is executed whenever an object of that class is instantiated.

context — In the Variables window, the context is the collection of variables that the window watches. The context can be a single thread, a single call, or an entire program. Unless otherwise specified, the context is the set of all variables in use at a given instant.

data hiding — Defining a data item in such a way that another data item (one in the outer scope) is no longer accessible; the one in the outer scope is hidden.

Debug workspace — A Visual Café workspace that contains debugging tools, such as the Watch window and the Breakpoints window. You automatically enter the Debug workspace when you test-run your programs in Visual Café.

debugging — The process of finding and correcting programming errors. Bugs can take the form of compile-time errors or, more dangerous, run-time errors. Visual Café provides a whole slew of bug-killing tools.

delimiter — A separator. Commonly, some character within a string of characters used to mark a division between the ones to its left and right.

Edit menu — A Visual Café menu that contains standard cut and paste commands.

Edit workspace — The Visual Café workspace in which you write Java programs. The Edit workspace includes the Form Editor, the Property List, and the source code editor.

encapsulation — This refers to a characteristic of object orientation programming where the data within an object can only be accessed through the object's methods.

Environment Options dialog box — A Visual Café dialog box in which you configure the appearance and behavior of Visual Café. In the Environment Options dialog box, you can customize the functions of the source code editor and determine which components appear on the Palette toolbar.

event — Whenever there is keyboard or mouse activity, a message is sent to the Java application. This message is known as an event.

exception — The Java way of handling error conditions. An exception is thrown from the location of an error and is caught by an error handler designed to work with that particular kind of exception.

finalizer — The method in any object — named `finalize()` — that is called by the Java interpreter when reclaiming the object.

folder — A directory.

Form Editor — The Visual Café user-interface-design tool. By dragging components from the Component Library or the Palette toolbar to the Form Editor, you can create a complete user interface without opening the source code editor. After using the Form Editor, you'll often want to adjust the appearance of your components with the Property List and add behaviors with the Interaction Wizard.

fundamental data type — A built-in binary data type. One that does not require a reference and that is not constructed with `new`.

GAL — Get A Life. There is no such acronym. It was placed here as a message to people who read straight through a glossary.

garbage collection — The action automatically taken by the Java interpreter to reclaim unused objects.

hiding — See data hiding.

Hierarchy Editor — A Visual Café programming tool that gives a graphical representation to the classes that make up a Java program. You can use the Hierarchy Editor to define which classes derive from which other classes. Also see Class Browser.

HTML — HyperText Markup Language. The language that is used to design World Wide Web pages.

Huffman code — A text-compression method where the characters that are used more often have shorter internal representations than those that are used less often.

IEEE — Institute of Electrical and Electronics Engineers. `<http://www.computer.org>`.

IEEE-754 — The floating-point standard used by Java.

init() — The name of the method where all applets begin execution.

instance — This is the form of an object or an array that exists during the execution of a program. It is constructed from some descriptive element (such as a class or an array specification) by using the keyword, `new`.

instantiate — A term from object-oriented programming. It is the action of creating an object from its class definition.

integer — A whole number. It is a numeric value with no fractional part. In Java, an integer is a number without a decimal point. The Java integer data types are `byte`, `char`, `short`, `int`, and `long`.

interaction — A relationship between one piece of code and another. Usually, one piece of code will perform a specific action in response to an event that happens to another part of the program. Visual Café makes it relatively easy to create interactions with the Interaction Wizard.

Interaction Wizard — A Visual Café tool that makes it easier to create interactions. By specifying a component that something — such as a mouse click — will happen to, then specifying another component that will do something in response to that event, you create an interaction with the Interaction Wizard. The Interaction Wizard does all coding for you. You can create complete simple applications with the Interaction Wizard.

Java — A programming language, developed by Sun Microsystems and released in late 1995, that can be used to create secure, networked programs for use on multiple computer platforms. Java programs often take the form of applets, but can be stand-alone applications, too. Visual Café helps you write and test Java programs.

JavaBeans — A specification for sharable components written in Java. A JavaBean could be used as part of a C++ program, with a Motif Widget, or in conjunction with an ActiveX control.

JIT — Just-In-Time Compiler. A compiler (or translator) that converts Java bytecodes into native executable code for the local machine. This happens in a browser each time the bytcode is loaded from a class file for execution. The lag in load time is more than made up for by the speed-up in execution.

list box — A component that contains a list of items and occupies a fixed rectangular space on the screen. If there are more items in the list than will fit into the assigned space, a list box will grow scroll bars to allow users to peruse all list items. Compare choice box.

logical bug — See run-time error.

main() — This is the name of the method where all applications begin execution.

Messages window — A Visual Café window that displays information from the compiler about what it's up to and errors that have appeared. Visual Café also executes command-line applications in the Messages window.

method — Analogous to a function in C or FORTRAN, or a procedure in Pascal. It is a body of executable code that is given a name, and possibly a list of parameters, so that it can be called from other methods.

NaN — Not a Number. This is the name of any data pattern found in a float or double that does not represent a valid number. This is from the IEEE-754 standard.

narrowing — Converting from one primitive Java type to another that could cause loss of magnitude information on the data. An example of this is the conversion of a `long` to an `int`.

object-oriented — A general term that refers to a method of organizing the code in a program. An encapsulation of data along with the methods that work on the data is called an object. In Java, writing a class is defining an object.

object — 1. In the Java language, an object is either the instance of a class or an array. It is an entity that contains data and the methods that operate on the data. 2. In Visual Café, an object is a graphically displayed item on the screen that will accept either mouse or keyboard input. 3. Anything else (the term is used so loosely it is becoming meaningless).

operator — The set of special symbols that are used in the Java language to copy data from one location to another, or to perform arithmetic operations.

overloading — Two methods in the same class can have the same name as long as the list of argument data types is unique enough that Java can tell which method is intended when one is referenced.

overriding — When a method in a subclass has the same name as one in its superclass, a call to the method will be to the one in the subclass — the one in the superclass is overridden.

Palette toolbar — The tabbed area of the Visual Café toolbar that contains components that you can drag into the Form Editor. You can adjust the contents of the Palette toolbar — and even add your own tabs to it — via the Environment Options dialog box.

parent class — Another term for superclass.

polymorphism — The capability for the same method call to work on objects of different types. In Java, this is achieved through both class inheritance and interface implementation.

program — A Java applet or application. Programs can involve many .class and .java files, but usually fit into one Visual Café project.

Project Manager — A Visual Café window that graphically depicts the classes and other pieces that make up a project. The Project Manager lists all applets and applications, the components that appear in those applets and applications and the HTML files associated with the applets.

project — A Visual Café organizational tool. Projects include all source code, HTML, text, and other files that relate to a single Java program. Files with the extension .vpj contain information about the files that belong to a project.

property — A trait of a component. A list box, for example, has properties that define the contents of the list it displays, the screen space it occupies, the font used to display list items and many other characteristics.

Property List — A Visual Café tool that makes it easy to see and modify the properties of components. For example, if you wanted to change the label on a button, you could click the button in the Form Editor and adjust the Label property in the Property List.

radix — The base of a number. For example, a decimal number has a radix of 10 and a hexadecimal number has a radix of 16.

real number — A number that has a fractional part. In Java, a real number one with a decimal point (it may also have an exponent). The real number data types are float and double.

run-time error — An error that doesn't stop a program from compiling but causes it to give an unwanted result. Run-time errors include those that result from faulty program design. Compare compile-time error.

source code editor — The Visual Café tool with which you write Java code. The source code editor has the ability to move the cursor automatically to methods.

source code — Human-readable text contained in a .java file that is to be compiled into a machine-readable .class file.

subclass — A class that is defined based on some other class by using the keyword extend. See superclass.

superclass — If class B derives part of its definition from class A by use of the extends keyword, class A is said to be the superclass of class B — class B is the subclass of class A. The superclass is also called a parent class.

text area — A component that handles multiple lines of text. Text areas can be made to be editable or not, and can be used for either input or output. Compare text field.

text field — A component that can handle a single line of text. Text fields can made to be editable or not, and can be used for either input or output. Compare text area.

thread — A sequence of program execution, independent of other, simultaneous sequences of program execution inside the same loaded program. One program runs as if it were two or more. One thread might keep the screen updated, while another prints a document in the background. You can monitor threads and the conflicts they sometimes cause via the Threads window.

Threads window — A Visual Café debugging tool that displays a list of threads that are active at the moment. You can use the Threads window in conjunction with the Variables window and Watch window to see if threads are conflicting with one another.

Unicode — An international standard set of numeric representations of characters from the alphabets of many languages. It enables software to unambiguously represent the characters of any combination of these languages. It has 16 bit character codes intended to cover all of the world's writing systems, including Roman, Greek, Cyrillic, Chinese, hiragana, katakana, Devanagari, Easter Island "rongo-rongo", and even Elvish (the character set invented by J.R.R. Tolkien in *The Lord of the Rings*). The specification appears at <`ftp://unicode.org`>.

UTF-8 — UCS Transformation Format 8-bit form. An encoding method that compresses Unicode data into 8 bits. It saves space if the Unicode content is mostly ASCII.

Variables window — A Visual Café debugging tool that displays the names, data types and values of all the variables active in the current context. The Variables window displays information only when the program it's watching is stopped at a breakpoint. Compare Watch window.

Visual Café — A rapid application development environment for Java programs. Symantec Corporation scored a serious win with the release of Visual Café, which brings Java programming out of the exclusive domain of geeks and closer to the grasp of a wider range of programmers.

Visual Café Enterprise — A powerful version of Visual Café thats good for building high-volume networked applications.

Visual Café Pro — An enhanced version of Visual Café, complete with database-connectivity programming tools.

Watch window — A Visual Café debugging tool that displays information about only those variables you specify. Compare Variables window.

widening — The Java term for converting data from one fundamental data type to another that will guarantee no loss overall magnitude (although there could be some loss of precision).

Workspace — A collection of programming and/or debugging tools in Visual Café. There are two standard, pre-configured workspaces — the Edit workspace and the Debug workspace — but it's not hard to create your own workspaces, populated by the windows you like best for certain tasks.

WWW — World Wide Web. If you don't already know this, go back three spaces and roll again.

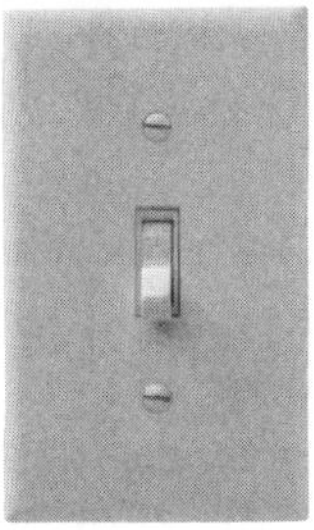

APPENDIX

USING THE CD-ROM

Sealed in a plastic pouch inside the back cover of *Discover Visual Café* is a CD-ROM. On it you'll find all the code listings in this book, plus a few more. You'll also find a file called `CH14CD.HTML`, which contains the Component Property Guide discussed in Chapter 14.

System Requirements

To run Visual Café and take advantage of these files, you should be using Windows 95 or Windows NT on a 486, Pentium, or Pentium Pro computer, with 16MB of RAM, 20-30MB of hard disk space, a VGA display, and a CD-ROM drive.

To run Visual Café on a Macintosh, be sure you have a PowerPC processor, System 7.5 or later, 24MB of RAM, 30MB of free hard disk space, and a CD-ROM drive.

How the Files Are Organized

The files on this CD-ROM are organized into Visual Café project files, so it's easiest to work with them that way. You can, however, use individual .java and .class files — everything is there. The program files are organized into directories that correspond to the chapters in which the listings appear.

For example, in order to work with the `booleanShow` class covered in Chapter 3, open the Chap03 directory on the CD-ROM and look for a file called `booleanShow.vpj`. Open it with Visual Café and you're in business.

Alternately, you can import .java or .class files from the CD-ROM into your own Visual Café projects. To do that, choose **Project** → **Add Files** and pick the files you want to import from the dialog box that appears (you can bring in more than one file at a time).

To compensate for a shortcoming in the way Visual Café deals with command-line applications (they'll run and disappear in an instant if you're not careful), always run the command-line sample code from this book by clicking the Run button, rather than choosing **Run** → **Execute**.

To be able to use example programs on the CD-ROM, it will be necessary to copy them to your hard disk. There are two reasons for this: First, Visual Caf=E9 expects the source and project files to be resident on a writeable medium. It likes to compile each class right before it runs it. The advantage of doing it this way is that it eliminates the possibility of accidentally running an old version of a class. You always know that you are executing the latest version of your program.

Second, some of the programs will not run in the applet viewer right off of the CD-ROM. This is because the programs were designed to generate slightly different versions of the same class files as the book proceeds from one example to another. The compiled class file on the disk may not be the right one for a specific example. This problem disappears if you copy the code from the directories to your hard drive and run all of the examples from inside Visual Caf=E9. Once you run a program from inside Visual Caf=E9, that program will run fine in the standalone applet viewer (that is, until you compile and run a different program in the same directory).

NOTE: The CD-ROM's Chap11 directory holds a few simple JavaDoc-generated HTML files. For full hot-link functionality, these files should be installed to the directory that holds the Java API docs (the ones you installed along with the rest of Visual Cafe). Do this by naming the output directory on the JavaDoc command line:

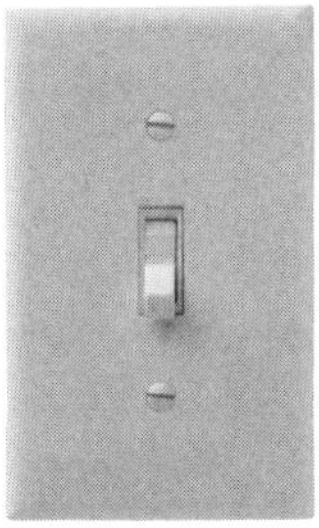

INDEX

(*continued*)

D

E

(*continued*)

I

J

(*continued*)

S

T

U

IDG BOOKS WORLDWIDE, INC. END-USER LICENSE AGREEMENT

Read This. You should carefully read these terms and conditions before opening the software packet(s) included with this book ("Book"). This is a license agreement ("Agreement") between you and IDG Books Worldwide, Inc. ("IDGB"). By opening the accompanying software packet(s), you acknowledge that you have read and accept the following terms and conditions. If you do not agree and do not want to be bound by such terms and conditions, promptly return the Book and the unopened software packet(s) to the place you obtained them for a full refund.

1. **License Grant.** IDGB grants to you (either an individual or entity) a nonexclusive license to use one copy of the enclosed software program(s) (collectively, the "Software") solely for your own personal or business purposes on a single computer (whether a standard computer or a workstation component of a multi-user network). The Software is in use on a computer when it is loaded into temporary memory (i.e., RAM) or installed into permanent memory (e.g., hard disk, CD-ROM or other storage device). IDGB reserves all rights not expressly granted herein.

2. **Ownership.** IDGB is the owner of all right, title and interest, including copyright, in and to the compilation of the Software recorded on the disk(s)/CD-ROM. Copyright to the individual programs on the disk(s)/CD-ROM is owned by the author or other authorized copyright owner of each program. Ownership of the Software and all proprietary rights relating thereto remain with IDGB and its licensors.

3. **Restrictions On Use and Transfer.**

   (a) You may only (i) make one copy of the Software for backup or archival purposes, or (ii) transfer the Software to a single hard disk, provided that you keep the original for backup or archival purposes. You may not (i) rent or lease the Software, (ii) copy or reproduce the Software through a LAN or other network system or through any computer subscriber system or bulletin-board system, or (iii) modify, adapt or create derivative works based on the Software.

   (b) You may not reverse engineer, decompile, or disassemble the Software. You may transfer the Software and user documentation on a permanent basis, provided that the transferee agrees to accept the terms and conditions of this Agreement and you retain no copies. If the Software is an update or has been updated, any transfer must include the most recent update and all prior versions.

4. **Restrictions on Use of Individual Programs.** You must follow the individual requirements and restrictions detailed for each individual program in [the shareware section] of this Book. These limitations are contained in the individual license agreements recorded on the disk(s)/CD-ROM. These restrictions include a requirement that after using the program for the period of time specified in its text, the user must pay a registration fee or discontinue use. By opening the Software packet(s), you will be agreeing to abide by the licenses and restrictions for these individual programs. None of the material on this disk(s) or listed in this Book may ever be distributed, in original or modified form, for commercial purposes.

5. **Limited Warranty.**

(a) IDGB warrants that the Software and disk(s)/CD-ROM are free from defects in materials and workmanship under normal use for a period of sixty (60) days from the date of purchase of this Book. If IDGB receives notification within the warranty period of defects in materials or workmanship, IDGB will replace the defective disk(s)/CD-ROM.

(b) IDGB AND THE AUTHOR OF THE BOOK DISCLAIM ALL OTHER WARRANTIES, EXPRESS OR IMPLIED, INCLUDING WITHOUT LIMITATION IMPLIED WARRANTIES OF MERCHANTABILITY AND FITNESS FOR A PARTICULAR PURPOSE, WITH RESPECT TO THE SOFTWARE, THE PROGRAMS, THE SOURCE CODE CONTAINED THEREIN, AND/OR THE TECHNIQUES DESCRIBED IN THIS BOOK. IDGB DOES NOT WARRANT THAT THE FUNCTIONS CONTAINED IN THE SOFTWARE WILL MEET YOUR REQUIREMENTS OR THAT THE OPERATION OF THE SOFTWARE WILL BE ERROR FREE.

(c) This limited warranty gives you specific legal rights, and you may have other rights which vary from jurisdiction to jurisdiction.

6. **Remedies.**

(a) IDGB's entire liability and your exclusive remedy for defects in materials and workmanship shall be limited to replacement of the Software, which is returned to IDGB at the address set forth below with a copy of your receipt. This Limited Warranty is void if failure of the Software has resulted from accident, abuse, or misapplication. Any replacement Software will be warranted for the remainder of the original warranty period or thirty (30) days, whichever is longer.

(b) In no event shall IDGB or the author be liable for any damages whatsoever (including without limitation damages for loss of business profits, business interruption, loss of business information, or any other pecuniary loss) arising out of the use of or inability to use the Book or the Software, even if IDGB has been advised of the possibility of such damages.

(c) Because some jurisdictions do not allow the exclusion or limitation of liability for consequential or incidental damages, the above limitation or exclusion may not apply to you.

7. **U.S. Government Restricted Rights.** Use, duplication, or disclosure of the Software by the U.S. Government is subject to restrictions stated in paragraph (c) (1) (ii) of the Rights in Technical Data and Computer Software clause of DFARS 252.227-7013, and in subparagraphs (a) through (d) of the Commercial Computer--Restricted Rights clause at FAR 52.227-19, and in similar clauses in the NASA FAR supplement, when applicable.

8. **General.** This Agreement constitutes the entire understanding of the parties, and revokes and supersedes all prior agreements, oral or written, between them and may not be modified or amended except in a writing signed by both parties hereto which specifically refers to this Agreement. This Agreement shall take precedence over any other documents that may be in conflict herewith. If any one or more provisions contained in this Agreement are held by any court or tribunal to be invalid, illegal or otherwise unenforceable, each and every other provision shall remain in full force and effect.